How to Make Enemies

A second volume of autobiography

Poetry
Postcards to Pulcinella
The Mongrel
The Solitudes
Judas

Plays
The Dull Ass's Hoof
This Way to the Tomb
Stratton
The Rape of Lucretia
Don Juan
Our Lady's Tumbler
The Death of Satan
Abelard and Heloise
The Catalyst
O.B.A.F.G.

Prose
Journal of a Husbandman
Home-Made Home
Tobacco Growing in England
Where I Live
The Blue Fox
Jan at the Blue Fox
Jan's Journal
The Last Adam
Saint Spiv

Adaptations
The Eagle Has Two Heads
The Typewriter
The Apollo de Bellac
The Rabbit Race
Beauty and the Beast
The Trojan Women

Editions
The Selected Writings of Mahatma Gandhi
The Poems of Ben Jonson
The Songs and Satires of the Earl of Rochester

Autobiography
All Men Are Islands

The Author by Epstein

How to Make Enemies

Ronald Duncan

RUPERT HART-DAVIS *London 1968*

© Ronald Duncan 1968
First published 1968

Rupert Hart-Davis Limited
3 Upper James Street London W1

Printed in Great Britain by
C. Tinling and Co Ltd
Liverpool, London and Prescot

SBN: 246.64472.9

Acknowledgements

Acknowledgements for permission to
reproduce copyright material are due to:
Mrs Dorothy Shakespear Pound, duly appointed
Committee of Ezra Pound, for permission to
print a hitherto unpublished draft of *Pisan
Canto LXXXI* (both in the text and in the
part titles), the poem on Wyndham Lewis
and an unpublished letter from Pound to the
author; to Messrs Faber & Faber Limited,
for *The Rape of Lucretia* by Ronald Duncan; and
to Messrs Vision Press Limited for Ronald
Duncan's adaptation of *The Eagle Has Two
Heads* by Jean Cocteau.

Contents

A*

Illustrations

(between pages 192 & 193 and 224 & 225)

The author at West Mill
Photo, Reveille

Kathleen Ferrier at Mead Farm

The author and Benjamin Britten at Glyndebourne
1946, preparing the Rape of Lucretia
Photo, Radio Times Hulton Picture Library

Our Lady's Tumbler, Salisbury Cathedral, 1953
Photo above, Salisbury Journal
Photo below, Bosio

Part One

The ant's a centaur in his dragon world

AN autobiography cannot give an accurate picture of a man's life if it is to be readable. However eventful our life may be it has some very dull chapters: day after day in which we achieve nothing worth recording; month after month in which we think of nothing but trivialities; and year upon year in which we do little but age. Tedium, repetition and trivia make up most of our life. An accurate autobiography would never find a publisher; if it did, it would never hold a reader. So when we write our life we falsify it by recording only those incidents which were amusing or eventful thus giving the impression that our lives were wholly made up of such anecdotes. It is not true, and we write this way not because we have one eye on the reader, but because it is impossible to draw what has no shape or record what was uneventful. If a man lives twenty-five thousand days or so, how many of them can he remember? Not more than a couple of hundred at the most. But the rest were days he lived: they fell like leaves trodden under. Hannibal did not spend all his life crossing the Alps, nor Leander swimming the Hellespont.

There is a steep hill in Devon running from West Mill to Mead; it is about a quarter of a mile long: I have ridden or walked up and down it two or three times nearly every day since I was twenty. How many of those innumerable journeys can I recall? Not more than a dozen or so: the time I carried my new-born daughter down in her carrycot; the first time I rode up with my Arab; the time when, during the war, an old Sunbeam lorry stopped on the hill and then ran backwards down it, to overturn at the bottom; but for the rest I have walked up and down sleepwalking, without even a dream to remember. To record accurately we would have to write most of our lives on water.

There was one journey up that steep track from West Mill which I remember vividly. I was only twenty-nine but I was so crippled I could not walk a step. A neighbouring farmer had to lift me into his cart then haul me up the hill like a sack of potatoes. A series of petty follies had reduced me to this ridiculous state. Rose Marie was expecting her second child. In anticipation of this event, and remembering the precipitous hill, we had thought it wise for her to mount it while she could still walk. Accordingly she had trundled up with her burden a week before the birth was expected. She stayed in Bude with her mother in a house near the nursing home. Unhappily our calculations must have been at fault. To my extreme irritation, a full week elapsed without the child being born. And another week of waiting followed. This annoyed me: it meant I had to live alone. My daughter Briony was then only two: my mother and sister were looking after her at their cottage five miles along the coast. And I always find living alone intolerable. That is not because it entails cooking my own meals: I always enjoy cooking. It is simply that I detest my own company, especially when it is imposed upon me like an unwanted guest. My ideal is to have solitude knowing that somebody is in an adjoining room, and that, when I have bored myself, I can go in to annoy them. But the prospect did not please me of having to sit like a monk without a vocation for a whole fortnight. Consequently, when a couple of honeymooners, hiking along the coast, knocked on the door of West Mill and asked if I could accommodate them I readily agreed. It was better, I thought, to become a boots than be a monk. I offered to give them full board and lodging for £2 a week. They seemed very pleased. It did not occur to me that I had undercharged them. Indeed, had they known it, I would have paid them to be in the cottage. The man's name was Denys Val Baker. I gathered he was a writer too. But for all that, he seemed quite agreeable. I now busied myself preparing menus, and concocting lethal dishes of aphrodisiacs. I would pour half a bottle of wine into the sauce and then fall into a reverie about the profit I was now making as a lodging keeper, but of course fail to deduct such costs as the wine. My P.G.s seemed satisfied with their diet and were so impressed with my breakfast trays that they never suspected that I was also a writer: I do not enjoy talking shop with other untouchables. This omission no doubt led my guests to put out their filthy shoes every night. Cleaning shoes and scraping mud from soles is a job I do not enjoy, especially when I can't find the right brush and then apply the wrong polish. And the Val Bakers tramped the muddiest country and occasionally changed their hooves during the day, so that the next morning I had half a dozen pairs to scrape, brush and burnish. It being sunny weather I thought foolishly it was better to sit out on the grass while doing this chore than dirty the kitchen floor which I would then have to sweep. Consequent to this domestic forethought, I contracted a severe bout of rheumatism, and if my guests hadn't come to the end of their honeymoon, they would have gone hungry for I became too crippled to stand by the stove, let alone balance a tray. I could not even bend down to put my own shoes on. In this state I received the news that my son, Roger, had been born. But I could not move towards him until a cart took me up the hill and my sister drove me into the nursing home in Bude which stood near the golf course.

I hobbled to Rose Marie's bed and, as she said at the time, successfully distracted the nurse's attention from her. The child looked like a miniature Joe Louis. Perhaps the acute pain in my back prevented me from having any paternal feelings. I was glad that the birth was over: now Rose Marie could hurry home and I wouldn't be alone any more or be driven to such excesses as taking paying guests. And it occurred to me that she would now get her splendid figure back. But no lofty thoughts about seeing my cradled immortality intruded into my self-obsession. Though I had taken Rose Marie some flowers, I often noticed that on these occasions when it might be assumed that I would feel something deep, I felt nothing at all. The first sight of my son occasioned no transports within me. If anything, I felt a slight resentment at his appearance and some sense of rivalry. Young bull frogs strangle their fathers to mark their adolescence. But perversely though I often feel little emotion when I am supposed to, I can suffer when I am not personally involved. The birth of other people's children has often moved me deeply: naturally Rose Marie resented this aberration on my part. In justice to myself, I suppose I never crowed over a poem I had written, but often got excited over other people's. Perhaps my English sense of restraint and understatement operated within me as I looked down at this bundle which came in with a cry to go out with a groan. And perhaps I felt something like guilt for creating that which is synonymous with suffering? When the cooing nurse handed the bundle to me and asked if I felt proud I thought she was being excessively silly and sentimental.

Injections of novocaine relieved the constriction in my back and I was able to visit the nursing home every day. Frequently I would see John Baird, the inventor of television, as I went in and pass the time of day with him. At that time he lived next door. A muffled man, abstracted and embittered. His appearance reminded me of Aldous Huxley.

I had been told that most men want sons: I could not understand that. For me a son was a rival, an intruder, whereas a daughter had been an addition to my harem. I had decided some months before my daughter had been born to call her Briony. The reason was I liked the sound of the word, not because Briony is a poisonous berry which grows in the Devon hedgerows.

The joy this pretty creature gave me as soon as she could toddle around the cottage was almost as great as the pleasure I'd found from my first Arab horse. My eyes were rinsed with every pout, dribble, tumble and movement she made. But the unique gift this child brought me was not the delight I found in her careless grace or casual looks, but the astounding revelation of a quality I had never met anywhere in life before: her innocence. Ignorance I had met, innocence, never. And by innocence I mean that Briony's gift lay in her trust. She was credulous of anything so long as it was good, incredulous of evil. She was born with a sense of absolute good. Every child has this to some degree, but not to hers. Before she could talk, I used to make up stories for her, and when she was able to ask questions I would improvise fantastic answers: she would nod her head if my explanation seemed good and shake it if it offended her sense of virtue. She was utterly naïve; to her, people always have the right motive; she seemed incapable of believing evil in others because there was none in herself.

No other woman *gave* me affection—some have returned it for a time. But this child gave before she received. If she had three strawberries, she would run to me with two. We were more or less inseparable. I liked to have her crawling about on my desk and her paw signed most of my manuscripts. When I rode up to the farm she clutched the mane. And when I gardened she toddled behind me dropping the spuds in the holes, believing every story I told her: that the penny I planted would grow into a shilling; that some horses have wings and the earth had been created by being laid by a huge peacock; that the stars were holes in the fabric of heaven made when violets were picked out of it; that the sea was made from the tears of crocodiles and the tide turned because the ocean missed the river's embraces. There was nothing good she could not believe. This innocence made her a receptacle for poetry, the poetry of make-believe.

It was largely to keep Briony amused that I went back to writing *This Way to the Tomb* long after the Community Farm which I had founded along the valley had collapsed in chaos. I had started it as something for the members to perform. As we had no theatre I had chosen a theme which required no sets: Saint Anthony was to meditate sitting on a mound which, with poetry to describe it, would do as a mountain.

My writing was, as it were, fully orchestrated by interruptions. Some self-made, others imposed—like the interval I had to spend in Stratton gaol on a silly charge of stealing a barrel of petrol which I had laboriously salved from the sea, or the ordinary day-to-day distractions which running a derelict farm single-handed during the war imposed. It was 1943: things which we now take for granted were then major achievements. For instance, with fuel rationed, I used to run the water wheel to produce light and heat. This entailed clearing the mill leat, greasing the bearings, mending the leather belts which drove the generator: not to mention looking after the bees which I kept because sugar was rationed, growing vegetables, editing and printing *The Townsman* on the kitchen table and feeding my horses which had to carry everything, including their own feed, up and down the hill. I got to my desk so rarely that it would be truer to say that my writing was an occasional distraction from my chores than the other way round. And indeed I did not even have a desk at that time, though I had built a study and nursery onto the cottage with the help of a jobbing mason and the deck timbers from a boat wrecked along the coast.

But it was appropriate that I had had to build the room in which I wrote. For writing poetry today entails making everything yourself again: coining the words, or trying to sharpen those with meanings blunted by usage or misusage; forging something like an idiom with no living dramatic convention to support you and even having to weave a home-spun fabric of values out of the scraps of faith or straws of belief gleaned from the wayside in the materially affluent wilderness around, before even three lines of it can be written.

Though I had written three plays previously I knew next to nothing about how to construct one. I had no synopsis, only the vaguest idea of what the play was about. I merely had Ben Jonson's Masques in the back of my mind as a form which I wished to use, and the certainty within me that if poetry moved on the muscles of thought as opposed to slithering along on verbal clichés and emotional gestures, it should be possible to make it an inconspicuous vehicle for drama again, and not merely the decoration on it.

And so when I'd done the farm work I used to squat Briony on to the table, give her a sheet of paper to scrawl on and then take another for myself. Neither of us knew what we were going to write. My difficulty was that some lines insisted on appearing though I did not know in what part of the play they belonged, nor even which character owned them. But these images were there like bits of timber or tallow I'd picked up on the beach. Indeed it was while beachcombing that most of them occurred to me. One of these bits of flotsam were the lines:

> And my mind clings to the past
> Like a velvet train dragged on wet grass

At first I had thought they were a quotation. I could not think who the author was. I had written to ask Leavis. He had replied: "You." These lines stayed at the back of my mind for months and the image of the velvet train and the feel of the velvet being dragged over the wet grass was a vivid and recurring sensation to me. The only literary association to me was Marvel's line:

> Ensnared with melons I fall on grass.

At this time, I had four Devon calves. Three I fed on linseed gruel from a bucket and the other I bussed on a shorthorn cow. The cow got mastitis; I had to dry her off before the calf was weaned. This calf used not to come to the pail but would nuzzle the cow's udder violently. Standing there in the stable waiting for the calves to finish their gruel one frosty morning, I heard myself say aloud to the cow:

The blind mouth of the earth sucks a dry udder

And a few evenings later when Briony and I were set with our pencils, I wrote:

It is winter. Again winter.
The blind mouth of the earth sucks a dry udder.
Only leaves falling over and over disturb the year's slumber.
And my mind clings to the past
Like a velvet train dragged on wet grass.
Once it was spring...

I paused for an image. Then in my mind saw a tree on the road outside Cotignac where Rose Marie and I had stayed before the war. And I continued:

...The almond broke
Out with a mad frail enthusiasm from its tight bark;
And the cherry and peach stood within my reach.
My glad eyes grazed on the glory of it.
And my heart held part of the power of it.

It was summer. The sun shining.
A slow wind walked the cornfields combing
Wheat into waves, which followed one after another, till the whole
was flowing.

Then some of the chickens came to the window so I put them in:

Then my soul crowed like a cock aloud
And trod the future like a lot of hens, proud.

There was a vine growing round the window. I was writing too quickly to search far for images. The nearest to hand would do.

Autumn's a woman. A woman's a vine.
Carrying the soil's lust into the pressed wine:
Both blood and the grape, incarnadine.

Now I paused, again made self-conscious by having used the word "incarnadine" and wondering whether "multitudinous" was accurate or Shakespeare had used it more for ballast. Then a couple of lines of Pound's came into my mind:

I have sung of women in three cities
But there is not one
So now I'll sing
Sing of the sun.

There seemed no connection. But my unconscious mind found sufficient material here for me to finish the verse pattern with:

I heaped a girl's lap with lemons.
Oh who could not sing of such a season?

and to go on as with a string of beads:

It is winter. Again winter
And I am an old man with a fixed future
To which the sand in the glass dribbles as I sit by the water
    Dreaming, resisting contemplation
    On the precise point of meditation.

It was not until I had written that verse that I realised that the passage I was writing was, in fact, one of Saint Anthony's meditations. There had been no full stop after the verse. I felt the rhythm had to run on against the verse structure and, as it were, to add emphasis on whatever the point of his meditation was that was easy to find.

"Which is my fear. What are my fears?" I wrote and then I looked into myself and my feelings I had had when I had thought I would have to live alone a few weeks before. It was easy to continue:

Of all my fears it is loneliness which wears
The worst mark, with lips bitten and bleeding, and its eyes red
    with tears

22

The extreme feeling of the image of "the eyes red with tears" surprised me. I now tried consciously to objectify the Saint, his belief and condition, as opposed to my own.

> *Loneliness is the soul's wilderness and I*
> *Am alone, Jesu, unless in Thy Company*
> *Which I have known when You had left me,*
> *For when You were with me, I was not lonely,*
> *But then I, full of the strength of You, denied I needed You;*

And somewhere behind the Bosch picture of Saint Anthony I was aware of Gandhi. I recalled an incident when I had motored to Wardha with him from his Ashram *Segoan*, and how some girls in saris had jumped on to the running board of the car for the privilege of touching the Mahatma's clothes and how he had deliberately destroyed the image they were creating of him as a Messiah by grinning broadly at me and then pinching one of the girls' nose.

"They call me a saint," he often said. "To me I'm no more of a saint than they are." And so I completed the verse:

> *and I*
> *Blind fool and prig and called a Saint*
> *Am lonely now and cry of this complaint.*

I now made a conscious decision which was to try to give Saint Anthony an ordinary man's emotions and regrets. I had felt that Eliot's St Thomas failed in this respect and that the tensions and conflicts within that character were weakened by being too intellectual. I knew that the asceticism I was imposing on Saint Anthony would be meaningless unless a sensualist was imprisoned within them. I was certain that the spiritual vigour in a man was unlikely to exist without emotional and even sexual vigour in him too. I did not believe that vitality could exist in one part of a man and not in the others.

Gandhi came to my mind again. I recalled his admission to me that his wife remained illiterate because they had married young, and how he had insisted on their going to bed together every afternoon, and consequently by excessive copulation he had prevented her from learning to read or write. His vow of chastity was to be seen against this background and inherent appetite. Though I had commented that there was less virtue in it now that he was nearly seventy. Then I found myself thinking of Villon. This did not surprise me. Villon was my favourite Saint, though only I had canonised him. I suppose for no other reason than that I had seen a woodcut somewhere of his hanging from a gibbet.

> *Je suis François dont ce me poise,*
> *Né de Paris, empres Ponthoise*
> *Or d'une corde d'une troise*
> *Saura mon col que mon cul poise...*

> *I am François wretched clown,*
> *Born in Paris near Ponthoise town.*
> *My neck in this noose swings to and fro*
> *And feels the weight of my arse below.*

To these two images of Gandhi and Villon a third came to my mind, not as an idea, but as an emotion, almost a sensation. It was the memory of the pain I had experienced at Cambridge when I had fallen in love with a girl called Laura and how completely frustrated I had been by her frigidity towards me. I had compensated for this experience by creating the masochistic fantasy that she would eventually desire me as I had once desired her. And within this day-dream was the painful realisation that her looks would not last and that she would turn back to me as an old woman. I found this thought too painful to pursue, and the image of Laura as an old hag was immediately replaced by an invisible portrait of Rose Marie ageing on the paper before me. A few months before I had had the terrible experience of waking up one morning in bed with her and seeing maggots on her face on the pillow beside me. They were not imaginary, though at first I thought they were. The maggots were dropping from the ceiling above us from a decomposed rat which had died beneath the thatch. Perhaps it was thinking of Villon that had let loose this train of macabre imagery. *Regrets de la Belle Heaulmière* lay behind them:

> *Advis m'est que j'oy regretter*
> *La belle qui fut heaulmière,*

Soy jeune fille souhaiter
Et parler en ceste manière:
'Ha! viellese felonne et fière
Pourquoi m'as si tost abatue...

These various images and recollections occurred simultaneously in me within the space of a couple of minutes. I now felt an immense sadness within me and wrote the next three verses with tears behind my ears.

Now I must sing the oldest song
That was ever sung in this or any other tongue.
It is the song of her short sweep of beauty, and what it did become
    And always will, as if as punishment
    To those who love, their love keeps time's appointment.

How I fear time which is all change.
Oh where is there a fair face found to challenge
Advancing age, with his full equipage and cortège, and not surrender?
    I have pressed my lips upon
    Helen's mouth and kissed a skeleton.

And who owns the eyes which do not show
The faint lines like a bird's feet in the snow
Which deepen perceptibly, as time leads and we follow?
    An old crone cutting the heads off a pail of fish
    Stands on the feet that were my mistress's...

I read these verses aloud to Briony. She seemed suitably un-impressed. She had drawn a dog in red crayon. We both took our paper into the kitchen to show Rose Marie.

I had been at Cambridge in the early thirties: a bad period for poetry. I was lucky to have Leavis as my supervisor and had, in fact, chosen to go to Downing only because he was there. He was the only Don with a live interest in contemporary poetry. He had read *Hugh Selwyn Mauberlay* to me. He knew his *Waste Land* and *Sweeney*, while the rest of the English Faculty were paddling in the shallows of Sir John Squire. Apart from Houseman, I found most of the Georgians twee: as irrelevant as doodles on a Christmas cake: mere poetical decorations. The other influence at that time was the flood of so-called free verse which such magazines as *Transition, New Verse* and the American magazine which Ezra Pound called *Nude Erections* pumped over the landscape like so much sludge. I reacted strongly against this verbal diarrhoea: obscure without depth, feeble without form. Leavis, and the influence of Edgel Rickwood's *Calendar* criticism, helped me to ford this bog. Rickwood deserves rescuing from obscurity: to a poet, he is one of the three useful critics of this century.

By the time I came down from Cambridge, I was nauseated with literature that was written as literature and artists who lived as artists. It struck me as frivolous and degenerate. For me, poetry was not a flabby decoration to life but an axe, the only tool to hand with which I could try to swipe at some of the inarticulate undergrowth around me. It was a window in my cell, not a pretty picture on the wall. I did not want to be a poet but I knew that for me the only way out of the prison of my self was through poetry. I saw it as a crowbar, not a parasol. I was only interested in poetry that was as lucid as plate glass—something to look through, not at; as sharp as an axe, like Dante, Pope and Donne, and I realised that no tool could be tough or sharp unless it had form. You cannot chisel with something that has no definition, or drive at the inarticulate with something which itself pretends to be abstract. You cannot carve wood with wood. And most of all I despised the poetry that was not controlled and conscious, stuff written under the trance of beer, dreams or drugs or the piffle of the planchette. If the universe about us is unconscious, then we can only make some meaning of it by being conscious ourselves. You cannot carve wood with wood. At times I regretted that I had not become a scientist. At least they had method, tried to be articulate and lucid. But science was obsessed with things and limited to things. Five bars of Schubert meant more to me than *Principia Mathematica* which I read and could not understand (which is no criticism of the author).

Two experiences reinforced these ideas I held about poetry. The first was when Ezra read Guido Cavalcanti's Canzone to me, *Donna mi priegha:*

26

Donna mi priegha
       Perch'i volglio dire
D'un accidente
      che sovente
           é fero
Ed é si altero
      ch'é chiamato amore
Sicche chi l'negha
      possa il ver sentire
Ond a'l presente
      chonoscente
           chero
Perch'i no spero
      ch om di basso chore

Atal ragione portj chonoscenza
    Chè senza
      natural dimostramento
Non o talento
    di voler provare
Laove nascie e chi lo fà criare

E qual è sua virtu e sua potenza
    L'essenza
      e poi ciaschun suo movimento
E'l piacimento
    che'l fà dire amare
E se hom per veder lo puó mostrare.

He gave me his edition to study at Rapallo.

The other was when I was watering the vegetable garden at West Mill with a rubber hose fixed on the kitchen tap. By putting my thumb over the opening of the hose, the pressure of the water was increased: I could produce a fountain whereas without the form of the hose and restriction of the thumb, the water would have been an inept dribble. I realised that the pressures in poetry were wholly dependent on being run against a form. I therefore decided to write some of Anthony's meditation in the strictest and most complicated verse form I could lay my hands on. This, of course, was Cavalcanti's Canzone which is of five repeated strophes, each of which is divided into four parts, the first two repeating one interlocking rime pattern and the last two another. I was not interested in rime per se. Milton had referred to the "tyranny of rime." But rime helps to define some forms and is justifiable when it is inconspicuous. I analysed *Donna Mi Priegha* and found it depended on the rime scheme A B C C D D E A B C C D D E. In Italian, this is of course easier to maintain than in English; but I decided to use it as a model. I wanted the form to give tension to the thought, yet not be conspicuous itself. I wrote the first line aware that it contained an echo of Eliot, but did not let that bother me. What is the use of friends unless they are useful? So I continued:

> *How still the valley:*
> > *this is the dead end of the year*
> *And the cut back vines*
> > *show no signs*
> > > *of life, leaf:*
> *Even the olives have felt the grief*
> > > *of the cold mistral.*
>
> *The pruned trunks stand ugly.*
> > *Sometimes they appear*
> *To shake as a fist; Thine*
> > > *Hand Divine?*
> > > > *Raised in wrath?*
> *Then held for a brief*
> > *moment which was merciful.*

I read this over to Rose Marie to make sure that the rimes were unobtrusive as such but helped to give tension. Then I continued with the third part of the strophe which requires a pattern A A B B C C repeated in the final part:

> *Not even the nettles lolling up against the wall*
> *Have strength to fall.*
> > *Only the wind, now shepherding*
> *The shaggy clouds going*
> > *Over the hill for the night*
> *Has any energy as it flees from itself in flight.*

28

But it is not deadness nor is it tranquil.
It is all
        appetite the blind roots seeking,
Twisting and desiring;
        Sensualism out of sight
Like a saint who fasts when hunger's his perverse delight.

Having completed this strophe, I now had to write another four to complete the Canzone. When I had done this I read the whole four to Britten and considered it successful, since he was not made aware of the form itself, but only of the tension that the form produced. This made me decide to write other canzoni in the play, and also experiment with other strict forms. I toyed with the sestina but abandoned that in preference for others.

When I had written these meditations for Saint Anthony, I began to tackle his temptations. The play had still only one character. But having noted sadly on more than one occasion that I myself was made up of several people inhabiting one skin, I decided that the other characters in the play should be projections of facets of Anthony's own personality.

        ...I have turned over my heart
Like a coin in my pocket.
        I now know my nature,
But to know oneself is not to change one's nature.
It is to discover extreme disparity
And the dishonesty
        of a Prince's Court
Where vanity's the fashion and flattery's an art.
        The soul's a state in miniature;
In each of us all: slave, both rich and poor.
All the diversity of a city street walks
And talks
        Up the bazaar within my brain.
Some laugh some beg some crawl in pain.
        Then how I am alone or free
Until I clear this rabble which live within me and consume me?

From this point, the other characters became dramatic personifications of aspects of Anthony: Marcus, a peasant, representing the

Saint's physical nature; Julian, a poet, his sensuality, and Bernard, a scholar, to represent his spiritual pride. Having externalised the central character in this way, I planned to make the play a conflict between "the motley crew who climb on board and few obey the captain," and then to kill these projections finally as the Saint's spiritual conflict resolved itself and his personality became integrated.

Naturally I was aware how closely I was following Eliot's *Murder in the Cathedral* where St Thomas has also his four tempters. But I saw this parallel as a stimulating challenge. It never worried me nor occurred to me that I should try to find a theme further removed from his. I knew that Eliot and I had such different temptations that the two plays could only have superficial structural resemblances, and these I counted no disadvantage. And when I told Eliot what I was writing, unlike a mediocre talent, he showed no resentment or thought that I was muscling in on what he might have regarded as his own preserves. I sent him the two central canzoni soon after I wrote them. He asked Philip Mairet of *The New English Weekly* to print them and wrote to congratulate me on the technical achievement. A few weeks later I had a letter from Martin Browne who had produced *Murder in the Cathedral*. Martin Browne was at Bude, touring with a play by Ghéon, and he said that Eliot had told him I was writing a Masque and he would like to see some of it since he was looking for a play to present at the Mercury Theatre, where he was planning a season. By the time Martin came to West Mill, I had completed the Masque and sketched the satirical Anti-Masque. But it was only three or four pages in length. He persuaded me to lengthen the Anti-Masque so that the play could be a full evening. I agreed to do this and told Britten that consequently his work would also be extended. He was pleased. He also told me that he had written to Robert Speaight, whom he knew, to try to persuade him to play Saint Anthony. This was a help: I had not thought then of the problem of casting, though so much depended on it.

Eliot now offered to publish the play and his office sent me a contract. I signed it with alacrity. The advance was £25. Sometime later when I had to assign the dramatic rights to Ashley Dukes, he discovered from my contract that I had, in fact, sold

Fabers all rights in the play for this paltry £25. Eliot told me that in future I had better read contracts more carefully and gave me my dramatic rights back again.

Eliot was not a typical publisher. He took an author's interest in one's work, never minded how much one corrected the proofs or delayed marking them, but even he did not respond to the opportunity of publishing the Gita.

When I was staying with Gandhi at Segoan he had given me a translation of the Gita. I had told him that I did not think it was a very good translation: the English was too flowery and not in keeping with the austerity of the text. Two or three years later, Gandhi sent me his own translation to which Mahadev Desai had added a commentary. Gandhi agreed to my suggestion that the work should be published in England. He suggested that I wrote an introduction. It seems hardly credible, but though I peddled this work round London publishers, none accepted it. Eventually I returned it to India. It is as if a thesis by Einstein on physics or an essay by Stravinsky on harmony failed to get printed. Surely this disproves the complacent notion—advanced by publishers— that anything of value gets into print?

During the first year of the war Britten had been in the United States. He had gone there in the summer of 1939, a few months before war was declared. Auden and Christopher Isherwood had settled there a year or two earlier and taken out American naturalisation. They had urged Britten to follow them. When he left for America he too intended to emigrate permanently. I never took this intention seriously. When we had gone to Paris together a couple of years before the war, he had been homesick before he reached Calais. The Press had commented viciously upon how some intellectuals were ratting on the country. But Ben's letters to me showed he missed everything English including the air raids. He tried to settle down on Long Island: living at Amityville because he had noticed a signpost nearby bearing the nostalgic word, Suffolk. He wrote and told me he was setting some poems of Rimbaud and, besides *Les Illuminations*, had composed his first opera, *Paul Bunyan*, to a libretto by Auden. He was busy enough but homesick for Snape and the Fens. I could detect from his letters that being a conscientious objector, like myself, he suffered from a similar feeling of guilt for not being at home and in prison there too. We both knew that is where we should have been since so many people, convinced by our opinions, had suffered the imprisonment which we ourselves had escaped. Amongst them was Michael Tippett. Britten tortured himself whether to return home or not. But eventually he had decided to return. This decision was made after he had picked up a copy of Crabbe and read the Suffolk poet for the first time. "To think of Crabbe is to think of England", E. M. Forster had written. Crabbe had been born at Aldeburgh. *The Borough* is a documentary in which the details of the Suffolk scene are accurately and vividly nailed. Reading the poem made Britten realise that he wanted to return immediately. For nearly six months, he waited for a boat. During this time he conceived the idea of writing an opera based on Crabbe's poem centred round the character of Grimes.

"I didn't suppose anything would come of it," he wrote to me, "but I mentioned the idea to Koussevitsky and he's giving me $1,000 as a commission!"

Soon after, Britten arrived home in the late spring of 1942.

He immediately went before Tribunal at which he was exempted from military service on the understanding that he would appear at the war-time concerts. I met him in London, and a few weeks later he came down to West Mill. I was delighted to see Ben again. So was Rose Marie.

"Now you can tune my piano, which you chose for me," she told him. When he said he did not know how to do that she was quite surprised.

"But I thought you were supposed to be a musician!"

It was a desperate time: the Germans had penetrated almost to Moscow; our forces in North Africa were being routed; our ships were sinking. One evening I had watched twelve disappear from a convoy as they were bombed in the Bristol Channel; every morning the radio informed us which city had 'had it' the night before: and finally invasion seemed probable and imminent; but in spite of the hourly and depressing news bulletins over the radio, Ben kept Rose Marie and me literally rolling on the floor in helpless fits of giggles.

Apparently in the States he had come across a book called *Guide to the Classics*, a typical American publication, the purpose of which was to popularise classical symphonies and help the morons of Maryland and Wyoming to remember the themes of these musical gems. Accordingly, the author had written words to all the major works of Beethoven, Brahms, Mozart, Chopin and Schubert. Ben had this entire volume of bathos by heart. Like a Chinese torturer he would not let us suffer the whole in one dose, but would let us recover from his singing:

> *"This is the symphony*
> *which Schubert wrote and never finished...*

only to reduce us to another fit of the giggles with the aid to remembering Mozart's Jupiter Symphony:

> *"Once more we are Mozarting"*

The worse the news became, the more relentless Ben would be. If the invasion had occurred on our own beach, if the cottage had been bombed, we would have been too helpless with hilarity to pick up our remains.

When I had seen Ben in London a few weeks before he came to Devon, he had told me that he had run into difficulties with the libretto of *Peter Grimes*, and was particularly dissatisfied with the lyrical passages and especially the end of the last act. He warned me that he expected my help and was going to try and finish the opera in Devon. Meanwhile he had given me Montague Slater's libretto to read. I had not been impressed and, as I had not at that time written a full opera libretto myself, I thought his work could easily be improved. The dramatic structure and the characterisation was firm enough but, as Ben complained, it failed to provide him with any springboard in the lyrical passages. Also, the final scene where Peter Grimes goes mad was unconvincing.

Five years of war had done little to improve the comfort of West Mill. Prison had discouraged me from salvaging any more petrol from the sea: we had therefore none for the car. Dil Fareb, my Arab, had been degraded to a mule and, with some panniers which I had bought in Fez before the war over her back, we had loaded Ben's and Peter Pears' luggage into them.

"I'm sorry it's so heavy," Ben had said as we had heaved his suitcase into one side causing the girth to slither, "but I've had to bring a lot of paper to write the score on."

The cottage was little more than a chaos of wreck wood, barrels, and lumps of tallow surrounding a grand piano. I soon saw why Ben had taken such enormous care in choosing this instrument at Chappell's for me when I had given it to Rose Marie. Merely waiting to down half a pound of Devonshire cream which he used to eat with a spoon and without any bread, he immediately settled at the instrument and asked if Rose Marie and I could bear to hear the opera. Peter volunteered to sing every part. There was some delay before we could begin; Ben had to remove one of Briony's dolls which had been put to bed on the strings; I had to rush out to feed the pigs and milk the goats and the new blue Shorthorn cow while Rose Marie tried to quieten Roger who bellowed in his cot. Other duties to be performed before the recital could begin on the untuned piano included my disappearing into the water wheel machinery with a hair pin which served to hold the join of the leather belt which drove the electric generator to provide the composer with light, and the hasty removal of one hundred week-old cockerels which Rose Marie was rearing round a couple of hurricane lamps in a box beneath it. But eventually we were ready. Ben warned us apologetically that he wanted to play the piece right through and that this would take him at least a couple of hours. He promised to play it as fast as he could so that Rose Marie would not have to delay getting the dinner.

Few hours in my life excited me as much as these. I was immensely impressed by the emotional intensity behind the music, particularly by the haunting and subtle gentleness of the trio for the four women, the *Interludes*, especially the *Passacaglia*, and the terrific impetus behind the whole work. I was aware that I was listening to a masterpiece. Even Roger and Briony remained comparatively silent throughout. I was also struck by the originality of the work.

"The last scene is missing," Ben said, closing the piano. "That's why I'm here."

Having congratulated him, I berated him for his profligacy.

"My only complaint with the work," I said, "is that you never gave one a second chance to hear some of the melodies again. Verdi isn't so spiteful."

For the next week or so I happily abandoned *This Way to the Tomb* which was unfinished on my desk and devoted myself to doing any cobbling to the libretto which Ben required. This was not easy, since the words were, apart from the last scene, already set. It entailed finding lines to fit the precise run and stress of the music.

"What I need here," Ben said, "is a line with the same number of syllables as 'Guinness is good for you' but something less bathetic than what Slater has given me."

When we were not absorbed in this kind of crossword puzzle, Ben was scoring the work. Briony was fascinated with the pen he used which drew five lines across the page with one stroke. The nib was like a five-fingered claw. Somehow or other, he managed to keep her amused and her chatter never seemed to distract him. Indeed, scoring seemed to be such an automatic and easy process to him that he was able to talk at the same time, seldom pausing to go to the piano.

Meanwhile I sketched out a last scene, deliberately echoing phrases from arias and numbers in the earlier part of the opera so as to force Ben to take the opportunity of recalling phrases of the music which had captivated me. He fell in with this pressure.

I had few qualms about altering Slater's libretto. And those I had were allayed by Ben who promised he would put things right with him. I little realised then that I was establishing a precedent; and that the same kind of liberties, though less extensive, would one day be taken with my own work.

When Ben and I were not working on *The Tomb* or *Grimes* we were busily hatching up another opera. He had said he wanted to write a comedy or two or three one-act comedies which might somehow be linked together. Eventually we settled on *The Canterbury Tales* and decided on selecting three, using the pilgrims as a link through an overture, two interludes and an epilogue. We drafted out a synopsis and later I started to write a libretto, basing the first part on the *Nun's Tale*.

With a play and an opera almost on the table, Ben and I boiled with other ideas. Every day produced the germ of a work which we enthused over at dinner and forgot by breakfast. But what we did see was that there was little point in working on grand operas when the expense of staging a new work was so astronomical. Ben wanted to turn his back on that Wagnerian circus and write for a smaller ensemble such as Mozart had used. He talked to me about the technical problems involved: how a composer of opera has two alternatives, either to find a musical idiom which he uses throughout his piece such as in Wagner, Verdi or Puccini or to return to the style which Mozart had used in *Figaro* where the arias, duets and ensembles are set as distinct numbers with accompanied recitative and *recitativo secco* to move the action along. I had, of course, run into precisely the same kind of problem in writing verse plays. I had found it comparatively easy or straight-forward to write Anthony's meditations but had laboured over writing passages where one of the characters had to do something pedestrian such as to tell somebody to shut a door or announce that he was going up the hill to milk a goat. Eliot and I had often discussed this question of style and had both tried to solve it by finding an idiom sufficiently flexible to carry the run of con-temporary language, including the 'one lump or two' moments. In a sense we had settled for the Wagnerian solution. Neither of us wanted to see poetry stuck on to the wall of drama like so much decoration or stucco that is used only for lyrical moments. But for the poet, opera poses another problem altogether: it is how to be heard or understood at all. When Ben said that he could get greater musical clarity in a Mozartian ensemble, I saw that it would also provide some possibilities for verbal precision too. In Wagner few words are heard or understood: in Mozart, whatever happens to the language in the numbers themselves, at least the words in the accompanied recitative are audible. I therefore en-couraged him in this line, for opera, though it was opposed to the course I was pursuing in drama. But it was, of course, the economic factor that was decisive: he wanted to write new operas. I urged him to form a small mobile group that could take opera round the country to offset our lack of opera houses. We walked miles dis-cussing this, and The English Opera Group eventually emerged from our hikes.

I was immensely fascinated watching Ben score. I had had no

idea of the amount of physical work it required. He used to say that a composer was a manual worker, and remind me that there were more notes in one opera of Wagner than there were words in all of Shakespeare's plays. He sat for about eight or ten hours a day at this chore, as he called it. He finished the score at West Mill. Rose Marie and I sensed that we had to celebrate the occasion somehow to avoid an anticlimax. We had no petrol, and even if we had there was then nowhere to go. We had eaten the snipe which Pears had plucked the day before. At Rose Marie's suggestion we decided to have a full dress performance of the opera. She had a black velvet evening dress. I managed to find my black tie, and Ben and Peter also put on dinner suits. This gave the evening a sense of occasion. We all felt very self-conscious as we sat dressed up in the tiny sitting room. Ben was extremely nervous. Peter sang every part. It was the most memorable evening I remember.

When he took a rest from scoring I read Ben some of the pages of *This Way to the Tomb*. Thinking of the costs he suggested some songs that could be sung unaccompanied, and offered to write a piece for a small choir at the beginning and end of the play.

"Maybe," he said, "you will find other opportunities for music before you finish the piece." He wanted to collaborate as much as he could and to find as many opportunities for music on the stage as possible.

"If I extend the anti-masque," I said, "you will have to write jazz for that." This possibility intrigued him.

A week or two after Ben left West Mill with the completed orchestral score of *Peter Grimes*, he asked me to come up to London to talk about the possibilities of our writing an opera. I went to lunch at the flat he and Peter had taken on their return from the United States in St John's Wood High Street.

Lunch was served soon after I arrived. Only the three of us sat down to the meal. Ben immediately continued the discussion we had started in Devonshire about the possibility of forming a small group to perform chamber opera. I maintained that the best way of achieving this organisation was to write a new chamber opera first and the group would then gradually form itself round this work. As usual in this sort of discussion, I produced the same analogy: that an axle is first needed if the spokes are to be attached to it. Ben accepted this and we started to discuss possible subjects. But interested as I was, my attention was almost wholly focussed on a girl of about nineteen who served the meal. She was so pretty, with black hair down to her shoulders, ivory skin and the most beautiful dark brown eyes. I could not keep my eyes off her every time she came into the room from the kitchen. Only dimly did I hear Ben asking me if I thought we might find a subject in Euripides or Shakespeare.

I remember asking for some more coffee just for the pleasure of seeing her come into the room again. I left the flat after an hour without having got any nearer to finding a subject for our opera, full of envy for the way Ben had solved his servant problem.

The next morning I phoned him and suggested we should meet sometime during the day to work on *This Way to the Tomb*. He said he was going out to lunch with Ralph Hawkes, his publisher, and would be back in his flat at four o'clock. I therefore arrived there at three.

The girl opened the door. She led me into the sitting room and asked if I would like some coffee. When she returned with it, I noticed she had two cups on the tray. She poured a cup for herself then sat down opposite me. I admired her for this and noticed how gracefully she sat and how well poised she appeared to be. I offered her a cigarette, she accepted. Observing her relaxed manner, I concluded that this was not the first time she had sat in the arm-chair opposite with one foot curled carelessly under her. Even a blind man would have noticed how attractive she was. The girl made no effort to talk to me. But as I did not want her to think I resented the liberty she had taken by sitting down and having coffee with me, I thought I had better make an effort at conversation myself. My first attempt led nowhere: she was obviously shy. I tried again and again received only a mono-syllabic reply.

Of course we had not been introduced. I asked her name.

"Marion," she replied. "Didn't Ben tell you?"

Ben! It had slipped out. So ... she was on Christian name terms with her employer.

"No, Mr Britten didn't tell me your name," I replied shortly, reprimanding her with my tone, not because I did not approve of the intimacy she had achieved with him, but jealous it was not with me.

Just then I heard the front door open downstairs. Marion got to her feet quickly, picked up the tray, put the cups on it and left the room. Ben bounded in a moment later. I let him apologise for being late because I was annoyed: he was, in fact, ten minutes early.

He got down to work; he played me the *Blues* and the *Boogie Woogie* he had written for the anti-masque, then Marion returned, this time with a tea tray. She put this on a small table beside the fire and withdrew. My attention wandered.

"Where did you find such a pretty maid?" I asked.

"Maid?"

"You can hardly call her a char."

"Do you mean Marion?"

"Yes."

He laughed. "What gave you the idea she's my maid?"

"She waits at table. You don't introduce us. If she's not your servant, what is she?"

"I told you in Devon; when the Steins were bombed out of their flat in Kensington I asked them to share the flat with us here. Marion is their daughter. Her mother, Sophie, is upstairs, her father, Erwin, works in Boosey and Hawkes."

"Tell me about Marion."

"She's nineteen; she's at the College and is quite a pianist; she was at Kensington High School. There isn't a trace of a German accent, is there? She'll probably make the grade of a concert pianist. Kendall Taylor is teaching her ..."

"But why do you make her wait at table? Why did she carry that tray in and then walk off without saying a word?"

"Out of respect. She's terribly fond of poetry: she adores music."

"Doesn't she eat? Then why doesn't she eat with us?"

"She usually does. But we're supposed to constitute genius at work. So let's stop gossiping."

I snorted. "She's too pretty to play Martha," I said.

I attended a good many of the rehearsals of *Peter Grimes* at Sadlers Wells. And long before the Dress Rehearsal I knew the work almost by heart. I found the rehearsals immensely exciting and stimulating. I enjoyed the atmosphere of conspiracy which pervaded the proceedings. The chief conspirator was Joan Cross: it was she who had somehow managed to persuade Sadlers Wells to produce a modern opera against all precedents. I had the impression that though the Administrators had given their permission for the opera to be produced, they did not approve of it and they managed to show this attitude in small but irritating ways.

The critics now refer to the ovation that this work received at its First Performance, as if to give the impression that they had led it. But the opera received only a mixed reception. When Tyrone Guthrie, Director of Sadlers Wells, appeared to take a curtain, he received cat-calls from some parts of the house. Thinking of the way the public and the critics had received *Sacre du Printemps*, I had sent Ben this impromptu First Night telegram:

> *If this noisy city should,*
> *arriving late from some debate,*
> *seek some argument in your lucidity*
> *and, finding it not there, then say*
> *it should be there; and*
> *if amateurs become choruses,*
> *and choruses form unions,*
> *and unions committees*
> *of managers and saboteurs;*
> *or, if the critics come*
> *to beat their own fantastic drum*
> *entombed in tomes of theory, deaf,*
> *without a single thought as an impediment to speech*
> *which flows from paragraphs to columns and grows*
> *in verbose vacancy and overreaches sense*
> *by the measure of their ignorance;*
> *If Turd of the "Times" comes and compares*
> *The subtle Grimes to Madame Flybuttons,*

And if old Newman escapes from St Dunstan
to soil tonight with his begrudging praise,
Then send these dialectical deaf mutes
to me who'll answer jealous critics of your art
with peas and beans, much wind and the resultant fart,
for I know your music is
what poetry just describes.

I had only intended to write a conventional first night message. The girl in the Post Office counted the words spitefully. From her look of disapproval I thought she might charge me double for one or two.

But when the curtains fell that night, I thought that even the dimmest and deafest would be aware that they had heard a masterpiece. They were sanguine hopes. Professor Dent's comments the next morning were to the effect that the music reminded him of the noise of a motor bike starting up. But fortunately there were two or three musicians present of the calibre of Erwin Stein who could make a more accurate assessment. Ben's only apprehensions were that the opera's reception would let down Joan Cross and Guthrie, who had shown faith in the work and risked their reputations on its account.

Back stage, whatever his achievements had been that night, he looked like a schoolboy about to receive fifty lines for having sent in an essay for his homework on the wrong subject. And the evening ended on a note in that key.

Boosey and Hawkes, the publishers of the opera, had arranged a First Night Party at the Savoy. Innumerable cars had waited to convey important guests, including the cast, to the hotel. Ben and I saw several of our friends off in these limousines and then turned to take a car ourselves, only to find we had been left stranded. We sought a taxi, found none, then started to walk disconsolately through the rain down Rosebery Avenue.

"Lucky I bought a raincoat," Ben said philosophically, as another taxi passed us with its meter flag down. "At any rate, I don't suppose it's a very good party."

We eventually managed to get on a tram and finally reached the Savoy about an hour after the last guest had arrived. The door-keeper looked at our muddy shoes, hesitating to allow us in. Fortunately one of the people celebrating happened to recognise the composer.

As we entered the room, a figure looking like Genghis Khan bore down on me. It was Gabriel Pascal.

"A film producer," Ben whispered to me.

Pascal immediately congratulated me on my performance. Never having sung a note in my life I looked bewildered, and disclaimed such pretensions.

"But were you not the boy, Peter Grimes's apprentice?" he asked.

I shook my head.

"Then you should have been," he said, with Pascal finality.

I realised that that was not going to be the last I heard of him.

I had bought Mead Farm, which adjoins West Mill, just before the war. At that time, my sister and I, who were founder members of the Peace Pledge Union, had profoundly shocked our trustees by insisting that our joint holdings in firms which we considered were profiting from the rearmament race should be sold and reinvested in something less militant, like land. But that was, of course, only one reason for my purchase. A more basic one was the drive everybody feels, if they are honest, to own the land immediately around them. That is clearly a fundamental impulse: in addition I had known every field on this farm for most of my life.

The owner of the farm was a man called Hancock, whose father-in-law owned West Mill too. When Hancock sold Mead to me, he stayed on as tenant. The farmhouse had been divided into two separate parts: Hancock lived in one, and Dr Radford and his family moved into the other. They had been my neighbours at Gooseham Mill.

Hancock was more of a cattle dealer than a farmer. On the hundred acres, he ran less than six cows, two sows and a carthorse. The land was not farmed but ranched: he paid his rent to me of £75 a year by selling the rabbits which infested every hedge. If he grew a field of dredge corn, the rabbits ate their way to the centre of the field. But like most Devon farmers at that time, he would not clear the land of the vermin because he relied on them to pay the rent. It was a situation analogous to a man living on the fat from the fleas which thrived on his own back. Riding by the Mead fields every day on my way to and from Gooseham Mill, which I farmed myself after the Community had collapsed, I found it very irksome to see Mead becoming more and more derelict. I was eventually driven to rent fields back from my own tenant. I could not give him notice to quit since the Agricultural Act had made him a protected tenant. I could, theoretically, have appealed to a Tribunal on the grounds of bad husbandry, but since he was in effect my own landlord at West Mill that course would have brought counter-measures against me. So at exhorbitant rents, I took back one field after another until Hancock was living rent free on the remaining fifty acres.

The situation at West Mill was no better when Hancock refused to do any repairs or improvements. And though Rose Marie had been content enough for several years with a bucket outside for a lavatory, a garden hose pipe with one end in the mill box siphoning water continuously into her sink which consisted of a basin in a state of perpetual overflow, now that she had two children she had rightly insisted on some improvements to our gypsy-like existence. My friend Nigel Spottiswoode installed a bathroom and hot water system. With the timber from a wreck we had also built a nursery on to the cottage. But Hancock had not paid for any of these improvements and had refused to sell the cottage to me. Eventually, when I finally persuaded him to do so, I found I was in effect paying twice for the improvements I had made myself to the cottage. But we were glad to get the place at any price. Soon after I had bought it, I realised that our best plan was to buy both my tenants out at Mead and move up the hill into the farm myself. West Mill was too inaccessible with two small children; everything had to be taken down to it, including coal and groceries, in the two panniers slung over the back of Dil Fareb, who, in spite of her pedigree, suffered these indignities patiently. Accordingly Hancock again had me by the short hairs and put me up to ransom, forcing me to pay him £1,000 for the inconvenience of moving to another holding he owned in Welcombe. Dr Radford was less difficult to deal with: he himself was in the forces, but his wife merely insisted that I should buy all her furniture. As she was a rent restricted tenant, I had to agree and paid, not only for her furniture, but for a boxroom full of hat boxes containing bonnets belonging to her late mother. Having acquired this junk so expensively, I now hated to throw any of it away. For years I hoarded these hats, fans, knicks and knacks, hoping they would come in useful someday. Many of these ridiculous objects still surround me like ghosts from a past in which there was no pleasure. There are albums of photos in which nobody I know is portrayed. But they have not been flung away; for who knows when a crocodile skin album might not come in handy, or when an ivory fly whisk will not be the one object you need?

When I lived with Gandhi, he taught me two things which cancelled each other out. He believed that one should live as simply as possible. He used an old orange box for a writing desk. But he also instructed me on the need to be self-sufficient, to grow things for oneself, to make things at home, and indeed, he was a prophet of the do-it-yourself movement. The paradox is, I discovered, that once you have taken to doing your own carpentry, house building, gardening and plumbing, your life of simplicity has gone by the board. For every old bit of wood, screw, pot or chunk of iron might one day be just the thing you are looking for; consequently, your barn overflows into the kitchen and the kitchen walks upstairs into the bedroom. The old stove is not thrown away but put under a bed because its iron top might make a lid for an inspection pit cover if, and when, you made an extension to your drainage. My desk, too, became full of coffee tins filled with old rusty screws which I had rescued from timber I had dragged up from the beach. Indeed, one of the reasons why we had to move from West Mill to the farm was this disciple of simplicity had no longer any room himself to turn round among his junk. The pity was, Mead was filled with Chinese fans, hat boxes and bonnets, before I even moved in with my lumps of tallow, coils of rope, ships' lanthorns, African drums, not to mention all the clutter Ezra Pound had given me, including cushions hung with beads inscribed with quotations from Virgil. How could I have thrown these away?

It was June, a blue skylark of a day with an oyster heat-haze on the horizon; the herring gulls listlessly scissoring the cliffs: I was happy. It was just the sort of day I wanted because I had ten acres of hay down on the cliff fit to carry—or it would be if it was all turned as soon as the sun had dried out the dew.

I explained this to Rose Marie and handed her a prong: we had no hay turner on the farm. There was not a dozen bailers in the whole of Devon then.

"We'll have to turn it by hand," I said, "and then put it into pokes, in case it rains tomorrow."

"But I must finish the bathroom ceiling," she complained.

"That will have to wait. Anyhow, it will do you good to be out in the sun," I added, thinking of my hay.

Indeed, I did not even notice that she looked tired. Actually she was not tired, she was exhausted. No wonder, she had kept pace with me for seven years. And only the day before had turned navvy and carried out sackfuls of lime and rubble from the bathroom where the old lath and plaster ceiling had been taken down by the carpenter in preparation for replacing it with plaster boards.

But in spite of that effort, besides the work of running the ill-equipped farm house, feeding and fending the children and acting as secretary, Scheherezade, mistress and monitor to a manic poet, she gamely followed me out to the field. We each took a row, turning the hay still wet underneath where it was heavy with clover.

We worked for a couple of hours, and then I left her and went off to another field to ask a neighbour if he would lend me his tractor. I was not away more than half an hour. But when I returned to the hay field, Rose Marie was not to be seen. I feared she was lounging in the hedge. I shouted for her impatiently. It was too early for her to have gone in to get lunch. Feeling martyred at having to work alone, I picked up my prong to turn the hay on my row when I saw a splash of blood on hers.

As I ran to the farm, I tried to think how she could have cut herself. Had she pierced her foot with the prong? Found a hook or scythe in the hedge and severed a finger? I ran on into the house calling her name as I entered the kitchen. The sink was bespattered with blood. A tea towel covered in it. I shouted for her again. Then rushed upstairs.

She was lying on the bed white as a corpse, her eyes closed. For a second I thought she was dead.

"Where have you cut yourself?"

"I haven't," she whispered.

"Then who has?" I demanded, already feeling resentful for the fright she had given me.

"Nobody."

"But all this blood?"

"I began coughing out in the field, suddenly I felt a bubbling feeling in my throat and then started to spit blood."

"Probably that lime from the bathroom ceiling caused it," I suggested unconvincingly.

An hour later, the local doctor told me that Rose Marie's haemorrhage indicated that she probably had T.B.

"It looks rather serious. Her temperature is up, her weight is down. She must have an X-ray immediately. Do you want me to arrange that?"

I did not hear the doctor's question. I was listening to the funeral march of *La Bohème* which persisted in accompanying Elizabeth Barrett Browning's death scene in *Traviata*.

"People die of T.B., don't they?" I said.

His answer was to turn away and shut his bag with a click. Antibiotics had not been discovered then.

"She should have an X-ray as soon as possible, meanwhile complete rest. We must avoid another haemorrhage. And we must get her weight up. It's under eight stone, two stone below her normal weight."

The music had stopped. This time I heard him and read the grim expression in the man's eyes.

"That's a lot," I said.

"Yes. A pity you hadn't noticed it. She should have been in bed for months."

He left. He did not like me. I did not like myself. I ran upstairs and looked down at the flushed face asleep on the bed.

I woke her up. I needed her sympathy. The doctor's remarks had quite upset me.

"That fellow almost accused me of starving you," I complained. "He says you're under eight stone."

"I've been telling you every day for months that I was losing weight," she said between coughs.

"Have you?...I thought you were trying to slim."

"You never thought about it at all," she said, getting up. "You were thinking about your work."

It was true. Her remark did not make me feel guilty, it only made me start worrying about the poem I was writing...

She was downstairs before I noticed she had left the room. She was at the sink.

"What are you doing down here?"

"Clearing it up. I know you can't bear the sight of blood."

"You must go back to bed immediately," I insisted not too vehemently as she reached for a cloth.

"Don't look at it," she said, "you'll only faint."

"It's a brighter red than ordinary blood," I observed.

"It's not ordinary blood, it's my life's blood."

The funeral march started up again. I stopped her reaching for a pail and propelled her out of the room. Even at eight stone, I could not have carried her.

"You're going to stay there," I said, fuming as she got back into bed. "I'll get the lunch." I tried to keep the magnanimity out of my voice.

"What about your hay?"

"Bugger the hay."

There was no sacrifice I would not make for myself. I knew I could not bear my own life without her. When another person's life reminds us how vulnerable and precious is our own, it is as near to love as most of us can get.

Now frantic with worry, I sloshed eggs into basins and threw empty shells into frying pans. Then remembered Gamel. The Brenans were still at Home Farm.

I had an idea that Gamel had had T.B. herself. Or was it that she wrote poetry as good as Elizabeth Barrett Browning? Perhaps it was both?

Within ten minutes she was around making the omelette and giving Rose Marie the sympathy I deserved.

Now my security was threatened. *Operation Tuberculosis* was put into action. My mother and sister took Briony and Roger.

Risking a second haemorrhage, I rushed the poor girl to London and took her straight to the Brompton Chest Hospital for X-rays, blood and sputum tests.

They said it would take a day or two for them to tell whether the disease was still active.

The delay irritated me. If it was to be bad news, I wanted my bad news there and then. The delay made a poor curtain.

Fretting with worry and farming by phone, I waited. She waited too, I suppose, down at Aldbourne where the Brenans had a cottage and had taken her there by ambulance from London. Of course the tests were positive. Anybody could have foreseen that.

"She will need to enter a sanatorium immediately."

"So she will," I said grandly and innocently, only to be told that the hospital had no bed. Every sanatorium and hospital was full. Ordinary nursing homes were not allowed to take T.B. patients as it is a notifiable disease.

After spending days on the telephone, I found a bed at St Ignatius hospital. I learned from the porter who carried the bag up to the grim and hideous ward that I had been lucky because another young man had been unlucky—his wife had died of the disease the day before.

With unusual restraint, I did not tell her this. She got into bed. I had a word with the house doctor who was looking at her X-rays.

"She's got a hole in her lung all right," he said cheerfully.

"How big?"

"About the size of a penny. We'll have to collapse the lung."

"How?"

"Give her an artificial pneumothorax."

"When?"

"When she's strong enough."

I returned to the morgue-like ward where Rose Marie lay beside twenty-three other women, many in the last stages of the disease. I compared her with the occupant of the bed opposite her near the door. They were of the same age. Both their skins were taut over their cheekbones and flushed, giving the impression of a glaze to the texture. Their eyes had the same kind of brightness, as though each had just drunk half a bottle of champagne; their hands had similar long fingers with their bones wearing the flesh like a kid glove. There was the same clamminess too. An enamel mug as a sputum cup stood on their bedside tables. And their coughs were identical too. And both had something like green rubber in their mouth after each cough.

But Rose Marie was not depressed by her condition: it was the bullying sister who reduced her to tears. This starched woman was disliked by the nurses and patients alike: she had a talent for humiliating both her patients and their visitors.

A few days after she had entered this hospital I noticed on my daily visit that screens had been placed round the bed opposite Rose Marie's.

"She had another haemorrhage during the night," Rose Marie told me. I took her hand and even while I sat there I could hear the poor girl opposite:

"I don't want to die. I don't want to die," she kept repeating. But both the screens and the bed were gone the next day.

"They always move hopeless cases towards the door," Rose Marie said ominously, and aware that she had been placed there on her entrance.

During this time, Ben insisted that I stayed at his flat in St John's Wood High Street. He gave me the room which Auden had just vacated. Pears and the Steins also still lived in this small flat. It was a great help to be there: Ben was not just sympathetic, he shared my concern. He had known Rose Marie almost as long as I had. He saw I was distracted with worry. To lessen it, he worried too. There was nothing else he could do. Neither of us mentioned our sense of foreboding. I would not have felt this so deeply if Rose Marie had not been so beautiful. Death is a lecher.

Everybody told me that whatever the outcome of her illness, she would be on her back for at least a year. I arranged for one neighbour to harvest my barley; another grazed my stock; my mother and sister had Briony and Roger who were then under four. It seemed that I might never return to Devon: I knew I could not go back without her.

I remembered a strange letter I had received from the BBC

some weeks before Rose Marie had had her haemorrhage. In this, Laurence Gilliam had asked if I would consider applying for a job with the Corporation if it were advertised. I now replied that I would. And met him for the first time at Broadcasting House. He told me that their Features Department, of which he was director, had decided on an experiment. They were going to invite three writers to join the staff and learn the technique required for writing for the radio. Another poet, Louis Macneice, worked in the department, and had written one or two successful scripts to which Ben had written incidental music. I was offered £12 a week and a secretary. I accepted, not because I could see I would need the money, but because I was so distracted with worry I could not sort out my mind sufficiently at the interview to find reasons to refuse. At this time I would probably have agreed to anything that was suggested to me: the world was remote; I was in a cocoon of anxiety, and lived only for the visiting hours.

At each of these, I saw Rose Marie's condition rapidly deteriorating. The eyes more hollow, the flush more marked and the cough... As I used to put the flowers beside her bed, I would squint into the sputum mug, then stare sadly down at her, already seeing the 'bracelet of bright hair about the bone'. And what was so impossible to bear was her unhappiness: not caused by her illness, but by the petty bullying of the sister who seemed to wish all her patients dead. Rose Marie had been in the ward about ten days when I arrived to find her sobbing with hysterics.

"The old bitch seems to hate her even more than the rest of us," a girl in an adjoining bed told me. "Maybe because she's so pretty."

I could see that this morbid persecution would kill her, even if the virus did not.

"Get dressed," I said. "I'll take you to Ben's flat for tonight. We'll find another hospital somehow."

The house doctor tried to dissuade me. He pointed out my grave responsibility in discharging a patient in such a condition. Rose Marie continued to dress.

"And I must warn you that tuberculosis is a notifiable disease."

At least her spirits revived in the taxi. Marion helped her into bed; then Ben amused her by playing the jazz songs he was writing for *This Way to the Tomb*. Sophie Stein smothered her in tears of affection. Even the cough seemed temporarily quietened.

But the Clinic at Marylebone to which I reported her condition the next day insisted that she went for another X-ray. And though these had been taken so many times before, the routine of red tape could not be evaded. For dozens of hours we sat in dozens of waiting rooms, becoming more and more depersonalised in each. Eventually an ambulance containing several women in a similar condition collected her and she was conveyed to a sanatorium at Pinewood, about an hour's train journey from London.

It was a barrack-like single-storeyed building set in a pine wood because the air from these trees was then supposed to be beneficial to the disease. It contained a couple of hundred patients, most of them in their twenties and looking forty: shop girls worn out by drudgery and childbirth. But Rose Marie seemed more content there, and biting her lip she did her best to accept the news that she would probably be there for at least a year. I was allowed to visit her twice a week for an hour. The male visitors, each with their pathetic bunch of tired flowers, trundled out of the bus, docking their cigarettes as they did so. These were painful hours; the clock skidded through them. She would try so hard not to cough while I was there, often almost choking from the effort of withholding it. We were now very much in love: insecurity had heightened our awareness, our hopeless interdependence—how can there be any hope for that? Sometimes she would tell me a dream, only to find it was I who had dreamed it.

I took my appointment with the BBC. It was the first and only job I ever had—apart from my spell as a coalminer. So I began by taking it seriously, arriving promptly at Rothwell House and sitting down before my secretary and a blank blotter. But the in-tray remained empty and the out-tray carried only a few of my farm bills and the proofs of *This Way to the Tomb*. After staring blankly at my secretary for a few days, I suggested she knitted me some socks. Eventually I asked Laurence Gilliam what I was supposed to do and was told to hang around and get the feel of the place.

"If you'd like to go to any films or plays in London, do so and charge them to expenses," he said. "Seeing something may give you an idea." The orbit of my sinecure remained so vague I did not know how to abuse it. I interpreted the directive literally. After several weeks of going to the BBC and nobody ever giving me anything to do, I got into the habit of using my room there as a place to dump my shopping. But I always remembered to look in on a Friday afternoon, when my cheque with its generous and un-questioned expense allowance was on my desk. This was helpful. I had often sought a beneficent deity and found it in the BBC.

While I was living at Ben's flat he was working on the *Donne Sonnets*, and sometimes used to consult me about the texts. I believe his sympathy with me in my concern over Rose Marie was expressed consciously in his setting of the sonnet:

> *Since she whom I lov'd had paid her last debt*
> *To nature, and to hers, and my good is dead,*
> *And her soul early into heaven ravished,*
> *Wholly on heavenly things my mind is set...*

He played this to me immediately he had composed it. I thought that this was the most beautiful thing he had written. I still think it is—that, and the *Passacaglia* from *Grimes*. To cover my emotion, I picked up his manuscript and remarked that I would still try and check the line of the poem:

To Nature, and to hers, and my good is dead.

I was not satisfied that the phrase 'and to hers' was correct. We had been using John Hayward's Nonesuch edition, and I sus-pected that he might have been as grossly careless with Donne as I had discovered he had been in his de luxe edition of Rochester.

It was while I was staying at St John's Wood High Street that Ben gave me the advice for which I shall always be grateful. I had never kept any accounts. The income tax had made an exhor-bitant demand.

"You'd better go and see Leslie Periton," he said. "He has looked after me for years."

Periton became a close friend and my main financial prop. He is a sort of St Christopher for writers, actors and composers, ferrying them from certain bankruptcy to precarious solvency.

Soon after *Peter Grimes* was launched at Sadler's Wells, Ben and

I started on his next opera. As he had done all the music for *This Way to the Tomb* it seemed only fair that I should do a libretto for him. We worked so easily together that we were quite confident that we could write the opera within three or four months, and started to discuss where we would try and get it staged long before we had even found a subject.

It was Eric Crozier who suggested *The Rape of Lucretia* as a theme. Ben and I liked the idea immediately, and a few days later drafted out a dramatic synopsis which, the same weekend, we broke down into musical synopsis, that is, aria, duet, ensemble, etc.

My schedule was to write the Lucretia libretto in the morning, then go down to the sanatorium when allowed.

As soon as I had done a few pages of the libretto, Ben would start composing. I managed to keep a few pages ahead of him. He seldom asked for any alterations. The only thing that disturbed us while we were writing it was how we were going to find the money to put it on and who could possibly sing the part of Lucretia. We knew that Peter Pears would sing the Male Chorus, that Joan Cross would sing the Female Chorus, but it was not easy to think of a contralto.

One day when we were composing the Second Act, Ben suggested that we ought to hear a girl whom he had been impressed with about a year before. He asked me to come along to audition her with him.

We were sitting upstairs in his little studio when a girl came in, looking very much like a provincial schoolteacher. She was so terrified she could only whisper. We wondered how she could possibly sing. Glancing at her clothes I was not impressed. I could see no signs of Lucretia there. I noticed the beautiful bones of her face, though I thought the jaw was a little strong. I remember she had a particularly ugly hat. Ben and I were both feeling almost as embarrassed as she. He cut the talk to a minimum and handed her the score. She read it through once, then went to the piano and sang part of the Spinning Aria. We were both so moved by the quality of the voice that neither of us spoke. I had been impressed, too, by the genuine feeling of purity which came over. This was a very necessary quality for the part. The poor girl waited for us to speak, not knowing why we were silent. Thinking that she had made a mess of her audition, she burst into tears. We then had a job to reassure her, and the more we did it the more she thought we were just being kind. We had been extremely lucky. She was not only vocally perfect, but it could not have been better casting from my point of view. True, she had never been on the stage, but I did not feel that that would be a disadvantage. Oddly enough, though Ben and I spent the next few months repeating to Kathleen Ferrier that we adored her voice, we never managed to convince her after the first audition.

The technical problems of writing the opera were nothing compared to the worry of finding the money to stage the work. It is always this way, one-tenth of one's energy to creative work, nine-tenths of it dissipated in finding the pennies. But, as with our contralto, so were we lucky with the financial side. We decided that we needed £15,000. The Arts Council agreed to find £5,000 if we could find the other £10,000. I knew of a stockbroker who had made sufficient money to give the City up and take to farming. He was called Jimmie Bomford and he was interested in the Arts in a vague way—he had sufficient acumen to be collecting impressionists in the 1930s. Ben and I approached him and he agreed to find another £5,000. I was surprised at the ease with which he agreed to do this, but found the snag a week later when he produced two unacceptable conditions: one was that a friend of his should sing the part of Tarquinius and the other that he should have the job of designing the sets.

There was nothing for it but to approach John Christie. Ben and I arranged to meet him for tea at Debenham & Freebody's. That must have been at his suggestion. We were surrounded by buttered toast; Christie, as usual, wrapping the handkerchief round and round his right hand and asking us what we wanted. On these occasions Ben was always silent. With some temerity I explained that we had written a chamber opera, that the Arts Council had agreed to find £5,000 and we were looking for another £10,000. Christie helped himself to more buttered toast and pondered the matter for less than three seconds.

"I will give you the money," he said, "on one condition." Ben and I looked at each other. Was he going to want to sing Tarquinius too, or had he ambitions to conduct?

"I will come in and stage the work for you, on one condition, and that is that you don't ask the Arts Council for a penny piece, and let me do it all."

We could hardly believe our ears. Christie then expounded on his hatred for the Arts Council, and arrangements were made for us to stay at Glyndebourne for six weeks to rehearse the piece the following summer.

At this time I had a letter from Michael Tippett asking me to meet him at Fullers tea shop at Victoria.

He too wanted me to write a libretto for him and suggested a Masque in a similar form to *This Way to the Tomb*. Over more buttered toast we discussed a possible theme: unlike Ben, whose mind always kept to the simple dramatic elements without any intellectual overlay, Tippett rushed to see a metaphysical or symbolical connotation everywhere. We sketched out a possible subject which he became more and more enthusiastic about as he perceived more complexities within it. But I told him I could not go any further with the idea then because I was still busy writing a libretto for Ben.

"What's the subject?"

"The Rape of Lucretia."

"Would you mind if I set it too?" he asked.

I looked dubious. Such an idea had never occurred to me.

"In the 18th century composers often set the same libretto," he assured me. "There's quite a tradition for it." He gave many examples; I felt almost convinced.

"Send me the first act," he urged.

I promised reluctantly to do this, but said I would have to tell Ben of his plans.

Tippett agreed to this but was confident that Ben would not mind.

"Of course he'll finish his score a couple of years before me," he said, "it's all so easy for him."

The next morning, without any undue apprehensions of Ben's reactions, I told him of Tippett's idea. He was completely crest-fallen and miserable.

"I suppose you think Michael could make a better job of it than I can," he said, suspicious that I had originated the idea. "Well, you may be right," he said with genuine modesty. "Michael's got some sort of depth I think I lack."

I hastened to explain that it had been wholly Michael's suggestion and that he had assured me there was a tradition of composers setting the same book.

Ben admitted there were many precedents. I never referred to the idea again.

After I had been sitting in Rothwell House at the BBC for a couple of weeks or so, the first atomic bomb was dropped on Hiroshima. I remember I was walking along St John's Wood High Street when I read the news on the placards. It made me feel sick and depressed at first. I then became violently angry and indignant. It was in this mood that I attended for the first time the weekly programme conference. I listened astounded at the frivolous subjects for immediate programmes, and then suggested that some programme should be improvised on Hiroshima. Laurence Gilliam reminded me that this was the feature department, and not suitable for political or, he added wryly, pacifist comment. Not caring whether I was sacked on the spot, I replied if they did not feature Hiroshima in some way they were a lot of ostriches broadcasting out of their fundament. The meeting was terminated. Mr Gilliam told me to stay behind.

"If you're so keen on doing something on Hiroshima you'd better tell me precisely what you have in mind."

This was fair. But I had nothing more than fury in my mind.

He sensed this. "A programme that's broadcast has to have a shape and a script. It has to be rehearsed and scheduled."

"Couldn't we do something tomorrow?" I urged, "while this savage atrocity has laid bare the whole conscience of mankind? If we wait weeks, indifference will have covered the wound."

"I can't see what we could do by this evening," he said dryly.

"To begin with we could send cables to a dozen people of known spiritual integrity and then broadcast their reaction to the bomb."

"Such as who?"

"Gandhi, Einstein, the Pope, Albert Schweitzer, Nehru, Bertrand Russell..."

For a moment Gilliam pondered the idea. I could see him thinking how good these names would look on a programme.

"It's an idea," he admitted.

"I'll go and draft the cable."

When I returned five minutes later, I found Gilliam had already returned to the shallows of *Desert Island Discs*.

I put my cable before him. He did not read it.

"I had a word with the Programme Director," he said, "and the idea didn't appeal to him."

"You mean they don't think the dropping of the first atom bomb on a town is news? Or don't they consider the reaction of this list of people is worth hearing?"

"I don't know, they just said it wasn't a frightfully good idea."

I slammed out of the room. My anger and frustration made me actually weep as I walked blindly to Hyde Park. I felt like an atom bomb myself. But as I charged round and round the Serpentine I saw that my first idea for a programme on the bomb was a mistake. Here, I realised, was a supreme opportunity: humanity was now anaesthetised with shock and was, as it were, lying prostrate, ready for music and poetry to perform a major operation on it. Now was the chance to use poetry as a knife and music as a scalpel and cut some of the cancer out of the belly.

As I ran from the Park the words of the poem came like telegrams into my head. I went to Ben.

"We must immediately write an oratorio about Hiroshima," I said, "something as artistically painful as the burns we've inflicted on the Japanese."

"Of course we must."

He closed the second quartet which he was composing. This piece had been causing him trouble.

"Let's go for a walk and work something out."

By midnight we had sketched the plan for an oratorio in three parts. It was to be a full scale work with full chorus, soloists and symphony orchestra, almost like the *Messe des Morts* in scope, with a pastoral symphony which Ben insisted should be in the first part. He was then already feeling his way to the Spring Symphony. The tenor was to be Peter Pears, and he planned a big contralto part for

Kathleen Ferrier, and a soprano role for Joan Cross. It was all in our hands.

The next morning I told Gilliam of our plans.

He listened cautiously. "I shall look forward to reading the script," he said. "How long will it take you to write it?"

"I shall be three days and nights on the libretto. Britten will compose immediately. I think we can have it ready in a couple of months."

"Well," he said, "you're already under contract to us, but Britten's another matter. The first thing is to let me see your script."

I went straight to my room and began to write. 'Mea Culpa, an Oratorio'. *'Dedicated to an unknown child whose severed hand I had found like a glove on the floor in a bombed house in Brixton in 1943.'*

I wrote quickly as though for the Stop Press, fearing that the patient would come round from shock and get off the operating table before Ben and I were ready to operate on his conscience. Within two days I had the nine pages completed. Ben said he was ready to go.

A copy of the libretto was placed on Gilliam's desk.

Boosey and Hawkes advised Ben not to start composing till they had negotiated a contract for him with the BBC. The BBC meanwhile intimated to his publishers that they would consider giving a contract for the work when he had submitted it. These negotiations continued over twelve months. The patient got off the operating table and started juggling with atom bombs and, where there had been a wound of a conscience, there was now only a grin. It was a pity: the *War Requiem* could have been written in 1946 instead of 1963.

This was one incident. There were many. They were all the same. A gradual wasting away of enthusiasm, the dissipation of creative energy. Like a befuddled old grannie, the BBC and similar besotted bodies sit knitting with committees. A Diaghilev would have given Ben and me our head: a mogul like Gabriel Pascal would have done the same. Art is served better by the reckless mistakes of tyrants or tycoons. Anything is to be preferred to the fumbling caution of democracy which is the blind rule of the lowest common denominator searching for mediocrity. Even com-

plete neglect of the artist is preferable to this piffling depart-
mental patronage in which everybody passes the buck till the
original idea is nibbled to death by the antennae of annotations and
memoranda. 'A camel is a race horse designed by a committee.'
Seventy per cent of my energy, whatever its value, has been
wasted, frustrated, and spilled on this rock. 'One bad general is
better than two good ones.' Give me an editor suffering from
dipsomania in preference to a sober editorial board.

I used to see Dylan Thomas a good deal when I was supposed to
be working at the BBC, but we never met, although we were in the
same department. I do not suppose this was any loss to either of us.
I did not admire his poetry. He had submitted several poems to the
Townsman (a quarterly magazine which I had edited from 1937 to
1945) which I had rejected. I was irritated by the echoes of
Hopkins. Hopkins is a poet who cannot be imitated, only
parodied. I admired Hopkins a great deal, in spite of Pound's
attempts to wean me from him, and my verse had been strongly
influenced by Hopkins' style when I was up at Cambridge; and
even later, when I came to write my first verse play, *The Unburied
Dead*. But it is one thing to tolerate a fault in oneself, another
when we see it in somebody else. And the mixture of Hopkins and
Johnny Walker in Thomas was not to my taste. Several people
suggested that I join them at a bodega opposite Rothwell House,
where Thomas went, but I never did. I suppose my failure to get on
with my colleagues at the BBC was due partially to my inhibitions
to boozing; I had witnessed two cases of D.T's before I was
fourteen.

While working on Lucretia, Ben asked me what our next opera
was going to be about. I had forgotten that we had already
sketched out a full synopsis of *The Canterbury Tales*, or that I had
scribbled part of the first act, so I suggested Abelard and Héloïse.
It was a subject that kept coming to my mind. I had been ravished
by the music of Abelard's *O Quanta qualia* when I had found it in
an anthology at school, even when Latin had nauseated me. Years
later I had picked up an old copy of a translation of the letters of
Abelard and Héloïse in Harpers' excellent bookshop in Bideford.
I gave this book to Ben to read. He was enthusiastic but said he

could not see how we could solve the problem of Abelard's castration.

"It can't happen on the stage. What do we do—have a baritone in Act One who suddenly sings counter tenor in Act Two?"

"There must be a solution," I said.

For the next week or two I thought of little else. The subject obsessed me. To my mind this is the greatest love story in history, or at any rate better articulated than any other which is perhaps the same thing. It occurred to me that there was a solution to Ben's problem.

"What we must do," I suggested eventually, "is to establish a sort of *Otello* love duet for them in Act One."

"Yes," he replied, unconvinced.

"Then we can extend this same duet again in Act Two."

"And then?" He was looking a little worried.

"In Act Three we can restate it. But this time the duet will be sung by Héloïse alone. Abelard will be silent, his part will *be sung by the orchestra*. It will be clear what has happened to him and give you opportunities to write something very exciting. After all, you like writing Lucretia's unsung entry at the end of the *Rape*."

"It could be very dramatic," he said, now as excited by the idea as I was. "That's what we'll do, establish the duet and then repeat it with Abelard silent."

I also told him that I intended to reveal in the last act that the Canon Fulbert, Héloïse's uncle, was really her father, and thus motivate the castration by paternal jealousy.

My pen now had St Vitus' dance. No project ever excited me like this one. The right subject and the right composer...

(I suppose we write an autobiography to reveal ourselves. It occurs to me that I cannot do that more effectively than by confessing that while I have been writing the previous three pages with one hand, I have been making marmalade with the other. I have never been able to resist the fascination of bubbling cauldrons of jam, then the triumph of scooping the stuff into jars. I find it impossible to do only one thing: it seems such a waste of time. I might as well be slicing fruit while thinking. I admit the marmalade boiled over and probably will not set. Let's hope these pages will. They are certainly sticky enough.)

I was too worried about Rose Marie's condition to give more than half my mind to the rehearsals of *This Way to the Tomb*. But I enjoyed hearing Ben's music; and what time I spent in the theatre I devoted to trying to ensure that his music did not get the sort of shabby treatment it usually does in a production. This was not difficult: Martin Browne was as concerned as I and gave Arthur Oldham, the young musical director, his arrogant head. Oldham knew precisely what effect Ben wanted, managed to find an excellent choir and rehearsed them without mercy. Meanwhile Bobby Speaight struggled to learn his long Canzoni. I could not understand how he succeeded in doing this. An actor's ability to learn lines has always bewildered me. I have never been able to quote even five lines of my own, even a day after I wrote them.

Marion, Ben and Eliot came to the First Night. It was sad that Rose Marie was not there in the black velvet dress she had worn for the first performance of *Peter Grimes* at West Mill and then at Sadlers Wells. I hurried to the sanatorium the next morning and told her how well the play had been received, carefully censoring the notices, most of which were patronising or carping. It seemed probable from them that the play would be off in a couple of weeks.

Like most people who have their first play produced, I used to go to the theatre every night, at least for the first week. This was not because I got any perverse pleasure out of seeing my own work but because odd relatives and friends had announced they were doing me the considerable favour of seeing my play and intimated that they hoped to see me in the foyer. Doubtless they would have been offended if I had failed to reward their attendance by not buying their drinks in the interval. Consequently I had to attend the first five performances: but by the time I had got to the fifth I had come to arrange my arrival at the theatre about ten minutes before the interval, when I could greet my thirsty friends on their way to the tiny wine bar.

I had just left my coat that evening when I heard a great disturbance in the foyer. Both the doorman and the manager were doing their best to silence and support a late arrival who was so drunk that he couldn't stand. Shouting at the top of his voice, he insisted that as he had a ticket, which I noticed was stamped complimentary, he had every right to enter. I recognised the drunk as a well-known critic. He did not know me. My impulse was to assist the doorman to hurl him out into the street. But as he was making such a din and was already disturbing the auditorium, the manager thought it advisable to let him in, hoping that would quieten him. So together we put him into a gangway seat at the back row. I sat beside him to prop him up. But my efforts were in vain: the eminent arbiter of fashion or taste slumped in a stupor and began to groan loudly and punctuate St Anthony's soliloquy with belches. I called the manager and together we lifted him and eventually dumped his critical faculties on the floor of a waiting taxi.

Two days later when the weeklies appeared, we read this twerp's long attack on my play. The management protested to his editor. This critic has never given me a good review since. Any dramatist I know could cap this story.

I have always risen early. I count this a bad habit because it is a nuisance to others, and a bore to myself, to be wandering about a house, especially other people's, two hours before they rise. It does not matter how late I go to bed, I wake soon after seven with an urgent need for tea and cigarettes. I then have to pad around their kitchen searching for caddies and sugar. My early rising derives from years of beachcombing: the scramble to be on the beach before my predatory neighbours.

One morning at St John's Wood High Street, I thought I might take a cup of tea into Marion. Her bedroom was next to the kitchen. Noiselessly I opened her door. She did not wake. I put her tea down beside her. There was a wooden carving of a crocodile on the mantel shelf. I picked it up to look at it, then replaced it and sat down to watch Marion sleeping. Ben had the previous evening told me that he wanted me to write a lullaby for the Female Chorus to sing over Lucretia. I picked up a pencil and just described what I saw before me:

> She sleeps as a rose
> Upon the night

And light as a lily
That floats on a lake
Her eyelids lie over her dreaming eyes
As they rake the shallows and drag the deep
For the sunken treasures of heavy sleep.
Thus sleeps Lucretia.

Then I tiptoed out of the room and put the lullaby on Ben's piano.

An hour later Marion came into the kitchen to get the breakfast. She thanked me for the tea, and asked why I had not woken her to drink it.

"And you did something else in my room," she said.

"What was that?"

"You must have moved my crocodile."

That much I admitted.

Erwin Stein had been a pupil of Schoenberg and a friend of Mahler. He was one of the most foremost musicologists in Europe. Ben had met him on a visit to Vienna before the war, and was instrumental in obtaining a position for him at his publishers, Boosey and Hawkes. Stein and his wife, Sophie, and Marion, managed to escape from Vienna on one of the last planes to leave the city before the Nazis took over Austria. When they reached London, they lived in a basement flat in Kensington, Erwin Stein working at Boosey & Hawkes, taking a special interest in Britten and Stravinsky; his daughter attending Kensington High School. When this flat was bombed, Ben had invited them to share his at St John's Wood High Street. Erwin's musical knowledge and taste was an invaluable support to Ben. It was he who did the piano score of *Peter Grimes*, and he had a considerable influence on the composer, and anybody who came to know him. He was one of the most unassuming men I ever met, and his knowledge of music was something I have not seen equalled. Besides these attributes, he had another: he was essentially European, by which I mean that one sensed that many influences and traditions were alive in his personality. He was mature: he never made claims: he was tolerant: he never made judgements. A specialist in the 12-tone system, yet not unfamiliar with the philosophy of Hegel and Schopenhauer.

Sophie, on the other hand, was in many ways his antithesis, a handsome Aryan with as much emotional content as he had intellect. She was one of the largest-hearted women I ever knew, and was moved to tears at least three times a day. She had an inexhaustible supply of pity for others. One of her eccentricities was that she never learned to speak English properly, and commenting at this time on my somewhat nomadic existence in bedding down wherever I could find a couch, she, intending to say that I was like a wild flower in the field, announced that I was like a weed in a ditch. The epithet stuck.

In retrospect, I dimly perceive that I must have outstayed my welcome at St John's Wood High Street. At any rate, one evening I had taken Marion to a concert at the Albert Hall. We were having a drink at the bar when Joan Cross bore down on us. She looked like a woman with a mission. Then with deliberate casualness she enquired if I had had any luck in finding a flat.

"Absolutely none," I replied.

"He's looked everywhere, there's not a thing to be had," Marion said.

"Then I think I can help you," Joan smiled. "I've heard of a woman who has a small cottage, overlooking Hampstead Heath. It's very old, National Trust property. You'll think you're back in Devon. She lives alone, and is prepared to let you have the front bedroom and will give you breakfast, all for 26s. per week."

"How many bedrooms are there in this old cottage?"

"Two," Joan said, "and the woman is over seventy."

"Why should she want me as a tenant at such a ridiculously low rent? Is she lonely?"

"She likes living alone. Promise me you'll go and look at the cottage in the morning?"

I could only agree.

The cottage at 14 East Heath Road overlooked the Heath. And it was certainly old, proudly bearing the National Trust plaque on its front like a medal for services rendered.

"It looks like one of those places that you wind up at the back," said Marion, "and a cuckoo pops out from under the eaves."

We opened the wicker gate where michaelmas daisies and

chrysanthemums flopped in a tangle over the unweeded path. Then we stood still, listening. Somebody inside was playing a Beethoven piano Sonata, banging it out accurately but without any shading at all. The *pianissimo* passages were as loud as the *forte*.

"Whoever it is must be deaf," Marion concluded.

"Very," I said, having knocked four times.

Eventually a white-haired woman, aged about seventy, came to the door; she was dressed in black. She looked like a Victorian miniature and wore a band of black velvet round her neck to complete the image. I expected to see a group of gnomes sitting on red mushrooms in the kitchen, industriously hammering gold leaf or manufacturing silver ear trumpets.

Instead we saw that the living room of the cottage was so crowded with knick-knacks and ornaments that there was no room for chairs. It contained no furniture but a concert grand piano.

She showed us up to the small front bedroom which was filled by an enormous brass-balled double bed and a madeira wicker chair. Lace, and odd bits of pampas grass covered the mantel shelf. Obviously nobody had entered the room for many, many years. But it did not smell fusty but of concentrated lavender.

"I couldn't stay here anyhow," I whispered to Marion as we followed the old woman down the stairs. "I'd be too cut off without a telephone."

"And there is a phone too," Queen Victoria announced, glancing disapprovingly at the gadget she had obviously never used, which we now saw in a niche at the bottom of the stairs.

Clearly my one valid objection to the place had been anticipated. The phone had definitely been put in especially. Someone must have been very energetic, Erwin himself, or perhaps it was Joan?

In these circumstances I could do nothing but capitulate. I told Queen Victoria—I don't think I ever knew her name: at any rate she resembled the Queen too closely to have a different identity— that I would move in the next day. She confirmed that the rent with breakfast was 26s. per week.

"But I presume you'll pay for the telephone," she said, and then bit her tongue as she added "I never use it."

I gave her a week's rent in advance. I worked better in this cottage than anywhere I have ever lived. Or at any rate I got more done and managed to complete *The Rape of Lucretia* and *The Eagle has Two Heads* there, scribbling at each alternately, sitting in the wobbly madeira chair at the foot of the bed. Queen Victoria was a perfect person for a writer to live with. Immediately we fell into a routine. She must have always got up before it was light because we never clashed in the bathroom. By the time I was dressed, my breakfast was served on a card table beside the piano. She must have already eaten. Not a word was spoken. Then I would go upstairs and by nine o'clock was at work. By nine-fifteen precisely, Queen Victoria, having washed up, would start on Beethoven's Piano Sonata in D. She would always play it straight through three times; every passage was emphatic and *forte*. Occasionally there was a wrong note, but these were few enough to be noticeable. At ten-thirty, Her Majesty would puff up the stairs with an enormous battered aluminium pot of black coffee which was so strong you could almost stick a spoon upright in it. The old coffee pot stood on a tin tray covered by a lace cloth. She would put this before me silently and then ease her way down the precipitant and narrow stairs again. As I tried to stir my concentrated caffeine, Beethoven's Sonata in A would begin. This routine was rigid. She would work at a sonata for a fortnight, then turn to another, never varying her composer. Sometimes the phone would ring; it would ring a long time before I could hear it. Although its bell was beside her, she was either too deaf or too absorbed to notice it. Those who phoned me heard only Beethoven. Oddly enough, her playing did not distract me. It was always there, as permanent as a solid writing desk: I could almost put my elbows on the sound. I would have worried if it had stopped.

Naturally enough, Ben and Marion were intrigued. Ben had heard of old women taking to gin, never Beethoven. In those days he thought gin was better for them. Many theories were produced. The saddest was Marion's: she suggested that Queen Victoria was determined to give a concert at the Wigmore Hall. For weeks I sat happily writing on this solid surface of sonatas without having the courage to enquire to what end this dedicated practising was aimed. And though I used to go out every day for lunch and then seldom return until late, my occasional reappearance in the afternoon confirmed that she played sonatas all the afternoon too.

66

I never discovered what she did in the evening. But eight hours at the piano for a woman of seventy seemed obsessional. After about six weeks I could bear my curiosity no more. And as she put the black brew in front of me I blurted out the question.

"Why do you work so hard on Beethoven?" I asked.

"Because of Epstein," she said.

"Eh?"

"Epstein likes Beethoven," she explained and sidled down the stairs again.

This was too much for me. My curiosity had been doubled. It was impossible to imagine any woman less likely than her to be interested or obsessed about Epstein. Could it be that Queen Victoria suffered from two illusions? Was she trying to sculpt the sonatas and carve Beethoven? There was not a sign of the sculptor in all this ingle-nookery of lace and pampas grass.

While I sat writing the libretto, I would pause and turn this problem over in my mind. I think I became obsessed with it too.

Then one day, a few weeks later, just as I was going out, Queen Victoria actually stopped playing in the middle of a bar.

"Epstein wants to know if you will take tea with him next Thursday," she said and immediately began playing where she had left off.

"Tell him I shall be delighted to share a scone with him," I shouted.

Walking down to the tube station, I was not sure that Queen Victoria was not mad. I had never met Epstein but was certain that he did not hold little tea parties for an obsessional pianist of seventy, dressed like a black marquee. I was mistaken.

The following Thursday, I was reminded that I had promised to take tea with Epstein and told that I was expected at Hyde Park Gate at four o'clock.

Even so, as I approached the house that afternoon I began to prepare my apologies. It seemed probable to me that the sculptor had never heard either of me, let alone Queen Victoria.

A man opened the door who looked like a down-and-out docker or a Chicago gangster. He wore a cloth cap and carpet slippers. I expected him to be armed with a cosh.

"Good of you to come, Duncan," Epstein said, and ushered me into his dining room. Tea had just been served on the long dining-room table which carried thin bread and butter, cakes and scones. I looked for Alice and the White Rabbit but found myself being introduced to Mrs Epstein, who sat at the head of the table. She was a severe looking woman dressed in black and of Old Testament dimensions. Epstein himself sat at the other end of the table. I observed that Queen Victoria was on his right, clutching a piece of fruit cake with a Beethoven Sonata tucked under her arm. Matthew Smith, the painter, was on my left. Before hearing his name, I had assumed he was a general.

"I saw you in the Mercury Theatre a couple of months ago and immediately wanted your head," Epstein explained, "then last week Gladys happened to mention that you were lodging with her."

Queen Victoria beamed.

"And so I asked her to persuade you to come along one week. We do this every Thursday."

After we had nibbled our way through the buns, Epstein turned to his right and asked Gladys if she were ready. She rose augustly and we all trouped behind her into the drawing room. She sat at the piano and sailed straight into the Sonata in A. I had heard it all that morning and every morning for the past two weeks. She played it as she always played it with unrelenting emphasis and unnatural vigour. Epstein himself sat as still as one of his own statues. The only time I ever saw him chain his restlessness. He was moved by the music. He seemed unaware of the lack of any soft passages or the occasional wrong note. Or at any rate, he applauded as energetically as she had played.

"Come and look round my studio," he whispered, and we tiptoed from the room.

"Have you known Gladys long?" I asked him, feeling a sense of lèse-majesté about using her Christian name.

"Years. I like Beethoven. And so she comes along every week to play some to me."

"Do you know she practises eight hours a day, every day?"

"I guessed that. But what else has she to do?"

He then turned and confronted me with the head of Aneurin

68

Bevan which he was working on. Churchill glowered from another pedestal.

We didn't mention Gladys or Beethoven again. I never discovered the rest of that story, being satisfied with its end: devotion from one, kindness from another. And the fact that she played so badly made the story more precious to me.

"As I say, I want to do your head," he went on, quite unaware he was doing me any honour. "Will you please sit for me? I shall need about a dozen sittings. You won't have to sit still, and if you like, you can bring a secretary along and dictate while I work, like Lord Beaverbrook did."

"I'm not that busy."

"Well, I don't want you to look bored."

"Can't we talk?"

"I never stop."

"Then when do you want to start?"

"Tomorrow," he said. "Could you give me a couple of hours tomorrow?"

I smiled at his humility.

"Tell me, why do you want to do my head?" I asked him.

"I don't often want to do heads," he said, "sometimes I accept commissions. But yours is another matter. I want to do it."

"Why?"

He sat down in front of me. "Because it's a beautiful head," he replied simply. "I can't explain why, but what I'll do with it will be the explanation. No, you needn't worry, it won't be like that thing behind you."

I turned to observe a cast of a woman naked to the navel.

"That's Princess ——," he said. "She commissioned me to do a portrait head, then once I'd started insisted I should include her bust; later we descended to where you see. Fortunately she committed suicide before we got down any further. Odd how women like undressing in this climate."

The next day I presented myself at Epstein's house. He immediately hustled me through to his studio at the back and sat me down on a chair placed on a dais about a foot from the ground. He began talking voluably, raking his mind for chit-chat and anecdotes about the theatre, as though he were frightened

69

that I would become bored and leave. And while he talked, he padded round me examining my head from every angle as though it were some strange object, the first head he had ever seen. A look of concentrated wonderment in his eyes, while frivolous anecdotes poured from his lips.

He had a lump of clay ready and a wire support nailed clumsily to a board. Still talking, he began to fix tiny pellets of clay, each about the size of a small fingernail, to the frame. Fascinated by what he was doing, I failed to respond to his stories; this made him think I was getting as bored as he feared I might, and so he redoubled his efforts to entertain me. The anecdotes became more indiscreet and he worked even more frantically as though he had to finish it before I disappeared.

After half an hour, sweat was pouring from his face. He looked like any one of the coalminers with whom I had worked down the mine at Holmwood. He too was entombed, within a vision in his mind and he sweated to emerge; his only way of escape was to create the reality he imagined—which is, I suppose, applicable to any artist and makes frantic buried moles of us all. But I never saw any man, coal heaver, pneumatic drill driver, or navvy, work as hard as Epstein did. My head had been done before when I was twenty by a Royal Academician, David Evans; but that sculptor had worked leisurely beginning with a large lump of clay and gradually reducing it down, producing my likeness by taking bits away. Epstein had an entirely different technique. After an hour he had placed about a thousand tiny pellets on to his wire frame and created something about the size of a hen's egg. It was already a likeness of me, the embryo of the finished head. I commented on his method.

"It has to grow organically," he said. "Just as it does in the womb."

Two sittings later the head was the size of an orange, the sweat still pouring from his face as he worked without pause and talked without restraint. His fingers more gentle than a child's, his tongue becoming more vicious than a whip. Nobody escaped his lash: his previous sitters, Churchill, Bevan, Beaverbrook, were all paraded in their foibles before me.

"I was paid to do them," he said, excusing his contact with such tycoons. "Yours is the first head I've enjoyed for years. I think it'll be the best I've done."

As sitting followed sitting, Epstein and I became firm friends, or rather, in his eyes, fellow conspirators. He thought of the whole world as being divided into three classes: ordinary people, who were damned; the artists who had sold their souls to Mammon, who were also damned and to be hated; and lastly the few creative artists who, like himself, had somehow retained their integrity and been rewarded by the world's derision. It was a simple and untenable philosophy which served to feed his persecution mania and yet, at the same time, it gave him a sense of closeness to the half-dozen people whom he elected to his untouchable élite.

While I was sitting for him, his great carving of Lazarus stood in the studio behind me. It impressed me greatly, and sometimes Epstein would catch me staring at it. He was pathetically grateful for those glances. The sneers which such masterpieces received in the press hurt him where they were meant to hurt. May those cheap-jack journalists who wrote such articles be condemned to read their own piffle over and over beneath his graceful prayers in stone, either in Cavendish Square or Cardiff Cathedral. I once saw this tough man weep involuntarily as he re-read the sneers against Genesis in the press. They were: 'Oh you white foulness' (*Daily Express*); 'Epstein's latest and his worst' (*Daily Mail*); 'Unfit to show' (*Daily Telegraph*). I wondered then what those writers had ever carved beyond some lecherous limericks on lavatory walls.

One morning a few weeks after *The Tomb* had opened, Queen Victoria told me that a foreign gentleman with a bellowing voice had phoned me repeatedly the day before. She was not sure of his name, but thought it was something like Muscatel. It was obvious she neither approved of his manner nor his accent. Before retreating down the stairs again, she grudgingly informed me that he had left a message asking me to meet him in some café at seven o'clock.

"Which cafe?" I asked hopelessly.

"I think it was called Claridge's," she said.

"And he didn't say who he was or what he wanted?"

"He said he wants to give you a castle in Italy," she replied suspiciously.

"Must be some mistake," I said, settling down to work. "I know nobody of that name and people don't give castles away."

Ten minutes later the phone rang. I heard the Beethoven Sonata eventually skid to a halt.

"It's that foreign gentleman again," Her Majesty called.

I gingerly took over the barking phone.

"Do you like Saint Francis of Assisi?"

"I've nothing against him."

"Good, it's a deal except for the details."

"Oh, don't worry about those," I said facetiously, "but do tell me who's speaking."

"Pascal," the voice announced, imitating a Deity.

"Who?"

There was a minute's silence while God digested this heresy.

"Pascal," the voice boomed.

The phone went dead. I had a picture in my mind of him like Prometheus—it would have been appropriate if it had then thundered.

Even so, the name meant nothing to me.

That evening I had arranged to take Marion to one of Ben's concerts. When I met her I told her of the mysterious phone call and she quickly reminded me who Pascal was, and that I had, in fact, met the film mogul at the First Night Party of *Peter Grimes*.

We decided to call in at Claridges on our way to the concert and arrived at seven-thirty.

From the frantic atmosphere in the Hotel foyer, we thought that a fire had broken out. Porters were scuttling about looking worried, and the band was playing energetically and loudly, as it does when a ship is going down. Page boys were darting about as though they had hot coals in their trousers. The source of the disturbance was Pascal. Pascal had been kept waiting. It had never happened before. Like a harpooned whale he sat in one corner of the lounge spouting impatience and belching invective to flunkies and secretaries, who circled the wounded monster. But as Marion and I approached, the whale suddenly collected himself and assumed the posture of Buddha whom we had disturbed at his meditations. For a few moments he stared through us, then came out of his trance and studied me through his dark, diabolic and almost hypnotic eyes.

"I've seen your play about Saint Anthony," he said, as though that in itself was an honour I didn't deserve. "You are a great poet. I will do for you what I did for Shaw."

"And what was that?"

"Discover him. First I will present your play in New York, and Rome. Then I will make the picture of it."

He snapped his fingers. A terrified shoal of secretaries brought pads and pencils.

"Now we cast it. Tell me who you want in New York. Gielgud could enunciate your poetry but lacks the humanity. Nobody would believe he'd been tempted. Orson could do it. Make a note, ring Orson this evening. Britten's music couldn't be bettered. But your décor is shit and your costumes are worse. Whom do you want for your décor?"

"Bérard," I murmured.

"Bébé would be perfect. I'll send him some chocolates. That's all settled then. Now when can you go to Italy?"

"Why?"

"Because first I film your *Life of Saint Francis.*"

"I have never written one."

"Tomorrow you start. I place a castle at Ferrara at your disposal. You sit there and write it. In six months we shoot it."

"But tomorrow I've got to go to Pinewood," I said feebly.

"Pinewood? Where's that? Who's there?"

"My wife. She's in a sanatorium with T.B."

"So, we must move her to Switzerland. And then...who's that?" he demanded, suddenly noticing Marion beside me.

I introduced her.

"So," he said rudely, "you're a little Viennese?"

Marion ignored the comment and reminded me that the concert began in ten minutes.

"But you're both dining with me," he announced with imperious finality.

"Thank you, we can't do that," Marion explained. "We're going to a concert."

"You should go back to Vienna," he shouted with inexplicable rudeness.

I had never seen two people take such an immediate and unrestrained dislike for one another.

I rose and escorted Marion out of the hotel. As we left we could hear the whale foundering, waiters scurrying to administer to his gigantic needs, and secretaries scrambling to patch up his punctured pride.

Half way through the next morning I was again interrupted writing the libretto when Queen Victoria called up to announce that the car had arrived.

I did not own a car. I peered through the dirty lace curtain and perceived a large limousine outside the cottage with a uniformed chauffeur at the wheel.

I went and asked the man what he wanted.

"Mr Pascal said you wished to go to Pinewood," he said.

I got in. It seemed better than going by bus. But instead of going straight out of London I was driven at great speed back to the West End.

"This isn't the way to Pinewood." I felt that I was being kidnapped.

"Mr Pascal wishes to accompany you," the chauffeur said as we drew up at the Savoy Hotel.

In a few moments Kubla Khan himself appeared, bearing gifts of fruit and flowers.

"My own mother had tuberculosis too," he said, reverently, as he sat down beside me.

As we drove to the sanatorium Gaby continued to arrange my life without any sustained regard for my inclinations and how I myself might wish to live it.

"I have seen your agent, Margery Vosper, and agreed to acquire the American and Italian rights of your play," he said proudly without mentioning any figures.

I had an uncomfortable feeling that I myself had been bought. I resented this Tartar but at the same time was fascinated by him. Energy has always appealed to me, even when it has been almost criminal. Being almost incapable of making a decision myself, the man of action, even the wrong action, produces a sense of awe in me. And to increase my naïve response, Gaby told me that he was an ex-cavalry officer and a great admirer of Arab horses. I believed him. He was a great talker and peppered his conversation with well-known names with such an air of condescension that you did not feel he was name-dropping, but doing those he mentioned a favour. Within half an hour I learned that Brancusi had cooked for him, Bérard had designed his ties, Shaw had found him a secretary and Rilke was his uncle.

At the sanatorium, I left him in the car while I bore his gifts in to Rose Marie. I was surprised to find him still there when I came out an hour later.

Touched by his patience and his concern for Rose Marie, I allowed myself to be conveyed to Mumfords Farm, his eyrie at Beaconsfield. Gaby played many roles: one, the gentleman farmer; of course he bred only bulls. When I had admired his shorthorns he led me across the immaculate gravel drive to his Tudor mansion with its hall hung with several paintings of the Madonna. I was then subjected to one of the most embarrassing moments I ever experienced. Standing in the hall, Gaby pulled a velvet cord. I heard a gong-like bell toll. Promptly a good-looking woman appeared aged about forty. She clasped her hands in front of her and looked scared, as if expecting a beating.

"This is my cook," he said, "she will prepare you a dish you will never forget."

He then turned on the woman and spoke to her in Hungarian. She now looked even more terrified.

"I really am not very hungry," I interposed, thinking he must be ordering a braised peacock or a sauté of leopard when the poor woman had only got a steak in the fridge.

But Gaby ignored me and continued to lash at her with his tongue.

"Just a couple of boiled eggs will do," I continued, feeling miserable at the sight of the cook's punishment.

The tirade continued. The woman now on the verge of tears suddenly knelt before me.

"I really am not hungry at all, not at all," I said lamely.

Her hands reached for my shoe. For a second I thought she was going to do up my lace or something, then I realised I was wearing shoes which had no laces.

"Now kiss the poet's feet," Gaby commanded in English, and the poor woman bent her head and did so.

Astounded, I turned to expostulate at the maniac beside me, but having achieved his will on the woman, he now stood relaxed and apparently sane. The woman had risen and scuttled off.

I protested and made a move to go.

"She will be very hurt if you don't stay and eat what she's cooking for you," he said quietly.

I went to the door. I had to escape. My impulse was to hire a car, pick Rose Marie up from her sanatorium and drive immediately back to the refuge and sanity of Welcombe. I felt physically sick, nauseated with every person and all the values to which my so-called success had led me. As I went through the door Gaby came after me.

"You can't go like this," he said. "Can't you imagine how hurt my cook will be, when she finds you've left after she's prepared this very special dish for you?"

I stopped, incredulous that after the scene I had witnessed he should have the effrontery to accuse me of insensitivity towards the woman.

It occurred to me that if I left he would perhaps take his anger out on her and force her to some further indignity which I hesitated to imagine.

We returned to the house and while we waited for dinner Gaby discussed Buddhism; it was clear to me that this enigma had read widely on the subject.

"I once thought of becoming a monk," he said simply as we went in to dinner, to drink tokay from golden goblets.

I began to feel that my life had become a caricature, a Rake's Progress or a Poet's Regress. Gaby himself was so much the prototype of the Hollywood film director, international impresario, de luxe gypsy, that I found it difficult to accept him as a real person.

The cook appeared proudly bearing a dish made out of lobster, cream cheese and paprika. She stood by me while I tasted it, beaming with pleasure at my response. Gaby congratulated her and toasted her; she seemed to bear him no resentment of their previous interview. Obviously that scene was part of their routine, a relationship I couldn't fathom. But from the pleasure she got from our appreciation of her cooking, it was clear that I had been right to stay. It was always that way: my impulse to leave somewhere, to break with somebody was frustrated by the fear that it would be unkind: the consequence was that I began to be consistently unkind to myself, to the essential me who belonged by the stream running outside the door of West Mill, who was only fulfilled growing vegetables or messing about with derelict cottages in Devonshire.

Shortly after Beverley Baxter had written an article about *This Way to the Tomb* in the *Evening Standard*, he telephoned me one morning at Hampstead to say that Lord Beaverbrook wanted me to go and see him early that afternoon. I was not sure that I wanted to meet Lord Beaverbrook. I told Baxter truthfully that I had several appointments that afternoon. The voice at the other end of the line suddenly went very faint: when Baxter had recovered his equilibrium he informed me that Lord Beaverbrook was also a busy man and, as a matter of fact, had managed to sandwich me in between two important appointments. From his tone I assumed that one was with Winston Churchill, the other with General Eisenhower. Baxter paused to let this sink in to my insolent head. I was duly impressed, but warned him I would probably be late as I had arranged to lunch at some distance from Park Lane. I heard a stifled moan and he hung up.

And I was late, not out of deliberate casualness but because I had difficulty in finding the block of flats opposite Marble Arch. A male secretary, looking as if he was about to have a miscarriage, greeted me and propelled me hastily towards the Presence, past a pugilist whom I supposed was a body-guard.

Entering the room, my attention was immediately arrested by something more striking than Beaverbrook. It was his portrait by Graham Sutherland. I stood admiring the picture which was leant against a table: the model came and stood beside me.

"What d'you think of it?" he demanded.

"It's the best contemporary portrait I've ever seen."

"That's what I think too. Come and sit down. You're a poet. Tell me, what d'you think of Walt Whitman?"

Briefly I told him what I thought of Walt Whitman.

"I shall still read Walt Whitman," he said, "in spite of what you say. I hear you're a farmer too?"

We discussed Ayrshire cows. It was clear to me that he also knew more about cows than I did. After thirty minutes he stood up to indicate that I could take my leave. I did this with alacrity, fearing a tangle with any other of his appointments.

But going down in the lift I realised, to my surprise and in spite of my prejudices, that I had liked the man. Only a few years before I had written a savage lampoon against Lord Beavermere — 'skunk, pimp or profiteer' and I wondered whether the fact that he had flattered my sense of self-importance by wishing to see me had been enough to alter my opinion about him. I looked hard at this question but saw that it wasn't the reason. I still had no idea why I had been summoned. I supposed it was curiosity, but I realised that whatever his motives something about him attracted me. It was the same with Pascal. I could not approve of either but liked both for their energy, their enthusiasm about being alive.

Baxter telephoned me that evening.

"He liked you," he said almost gratefully.

"It was mutual," I grudgingly replied.

"He can be a great help to you."

"How? Does he know the best way to finish my new play?"

"Perhaps he'll ask you to write for the Daily Express?"

"But I don't want to," I added shortly. Thus unwittingly I forced Beaverbrook's next move.

It came two days later when his secretary rang to ask me if I would go down to Cherkeley.

"If you can indicate what time you will arrive at Leatherhead, Lord Beaverbrook will send a car to meet you."

"I'm sorry I can't be certain of that," I said.

Each brush-off got me further involved. If I had wanted a job, sought an appointment, I would never have got past the lodge. As it was, my indifference acted as a pass-key. Beaverbrook was waiting for me on the lawn, a second cane chair empty beside him. When his toadies had withdrawn he stared at me without saying a word. It was as if his eyes walked round me sniffing out my weakness like dogs. I stared back, wondering why some men have faces and others have caricatures.

"You're no better looking yourself," he said, reading my thoughts as well as his own, "or Epstein wouldn't have done you too."

The mongoose and snake act was interrupted by a minion with a draft of a leader and a few cables.

The Beaver glanced at them and then dropped one after the other on to the ground. It was always his filing system.

"And what d'you think of the *Express*?" he asked when we were alone again.

"I only look at the cartoons. Osbert Lancaster carries it."

He pursed his lips. I half expected him to bite my calf. But I felt it was my turn to ask a rhetorical question.

"Tell me what you thought of Stalin?" I said.

"Why?"

"Not everybody's met him."

"He's a very clever knave. We talked the same language. At least I understood him. Roosevelt never did; only Winston knew the score..."

He talked on for half an hour without reserve and then suddenly turned and asked:

"Tell me why I should be telling you? I've refused to be interviewed."

"Don't worry, I shan't write it," I said.

Then another secretary approached with a telephone on a long cable.

The Beaver picked up the instrument and listened.

"Yes," he said, and put the receiver down again.

"I have to go up to London," he said, "we'll have a drink, then you can motor up with me."

In the car he seemed lost in thought and I assumed he was thinking of some urgent international affair that was taking him up to London.

"I hear your wife's ill," he said, "what's wrong with her?"

"T.B.," I replied, "she's in a sanatorium."

"Where?"

"At Pinewood. A place run by the L.C.C." We continued up

79

the arterial road. Then almost surreptitiously he produced some-thing from his pocket and held it under his hand on his lap.

"Is money any use for her?" he asked, opening his cheque book. "Here's £400."

"No," I replied, too surprised to be sensitive. "I can't take that."

"Why not, if you need it?"

"Then let me earn it," I said without thinking.

"All right," he said, "you do that."

He put his cheque book away. My pride had been mean. It would have been more generous of me to accept his generosity. As it was I had trampled clumsily on his impulse to help. He could afford it. But that didn't explain his impulse. I felt miserable at the hurt I'd caused. Sitting there in the car he looked suddenly crumpled. By not taking his £400 I felt as mingy as I would have done if I'd refused to give a penny to a blind beggar.

For the rest of the journey we discussed Wagner without interest.

A couple of days later a Mr Arthur Christiansen telephoned me to ask if I would meet him. He suggested the Savoy or his office.

"Where is your office?" I asked, never having heard of him.

"I'm the Editor of the *Daily Express*," he said, then added, "it's a newspaper, you know."

When I presented myself at that office designed like a flash urinal it was apparent that Mr Christiansen returned the compli-ment—he had not heard of me either. We looked blankly across his desk covered with telephones; a map of the world hung behind it.

"I'd like you to write for the *Daily Express*," he said without conviction. "Have you ever written for the newspapers?"

"No."

"Would you like to?"

"I don't think I could."

"Why?"

"I haven't any news."

Mr Christiansen regarded me very sadly.

"Newspapers do contain other things besides news," he said gently, "articles, columns and criticisms."

I shuddered.

"Perhaps you could write about the theatre?"

"No, I seldom go to it."

He glanced at a piece of paper in front of him.

"Why, I thought you were a playwright?"

"That's why I don't go. The plays make me too angry."

Again Mr Christiansen looked a little crushed. Then he began again. It was apparent that he had been instructed by the Lord, as Beaverbrook was reverently referred to by his stooges, to fit me in somewhere. I felt as if my life had become a plagiarism of Mr Evelyn Waugh's *Scoop*.

I decided that I had better be quite frank and deal the poor man a final blow.

"I really don't know much about anything," I said "except poetry...'

I was right. That word made Mr Christiansen wince.

"And cows," I added diffidently. At that his face lit up.

"There we have it," he said, "I knew we'd find something. You write us an article on Cowes. About a thousand words — you know the thing, yachts and the people who sail them."

"I meant dairy cows."

He winced again. I began to feel sorry for him. We drank a cup of tea in silence while he studied the map behind him. I assumed he was looking for somewhere to send me but there wasn't a war on just at that moment.

"I could go to Tibet," I said helpfully.

He digested this suggestion and turned.

"You could go to Tibet," he repeated flatly. He bit his tongue and sat down again.

"But you are living in London for the time being?" he asked hopefully.

"Yes."

"And having written such a successful play you must get around a good deal to parties and things and meet a lot of people?"

"No."

"Why not?"

"I'm writing another play."

This finished him.

"Look, Mr Duncan," he said firmly, "we run a column in this newspaper called 'William Hickey'. I don't suppose you've ever read it, but it's about personalities, peers, débutantes and people in the news. I want you to write it."

"But I don't meet these people."

"That's your problem."

"I can't do this every day."

I could see the man greying before my eyes.

"You can't do it every day?" he repeated, stabbing a pen nib furiously into his desk. "No, I do see that would be hoping for a good deal from you, but since it is a daily feature, perhaps you would write it once a week—say on a Friday?"

"I'd prefer a Saturday," I said.

"Would you. But we don't appear on a Sunday," he said, waving his hand weakly above his head.

I thought of Lord Beaverbrook's generous gesture in the car. 'I'd prefer to earn it,' I'd said. So this was his way of taking me at my word? I didn't want to offend him again.

"All right, I'll do it on Fridays."

Mr Christiansen looked relieved.

"That's very helpful of you," he said. "Let me have your copy by ten p.m. and remember, type it all in capitals."

"Why?"

"Lord Beaverbrook wants to read it personally. He's short-sighted."

I left Mr Christiansen to nurse his embryonic ulcer and bought a copy of the *Daily Express* to study William Hickey in the tube going back to Hampstead. I thought the column was very dull, failing as entertainment and lacking both the spice or spite of gossip. Of satire there wasn't a trace. I decided it would be amusing to enliven it.

That evening, while Queen Victoria played through the Sonata in F minor, I resurrected Major-General Marsland, his brother the Bishop, and invented the Earl of Morwenstowe, the Marquis of Hartland and his débutante daughter, Lady Frigidity Stanstead, and a bright young thing called the Hon. Clitoria Lunt. I needed a hostess and without much effort summoned my Aunt Henrietta up from her suite in Hades to entertain these imaginary nonentities on a barge moored off Hampton Court.

My description of this party got rid of a couple of paragraphs. Next I visited a Gallery in Brook Street where a Serge Flamsky was holding an exhibition of abstract painting which he'd painted with an egg whisk. Having got into the swing of this social whirl I found I was enjoying myself immensely. I got it typed in capitals and as I posted it almost regretted that I had agreed to do it only once a week. I felt relaxed, it had drawn off some of my spleen. A column like that, I said to myself, is almost as comforting as having a portable urinal.

The next morning I hurried to the newsagents for the pleasure of seeing my motley gang in print. I was not merely disappointed, I was furious when I saw that not a word I had written had been published.

I marched into a phone box and asked Mr Christiansen if he had received my copy.

"Yes," he admitted.

"Then why didn't you print it?"

"It contained twelve libels, four slanders and two instances of probable obscenity," he said.

"How can there be any libel or slander in it?" I demanded. "None of these people exist."

"What did you say?"

"I said, none of these people exist."

"Oh dear," he said, "what are we going to do with you?"

But I was immensely cheered when I returned to my cottage to find a cheque for £50 waiting for me. I had earned that in an hour. It had taken me a year to write *This Way to the Tomb* and I had sold both the publication and dramatic rights to Eliot for £25. In my usual manner I worked out what my annual income would be on the assumption that I could obtain £50 per week as easily as this. With such fanciful thoughts in my mind I flew down to see Rose Marie in the sanatorium to give her the news. It depressed her. She called me a gossip columnist, and when I pointed out that none of the people I maligned existed she argued that that was worse, since "they can't defend themselves against your spiteful tongue."

I could hardly wait for the following Friday to write up further adventures of the Hon. Clitoria whose social round was again accompanied by a Beethoven Sonata. Having avoided anything obviously libellous and included a paragraph or two about some real personalities whom I had never met, I ran out the next morning, confident I should now see my tribe in print. But again it wasn't published. Nevertheless my cheque arrived. I didn't complain to Mr Christiansen. Beaverbrook himself telephoned me. To my surprise he never mentioned my abortive column, he merely asked me to lunch. Not knowing his methods, I assumed that this was his method of firing his employees. When he greeted me I suddenly realised where I had seen his mischievous face before: it was the exact replica of one of the satyrs carved over the maindoor of Notre Dame. He picked up my typescript, all in capitals, and joined his ears with a slice of melon grin.

"Splendid stuff," he said, "that'll take the skin off their backs. Keep it up."

During the meal he never mentioned Mr William Hickey and I began to wonder whether he had realised that I had filled the column with fictitious characters and libelled these to such a degree that his Editor had refused to publish it. Could it be, I wondered, that Beaverbrook had enough good taste not to read his own papers?

All he said when I left him was that he was looking forward to 'his next instalment of salacious slander'.

To satisfy his appetite and my own inclination, I invented a few more characters. Once again they failed to find their names in print. Nevertheless the cheque appeared promptly. With a few prods from Rose Marie my conscience began to stir: how could I go on taking £50 per week for some rubbish which was never published? My alternative was, of course, to apply myself seriously to the column, and write the sort of inane gossip about genuine nonentities that was printed daily. I decided that that would bore me. Consequently I went to see Mr Christiansen. From his expression it was apparent that he had prepared himself for any eventuality. I merely told him that I wasn't going to write the column any more. He seemed very relieved and hoped that we would meet again. At any rate that is what he said.

Having relieved this burden on my conscience I found it even heavier the next week when my cheque arrived without my having written anything. I assumed it was an error in the *Express* accounting department and eventually got myself to phone them. They were indignant at my suggestion that they made an error.

"We've been instructed to pay you £50 per week and our job is to carry out our instructions."

I telephoned the Editor and complained that I was being paid for doing nothing.

"That was your decision," he said enigmatically.

For the next five weeks my cheque continued to arrive. When I had received £400 the payments stopped. Beaverbrook had had his way.

I did not hear from him for several weeks. Then, one afternoon just after luncheon he telephoned me and in his gruff manner asked me to come round to his flat to see him.

"I'm sorry I can't do that now," I said.

"Why not?"

"Because I'm dressing..."

"A little late?"

"To go to the opera," I explained.

"Early for that," he growled and slammed the receiver down, not giving me time to add that I was going to Glyndebourne and the train left about four o'clock.

I thought no more of the incident but the next morning Beverley Baxter phoned me.

"You've properly upset the Old Man," he said. "Can you meet me at the House of Commons for tea to talk about it?"

Baxter looked as grave as any Ambassador presenting an ultimatum.

"You've no idea how much you've hurt his feelings," he said. "He's not used to people saying that they can't come when he whistles. I myself have left my family in the middle of dinner on Christmas Day to go down and see him. But you not only refused, apparently you fobbed him off with some damn silly remark about dressing for the opera at three o'clock in the afternoon."

"If he hadn't rung off I would have told him that I was going to Glyndebourne."

"I see. He thinks you were telling him to go to hell."

Baxter still looked very worried. Like all of Beaverbrook's aides and editors, he both feared and hero-worshipped the Imp.

"I'll try and straighten it out," he said. "You've no idea how upset he is."

I left the House of Commons. It looked as if the War of the Black Tie might yet be averted.

The next day the 'Ambassador' phoned me and told me that he'd given my explanation to Beaverbrook.

"Well?"

"He's very much your senior," Baxter went on, "and not used to being treated casually...maybe you could break the ice and phone him?"

This seemed a small thing to do.

"Can you come to lunch?" Beaverbrook asked.

"Thank you," I said, not unaware that he had made an effort too by asking a question.

We lunched alone. He talked freely about his early life, his affection for Bonar Law and the Duke of Windsor and his dislike of Lord Mountbatten. And throughout his fascinating reminiscences I found myself wondering why I, a mere pup-of-a-poet, should be the recipient of them? His concern for Rose Marie whom he had never met was genuine. I never understood the reason why he seemed to like me. I never wanted anything from him. Perhaps that was one reason for it?

At any rate, before I left he asked me if I liked films.

"Sometimes."

"I'm very fond of them," he explained, "and have my own little cinema down at Cherkeley. I wonder if you would like to keep me up to date with any you see so that I know what to choose to have down there?"

It seemed a small thing to do.

"Perhaps you could let me have a note once a week or so?"

"Certainly."

"And don't forget, typed in capitals."

I did this little chore every week and the cheques began to arrive again, this time from the *Evening Standard*, with a generous expense allowance. Nothing, of course, was ever printed; indeed, I used to send my criticisms straight to Beaverbrook himself.

When Rose Marie had to go to the sanatorium, Roger and Briony had gone to live with my mother and sister at Docton Mill. They stayed there until eventually they went to a nursery school at Swimbridge. As I used to go to the sanatorium nearly every day, I could only get down to see the children and my horse, Dil Fareb, occasionally. On one of these occasions Gaby Pascal offered to lend me his car and chauffeur to get down to Hartland. Then, at the last minute, he insisted on coming too. At Taunton, he stopped the car, rushed into a toyshop and bought half the store. He had never seen Roger or Briony. I could not understand his generosity. He enjoyed giving these presents. My children mistook him for Santa Claus. He had had no children of his own. There was no room to put him up at Docton Mill, so I decided to stay with him at the local hotel, dramatically situated at the bottom of the cliffs. From the outside it looks inviting. Gaby and I were put into one room. It was damp, it was cold, it was dirty. He was a long way from Claridges. At breakfast, the bacon was congealed and the coffee cold. We decided to spend the next night at West Mill, although it had not been occupied for a year or more. It was a fine morning. We got down to the Mill, and put a couple of chairs out and sat by the stream. Suddenly I noticed that Gaby was sitting hunched up. I thought he was coughing. I found he was crying.

"I can't bear this place," he said. "It reminds me of the house where my mother died." There was nothing for it but to walk up the hill again and drive back to London. But one could not be cross with him; he had meant to be helpful. He soon recovered on the drive back, and spent the time trying to persuade me to write the play on the life of St Francis. I often wonder how I avoided it. But I did find myself agreeing to make an English version of Pagnol's *La Femme du Boulanger*, and also his *Birth of Love*, although neither films were ever made.

Pascal fascinated me in a way I have never quite understood. He was a mass of inconsistencies and incongruities. Sometimes a bully, at other times gentle and understanding; a vulgar charlatan with moments of sensitive intuition. I think I saw him as a sort of Falstaff—ridiculous but genuine—with definitions broad enough to be seen. I suppose I can tolerate anybody but so-called normal people and can forgive anyone but those who bore me. At this time, Pascal could even persuade me to jump out of cars and pick up girls walking along Piccadilly or Regent Street. I found myself doing this on innumerable occasions when he would suddenly spot some girl on the pavement and tell the chauffeur to stop, at which I would leap to my cue. I would then approach the girl and say: "Have you ever thought of going on the stage?"

If the frightened typist, for that is what she generally was, did not walk off, and that is what she seldom did, she would appear immensely flattered by the thought and admit that it had at times occurred to her. Meanwhile Gaby watched from the car while I explained to her that Mr Pascal thought she would be ideal to play St Joan. I used to take the names and addresses of these girls and, strange to relate, no harm came to them other than that Gaby arranged to send them to a drama school and pay all their fees. They never heard anything further from him. He never made St Joan. I suppose most returned to typing after an interlude of Hollywood dreams.

While playing at impresario, I was farming by phone. This year there was one of the worst harvests for a decade. After I had taken over the whole of Mead I had to clean it, plough some fifty acres, and sow it all to barley. That summer all the corn was laid. I could see this from the train as I travelled up and down to Rose Marie's sanatorium. I knew the corn would be laid even worse in Devonshire. When I went down there, I found not a single acre standing. There were no combines then, just the old binders that worked across the field like rheumatic windmills. I took a match and watched the whole lot burn fiercely as a breeze came up over the cliff. Townees think of farming as a comfortable background. I would like to put them to stooking sheaves for a few days.

I had just got back to my lodging in Hampstead one afternoon from visiting Rose Marie when I received a phone call from the Manager of the Mercury Theatre.

"We've just been informed that Queen Mary is coming to the play tonight. Of course you will have to be there too."

"All right," I said, wondering whether I should be able to find a clean shirt.

I remember having a leisurely tea, a more leisurely bath, then changing and taking the tube. From Hampstead I had to change at Oxford Circus for Notting Hill Gate; as I settled onto the Central Line I glanced at my watch. It was seven-thirty.

"That gives me half an hour," I thought, picking up an evening paper. I passed three more stations and then suddenly I remembered that the curtain of my play went up at seven-thirty and not at eight o'clock. I would inevitably be thirty minutes late. What was worse, I realised that nobody would believe I had actually forgotten the time my own play started. The management would just think I was rude and unco-operative: the Queen would ask for my head. I was miserable: it was no way to return the compliment of her attendance. I ran from the tube station a full thirty minutes late. But there was worse to come.

Unfortunately the Mercury Theatre has no boxes and certainly no Royal box.

"Your seat is beside Her Majesty," the manager said curtly to me. "Third row from the front."

I pushed open the door, interrupting one of Robert Speight's soliloquies and tiptoed down the aisle looking for row C and somehow expecting that I would be able to slip unobtrusively into my seat. I don't know why I thought my seat would be beside the aisle. It wasn't. That privileged position had been taken by Queen Mary. I saw with panic that to get to my seat next to her, I would either have to squeeze past her lap or she would have to stand and step into the aisle. There was, I suddenly realised, an alternative: complete retreat up the aisle again. I chose this and turned. But just as I did so Queen Mary looked round and drew herself back in her seat as far as she was able to, indicating I was to press by her. No author has ever interrupted his own play as I now did. Not a single member of the audience had any eyes for my play; indeed, two rows of pop-eyed stalls turned to observe my manoeuvre, which, as I tripped over her stick, nearly landed me on Her Majesty's lap. I was sweating with embarrassment and felt so small I wondered whether I would weigh enough to keep my seat down.

At the interval between the Masque and the Anti-Masque the lights came on but since there was no withdrawing room at the Mercury, Queen Mary elected to stay rigidly in her seat. I had hoped she would sweep out leaving me to banish myself for the rest of the evening in some bar in Bayswater. But she turned to me. Her expression painfully reminded me of my Aunt Henrietta's.

"You were late," she said.

"Yes, Ma'am," I said, "I thought this play began at eight."

She pondered this for a second and then smiled.

"Perhaps it did," she said, "but the curtain went up half an hour earlier."

I enjoyed that. She was just like my Aunt.

"But I'm enjoying your play. It's very beautiful."

While *This Way to the Tomb* was running, I was asked by Hugh Beaumont to translate Cocteau's latest play *La Mort écoute à la porte*. I read this script, and turned the suggestion down. Beaumont asked why—I told him that I thought the sub-plot was too involved, and the only thing I would be interested in doing would be to adapt the play drastically. I warned him that Cocteau would never agree to this, and thought that the matter would be dropped. But Kitty Black, who was running the Company of Four at the Lyric, Hammersmith, would not leave the matter there. She had already cast the play for a promising actor and actress; one, Eileen Herlie, who was completely unknown, and the other, James Donald, who was still in the Army. Miss Black had a great deal of energy and drive. A few weeks later I received an invitation from Lady Diana Cooper to go and stay with her at her château outside Paris. Never having met this social Miracle, I was a little amazed. At any rate I knew I could not accept her invitation as the public were not allowed before V.J. Day to travel to the Continent, and like most people during the war I had allowed my passport to lapse. Kitty Black phoned me to ask if I was going to accept the invitation. She told me that Cocteau would be a guest too, and the idea behind the weekend was to bring us together to discuss his play. We had met in Paris before the war. Kitty Black had certainly pulled some strings. I replied that I could never get a permit to go. She countered this by saying that as Lady Diana was the wife of the Ambassador to France, these formalities could easily be got round, including my passport. I was finally persuaded to accept. I refused to commit myself to doing the play.

I crossed the Channel in a boat full of American soldiers. Not only was I the only civilian on board, but almost the only person who was not sick. There was not only a gale, but a blizzard which carried us to the French coast. It was the coldest January I remember. I managed to buy a pack of precious American cigarettes from one of the Yanks. It was delicious to get my fist on a piece of the affluent society. The train to Paris arrived six hours late at the Gare du Nord covered in snow. Naturally, I expected a car from the Embassy. Typically there was not even a servant to meet me. And in those days there were no porters, taxis, or buses at the station. I had not been invited to the Embassy, but to the Château some forty kilometres away. I discovered there were no trains to that place. Lugging my suitcase through the slush, I proceeded to Cocteau's eyrie in the Palais Royal. I tapped on his door. It was opened by a man who was stark naked. As my hands were absolutely numb by the cold, I was surprised at his appearance. Jean Marais took me in, slung a dressing-gown on, and stayed by me as though magnetised. I realised he was attracted to the pack sticking out of my pocket. Cocteau appeared from his bedroom, hardly bothering to greet me. All he had eyes for was the carton of cigarettes. I gave them several packets each, and for a few minutes they did a tribal dance of glee. Cocteau, wishing to return the gesture, told Jean Marais to go straight to the kitchen and fry me a couple of eggs. He said this in the same way an Emperor might have ordered a fabulous delicacy. While Marais was in the kitchen, Cocteau and I sat on his bed. The bed had a white rug on it. The walls had been lined with red velvet. But the thing that fascinated me most was a child's blackboard above his bed, and a piece of chalk on a string beside it. "C'est trés pratique," he said.

I was very impressed by this, and have always meant to construct something similar. Next, my eye fastened on a statue of a mounted rider with a lance aimed at a dragon; the horse and rider were several feet above the dragon which was on the floor. Having got over the excitement of the cigarettes and eggs, Cocteau excused his being in bed by saying he was unwell. I asked him what the trouble was, and he said he had been suffering from carbuncles. I paled at the word; I have never been able to look at a boil. I fixed my eyes on the dragon, then at the blackboard and the dangling piece of chalk, anywhere but at Cocteau peeling off his pyjamas so that I could examine his ravages.

"It's the result of the opium and the bad food." He looked emaciated, his skin the colour of vellum. "I've been in a hospital to be disintoxicated," he said, and gave me a book, *Opium*. It was now about three o'clock in the morning.

"When are we expected at Lady Diana's?" I asked. He looked surprised. "I haven't heard anything about a weekend. Anyhow, Lady Diana is in Switzerland. This is typical of her, she gets these ideas to invite people for the weekend, and then goes off somewhere herself."

"She must make a good ambassador's wife," I said, now very depressed at a fruitless journey.

"Jean," Cocteau called, "we must cheer Ronnie up. Do go and put your riding things on. He'll love to see you in those." Cocteau really believed it; so did Marais, who skipped off and came back in skin-tight breeches and riding boots.

"Doesn't he look lovely?" Cocteau exclaimed with pathetic admiration. I again found myself looking at the dragon.

"Well, at least we got together," I said eventually, "which I suppose is what this exercise was about. For one thing, I don't speak French any better than you speak English, as you can see. Anyhow you'd never agree to the cuts I think are needed to the plot."

"What are they?" he said.

"All that about the Archduchess."

He sat quietly on his bed while I lumbered on. Then, when I finished, he stood up and flapped his arms like a bird.

"I don't mind what you do to my play," he said, "so long as it still flies."

"If you really mean that," I said, "I'll have a shot." He seemed very grateful.

I wandered round his room, peering at his treasures. On one

side table I saw two matchboxes fixed together with matches sticking out, and a knob of sugar stuck between them.

"This was the beginning of cubism," he told me. "Picasso and I were having a snack somewhere in 1913 and we were discussing formalism in Art, and he made his point by borrowing a couple of boxes of matches to illustrate his ideas. This was the first example of Cubism."

But most of our conversation was on a less artistic level. The war had reduced us both to belly-consciousness. He wanted to know how much eggs were in London. I told him about our meagre butter ration.

With no friends of my own in Paris and not wishing to stay in the Palais Royal, I left about four to find a hotel. That was a major operation. Eventually I found a small hotel on the Left Bank which had housed the Gestapo only a few months before. There were many interesting relics of the occupation in my room, including a swastika still emblazoned above the bed. But I was too tired to bother about that.

Cocteau had said he was keen that Christian Bérard should design the décor for the London production of his play, so I went round to see him in his studio. It was about midday, but of course Bérard was still in bed. He seldom got out of it. Most of his designs were scribbled with fantastic verve on scraps of paper littering the eiderdown; when he had completed a design he dropped it on the floor. Most of them were sticky with chocolate. Bébé Bérard was never without a large box of chocolates, even when he was in bed. His podgy little fingers used to scrabble in the box like a bevy of mice. Neither his hair nor his beard was ever combed: I expected to see a few chocolates in that too. I liked him immensely. He was warm-hearted, and could never refuse a request. This was his undoing. Bérard set out to be an ordinary painter, and was one of considerable distinction. I admired the landscapes that were stacked in his studio, but nobody ever bothered to look at these. All they wanted was his stage or costume designs which he scribbled in three seconds on the back of an envelope. Bérard is only known for the work he did before he got up to go to his studio. His serious work has not been noticed, and when an exhibition was given in London in the early fifties it aroused no interest, and was reviewed as the work of a stage designer.

I went with Bérard to *La Répetition* and to *La Folle de Chaillot*. I particularly admired his décor for the latter, where he had suggested two window frames against a blue back-drop. If you gave Bérard two yards of wrought iron and a string of onions he would bring Spain to the stage. Before I left Paris, he had agreed to do the décor for the French production of *This Way to the Tomb* and had scribbled out some ideas for Cocteau's play. The principle feature of his sketch for the latter was a bed with an enormous red velvet canopy running high above to suggest the height within a castle. Second class designers would have messed about with the wall of a castle, building buttresses and enormous fireplaces to give an impression of dimension. But Bérard achieved the exact effect with half a dozen yards of red velvet. I was thrilled, and certain that the London management would recognise genius when they saw it. Of course, I was mistaken. They refused his offer even when he said he would come over and paint the sets himself. I was reminded of the refusal of an orchestra in London to take any interest in Stravinsky when he had told me he had wanted to come over and conduct some of his works.

Before leaving Paris I decided to call on Brancusi on the off chance that he was still alive. I feared what the occupation of Paris had done to this dear old man. Naturally I had forgotten where he lived, and as usual lost my way getting there. When I eventually found him, still in the same studio, still with his smoking cap on, still turning his lovely shapes mounted on pieces of ebony.

"Tell me how you've managed to survive?" I asked him.

"Survive what?"

"The war."

"Ah, that," he said, turning a switch so that his brass duck could slowly revolve for me. "Well, as a matter of fact," he said, "the war seems to have passed me by, and I didn't know there was one till I asked somebody one day why there was such a long queue outside the butcher's. The Germans were in Paris several months before I knew war had been declared."

I believe this of Brancusi, though I would not have done of anyone else.

"But they tell me it is all over now," he said, as little concerned as he had been at the beginning of hostilities. As he said this he was running his hand over a piece of driftwood he had picked up from the beach somewhere. Shape absolutely fascinated him. I have met all sorts of artists, but never one so identified with his work as Brancusi. I do not think he saw me as a person, but as a shape.

On my way back to London, I decided to walk the deck of the Channel steamer. I have never been seasick. It always amuses me to exhibit this when the hearties are laid low in their bunks. I noticed that another man was walking in the opposite direction. After a few minutes we sat down together in the front of the boat. We talked for some time.

"Do you mind if I say something personal?" I asked finally. "You could be mistaken for Adrian Boult."

"I am Adrian Boult," he replied.

When I reached London I was still in such a fury over Lady Diana's absent-mindedness that some of my irritation overflowed against Cocteau's play, and I put it aside till Kitty Black caught up with me. I then found myself accepting the commission. I warned her that my version would be very free, as I could not read French very well. She provided me with a crib. I told her that I would not look at it. The thing that interested me was the principle theme, where love and death are identified, and I thought the final curtain where the Queen goads the Poet till he kills her was theatre in the grand sense, bigger than life, which was what I demanded of it, being bored by plays made up of sherry or tomato sauce reality. Cocteau had told me that he had based the play on a King of Bavaria, and remembering my father's bastard background, I was personally interested.

I wrote almost the whole of this play in the electric trains that run from Waterloo to the T.B. sanatorium. I did not decide to write it in verse where the original was in prose, but could not prevent myself from doing so. After I had written two acts, I met Eileen Herlie, and she read what turned out to be the longest speech that has been written in an English play. Some critic bothered to count the number of words, but it did not cause her any dismay. She said the verse helped her. I made her swear to keep that a secret as I knew the H. M. Tennant office had a deep-rooted prejudice against poetry because they thought it was un-commercial. A few days later I met James Donald, a lean young man on a bicycle. Everybody was pulling strings to get him released from the Army in time for him to play the Poet. I don't think I was more than three weeks in writing this script; I got particular pleasure in writing the Queen's confession, and interpolating anything that interested me. When I had completed it, I was aware that I had done more than take liberties with the original, and I warned the management that Cocteau would never pass the script for production. But apparently he had already signed a contract.

But I insisted that a copy of my version should be sent to him. Not trusting H. M. Tennants I sent one myself. Cocteau replied that he was delighted with it. Knowing how badly he spoke English, I guessed he had not bothered to read it.

Soon after I returned I told Epstein at a sitting how much I admired the carving which Cocteau had suspended by string from his bedroom ceiling.

He smiled. "I've thought of that idea too," he said, and went and opened a chest in one corner of the studio.

He handed me a bronze caste of lovers in the act of copulation.

"These are meant to be suspended in that way," he said. "I've done several of them as you can see."

I admired them greatly. "I wish I had one," I said. "I suppose they're not for sale."

"You can choose any one for £10," he said.

"That's absurd," I said, meaning the price was far too low.

He closed the chest sadly.

"It took me days to do one," he said, "and the bronze must be worth the price."

"I meant £10 is too cheap. I'll give you £25."

He did not believe my explanation.

"Anyhow I don't really want to sell them," he said, taking no offence, inured to disappointment.

Hurt had become a second skin to him. People say that Epstein had a persecution mania. It is true. The reason: he was foully persecuted, not only by the Press and public, but by colleagues anxious to reduce the mountain to the size of their dunghill.

Part Two

Pull down thy vanity
I say pull down

ASHLEY DUKES, who owned the Mercury Theatre, was also on the Control Commission in Germany. One of the duties which devolved on this organisation was to reintroduce into Germany some of the "culture" which the Nazi Party had excluded from the country and which the Allies were under the impression they represented. Having bombed Berlin into a heap of rubble, and gone on doing so long after the city constituted any threat to their own forces, the Allies wished to assure the bewildered Germans who now lay dead or buried in the débris of their homes that they came as liberators, and the fore-runners of a cultural renaissance. At this point in their deliberations, doubtless some asinine member of Eisenhower's staff had had the temerity to suggest that some example of this culture should be produced to impress the Germans with the validity of the Allies' claims. No doubt several generals blinked, some yawned, and Montgomery got to his feet. But eventually the policy was agreed and the order was passed down the pipe-line for some confused colonel from Wyoming to implement. This poor sot probably delegated the matter to somebody else. It was no easy matter for the Allies to produce anything that embodied the spiritual aims for which they had fought and in whose name they had blasted a city to pieces. But eventually some moron had the inspired idea to ask the advice of the dowager doyen of culture, the British Council. To them this was no problem. I gather that they immediately replied with the suggestion that the Sadlers Wells Ballet headed by Margot Fonteyn should be conveyed to the city and perform such flowers of American culture as *Swan Lake* and *Petrouchka*. This was agreed, arrangements went forward until some irritating person pointed out that since the Allies had destroyed all the theatres in the capital there was nowhere for the ballet to perform. Naturally, the British Council was only temporarily dismayed and countered this difficulty with the proposal that Sir Malcolm Sargent should conduct the BBC Symphony Orchestra in a concert of Western classics. But this bright idea looked a little tarnished when Sir Malcolm came back with a programme consisting of Beethoven, Brahms, Bach and Mozart. With ballet and music dropped, the Council turned to drama: this, of course, was an easy one. Plans were immediately put in hand to fly the Old Vic to Berlin. Everybody felt confident: Shakespeare was safe and untainted with any Germanic background. The prospect of one of the dames playing a refined Cleopatra in a Kensington Gore accent filled everybody with glee. This was clearly what we had been fighting for. These plans were in hand and the decision put back into the pipeline where it eventually reached the Supreme H.Q. again. Where to everybody's dismay Winston Churchill vetoed it.

"I am not Sir Francis Drake," he is supposed to have said. "We didn't fight this war for Shakespeare—but to put on a new play."

Pandemonium in high circles developed. At some point in the confusion Ashley Dukes received the simple High Priority directive to arrange that a new British play should be staged immediately in Germany. He flew to London. I was summoned to meet him at the Garrick.

"Culture is at stake," he said. "The Supreme Command want to acquire the German rights of *This Way to the Tomb* and fly you to Berlin."

"I always knew I was the person they were defending," I replied, pocketing £100.

Fortunately the German poet Rudolf Alexander Schroeder had just completed a translation of the play. It went into rehearsals immediately. The American Air Force now found themselves providing material to make urgent repairs to a small theatre they had bombed.

When my backyard persecutors in Devonshire heard that I was being flown to Germany, they thought their worst fears were joyously confirmed. Clearly I had been a Nazi agent all the time and was being taken out to stand my trial at Nuremburg.

My friend Richard March, who was an Intelligence Officer in the R.A.F., insisted on accompanying me. I was pleased at this.

He spoke German perfectly and I didn't want to travel alone. March grumbled at the irony of the situation — that he should have spent five years in the R.A.F. and been dropped by parachute on Normandy and should now only get to Berlin on a pacifist's back.

We were met at the airport by a representative of the British Council who said he had been detailed to act as my interpreter. He drove us to the Hotel Stephanie off Kurfürstendamm and then to the improvised shanty building of the British Council. But when he introduced me to people he had nothing to interpret: for I remained silent: the sight of the devastation in the city was still so appalling that to comment on it was impossible and to talk of anything else seemed facetious or almost irreverent. March and I went for a walk round the Western Sector, picking our way through oceans of grief and monuments of rubble. Only the hideously ugly Jewish Synagogue was left standing in the centre of the city. Even the Jews regretted that. I had been in Plymouth the morning after the air raid there — but that was nothing to the terrible devastation that was all around us. Nobody was sure where the streets used to run. Sticking out of one pile of rubble I spotted a boot and went to pick it up: it had a foot in it. These sights made me feel so ashamed of being a "victor" that I felt I ought to buy a trowel and turn mason. But even then the Berliners were already making tiny inroads on the chaos using even wicker baskets as buckets and trundling perambulators piled with rubbish where they had nothing else with which to shift it. They worked silently and ceaselessly: children scrabbling, old men and women carrying a bucket or two or dragging out a door, a bedstead or a tattered piece of clothing. I spoke to several: they realised I was English: none showed any resentment. I could not understand how they were not overcome with hopelessness or why nausea with a civilisation which had brought them to this did not drive them to abandon it and send them running back into the woods from which they had emerged two thousand years before. It was clear that the Germans as a people were not defeated. But I felt defeated standing there on the blasted fragments of a stained glass window. I felt bogus, so unsure of all the values I had accepted that I wanted to burn my books and ban my own plays. The feeling was very much *This Way to the*

Tomb, and the joke I had enjoyed of being brought to Berlin now seemed to me in the worst possible taste. I no longer felt sure enough of any values to be a writer. Where had writing and ideas brought us to but a thousand acres of broken lives, broken homes and bits of plaster? There seemed more sense in being a brick-layer in preference to a poet.

That evening March and I went to a nightclub in the basement of a house quite near to our hotel. Our purpose was to cheer ourselves up: the Himalayan piles of rubble around us lay on our spirits. The club was full of American officers and lit by candles, the atmosphere not unlike that of a morgue. Girls in nylon mesh stockings sloped around with that bored expression which is the mask of expensive gaiety. None of these dance hostesses attracted me: but the cloak-room girl did. While she checked in people's hats, I sat beside her. She was about twenty-five, a brunette, and pretty, but her features have left no impression on me. What had drawn my attention to her was that when she had taken my coat, I had noticed she was reading a Busoni score. Somehow or other she told me she had a child. I assumed that meant she was married.

"What does your husband do?" I asked her as I might have done at a Cheltenham tea party.

"You mean the father of my child? How would I know what he does? I was standing in a food queue in a street not far from here with about forty other women. A detachment of Russian soldiers came down the street, fell out and each man grabbed a woman and raped her standing her up against the wall. We hadn't the strength to resist. We were half-starved."

She spoke without any emotion in her voice, the way people do when what they have endured has drained them of all feeling. Her story was obviously true. I was silenced again. The dance band played in the background. There seemed to be no bridge between her experiences and my own. I thought of my own secluded and selfish war years down at West Mill and felt a ridiculous sham. What the hell had I been flown to this city for? Whatever the reason had been, I didn't seem able to take the punishment.

I stayed talking to the girl for an hour. March had spent the time dancing and drinking with one of the hostesses. We left even sadder than when we entered.

"That was about the grimmest evening I ever spent in my life," he said.

The next morning we walked to the Memorial where Russian soldiers stood on guard. I studied these sullen, moronic, round turnip faces. It was only too easy to believe the cloak-room girl's story. These dragooned Siberian oafs had never seen a city before. When billeted in Berlin houses they had not known what lavatory basins were used for and had washed in them. I was also told that they were only kept in the Berlin Garrison for a short while for fear that Western standards might debauch their proletarian principles. The Huns must have brought such soldiers into Rome. One day Peking will garrison the same soldiers in Moscow.

I walked across to Hitler's Bunker. And in spite of realising that this man had been the cause or instrument of all the misery and devastation I saw around me, I felt a strange sympathy for him. My feelings were in such opposition to my reason that I tried hard to analyse my reactions. First of all I had to admit that I had a childish admiration for any man of action – even if they were the wrong actions. All of us carry some sort of hero image along with our teddy bears. I remembered that a portrait of Napoleon on a white charger had been one of my most precious possessions as a child and had hung above my bed. Then, too, Hitler had been defeated and any defeated person produced from me the sympathy I felt for myself. Also his absurd gestures and moustache had made him an almost Chaplinesque figure – had not Chaplin himself parodied him in *The Great Dictator?*

I realised quite clearly that if Hitler had been a better water colourist and I had been a worse poet, our situations might have been reversed. His first impulse into politics had been to get a new opera house built in his home town. Frustrated by the Town Council rejecting his plans and their indifference to art, he had led into founding a National Party...I thought of my own efforts to get a theatre built in Barnstaple, my own feeble excursion into politics "to get something done". Where might this impulse have led if I had been better at it? If circumstances not in my control had moved my way, if my pamphleteering and the Pacifist Movement had flourished, if my Community at Gooseham Mill had survived? I resolved to write a play about Hitler. There is a Hitler in everyone. He is a universal figure, like Falstaff and Don Quixote. We all make his mistake of pretending ends can justify means. We all believe the world would have more Opera Houses or something if we had the power. Our good fortune and the world's is that we haven't.

This Way to the Tomb opened that evening and was well received. The production was admirable in its stylisation, except for one piece of ridiculous naturalism; the character of Lechery was presented stark naked. Consequently the girl playing the part looked interesting but chaste which is not what I had intended. After the performance I went round the back and told this girl I thought her costume looked a little tight from out front and suggested to the producer that things which left nothing to the imagination left nothing to be desired either.

A year or so later, March and I returned to Berlin when I went to a reception of German writers which my publisher, Peter Suhrkamp, had arranged. Since most of these poets and play-wrights were still in mourning for some close relative dispatched by my culture, I would not have been surprised if they had received me as a so-called flower of it with coolness or derision. But they increased my feeling that I was bogus by showing me considerable genuine respect. The reception struck me as ghoulish and macabre. As though condemned men had been dragooned to come along and recite eulogies to their Executioner. Little pots of flowers festooned the table which was laden with smoked salmon, steinhäger and chocolate éclairs. I remember thinking that whatever the situation, it is soon made ridiculous if you find yourself holding a chocolate éclair in one hand and a glass of gin in the other. I think a similar thought occurred to Bertholt Brecht who came to sit beside me, also burdened by a cake. Under these conditions our conversation was mere con-fectionery. Our respective comments oozed onto our own lapels. What might have been a serious meeting somehow lay under the spiritual auspices of Billy Bunter. Meanwhile I noted that what-ever philosophical or political differences there were between

Brecht and me our taste for éclairs was mutual. We did not agree to differ, we simply agreed to eat. There was nothing else we could do. But before I left I promised him that I would go and see his new play, *Der Hofmeister*, which he had just produced. He said he would arrange the tickets. The thing that impressed me about Brecht was his eyes. They were pensive eyes and you could see him thinking in his eyes. It was as if all the man was focussed in his pupils.

Some time later, March and I took a taxi through the Brandenburger Tor into the Russian sector to see Brecht's play. We had notified the Army H.Q. of the British Sector where we were going and carried our passports. But there was not too much red tape at the beginning of the occupation: there was a wall, but it was not yet of concrete blocks. It was still possible to take the Metro between East and West.

After we had travelled about a mile, a couple of Soviet soldiers stopped the taxi and flung the doors open and began to search the vehicle. Finding nothing they slammed the door and we drove on.

"What are they looking for?" I asked March.

"I don't know. Probably English newspapers. That's the one thing which gets you into trouble straight away."

"Is it?" I replied nervously producing a copy of *The Times* which I had stuffed into my coat pocket.

March went almost white.

"We must get rid of that. If they stop us again and they find that on you, we'll both be locked up for weeks and end in Siberia!"

"I find *The Times* difficult enough to read," I replied. "I don't look forward to eating it."

"We must stuff it in our shirts, in our socks."

"You can have the sports page," I said. "I refuse to be found with that in my bosom."

Quickly, with the cabby squinting round to observe our activities, we stuffed our shirts and packed our socks.

"I'm told tramps do this to keep warm on the Embankment," I said, "but maybe they don't use *The Times*."

Rustling with newsprint we took our seats in the stalls. When we did so the places either side of us were vacant. I was so impressed with the décor of the play and the first act that I did not notice when the seats were filled each side of us. But when the lights came up for the interval March and I saw that we had obvious Security men sitting solidly in front, behind, and each side of us. We went into the foyer for a cigarette. The Security men followed. We went to the lavatory; they came too. It was so much like a bad thriller that I began to giggle. March did not seem so amused.

"I don't like the look of this," he whispered, wiping the grin off my face as I remembered he'd been in Intelligence for five years. "It's lucky I came with you and that I've got our passports safe in my pocket."

We returned to our seats with our entourage. The curtain rose again. Then a thought unrelated to the play occurred to me.

"Where have you got our passports?" I whispered.

"In my coat pocket, of course," March replied.

"And where is your coat?" I said, remembering we had both put them in the cloak-room.

"Oh God," he murmured.

My faith in Bulldog Drummond diminished perceptibly.

Five minutes before the curtain fell, I received a nudge from James Bond; we made a dramatic dash for the cloak-room, retrieved our coats and left the theatre. March hailed a taxi as though we were in St James's. One drew up, we got in. I began to giggle again.

"It's too ridiculous," I said, "being able to take a taxi out of the clutches of OGPU. They can't seriously have been after us."

"You forget," March replied pertinently, "their Intelligence people are often as unintelligent as ours."

"You should know," I said, observing a car on our trail in the worst film manner. "Anyhow Brecht won't be very impressed by my manners, not going to see him after the show. I must rectify that in the morning."

The play had impressed me immensely. I had never seen a production to match it. The Berliner Ensemble, under Brecht, made the London Theatre look a shabby second-class touring company in comparison. I had liked the non-realistic sets where the walls of the house were only up to the knees of the actors. And the savage theme of the play so typically Brechtian appealed to me. The story was of a self-taught village tutor who had been taken in by the squire to teach his young daughter; though the tutor was clumsy and ugly the daughter fell in love with him; finding him unresponsive she was driven to get into his bed. Her father catches them, blames the tutor and flings him out into the snow. The poor man persuades the village butcher to take him in to teach French to his middle-aged wife. Again the woman falls for the tutor, again discovered, he is thrown out of work... eventually nobody in the district will employ him. Starving in his garret, he realises that so long as women find him sexually attractive, he has no hope of holding a job. He decides that the only way out of his dilemma is to castrate himself. This he did – on the stage. After which he returned to his first employer and informs him of the physical change he has effected on himself. The Squire congratulates him for becoming an acceptable member of society and gives him his job back again.

The savage comment on society that only the castrated, devitalised individual is acceptable to it appealed to me. It is, of course, typically Brechtian; but, oddly enough, the original play was written by Jakob Lenz in the eighteenth century and Brecht adapted it.

The following morning March and I took the Metro into the Soviet sector and went to see Brecht. He asked me if I would make an English version of the play and I agreed willingly, telling him that for the English stage the castration scene would have to be played off and various other alterations made to get it passed by our Cromwellian Lord Chamberlain. Brecht understood this and gave me *carte blanche*.

After leaving Brecht, we walked around the Sector watching old women clearing away rubble in baskets which they were tipping into trailers drawn by caterpillar tractors – an incongruous mixture of the mediaeval, or Chinese coolie, method with modern engineering. But even then the division between the East and West sectors was apparent. Then it was not that the West was cosmopolitan and materially affluent in comparison: it was wholly a difference in atmosphere. People in the West were poised like runners at the start of a sprint; in the Eastern sector they slouched around like sullen prisoners. But Brecht's theatre and the opera flourished, giving a false impression. As false as the newly built Soviet Hall of Culture which March and I went round. Apart from officials, we were the only people in it. The exhibits consisted of photographs showing life in contemporary England and America which were unfavourable compared to the equivalent in Soviet Russia. This method of using realistic documentation to make a social or political comparison is effective and convincing. Unhappily, this exercise in dialectics was a trifle biased since the photographs of modern England had been taken from Cruickshanks' illustrations of Dickens' *Hard Times* and from these it was hardly valid to conclude "that the British worker often went unshod." Incensed at this effective but stupid propaganda I went to leave the place when I noticed a small box hanging in the foyer marked "suggestions". I asked one of the officials for a form and on this made the suggestion that more typical photographs of life in contemporary Britain could be obtained from copying the illustrations of Piers Plowman and Chaucer. I popped my missive in the box and left the building, returning a minute later to see the official already extracting it.

"I think we'd better go while the going is good," March said. "Their sense of humour may not be any better than yours."

On the same day I returned to London I got in touch with Hugh Beaumont and told him that I had seen a wonderful new play in Berlin and that the author had offered me the English and American rights.

"Who wrote it?"

"Brecht."

"Who's Brecht?"

It was the 40s, not the 60s: in art we are always at least a generation behind. Nauseated with Shaftesbury Avenue, I longed to return to Devon.

My correspondence with Ezra Pound was of course stopped by the outbreak of war in September 1939. I knew that he was in Italy and that I had heard rumours that he was broadcasting for the Italian Government. Several American magazines came into my hands in which Pound was described as a traitor, "the American Haw-Haw", and one reproduced his photograph with the description beneath "Rat No. 1". I had every reason to doubt this assessment of the poet. For only a week before hostilities began, Ezra had written to me – a conscientious objector – urging me to join up "because the British Empire is something worth defending." I knew too that he was a fierce, though perhaps tactless, patriot. I suspected that what had happened was that Ezra had seized the opportunity of getting a microphone in his fist to broadcast about social credit or international usury. This, of course, proved to be the case, though it did not help to answer the charge brought against him of treason since he had, by accepting money from the Italian Government for his broadcasts, given technical comfort to the enemy.

I learned over the radio of his arrest, or capture, as it was termed. And a few days later while I was still living with Queen Victoria at Hampstead I received a letter from him. He said nothing of his own condition: typically he enquired about mine and asked how Rose Marie's health was. But the letter contained an enclosure: it was part of the Pisan Cantos.

> *Whose world, or mine or theirs*
> *Or is it of none?*
> *So thinking of Althea at the grates*
> *Two rose-like lips pressed down upon my own*
> *for the full eidos the form to*
> *pass and intercross*
> *each space full of its formal life*
> *that moved and keeps defined*
> *its clarity demarcations*
> *that though lovst well remains*
> *the rest is dross.*
> *First came the seen, then thus the palpable*
> *eliatum, though it were in the halls of hell,*
> *What thou lovst well is thy true heritage*
> *What thou lovst well shall not be reft from thee*
> *What thou lovst well remains, the rest is dross*
> *The ant's a centaur in his dragon world*

Pull down thy vanity, it is not man
Made courage or made order or made grace
Pull down thy vanity, pull down,
Learn of the green world what can be thy place
Pull down thy vanity
        Pacquin pull down
The green casque has outdone your elegance,
"Master thyself, then others shall thee beare"
        Pull down thy vanity
Thou art a beaten dog beneath the hail
A swollen magpie in a fitful sun
Half black, half white
Nor knowst'ou wing from tail
Pull down thy vanity
How mean thy hates
Fostered in falsity
        Pull down thy vanity
Rathe to destroy, niggard in charity
Pull down thy vanity
        I say pull down.
But to have done instead of not doing
        this is not vanity
To have, with decency, knocked
That a Blunt should open;
        To have gathered from the air a live tradition
or from a fine old eye the unconquered Flame
This is not vanity.
Here error is all in the not done,
all in the diffidence that faltered.

I remember reading this and, in spite of the inevitable accompaniment of Beethoven beneath me, was entirely captured by its music. I had admired parts of The Cantos but had thought it a very uneven poem. But I instantly realised that the page I held in my hand was Ezra at his best—which is as good as poetry can be.

The next post brought another chunk typed on flimsy pink paper with a scrawled note. Then others followed. I immediately went to see Eliot, taking the Cantos with me. He glanced at them and was unimpressed. I could not then understand his lack of enthusiasm. His attitude of restrained indifference bewildered me.

When Pound had been flown to Washington to stand trial for treason, there were rumours that he would almost certainly be shot. In the mood preceding the Nuremburg Trials anything seemed possible. People I was seeing at the time, even writers whom Pound had influenced and helped, seemed unworried by the prospect. Some called him a "Fascist", others an "anti-Semite". Epstein was sympathetic; Ben too wanted to help. But there was nothing we could do. For the most part opinion condemned him without anybody having seen the transcripts of his broadcasts. Having obtained his address at St Elizabeth Hospital I wrote, and, looking for something to send him, I found a copy of *The Journal of a Husbandman*. To my surprise I received this letter from him by return written in pencil stamped by the prison censor:

District of Columbia Jail,		*25*
C.B.1.	*Cell 216*	*Nov.*
	Washington D.C.	*1945*
	U.S.A.	

Dear Ron,
  Do send a copy of "Journal of Husbandman" to Olga and Mary @ Casa 60 Saint Ambrogio (Rapallo).
  All this is marvelous xperience if it dont break me and if the lesion of May cured (I thinks) in Sept. don't bust open under renewed fatigues.

Love to Bunny

& Rose Marie

Yrs
Ez
Ezra Pound

I passed it on immediately to Eliot who returned it with this comment:

My dear Duncan,
  Thank you very much for letting me see Ezra's letter which I

return herewith as it is a precious document of historical value. I understand from Miss Molton that the *Journal of a Husbandman* has gone off to Olga Rudge.

Yours sincerely,
T. S. Eliot.

But there was nothing anybody could do but write frequently to him or to his wife Dorothy, or to Olga, who was the mother of his daughter. Dorothy was living in Washington and visited him at St Elizabeth Hospital every day, whereas Olga was separated from him by being secretary to Count Chigi in Siena. She planned to get herself somehow to Washington but had no assurance that her position would enable her to see Pound once she got there.

With Rose Marie wasting away in the sanatorium, Ezra in gaol awaiting trial and probably execution, I felt acutely depressed and found it difficult to continue writing *Lucretia* and *The Eagle has Two Heads*. And to add to these difficulties there were others: concern about Briony and Roger who had been parked at a kindergarten; worry over my farm which I had on my conscience if not partially on my desk. But above all these urgent and personal matters I found that for some reason I could not keep my mind off thinking of Nuremburg. In particular I found the image of Goering kept coming before me. I could not understand this. I had, like most people, dismissed him as a medal-wearing poltroon, a sort of Gilbert & Sullivan figure with an ability for destroying the Luftwaffe. But now that he was captured and about to stand trial some quirk in my mind made me almost obsessed by his image. The other Nazi prisoners at Nuremburg did not impinge onto my consciousness.

At this time I was dining one night with my friend Gerard Portsmouth at his flat in Westminster. A cold, callous wind moaned along Great Smith Street; it blew away my resolution to go home. I knew I should do so; I had an important rehearsal next morning and I had yet to write some revision to the script. But the wind made me draw closer to the fire, and we sat there enjoying some Kirsch. I kept looking at my watch, thinking of the impending move. As usual, I quietened my conscience by a convenient compromise: I would have just one more cigarette, then go home for an early night so that I could get up very early to do the work before the rehearsal, which was not until ten anyway.

Gerard filled my glass again. The clock struck. This was terrible: I had missed the last tube train. And though I realised this, I left the flat at once and hurried to catch the train which had already gone. Such perversity can be observed on any day at any station: though we see the train move off, we still attempt to catch it, as if our effort redeems our fault for missing it.

The ticket-collector told me the last train had gone. I immediately went off in search of a taxi. I walked, I hailed, I cajoled, standing in their way. But to no avail. London cabbies have little mercy after midnight, especially if you are going to Hampstead and they've no return fare to pick up.

I went on walking. Indeed, I had to walk to Oxford Circus before I picked up a cab.

When I eventually put my latchkey in the door, feeling very tired and bad-tempered the clock struck two. At this rate, I thought, climbing into bed, I shall only get six hours' sleep if I am to be at my "desk" by eight to rewrite that scene. As a rule I need eight hours of intensive sleep. However, I composed myself and was just about to drop off when it began.

It started in the distance, then drew nearer. Now it seemed only across the road: the persistent and remorseless bark of a small dog. It barked its way into my pillow; it barked its way into my dream. I awoke, switched on the light and shouted out of the window. I got back into bed, pulling the blankets over my head. But the bark persisted, an intermittent yet regular yap at my consciousness. It seemed to have my mind tied to its tail.

"This will not do;" I said. "Mind over matter;" I said, wishing the damn dog dead, and seeking a fresh place on the pillow again.

Now, to get to sleep, I began counting sheep. One, two, three, bark, four, five, six, bark. Then the imaginary flock would scatter in panic, and I had to begin again. After this wrestling had gone on for an hour, I felt for a small bottle of veronal which I keep by my bed and, to spite the bark, took an extra tablet.

The drug had an almost immediate effect. I felt as though I were falling down a velvet wall to a cushioned oblivion. The bark receded...

The bark returned. I got up, put on my dressing gown, and went down the stairs, opened the door and strode to the corner of the street where a small wire-haired terrier stood barking at nothing. In a fury, I seized it by the tail, and, swinging it above my head, bashed its brains out against the lamp-post...

Then I woke up. I was perspiring with the violence of my dream and shocked by its details – for not only am I fairly docile, but I am quite fond of dogs, too. I could not think what had occasioned this outburst of subconscious horror. Then, seeing the unstoppered bottle of veronal by my bed, I immediately remembered the bark and the difficulty I had had in getting off to sleep. I smiled at this elementary example of repressed wishful thinking. I stubbed out my cigarette and sought sleep again, determined to catch up on the interruption.

By the time I had had breakfast I had forgotten the matter, and was soon at work tidying the scene for the rehearsal. This done, I felt quite cheerful and carefree, until I reached the corner. There, at my feet, lay a wire-haired terrier with its head bashed in, beside a bloodstained lamp-post.

I stood still. Was it a dream? Or had I, in my sleep, got out of bed and swung the dog above my head and...? I do not know.

This dream that carried over from sleep into consciousness with its image of blood on my hands somehow seemed to me to be connected with my sudden obsession about Goering. But I could not discover the connection: it was something I felt rather than thought.

Then about a week later, I had another dream which seemed important to me. I dreamed that I saw a faceless man pushing a hurdy-gurdy along the gutter. He stopped and began to turn the handle of his machine to produce a funeral waltz. Then another man, also without a feature on his face, appeared, together with a woman who had her back to me. The couple began to dance in the road to the music. Suddenly the music ceased: and the faceless dancer raised his hands to the woman's throat and strangled her. The body fell in the gutter. Then the faceless dancer turned in the direction of the faceless hurdy-gurdy player and they confronted each other, their features gradually formed until I perceived that they were identical. Then slowly I recognised the face: it was my own.

This dream spoke to me. I became conscious of something that I had known for some time, and that was that each of us is not one person but several people. My pen had known this for years. In *This Way to the Tomb* I had actually divided the several facets of Anthony into four separate characters. And some lines I had written in another poem came to my mind:

> *No one knows who is the mover or who is moved*
> *Or where desire begins.*

Also I became aware how much I had resisted the dictum of theatrical producers: that characters in plays had to be consistent throughout the play. I realised it wasn't consistency of character that interested me, but its inconsistency. Anthony had likened himself to a crew of a boat:

> *A drunken crew climbs on board*
> *And few obey the captain.*

Then over the next few days, my musings about this dream and my morbid and inexplicable concern with Goering, suddenly emerged until I saw that my fascination with the Reichsmarschall was because he was being projected as an archetype, the epitome of evil which I carried within myself. "There but for the Grace of God", etc. Instantly I realised that I wanted to write about the complete division in a man, and how each of us walks with a shadow, though some of us meet it and others escape it.

For a time, I considered getting these realisations into a play about Hitler. I wanted to examine the inconsistencies of his character, the problem how a water-colourist, with an ambition to build an opera house in his home town should, on the way to achieve that, exterminate six million Jews and end in a bunker – studying, not a map of the Russian front, but the architect's plans for the opera house he had originally wished to build. But every theatre manager in London begged me not to waste my time writing such a play. "People don't want to hear any more about him," they said firmly. "Nobody would produce it." I abandoned this idea not for their reasons but because I began to realise that neither Hitler nor Goering were evil enough, or divided enough to hold my interest or to suit my purpose. I wasn't sure what I was looking for. But over the next few weeks certain images and memories which I thought were irrelevant and unconnected came to my mind.

I found myself one day sitting in the tube remembering an incident which had occurred when I had been staying some years before with Lord Portsmouth at Farleigh Wallop.

Portsmouth had been showing me round a room at Hurstbourne which was hung with several family portraits covering three centuries. I had looked at the paintings then glanced at the face beside me.

"They're all portraits of one man," I'd said, "only the clothes differ."

Then his son, Viscount Lymington, had come into the room and we both looked at the same face again.

This connected with one childhood experience of being told I was so much like my father and one day actually being mistaken for him by one of his friends as I had walked down Piccadilly.

And behind your head I see
Rows of approving ancestry

I had written the day my daughter was born.

I also found myself recalling the shock and resentment I had felt against my father when my trustees had, on my seventeenth birthday, handed me a letter from him written fourteen years before, and I had mistaken his handwriting for my own.

But the clinch of this undertow of pondering about how much we are of ourselves and how much we are merely part of the pattern of continuity that holds us, came one day when I was still writing *The Eagle has Two Heads*. Cocteau had told me that he had based his original play on Ludwig II of Bavaria. I knew little about him except that by blood he was my great-great-uncle and had been a patron of Wagner. And so I got a book from the London Library on the Wittelsbachs and, going home, casually

116

opened it in the tube. "The male members of this family," I read, "are noted for their passion for horses and poetry."

I snapped the book shut, resenting this playing out of other people's lives through my own. But though a book is easily closed, its matter is not. I now found I was becoming obsessed by the question of individual continuity: worrying about the extent we are of ourselves apart from those traits and influences we have inherited. It was a concern with mortality: and I saw that, in so far as we are individuals, that is by derivation un-divided, so are we mortal, but in so far as we are manifestations of a tradition then we are, in that context, immortal. The paradox being that the part of us which is our own, and precious to us because it alone defines our being, we cannot keep, but those parts of us which we borrow from our forefathers and lend temporarily to our sons, we do keep.

Suddenly this concern with immortality and resentment against inheritance fused with my search for absolute evil. I had not far to look. I realised that if virtue was "assenting to God's will" or, to use another terminology, "the being in tune with natural law" or in the current jargon of Vienna, "the acceptance of reality," then evil was the other side of that coin. It was the rejection of God's will, the laws of nature or reality, call it what you will. The truth is we are of one another and we are most evil when, refusing to accept that, we wish to be unique. It was as if Beelzebub and Prometheus suddenly sat each side of me in the tube. In searching for absolute evil I was aware that in so far as crimes such as murder, rape, etc., are the result of circumstances and are generally unpremeditated they are as trivial as the circumstances which caused them. What I was looking for was evil not caused by the pressure of circumstances acting on the individual but arising out of his deliberate will. By this criterion Hitler, and such figures as Jack the Ripper, seemed to me creatures run over by history or maimed by a sickness within themselves but not evil as Beelzebub was, who challenged God's will by setting himself up as equal.

Then, as often happens when I am consciously worried over a question, my unconscious answers it, usually aloud, when I have quite forgotten what I have fed into the computer. So it was in this instance. I was sitting in a bus in Regent Street opening the

117

Evening Standard, I remember, when I suddenly announced to my own surprise as much as my fellow passengers:

"All men hate their sons."

One or two people looked round. I hurried off the bus.

On the pavement, my conscious mind rejected this generality. Convention has it that "all men love their sons". Then suddenly I saw that my unconscious mind had seen behind the camouflage and presented me with a telegram containing a dramatic situation, the essence of absolute evil.

As I have said, while living with Queen Victoria I worked well; the rent was cheap and I enjoyed the anachronism of living in a derelict country cottage only five minutes' walk from Hampstead Tube Station. But after living there for several months, I had to leave in spite of its convenience. The problem of finding alternative accommodation was exceedingly difficult immediately after the war. The reason why I had to abandon Balmoral was that I became stuck to it precisely like a fly on a fly paper. This occurred indirectly as a result of my constant worry about Rose Marie's weight. She was weighed every week. When I visited her in the sanatorium the question of whether she had gained or lost a pound was a matter of great concern to us. She had been nearly ten stone before she had contracted tuberculosis: when she had had the haemorrhage her weight had fallen to eight stone. One week, to help her with this battle with ounces, I bought a large jar of toffee flavoured cod liver oil and malt and urged her to take as much of it as she could bear. She agreed to do this if I would promise to buy another jar for myself. She was worried because I had had one cold after another that winter. It seemed a reasonable arrangement. At that time, I would have agreed to dose myself with any beastly confection if it indirectly increased her weight. I bought the jar, and borrowing a large spoon from Queen Victoria, I carried it up to my room and placed it by my bed. I took a dollop the next morning and placed the spoon on the top of the jar. Or that is what I thought I did with it. But a day or two later, when I had taken scene two of the libretto of *Lucretia* to Ben, he discovered that he was adhering even more closely than usual to my text. Another day, I found traces of cod liver oil and malt on my collar. Next the terrible stuff insinuated its way on to my pillow: the sheets became contaminated, clinging like a shroud to my form. But the last straw was when I found that I could not put the telephone down. There was nothing I could do, but move.

Through an advertisement, I found a room in Hertford Street. My rent was now increased to seven guineas a week without breakfast. As usual when I indulge in an extravagance, I manage to assure myself that it is, in effect, an economy. In this case, I told myself that I would be saving at least £3 per week in taxis on the long journey out to Hampstead—the fact that I had never spent that, but generally travelled home by tube, did not weigh in my calculations. I am adept as a confidence trickster when I myself am the gullible object. And perceiving all the delightful colourful barrows round the corner in Shepherd Market, I added the argument that I would now be able to buy food cheaply and have at least one meal a day in my room. This economy of 30s. per day showed me that my move to Hertford Street would give me a profit of £5 per week. This kind of financial idiocy marks every transaction I make. All my extravagances are economies. Of course the real reason why I took the room in Hertford Street was that it looked tidy and spacious before I moved in, and being near to Shepherd Market, I again felt less homesick for Devon because of the atmosphere of a village surrounding the barrows. I love barrows heaped with vegetables and fruit. I like everything about street markets, even the litter. Rupert Street, Portobello Road: these are my favourite haunts even when I've nothing to buy. It is the variety of the things, their colour and the way oranges and other fruit are piled in precarious heaps which fascinate me.

It was, of course, a disappointment when I returned with my first purchases from the barrows to observe that there was, in fact, no means of cooking in the room. I asked for a gas ring and was told that the housekeeper would serve coffee and tea but no cooking by tenants was permitted. This somewhat upset my budget.

My room on the first floor had originally been part of a large drawing room running the length of the house. Adapted for letting, the back part of the room had been divided by a thin partition of hardboard. My bed adjoined the partition. On my first night there I was woken by noises coming from the bed two inches away on the other side of the partition. It was the same every night. First, I would hear my neighbour teetering up the stairs with a heavy tread behind her. Then the light would switch on, the sounds of shoes falling to the floor, then a scuffle and the brief but audible creaking of the bed. This would be repeated half a dozen times a night. Most of the clients were members of the American Air Force. As I lay sleepless in bed it used to occur to me that my neighbour was probably more successful with her budget than I was with mine. After two or three chaste months in this room, I left with a feeling of sexual exhaustion. And I was also slightly depressed by the tenant in the room below me. He was a man called Jim Mollison who had, before the war, been a world famous aviator and had flown the Atlantic solo and then had married Amy Johnson, an equally well-known pilot. They had parted; she had been lost while ferrying aircraft during the war. He was a broken figure, now unknown, and apparently uncared for, drunk every night, often incapable. It was like watching a person commit suicide in slow motion.

Most of our life is like a blind man sleepwalking. For the greater part, which is, I suppose, the best part, we are unaware that this immediate step will lead in that ultimate direction. Drifting from triviality to frivolity we allow the pressure of circumstances to mount till we are driven one way or another. We seldom have to bear the burden of decision and when we take one, are often quite unconscious of having done so.

But some of us have not been so fortunate. We can remember the precise moment, even the details and the road where we were at the time when we woke from one dream only to run into a nightmare. These moments of emotional crises are like little deaths, because in them we stand momentarily outside of life. We then have to decide what to do in order to be able to continue to live. Perhaps they are the only moments we are truly alive?

For months I had been aware that Rose Marie might die. In my imagination I had stood by several of her graves. I had buried her on the cliffs of Devon, beneath a magnolia tree in the orchard and watched her fairness burn on a pile of sandalwood. I had written innumerable epitaphs, both hers and mine. Like my allowance, I spent my grief before I received it. Lucretia's death had been Rose Marie's, and as I wrote *The Eagle has Two Heads*, I found myself bending line after line to contain the same sad image.

I had some justification for this morbidness; the doctors had told me that her lung was not responding to treatment. The operation, artificial pneumothorax, had failed, the virus remained active, her weight decreased in spite of absolute rest. Every week I observed her skin take on a sort of ghostly transparency. Then one day when I had been down to see her and was just about to climb back into the bus, the House Surgeon asked to speak to me. He was a Scotsman with the tact of a swordfish. He told me as though discussing a puncture on a second-hand motor, that the hole in my wife's lung was increasing in size, and to convince me, casually showed me an X-ray photograph.

"In this case;" he said; "I think we'd better scrap that lung altogether to prevent the disease spreading to her other."

He went on to explain the gruesome details of thoracoplasty.

"I shall have to saw through and remove several ribs on her left side from the back;" he remarked affably; "to remove the entire lung. Of course I require your permission to perform the operation."

"Is it dangerous?"

"It is a major operation. But her heart is good."

"When do you think it should be done?"

"As soon as possible."

"Give me a few days to think," I pleaded. The doctor then showed me photographs of the terrible scars on the backs of women who had undergone it.

"Of course it's very disfiguring, especially for a woman like your wife, but it is a chance."

I pondered his use of the last word.

"How many survive this operation?"

"About half. Her heart is particularly good."

"How long will she live if she doesn't have this done?"

The surgeon took off his glasses and pursed his lips as though making a mental addition.

"She could go on for several months," he announced generously. It rained behind my eyes. I ran straight to Ben. He listened gravely. But to us this was not unexpected. We had imagined this, and both experienced the crisis months before. Events had caught up with what we had fearfully anticipated. This gave a sense of unreality to my dilemma.

I repeated my conversation with the surgeon to him.

"You mustn't let her go through this," he said firmly; "refuse to give your permission."

I was immensely relieved to hear this advice. It agreed with my intuition. I have always had a terror of surgery. And though reason, medical and family advice seemed stacked against me, with Ben's support, I felt fortified enough to delay and try and cheat destiny. We both knew that if she had the operation, she would die under it, because that had already happened in our imagination.

"I'm certain we mustn't allow it," Ben repeated. I was grateful, too, for the pronoun.

But my mind is like mercury. Within twenty-four hours I found I couldn't hold to this decision because I couldn't face the alternative. "Several months," he had said. And then, generously.

And so I began running up and down Harley Street seeking out the best surgeon in the country. He listened patiently and looked at the X-ray plates I had brought him.

"The advice you've already been given by the Sanatorium is correct," he said. "I too would advise thoracoplasty."

"Is it a dangerous operation?"

"Yes, a major operation. One I perform frequently. Often with success."

"Would you do it?"

"Yes."

"Would you have it done on your wife?" I asked almost savagely.

He turned to the window and was silent for some time.

"That was a strange question to ask a surgeon;" he said eventually.

"And your answer?"

"The answer's no," he said simply.

I thanked this man profusely for his wonderful honesty, hired a car and drove off to Pinewood. For a few miles I was almost happy. Finding the best medical advice confirm Ben's and my own intuition relieved me from the misery of indecision. My mind was now made up. And this produced a kind of gaiety in me at least for a few miles.

I was just driving round a roundabout at Bagshot when the full implication of "a few months" hit me. I had already realised that it implied her death. But now I was suddenly fractured with the consciousness that I would not be able to face life without her. She has a good heart, the surgeon had said. I saw then that we had only one between us. And oblivious of any direction I circled the roundabout entirely. Each building and every tree surrounding that place is nailed in my mind. In my abstracted state I was awake in a way that I had seldom been before. In that moment I found that beyond love for another lies love for oneself. That the impulse for self survival was an even greater anxiety. We grieve most for ourselves. As I circled that roundabout again I felt lost, homeless. The feeling was of panic, the panic I had experienced when I had been lost on the sands at Bournemouth as a child. If Rose Marie were to die, I realised I would not even have a deckchair to search for, and would be for ever running peering into the face of strangers.

"Like a lost child with tireless feet. To love as I love," I said aloud, *"is a kind of suicide."*

Hearing my own voice brought me to my senses, as we say mistakenly. I found the right road and it was along it that I realised consciously that if I was to survive I must not be in future so emotionally dependent on one woman. "It's safer to have two" the whisper said. I listened carefully. The message perforated my soul.

But by the time I reached the Sanatorium I had forgotten the experience. That is to say, I had filed that level of consciousness away within some secret drawer.

I went straight to see the House Surgeon who had a form ready for my signature on his desk.

"I've decided not to give my permission," I told him.

"You realise your responsibility?" he asked. "We can do no more for her."

"I'm taking her away," I said, forming my resolution after I had spoken the words.

"You realise tuberculosis is a notifiable disease? You're taking a grave responsibility."

There was nothing more to be said. I left his room and went and told Rose Marie, as I had done once before, to get dressed.

She did this gaily and quickly. To her any move from that place was an improvement.

"Aren't I going to be carved up then?" she asked.

"No."

"All because you don't like the sight of blood?"

"Maybe. Let's get going."

I bundled her into the small car and we set off happily for London like two children playing truant. The disease made her fair complexion even more delicate. She was happy. In the first traffic jam a lorry driver whistled at her. The policeman stared at her. It was always so. Her beauty was so conspicuous that one shared it as one admired it.

"Where are we going to?" she asked eventually. "We shall need a bed—a big bed," she added hungrily.

I couldn't take her to Ben's flat: the room I had occupied there was being used. Hertford Street was out of the question: it was too small, and I had made it too sordid.

"We'll find an hotel," I replied optimistically. We drove around for one till nearly ten o'clock. I telephoned another dozen. But none had a room available.

"It looks as if we'll have to sleep in the car;" she said gaily and then a coughing fit sobered her mood.

I continued to phone. I even tried the Ritz and the Savoy.

"What you lack is influence," she teased. "A pity. I think we could use a double bed."

It was then approaching midnight. It was cold. I began to realise what the doctor had meant by taking on a grave responsibility. Pondering her jibe about my lack of influence I immediately thought of Gaby Pascal. Gaby would know how to handle the situation. I immediately phoned him and told him of our problem.

"Take her to the Savoy," he ordered in his best Mogul manner.

"But I've tried there. They haven't a room."

"Take her to the Savoy," he repeated. "I will order them to find one."

"What if they don't?"

"Then I will tear the brothel down."

No man could use a telephone to greater effect than Gaby. When we arrived at the hotel the manager himself conveyed our single suitcase to a suite. Nor had the Mogul forgotten to order the champagne.

For the next few days, Rose Marie luxuriated in her suite and held Court. But beneath her laughter I could hear "a few months" tolling in my mind like a funeral bell.

Sophie and Marion Stein came along. The former with tears in her eyes, but after a few minutes Rose Marie had turned their visit to the invalid into a party. Her gaiety was desperate. I felt this desperation too. And I was aware that I couldn't go on living at the Savoy even though our honeymoon there was to end in a funeral.

And as often has happened my work, which had been postponed, now reached its deadline. In an atmosphere part morgue, part party, I had somehow to write the last scene of *Lucretia* and the last few pages of *The Eagle has Two Heads*. In both cases the rehearsals were already scheduled.

Ben had told me that he wanted me to write a soliloquy for Lucretia before she kills herself.

"Forget about me," he'd said. "I shan't even try to set it. It can be spoken. After all, I've written the music for her final entrance without words. Now it's your turn. But do let me have it by tomorrow morning."

There were too many people in the sitting room for me to think. Then I went and sat on the bed which now lacked its invalid, and with my eyes on Rose Marie through the open door, I scribbled the speech quickly for Lucretia.

Then turn away for I must tell,
Though telling will
Turn your tender eyes to stone
And rake your heart and bring the bones
Of grief through the rags of sorrow...

Nor had I far to look for Lucretia's final cry at the end of that speech.

> Oh, my love, our love was too rare
> For life to tolerate or fate forbear from soiling
> For me this shame, for you this sorrow.

Having completed this "speech," I glanced through the door again. Rose Marie was now sitting down. Her hand trailed over the arm of her chair. I wrote Collatinus' epitaph for Lucretia.

> This dead hand lets fall
> All that my heart held when full
> When it played like a fountain, prodigal
> With love liberal,
> Wasteful.
> So brief is beauty.
> Is this it all? It is all!

Ben had suggested that every character should have an epitaph to sing over Lucretia's body which he intended to set as a scene to bring the opera to an end. I could see that it was going to be only too painfully easy for me to write that part of the libretto. But the irony was that within half an hour of writing these two pieces which did nothing if not express my feelings for Rose Marie, she had quarrelled with me, accusing me of not loving her.

Her guests had gone, she came into the bedroom, and glancing at the paper on the bed needlessly asked me what I had been doing. Before I could reply, the phone rang. It was Chile Gray, a girl friend of my sister's whom I had known for many years. I replied in monosyllables and curtailed the conversation.

"Who was that?"

"Chile."

"So I gathered by your guarded manner. What did she want?"

"Merely to ask how you were."

"Liar. What does she care how I am? I suppose she wants me out of the way? I suppose you've been carrying on with her while I've been locked in the bloody sanatorium? Typical. You don't love me any more. You're still fond of her, that's why you're so secretive and have these furtive phone calls, isn't it?"

The tears came, the hysterics followed. But even so I couldn't tell her why Chile had phoned me. Not then; the news I had just received was that Chile had, at my sister's suggestion, been to see Briony in hospital and was letting me know that she was recovering from her operation. The child had had a gland removed from her neck. I couldn't tell Rose Marie about this because she would have blamed herself—especially since the gland was tubercular.

An hour or two later in order to reassure Rose Marie I showed her the verses which were still lying on the bed. She read them sulkily.

"I'm no longer jealous of Chile," she said. "Now you've made me jealous of Lucretia."

Nor could I tell her that writing about Lucretia's death I had been thinking of her own.

But before a woman's accusations it is never an advantage to be innocent: innocence is the one sin they can't forgive. Sometimes I felt I had let Rose Marie down by not providing her with a justification, a receptacle for her jealousy.

But within an hour I had reassured her and her tears were forgotten. It was like building up a house of playing cards for the slightest draught to topple, only to build again. The next draught was another telephone call. This time I decided to let her answer it. The conversation was brief. I observed the flush heighten; the tense mood reappear.

"That was a message for you," she said almost inaudibly; incredulously. "The wedding dress is ready, but the bridesmaids should have another fitting."

"Oh good," I said unguardedly. "I'll tell the bride."

"You do that."

I glanced at her. It was not possible that she was thinking I was bigamous? It was possible. Before she could articulate the thought "you might have waited" I hurried to explain.

"It's for Connie, you know."

"I know. Your secretary."

"Part time."

"Part time."

"Some time ago she told me she was getting married and

127

how much she would have loved to be married all in white."

"Did she?"

"Yes, she'd seen some film in which there was a wedding and was terribly envious of having a dress like that."

"So you bought her one?"

"No, I asked Gaby to arrange for the studio to loan the dresses from the wardrobe."

"Funny you'll go to such efforts for others," she said with considerable justification, "and yet you married me wearing rags and a pair of wellingtons."

Utterly routed, I smiled. She smiled too.

The bills at the Savoy are presented weekly. It took me that time to realise that we couldn't go on staying there indefinitely.

Rose Marie's condition had worsened. Her cough was more frequent: I caught her often swallowing the sputum rather than frighten me with the sight of it. But we had burned our boats: even if she had been willing I could not get her into a hospital or a sanatorium having removed her from one only a week before. We had set our minds against surgery. We considered moving back to the farm but decided against that as is it was too isolated and we could get no nursing or domestic help there. I tried several private nursing homes only, of course, to run into the fact that they could not take a patient suffering from tuberculosis because it is a notifiable disease.

"I'm sorry I'm taking such an expensive time dying," she said.

In this grim dilemma I remembered Archie Ling. I had first met him a few months before at Gerard Portsmouth's flat. Ling was a bachelor of about forty: at dinner he had intrigued me because his erudite conversation had contrasted so strongly with his conventional man-about-town manner. He struck me as a Yogi in a Savile Row suit. While mixing a cocktail he would quote the Gita accurately. I observed that his interest in philosophy and mysticism was not idle or superficial. I assumed that he was a well-to-do dilettante in letters and, after he had gone, Lady Portsmouth surprised me by telling me he was in fact a wine merchant who had a small business in Avery Row, behind Claridges.

He had written to me a few days after this first meeting and asked me if I would dine with him to discuss a commission to write something for him. Intrigued by his request, I was further interested by the meal he had prepared himself. It consisted wholly of raw vegetarian foods exquisitely prepared and served with excellent wines. To excuse his meal he explained that he adopted this diet as an alternative cure to the orthodox treatment for tuberculosis. When I had told him that Rose Marie was in a sanatorium he had shaken his head dubiously and said he had experienced two years of that routine, but had since been able to cure himself although the doctors had written him off as a hopeless case years ago. But at that time I had still some faith in traditional medicine, and had consequently written off his comments as enthusiastic quackery. We had then got down to discussing the commission.

"I'm issuing a Christmas card to my customers," he had said, "and I would like you to write a short poem about wine for it. No more than a dozen lines. I thought of asking Noël Coward but would much prefer you."

Amused that the success of *This Way to the Tomb* had put my reputation on the level of the fashionable Master, I agreed, and the next day had sent him precisely twelve lines. The payment for these had arrived at East Heath Row promptly: two bottles of wine for every line I had written.

I had never met anybody so appreciative of poetry; Mr Ling had stayed in my mind.

I phoned him and told him of my problem. He came to the Savoy immediately, applauding our decision to refuse surgery, and suggested that I should put Rose Marie in what he called a "health hell" where she would have a strict vegetarian diet. He gave me an address of one of these establishments at Hinton Charterhouse, near Bath.

We had nothing to lose. We had no alternative. I made arrangements with one hand and tried to write *The Eagle has Two Heads* with the other, finally having to dictate a scene of it to Connie in the back of a car. A traffic jam in Regent's Park gave me the only opportunity for writing the dialogue between the Poet and the Queen. But my emotions were in focus. Rose Marie was propped up in the front of the car. Archie Ling was driving. Where was he driving? He had a sort of death's head.

I would like this moment to become
The image of eternity. This is the moment to which we've grown.
And from this moment we must fall away.
When times as precious as this hour to us
How violent blows the tempest which tears each second from us.

THE QUEEN

Don't talk any more.
To boast of happiness is to tempt
The Gods to tear this moment from us
And turn it into stone and hang it from our necks
As a memory, making us mad with the weight
Of what is now so frail and light
A breath of fear can blow it all away.
A woman is speaking, Stanislas,
Do you understand?

STANISLAS

Dear God help me to understand thy will
And why our love's
          So strong and yet so fragile;
And why we two
          should reach this peace
                    to find it is all peril.
Like tired swimmers we
          struggle in a callous sea,
And for the most part
          drink indifference down
And drown our thirsty hearts.
          But for one or two this miracle:
To climb upon this little raft
          which is our mortal love.
Now, even God is jealous
          and clumsy Fate conspires
To wreck ruin and upset
          this raft of our desires

Great love is great in agony.
To it, pain is peace,
　　Those who are born slaves are free
Compared to us
　　who are imprisoned in this tyranny.

STANISLAS

Those who are burnt to death,
Never know this cruel flame
　　consuming all within, so pitiless is desire.

THE QUEEN

And those who freeze to death,
Do not feel so cold
　　as those who love and then, unloved
feel as they grow old.

STANISLAS

Oh God is there no mercy
For those who love?
　　Is this the punishment
Or is this the sin...

I suppose the traffic jam had lasted twenty minutes. It was never difficult for me to write: my difficulty was to find the opportunity. If I went to pick up a pen I usually found I was holding a lipstick.

Before we left for Bath, I saw Beaverbrook and told him that I couldn't do any more private film criticisms for him because I was going to leave London. He was disappointed.

"Then you'd better write something for me every week from the country," he said, "and don't forget, send it to me personally. All typed in capitals. How much is it costing you two at this 'health hell'?"

"Twelve guineas a week."

"Typed in capitals," he barked, trying hard to mask his kindness with severity.

Gaby Pascal also reminded me that he had an urgent commission. He now offered me £100 to do a rough film treatment of Marcel Pagnol's play *The Birth of Love*. This play takes place in the Ice Age. As usual Gaby was firing on six cylinders of enthusiasm and was already arranging with a studio in Rome to have models of mammoths made. I accepted this proposal too because I had enjoyed doing a similar adaptation of Marcel Pagnol's *Femme du Boulanger*.

The "health hell" was housed in an elegant small Georgian manor house in a Cotswold type village. We liked the place as soon as we saw the magnolia trees against the wall and the enormous copper beech in the well-tended garden. This vegetarian hostelry was run by a waspish-looking woman who perhaps not unnaturally took a strong dislike to me on sight. She gave Rose Marie a room on the ground floor and having examined her, informed me not unkindly that she could not allow her to stay unless I registered her with a local doctor.

"I will treat her," she said, "but you must do this to comply with regulations." I could see that Rose Marie's condition was worsening every day; there was more sputum; the coughing was continuous. There was a kind of blushiness about her skin and the cheek bones protruded. It was horrible to see her ribs. The pathetic thing was that I could see her appetite for life increased every moment as the probability of not having any became closer.

Now completely frantic with apprehension—I had already attended her funeral and imagined the panoply of my grief—I started to do research on tuberculosis. I didn't know where to begin and decided to look it up in the Encyclopaedia Britannica. There was quite a good library at the home. The Encyclopaedia informed me, amongst a lot of depressing details, that the Irish peasants used garlic as a cure for tuberculosis. I looked up garlic. It said "often used by peasants as a cure for tuberculosis." With this cross-reference confirmed, I decided to buy some garlic the next time I went into Bath. I did this the next day in order to take her to have an X-ray at the doctor with whom we had registered. The doctor glanced apprehensively at Rose Marie and said he would look her up from time to time. From the tone of his voice I gathered that he didn't feel he would have to make many calls. I asked the doctor if he had heard of garlic as a cure for tuberculosis. He hadn't.

"There isn't any cure," he said. "She's in a desperate state, and there's danger of another haemorrhage. The hole in her lung is the size of a cup. I would insist on surgery: but since you refuse, there's no treatment but complete rest."

After leaving him I rushed round Bath trying to buy some garlic, but couldn't find any in any of the shops. We went back to Hinton Charterhouse, both feeling extremely depressed. Before going back to bed Rose Marie insisted on a brief walk through the grounds. These ran towards what Jane Austen called a wilderness, a part of a garden deliberately left, wild and wooded except for a path through it.

We were sitting here when I noticed a strong smell. She asked me what it was and I plucked a handful of wild garlic.

"Try some," I said and made her nibble the green stems. And we gathered some to take back to add to the salad of raw carrot, watercress and seaweed with which she was being fed. The theory behind this treatment was that the diet cleansed the blood and that if the blood were clean it would create its own antidote to the disease. We were prepared to try anything. I tackled my nut cutlet with feigned enthusiasm. I had once been a vegetarian before. But Rose Marie was now a convert and with every mouthful of garlic which I gathered daily from the wilderness she saw herself getting better.

For the first few days I had not even the heart to look, let alone weigh her for fear of discouraging her. But after no more than a week I noticed that the tin sputum mug on the bamboo table at the side of her bed was empty. Naturally I assumed she was herself emptying it so as not to alarm me. I watched: her cough had decreased. I put her on the scales. On a diet of lettuce and wild garlic she had gained three pounds. We celebrated, Rose Marie making me promise if her weight continued to increase to let her attend the first night of *The Rape of Lucretia* at Glyndebourne.

As a matter of routine the doctor in Bath decided on another

X-ray, to check. He could not believe the plate when it showed that the cavity had begun to calcify.

"These things have happened before," he said, grudgingly. "We don't know the explanation."

"Garlic," I repeated. "I suppose the reason garlic is efficacious," I said, improvising an explanation as I went along, "is that it purifies the blood and that allows the blood to cure the disease itself."

He smiled tolerantly.

The opera was, I thought, finished and I busied myself happily writing *The Birth of Love* under the copper beech, and scampering up to London occasionally for the day to help Ben with auditions. On one of these visits I found him looking unusually sheepish. It was several hours before he could bring himself to the point.

"I've got an impossible problem for you: from your point of view the opera is dramatically complete with Lucretia's death and the finale of epitaphs sung over her body, but I've just discovered that musically it's not finished. I want to write a final piece beyond the curtain as it were to frame the entire work."

"An orchestral epilogue?"

"No," he replied; "if it were that I wouldn't worry about giving you an impossible task. I want something vocal, something for the male and female chorus. At the moment the piece ends with your line 'Is this it all? It is all! It is all!' —but for me it isn't."

"How much do you need? Two or three lines for each?"

Ben looked miserable, guilty as a schoolboy.

"No. I really want one or two pages. A big piece. The biggest of the opera. I can see it's impossible for you because the action is complete. What more can you find to say? I do see that."

We walked across St John's Wood High Street to the pub for a drink. He apologised all the time as though he'd done me some unforgivable injury.

"Yet I can see that it's impossible for you to write anything after that finale without it being a dramatic anticlimax, but musically I need it."

"The only way," I said eventually, "would be to give the

chorus some universal comment on the entire tragedy to frame it dramatically, as you want to do musically. That will mean making the chorus take up their position as commentators outside and beyond the tragedy itself. Perhaps reverting to the position as Christians."

Ben gratefully bought me a packet of crisps.

"Now I see why you insisted on making them Christian. It gives them a definite point of view from which they can objectify the pagan tragedy. You must have unconsciously anticipated my need to round the piece off with something beyond itself."

"Maybe I can do something."

Ben looked relieved and pathetically grateful. We returned to the flat. Marion gave us lunch, as unobtrusive as ever. There was a lobster for me. She'd obviously been primed.

Ben came to the station to see me off back to Bath. On the platform he began to look sheepish again.

"By the way," he said as I got into the train, "I've promised the score to the copyist by Monday, so try and let me have the stuff before the weekend."

"What's today?"

"Thursday."

He looked very guilty.

"I'll go to Snape and wait for it there. About four pages," he pleaded. "Something to top the finale. Make it as big as you like."

"I'll phone it through to you."

On the train going down I saw clearly that the only way of tackling this problem was to state that Lucretia's rape by Tarquinius implied a perennial violation by humanity. Without consciously thinking any more about the problem, I recalled the final phrase of the libretto as it stood:

> How is it possible that she
> Being so pure should die?
> How is it possible that we
> Grieving for her should live?
> So brief is beauty.
> Is this it all? It is all! It is all!

Then on the back of a menu in front of me I wrote:

> *Is it all? Is all this suffering and pain,*
> *Is this in vain?*
>> *Does this old world grow old*
> *In sin alone?*
>> *Can we attain*
>>> *nothing*
> *But wider oceans of our own tears?*
>> *And it, can it gain nothing*
> *But drier deserts of forgotten years?*
> *For this did I*
>> *See with my undying eye*
> *His warm blood spill*
>> *Upon that hill*
>>> *And dry upon that Cross?*
> *Was that all loss?...*

Having found the position the rest, of course, was easy. After spending the next morning under the beech tree I was able to phone the two strophes of this canzone through to Ben. The line was bad. To make the dictation more difficult I insisted that he got it down in the precise canzone form in which I'd written it.

"Cor!" he said. "I suppose I asked for it...But it's just what I wanted."

In a train to Bath, I realised that the only thing I could write for Beaverbrook from the country would be something about farming. But technical articles are dull and Beaverbrook had a horror of what he called "essays". The idea of writing a country diary in which one notes the first swallow or the last wasp seemed to me to be fatuous. Then the pleasure I'd got in writing about my fictitious gang of socialites, for William Hickey, suggested to me that it might be possible to invent some country characters and get them up to some scrape or rural spivery every week. I immediately scribbled out the first *Jan's Journal*, creating Amos, based on a neighbour in Devon, and the Colonel, who was a fusion of several farmers I knew. I sent this off to Beaverbrook, typed in capitals at least to show him that I'd taken note of his request.

He wired me that he was delighted with the invention and begged me to go on writing it. I was surprised to find the stuff published on Saturday in the centre page of *The Evening Standard*. The Editor, James Gunn, unlike Christiansen, was genuinely delighted to have the column. This way I continued *Jan* through that summer. I'd have probably shot myself if I had realised that I would write it every week for the next fourteen years. But as it turned out, writing it was easy and pleasurable. I became genuinely fond of Amos and used to invent his activities, especially his spivery, with uncanny ease. Indeed, it never took me longer than an hour to complete my sermon for the week, as Rose Marie called it. Although the column gained some sort of public for itself, I always felt I was writing it for Beaverbrook alone, since he occasionally sent me cables from various parts of the world indicating he'd particularly enjoyed an issue.

This column was only 800 words. I enjoyed writing it because of the technical problem to be solved in each, of establishing a story leisurely and giving it a snap, surprise ending within such a limited length. Journalism can be just as satisfying to write as anything else if you haven't a sub-editor or a proprietor breathing platitudes down your neck. And in fourteen years I never had a single *Journal* altered or censored by Beaverbrook or any of his editors. The opposite is generally supposed to be the rule. All the more important to state the exception.

After *This Way to the Tomb* had run at the Mercury Theatre for almost a year, it transferred to the Garrick. But before opening there the production with the original English cast moved for a limited season to the Studio des Champs Elysées in Paris. I took my mother over for the first night and we stayed for about a week. The play was well received; the British Ambassador gave a party at the Embassy after the first performance. But my mother was too shy to enjoy that sort of thing: we escaped from the reception and wandered about the streets admiring the barrows of flowers. I too liked doing that. It reminded me of the closeness I had felt with her when she used to walk with me to my prep school. It was the only week we spent alone. I remember nothing of all the writers I met. Probably due to my mother's sense of values, my only memory of that week is of a barrow loaded with mimosa and the childlike delight things like that gave her.

Part Three

What thou lovst well remains, the rest is dross

WHEN the *Lucretia* rehearsals started at Glyndebourne, the Company consisted of two entire casts which were to sing on alternate nights, plus several repetiteurs, the producer Eric Crozier, John Piper, Ben, the two conductors, Ernest Ansermet and Reggie Goodall, and myself. This large number of people did not seem to worry Audrey Christie, whose hospitality was never ruffled.

Even when Ben was composing *Lucretia*, he told me that he wanted Ernest Ansermet to conduct it. I didn't remember where they had met. I thought it was that he had been impressed by Ansermet's rendering of various Stravinsky scores. I believe he had also conducted the *Sinfonia da Requiem* in Switzerland. When the arrangements were made to present the opera at Glyndebourne, Ben was pleased that Ansermet had accepted the invitation to conduct, and he arrived at Glyndebourne for the rehearsals three weeks before the first night, and was there when Ben first played the score through in the Music Room. He was a man I took to immediately.

I enjoyed his sense of humour and the many stories he told me about himself and Stravinsky. I have forgotten most of them, but I always remember one.

Stravinsky and he were staying at an hotel in Switzerland during the First World War when work was short and both hard-up. Consequently they shared a bedroom. Both men were extremely interested in the opposite sex and Stravinsky gave Ansermet a long lecture on the necessity of keeping fit if you were to be a satisfactory lover.

"It is necessary," he told Ansermet, "to remember this and even do physical jerks to keep a good figure and to be always in good condition."

Ansermet was dubious but easily persuaded by Stravinsky's enthusiasm in this as in all other matters.

"Igor used to drag me out of bed and make me go through Swedish exercises, handstands and what-not, before we were allowed our breakfast. This went on for several days. However, one day I came in from rehearsals and asked if Igor was in.

" 'Yes,' the receptionist said, 'up in his room.'

"I went upstairs, but Stravinsky was not to be found. I went down to the receptionist again.'

" 'Are you sure M. Stravinsky is in?' I asked.

" 'Yes,' said the girl, 'he is in his room.'

" 'I have just been there and he is not.'

" 'He has a separate room on the top floor,' the girl told me.

"Bewildered I took the lift to the top floor and there was Stravinsky doing Yogi exercises on the floor.

" 'What is the idea of this?' I asked him.

" 'Well, Ernest, you don't think I was going to let you into all my secrets, do you?' Stravinsky said."

During these rehearsals of *The Rape of Lucretia* I received an urgent telegram from Beaumont asking me to think of a title for the Cocteau play. *Death Listens at the Door* would not do. Cocteau had changed this to *Azrael*—the Angel of Death. Beaumont had begged him to think again as he was frightened that this title would be confused by the public with Israel. But Cocteau was adamant, so Beaumont turned to me to invent something entirely new.

"He won't like this," I told his office on the phone, "it is going too far. After all, the title is really all that's left of the play." But they were in rehearsal and advance publicity would have to be done. With a wry thought about the authorship of the play, I scribbled the title *The Eagle has Two Heads* and sent it to London.

While we were rehearsing *Lucretia* John Christie invited Ben and me to write a new opera which he promised to present the following year. Ben agreed and said he wanted to write a comedy. This put Abelard out of the question and since the new piece was to be a chamber opera the *Canterbury Tales* wasn't suitable either. And during *Lucretia* rehearsals he had decided he wanted to write a work for Kathleen Ferrier. It was Joan Cross who eventually produced a subject for us by suggesting *Mansfield Park*.

She went off to Brighton especially to buy me a copy of the novel so that I could re-read it. As usual Ben was excited by the idea, especially because the story was suitable for Kathleen, with good parts for Peter and Joan too. They were both anxious to get Jane Austen's elegant urbanity on to the operatic stage. Ben's enthusiasm seemed to be mainly because he saw musical possibilities in the letter-writing scenes. Again we worked out a dramatic synopsis first and then broke this down into a musical synopsis: aria, duet, recitative, etc. When this was completed I began to write the libretto. We had settled on the title *Letters to William*. The Christies were delighted, mainly because Ben had said there would be a part for Audrey's pug.

Everybody became very nervous as we approached the first night of the opera at Glyndebourne; so much depended on it. It was the first new opera to be presented there. Kathleen Ferrier had some reason to be nervous: it was her first appearance on a stage. A feud had arisen between the producer, Eric Crozier, and Rudolph Bing, the Glyndebourne manager. Ben himself was making Christie a target for all his nervous tension. The peace was only kept by the extraordinary tact of two people: Audrey Christie and Ernest Ansermet. The night before the first performance I dreamed that Christie had told us all to leave Glyndebourne. Britten and I had then hired a large garage constructed of galvanised iron in which to perform the opera. We were apprehensive about the acoustics. As the opera started it began to thunder and hail. The noise of the hail on the galvanised iron roof made it impossible to hear a single note, but at the same time most of the hail managed to perforate the roof, and drench the singers. In the middle of this chaos I went to Joan Cross and handed her my sodden libretto.

"Don't give that to me," she said, "it's wet, anyhow."

I suppose I picked on Joan because she had been teasing me about a line in one of the female parts she had to sing: "Now every whore has the Emperor's ear." She had asked me whether "Emperor's ear" was a new name for syphilis.

After the performance, Ben, Rose Marie and I were having a drink with Sophie, Erwin and Marion. Reggie Goodall, who was to conduct the work on the second performance and thereafter on alternate nights, joined us. His wife was somewhere about the place. Poor Reggie had, within four days of meeting Rose Marie, become infatuated with her. He followed her about the house and gardens and frankly admitted to me that my wife had even put his beloved Lucretia out of his mind. I think he had identified them. None of us took his infatuation seriously: we cast Reggie as Malvolio and teased him mercilessly; he did not mind that, so long as he was at Rose Marie's side. Every ten minutes he would confide in me that he could not takes his eyes off my wife and apologise. I found myself sympathising with him in his predicament. This was not very altruistic of me because I was suffering at that moment from my attraction to Petra, a friend of Audrey Christie's. She was an art student. Her mother was Irish, her father Spanish. The result could not have been more felicitous. She had jet black hair and blue eyes, and a skin that looked as if she had a sun tan. The difference between Reggie and myself was that my feelings for Petra were secret, something I had not admitted even to her. I dared not look at her. For the last few weeks we had seen a great deal of each other: I did not think she reciprocated my feelings. But that evening, I had had doubts, not from any gesture she had made, but because of the lack of them. After the curtain had fallen and we were all back-stage, she had excitedly run up to congratulate Ben, Peter and Ansermet and kissed each of them. But when she had come up to me she had arrested the impulse, fallen silent and turned away, as if on the verge of tears. Even so, I thought that this was probably because she sensed my feelings for her and that they embarrassed and saddened her. At the table she addressed her remarks to Ben or Rose Marie: tacitly I ignored her...It was only too easy for me to sympathise with Reggie, and when he stood up and asked Rose Marie if she would walk round the lake with him—and then turned and asked if I minded, I found that my only apprehension was to make sure she took her wrap because of the night air and the danger of her catching a chill.

As soon as they had left the room, Sophie Stein turned to me and said she couldn't understand what I was thinking of, letting Rose Marie go off round the lake in the middle of the night with Reggie Goodall. Sophie sighed audibly; she was a determined romantic: the opera, the champagne and the gardens of Glynde-bourne were too much for her. It was a shame nobody had volunteered to show her the waterlilies or the swans. But something else occurred to her.

"I know," she said, "why don't you now take Petra round the lake? That will give Rose Marie something to think about."

It was as if she'd read my thoughts. This was what I had been wanting to do the whole evening. The girl looked away shyly. I got to my feet; Sophie urged Petra to hers.

"I'm sorry about that," she said as we walked towards the water.

"I had the idea an hour before she did," I said. She was silent, not believing me.

"Well, what shall we do to tease Rose Marie?" she asked with forced gaiety.

We could see her and Reggie in the distance walking at the far end of the lake.

"Let's go and sit on that bench," I suggested, "then they'll see us when they pass."

We sat down to wait. Neither of us spoke. I felt her tension but had no true indication of the cause. It was as if she had grown to that evening: she was beautiful but her sadness now enhanced her. I had the awareness that I was living a moment I would never forget. Consciously using my eyes as a camera, I took an indelible print of the girl with her black hair "like a waterfall of night over her ivory shoulders".

With infinite caution I put my arm round those shoulders expecting her to move away. But she stayed still. A white swan moved over the black lake. And she stayed still. It was an enamelled evening, the air indolent, shadows of velvet. Magnolia petals lay on the lawn.

I turned her head towards me. This first kiss with this girl of eighteen whom I expected to rebuff me, was the most passionate surrender I ever experienced.

Then we heard the crunch of gravel coming nearer and Rose Marie's voice.

"Was that merely to tease her?" she asked. Tears spurted from her eyes.

For answer I pulled her up and took her amongst some trees away from the lake.

When we went inside later, Rose Marie, Ben and Reggie Goodall, Marion and her parents, were still at the table.

"I hear you've been round the lake too," Rose Marie said to Petra. "We didn't see you."

"We must have followed you round," I said.

Ben and the Steins eventually made a move to go.

I then realised that as Rose Marie had invited Petra to stay with us she would be sleeping alone in her room that night and that room adjoined ours. I did not close my eyes all night: I lay there knowing she was weeping. I ached to receive those tears. Rose Marie slept deeply beside me. My impulse was to emulate Tarquinius and steal through the silent hall. I began to perceive that whatever I wrote, I eventually lived. Lying there I realised that Sophie's suggestion for a tease had released something that would never be contained again.

And lying there I became aware of something else: my feelings for the woman sleeping beside me and for the other in the adjoining room were similar. It is the platitude of literature and the false assumption in life that a man falls in love with one person because he has tired of or fallen out of love with another. This convention may be convenient. But it is a simplification without reality. My feelings could not conform to it. But all this time, I was unable to accept this realisation about myself and consequently damaged myself and struggled against the nature of my own being. Others struggled against it too. I suppose I was a born bigamist: not that that confers any particular distinction upon me. Monogamy was invented by women. If a man doesn't find at least two women who attract him, he's unlikely to find one. I was not a sensualist but acutely fastidious. Few women attracted me: a few can be too many. Of course I was emotionally insecure. Is there a man who isn't? I suppose the unconscious resolution I had formed driving round the roundabout when I feared that Rose Marie was to die was part of that insecurity.

After the season of *Lucretia* at Glyndebourne, John Christie toured the opera for four weeks. Ben and Rudolph Bing, the manager at Glyndebourne, encouraged him to do this. After all, one of the reasons why we had written a chamber opera was because it was less expensive to mount and tour. Christie agreed to finance the tour so long as the Arts Council was not approached. His gestures of independence cost him £14,000. He never complained of the loss.

We opened at the Kings Theatre in Edinburgh: Ben, Peter and I stayed at the Caledonian Hotel. An hour or two after we arrived, I went to look for Ben and found he wasn't in his room although the porter had said he'd just gone upstairs. I came out of the room and then saw him with his back to me a good way down the corridor. He seemed to be lame, moving slowly forward as though crippled in both feet. I went up behind him wondering what could have happened to him. It appeared to me that he was moving as though he had blisters. Whatever it was, he was so absorbed in his gingerly procession that he was unaware of my presence.

"What's up with you?" I asked.

He continued his slow and painful progress for a few moments, concentrating so much on his movements that he didn't reply at first. Then he paused as though balancing himself on some imaginary precipice.

"What I'm trying to do, Ronnie," he said, "is to see if I can get right down this corridor and back without touching any of the red lines on the carpet."

He continued his careful way, like an adept at hopscotch.

"And what," I asked, "do you hope to achieve by this exercise?"

He looked very seriously at me as if I had asked a particularly foolish question.

"If I can get right up and down the corridor without touching the lines," he said solemnly, continuing his progress, "it will mean that I am a composer."

He had already written *Grimes*, *Lucretia*, the *Sinfonia da Requiem*, the *Donne* and *Michelangelo Sonnets* and a dozen more major compositions...

Five or six years later, when Ben was staying with me in Devon, I asked him to witness my signature on some Conveyance. He wrote his name and address and then paused.

"What shall I put down where it says 'profession'?"

"Composer," I said.

"Or should I put musician?"

"Composer," I repeated firmly.

He wrote the word quickly, almost guiltily as though forging a cheque.

I understood this inhibition only too well; for years I thought I was an impostor if I described myself as an author on any form I had to fill up and generally wrote farmer instead.

The reception of *Lucretia* at Edinburgh did not give either of us a sense of confidence. There were less than a hundred people in the audience. Ben and I sat in the draughty stalls wearing our overcoats to protect ourselves from the chill of disapproval blowing down our necks. It would have been a depressing week had it not been for Joan Cross' ability to find good restaurants in unlikely places, and Kathleen Ferrier's gaiety as she hopped like a child from one antique shop to another.

The rehearsals of *The Eagle has Two Heads* proceeded comparatively smoothly. This was due to the fact that the management was content to manage, and the producer, Murray Macdonald, confined himself to producing: neither tried to rewrite the script. Macdonald was, what is called rather derisively now, a "professional" producer, by which it is implied that the person is limited to being able to stage a play effectively, direct the actors and plot the moves but lacks a creative flair or intellectual pretensions. In other words the play survives but without the producer's indelible stamp. Murray Macdonald was never invited to direct a play at Stratford and, because he didn't go around the stalls yapping about "alienation", "commitment" or some other pet theory, he never became fashionable. Like Noël Coward, he believed that an actor's job "was to speak the lines and not to knock the furniture over".

Eileen Herlie, who played the Queen was grateful for Murray Macdonald's direction and also for any suggestions I could give her about interpretation, phrasing or diction. But James Donald, the leading man, was another matter. He believed that an actor should understand. He was not content to learn his part, take direction and play the scene according to the script. Nor was he satisfied to discuss his character and motivation with me. After rehearsals, he would read Freud or Jung and, according to which he'd dipped into the night before, so did his interpretation differ. Rehearsals at the Theatre Royal, Haymarket would stop while Donald argued some abstruse psychological motivation with the producer who invariably used to pass the abstract buck over to me. Eventually I found that the shortest way back to work was to agree with any theory or interpretation Donald produced. But we were patient with him, knowing that his intellectualism was a smoke screen to hide a young actor's nervousness and uncertainty, especially playing such a big role. The management had great expectations of James Donald and had delayed presenting the play until they were sure he could get his release from the Army to join the cast. He was spoken of as the new Gielgud. The more I rehearsed this play and compared Donald with Noël Willman who played Baron Foehn, I became convinced that a good actor relies on instinct rather than on understanding.

After the usual inadequate three weeks' rehearsals we went to Cardiff prior to opening the following Monday at the Prince of Wales Theatre there. The management tried to mislead the company into believing this was a good date and one they had selected carefully. Whereas of course everybody in the cast knew we were only going to Cardiff because Brighton was already booked and nobody looked forward to opening a difficult verse play, as they called it, in such a barn of a theatre before an audience of dockers and coalminers. These apprehensions were grim enough, our accommodation even more depressing. We had all been booked into a sordid little Temperance Hotel overlooking a main street: the clatter of trams made sleep impossible. And without sleep my vitality is halved and my anxieties are trebled. I worried myself into a migraine whether the bed in act one would look right and whether the music would arrive in time.

When I had seen Bébé Bérard in Paris, he had offered to design the sets and costumes, on condition he was allowed to paint the flats himself. With his usual enthusiasm and instantaneous flair, he had picked up the wrappings of a chocolate box from the floor and sketched a design for the Queen's bedrooms in the Castle of Krantz, the setting for the first act. Bérard's sketch simply focussed on the bed: it was the most regal thing I ever saw, not a conventional four-poster with tapestry background and conventional carved crests; but a simple double divan with a circular canopy above it, unsupported from the ground, narrowing as it funnelled up beyond sight to the flies from which it was hung. Both the bed and the canopy was crimson. "Velvet, of course," Bérard had said. I had been delighted with this sketch; indeed, it was his conception of this magnificent bed which stimulated me more than anything else to write my adaptation. Velvet, black, red, green, whatever its colour, always pleases me. But Bérard's design was more than pleasing: it set the tone of the entire play. For his bed was more than life size: it had dimensions beyond the confines of naturalism. The canopy reached beyond the sight lines, hinting at infinity on the floor but untethered by reality. Bérard's sketch set the style I wrote—in realising that this bed called for poetry and not the flat prose Cocteau had written his original play in. And his sketch contained all his brilliant suggestive economy; with that canopy the dimensions of the room were implicit: one would have only needed that on the stage for the castle to be imaginatively suggested without the need for the confounded clutter of a tawdry box set. This design would have saved the management a thousand pounds. But Binkie Beaumont refused Bérard's offer. Lying sleepless on my iron bed in this Temperance Hotel I fretted, worrying what dreary furniture the "Times" would have sent down to Cardiff. I knew the designer was doing his best: but that best, for me, was not Bérard.

The play ends with the Queen and the poet lying dead on the stage and, as they fall, a National Anthem is heard. I had naturally run to Ben and asked him to compose this: he had agreed and as usual, like a good tailor, done his job on time and to the precise measurements and specifications. But the management had done nothing about getting his anthem recorded: they had made moves to hire a small string orchestra without noticing Ben had of course scored it for a brass band. In the end the band of the Household Brigade was approached: there seemed to be doubt whether we would have the recording for the opening of the play. The theatre had suggested that as an alternative, the house musicians, who consisted of a gnome-like pianist and a be-wigged violinist who usually played extracts from *Iolanthe* in the intervals, should, if Ben's anthem didn't arrive, render the Welsh National Anthem, or *Deutschland Uber Alles* from off-stage.

My migraine did not improve until the record arrived an hour before the curtain went up: as for the bed and the expensive and tawdry box set, all beams, carvings and stucco, I took one glance at the bed and remarked that it was only fit for copulation, quite inadequate as a springboard for poetry.

After a terrible get-in, the dress rehearsal was unusually chaotic. The target which was supposed to wind in and out from the wings when the Queen did her pistol practice in Act Two disappeared before she had fired, then reappeared without reason in the middle of another scene; the thunder was too early and too loud; the anthem, too soft to be heard. Macdonald and I had pages of notes. The entire cast had lost their confidence and were miserably apprehensive of playing such a poetic piece before the miners and dockers of Cardiff. Instead of blaming the inhabitants for their inadequacies, they suddenly resented me.

I had written the longest speech of any play for the Queen in Act One when she dines in her imagination with the King on the anniversary of his assassination. The speech runs for over a thousand lines. Any actress would be nervous of such a lengthy soliloquy alone on the stage. But even before rehearsals had begun I had taken Eileen Herlie through it line by line so that she had no fear of the language, and Macdonald had, by plotting her moves even down to the details of marking on which word she removed her gloves, snuffed the candles, enabled her to sustain the scene. But at this dress rehearsal all our build-up of our leading lady's confidence was punctured by her rendering of the very first line of the play: *I love moths and bats.* Instead of this, Miss Herlie announced: *I love boths and mats.* After this beginning I wondered whether the rest of the text had been rendered into Welsh behind my back. It was obvious that the prompt copy had been lost: the dries were frequent, the fluffs innumerable. Our apprehensions became as uncomfortable as our hotel.

Several of the cast sneaked off to phone London to inform their agents that they were sure to be available for another play by the end of the week.

But as often happens after a disastrous dress rehearsal, the first performance ran smoothly. During the acts I had found the cast still depressed because they thought the audience was bored because they were not reacting. But I was not worried; sitting among them I sensed that their silence was one of attention and not boredom. Even so, I did not anticipate the thunder of applause as the final curtain fell. Both the cast and the producer was so surprised by this reception that they had neglected to rehearse their curtain calls.

After the performance the management had organised a dinner for the entire company in some restaurant. The table was in the shape of a T with places marked for the stars, the producer and designer on the cross piece and for the rest of the company including stage hands on the supporting piece. The cast toasted one another and took their seats; nobody bothered to observe that no place had been reserved for me. I felt slighted, wounded and bewildered. Eventually I sat with the stage carpenter at a side table. I was reminded painfully of those occasions when at school I had been put into Coventry without knowing why. And I have never discovered why I was treated like that on this occasion. Perhaps it was because the cast had been so nervous about the language and the long speeches in the play that they had built up a resentment against me? But I never sensed it during rehearsals. All I know is that I had a very unhappy evening and the next morning hurriedly left Cardiff to rejoin Rose Marie.

After its successful week at Cardiff, *The Eagle* came on to The Lyric Theatre, Hammersmith, where the Company of Four were presenting a season. It was scheduled to run for a month. In spite of their enthusiastic reception in Wales, both the management and the cast were far from confident; they told each other that the Welsh had a taste for poetry which Hammersmith was unlikely to share. I spent the weekend resisting last-minute cuts and trying to persuade Eileen Herlie to go all out for a bigger than life performance.

"Don't let Vivien Leigh cast a brittle shadow over you,"

I begged. "Think of Edwige Feuillière. It's not Rattigan, it's nearer to Verdi. You'll be all right so long as you don't pull back, underplay or play against it." I put more energy into this Svengali act than I had in writing the text.

Rose Marie came up for the opening, and went in her favourite black velvet dress which she always wore when either Ben or I had a First Night. Archie Ling, who had been so instrumental in helping her to recover from T.B., accompanied her. Sophie Stein who had read the play, insisted on going because the play appealed to her Viennese background: Marion, of course, was there; and as I didn't wish to sit in the auditorium, Epstein went with them. Cocteau, peeved by my changing his title, refused to attend and had ignored the production. Although he netted over £10,000 from it, he failed to thank me. I spent most of the performance back-stage to make sure that no agents, friends or rivals got at Eileen with any sensible advice. I was determined that we should all go down in ridicule or burn a hole through the drawing-room comedy carpet.

In the interval, Marion and I eavesdropped in the stalls bar. But we picked up few comments: people are cagey, they wait for the critics who are without taste, and prefer what fashion dictates. I noticed Noël Coward in the bar wearing his Chinese mask and looking as sardonic and imperturbable as ever. I wanted to know his reactions to the play, but since I had never met him I could not ask him what they were: I mistook his urbanity for concrete boredom and was depressed, because though we had nothing in common, I respected his instinct for theatre.

I returned back-stage now nervous myself, knowing that the last Act which, with the Queen and the poet dying on the stairs, trod on the heels of melodrama and almost echoed the tradition of the *Revengers Tragedy*, laid us wide open to easy derision, especially from a First Night audience who prefer the theatre to be a digestive tablet and not an emotional experience.

But again the play was well received: or so it appeared from the number of curtain calls. Having congratulated Eileen, I went to the front of the house to take Rose Marie back-stage to do her customary oblations. Several people muttered something non-committal to me and with false smiles bolted for their taxis, but there was one person who stood waiting for me on the stairs. He looked very severe.

"Congratulations," he said in his clipped manner and not needing to wait for the morning papers before he made up his mind. "That's what I call theatre. I'm going to New York in the morning and, if you've no objection, I'll tell Wilson he ought to present the play there."

I had no idea who Wilson was, but I thanked Coward, grateful that he had been sensitive enough to say something to me after he had known I had seen him there.

The press treated the play itself with little respect. Cocteau got blamed for a Ruritanian melodrama; I, for the poetry and long speeches; but neither of us came in for much attention. The notices were all Eileen's: she was acclaimed as the greatest discovery since Sarah Bernhardt without a dissenting voice.

After its run out at the Lyric, *The Eagle* transferred to the Theatre Royal, Haymarket. And this completed my hat trick; for at that time, *This Way to the Tomb* had moved from the Mercury to the Garrick Theatre and the *Rape of Lucretia* was being given at Covent Garden. I was on what is known as the "crest of a wave": I didn't perceive the trough beneath it. I was in fashion: but because that fashion was me, I mistook it for good taste.

I resolved not to be distracted or debauched by this success but to leave London: this was no sacrifice; parties bored me, late nights were not good for Rose Marie, and apart from that consideration I was so obsessed with the play in my head that I had no further interest in those now on the stage, though their success, especially that of *The Eagle*, stimulated me: I felt I had proved that poetry could be commercial theatre; the play was booked up for months ahead. Not realising that its appeal was due more to the publicity Eileen Herlie had received, rather than the language and style of the play, I concluded erroneously that poetry had come into its own again and the future was wide open. I couldn't wait to get down to writing *Stratton* and another four plays began to germinate in my mind. Rose Marie and I decided to go to Switzerland.

Eliot encouraged me to do this: he had not wholly approved of my adapting *The Eagle*. He did not like Cocteau but grudgingly had to admit that the work had given me some more experience in the theatre. To mark his disapproval of my French flirtation he refused to publish the text "as Faber's are interested in your own work and not your adaptations", and he also excused himself when I offered to take him to a performance. But he said he would like to see *The Rape of Lucretia* instead. I asked Rose Marie and Nigel Spottiswoode, who had returned to Welcombe after the war, to accompany us. I was apprehensive that Eliot wouldn't enjoy himself: he wasn't very musical, he didn't like opera and, when he had given a luncheon to Ben and me a few weeks earlier, I could sense that he had not been particularly impressed by Britten. Eliot equated opera with Wagner and his New English puritanism made him averse to the sensuous excesses of that medium. I had tried to make him understand that *The Rape* was an austere chamber opera and without the clamour of a chorus. And was anxious that he should like the work—which he had offered to publish and had indeed got into proof before the Faber edition was cancelled as they couldn't promise to get the libretto out in time for the Glyndebourne première.

We sat in the Grand Tier, to the side. The opera commenced: every dozen bars the lavatory cistern in the Gentlemen's behind us made a most terrible noise for five minutes. I observed that Eliot was becoming bored: we couldn't move to the other seats: fortunately, Spottiswoode and I had installed many lavatories in many Devon cottages. There was nothing we did not know about lavatory cisterns, ball-cocks and valves. Leaving our seats, we went into the Gentlemen's and turned plumbers. Eliot was very impressed with our performance in the Gents but the opera failed to interest him.

As planned, Rose Marie and I went off to Switzerland very much to my agent's dismay, who thought I was being very perverse leaving England with three shows running in London. But I ached to write: no play I ever wrote obsessed me as *Stratton* did: as I slept, I saw scenes of it in my dreams; as I talked to people lines of the play intruded involuntarily into my conversation. I was entirely possessed by it. I was not writing it: it was writing me. We went to Montana-Vermala as it had been recommended to us: but the hotel was too flash for our tastes and we moved to a small pension called the Châlet du Lac. But as there was no place where

I could write in the *pension*, I used to go off every morning to a café where I sat for three hours drinking an espresso every half-hour and with a record player and a foreign language being spoken around me. The background was remote enough to constitute silence. And I found I could concentrate in spite of the records and clatter of crockery. Bad music doesn't intrude, it is like rain outside the window.

I realised that *Stratton* was the real challenge: the problems of finding an idiom which could carry poetry in a contemporary setting. *Murder in the Cathedral* and *This Way to the Tomb* had succeeded; but both plays were set in the past and had a religious or a liturgical background to make the poetry more easily acceptable. Similarly *The Eagle* was, in this sense, remote from the immediate: it was a Ruritanian fantasy. In *Stratton* I wanted to try to write a modern play with enough depth to it that the language had the density of poetry without being decorative verse.

Another problem, rather a different facet of the same one, concerned me. I rebelled fiercely against the ridiculous way the theatre had been truncated into religious plays, social plays, thrillers and so on. It nauseated me, too, to be called a religious poet. If religious meant "to connect" how could any poet not be religious? How, I asked Rose Marie over and over again as we trudged up and down knitting with skis, can a meaningful play not have a religious connotation, and a social implication too? People had urged me to write a modern play but their interest in getting me to write on a contemporary subject was the hope that I would produce a play with a strong political flavour, preferably left wing. But I could not interest myself in transitory social equations: the human problem, not the social background, interested me. I saw that the only problems that were vital were those to which there were *no* solutions. Anything that can be solved, like higher wages, greater educational facilities or whatnot, were for me subjects for ephemeral pamphlets or editorials in weekly magazines and not the stuff out of which *Faust* and *Lear* arose. Consequently I set myself to write a modern play, but one which was about issues that were permanent to the human dilemma and not dependent on frivolous topicality. I wanted the play to have the elements of a thriller on one level, and the structure of a Miracle play on another. I was determined to integrate these facets into one piece and damned the West End for dividing sensibility in such a way that we had a separate theatre for every aspect of it: the Old Vic for the serious; the Windmill for the bawdy; the Mercury for the poetic; and the Haymarket for the plush. Life is entirely empty if it doesn't contain the whole, I shouted. And I was angry at all those people who wanted me to write a play about ordinary people.

" 'Ordinary people' don't interest me!" I cried. "The unique person is the growing point of human consciousness, damn and blast the average man, confound nonentities and lowest common denominators." These screams from the Alps did nothing to make me popular with the *literati* in London who, from their dugouts in the Savoy Grill, were belligerent with cocktail sticks for the betterment of the proletariat.

I wrote at white heat, for I saw that all the work Martin Browne and Eliot had put in to getting depth back into drama would soon be swept away by those who wanted to turn it back into a Shavian soap box without Shaw's wit.

In this mental ferment, I marched Rose Marie up and down the mountains in an attempt to lessen my energy and only succeeding in over-taxing hers. The poor girl loyally listened and gave the answers my rhetorical questions demanded as I hectored her from the anguish of my certainties. To be as certain as I was certain is as uncomfortable as sitting on a circular saw.

"I want to climb the Alps of the human spirit," I cried, tripping over my skis once again, "not play hopscotch in the *New Statesman* gutter."

The Eagle has Two Heads introduced Cocteau to the English public, but even after it had been running six months at the Theatre Royal, Haymarket, I had not heard a word from him. The play had been touring America very successfully with Tallulah Bankhead as the Queen, and Marlon Brando as the poet. Brando was thrown out of the production before it opened in New York—by Tallulah, of course, who had got her own way so much during the tour that she had changed the final curtain of the play. After such a successful tour, the play was expected to be a success on Broadway. Cocteau flew over to see it: I was not invited. On his arrival, he gave an interview to the press referring bitterly to the other head, meaning me. I do not know what his bitterness was about. I had made him £20,000 by now. The original French play had still not been produced, but when it was put on, Cocteau changed the title from *Azrael* to *L'aigle à deux têtes*. With this he gave the impression that I had mistranslated the title (which I had invented). He enjoyed telling his friends in Paris this.

The French production with Edwige Feuillère was not a success, but in London we moved from the Haymarket to the Globe. Cocteau continued to draw his royalties and malign me across the Channel. I have always wondered whether Stephen Spender, who was a firewatcher in the war, might have been an incendiarist to this quarrel between Cocteau and myself. However, in spite of it, I agreed to adapt another play of his, *Machine à Écrire*, which was produced at the Watergate Theatre.

I have been hypnotised, I have been psychoanalysed, but still I cannot remember. All I know is that whatever happened, it left me with an invisible burden of heavy shame. I've been carrying it now for twenty years: I feel its weight, but cannot see its shape. I feel guilty, I dare say I am guilty: but I do not know what crime it was that I committed. It could not have been murder, at any rate physical murder.

I remember every detail of that day except the hour that mattered. Perhaps writing this will make me remember? It is the only reason that I write it. For whatever it was, I want to know what is was.

I had come up from the farm with Rose Marie. With only two or three days in London, my diary was full: the usual kind of urgent but unimportant appointments.

"No, darling," I had told Petra on the telephone that morning. "I can't meet you this morning because I have to see my publisher, and then I've promised to lunch with Margery Vosper."

"What about this evening?" she'd pleaded.

"Hopeless. I've promised to go to Boosey & Hawkes at six to hear Ben and Peter's recording on this magnetic wire they're developing."

"And after six?"

"After that I've to meet Kitty Black for dinner at the Caprice."

"Then you're free between three and six?"

"No, I've promised to be at the Savile Club at four."

"Quite a busy little bee, aren't you?"

"It's like that when I'm only up for two or three days."

"Of course."

"Tomorrow's all right."

"But I want to see you today. Where are you lunching?"

"The Moulin d'Or."

"Then I'll be at the usual place at two-thirty. That will give us an hour."

She'd rung off fearing that I would say I couldn't manage it. And I couldn't ring her back for she always ran round the corner then and used a coin box. But I knew I couldn't meet her at two-thirty because I'd arranged to meet Margery for a late lunch and I knew she would be late for that.

My agent, unlike agents, had some good news for me. In those days I didn't value it.

"Warner has persuaded Bette Davis to make a film of *The Eagle has Two Heads*. He's going to fly over to talk to me about terms. This calls for a bottle of champagne."

I can even remember that I ate whitebait, saddle of lamb and that I managed to refuse the proprietor's suggestion to have some treacle tart for which the Moulin d'Or is famous. But having done that, I did not like to hurt the man's feelings by also refusing some Cyprus brandy which he offered me.

It was already two-forty: Petra would be already standing in the doorway at Swan and Edgars. The usual place, but the day was unusually cold. I gulped the brandy down hoping doing that would terminate the meal. It didn't, it merely made the proprietor fill my glass again.

When I looked at my watch, what I thought was a minute later, it was in fact three-ten. Margery was still gossiping. Poor Petra would be frozen, she'd have been waiting for forty minutes. It never even crossed my mind that she'd have gone. I had kept her waiting before.

I got to my feet, told Margery I'd suddenly remembered an

appointment and went into the street for a taxi. The fresh air immediately made me aware that I was drunk. I couldn't understand this: I'd had nothing but two glasses of champagne and two brandies.

Perhaps the brandy wasn't good? The man had said it was Cyprus brandy. Lurching into the taxi I remembered the effect South African brandy once had on me in Johannesburg, "snake bite" they'd called it. I now felt sick, very sick; drunk, very drunk. The taxi stopped outside Swan and Edgars. I peered out. There she was, waiting. She'd been waiting almost an hour in the cold. I was too drunk to get out of the taxi. Fortunately she saw me in it, ran across the pavement and got in.

The taxi had to be given a direction.

"Shall I take you home?" she asked.

"No," I replied.

"Then shall I take you to your hotel?"

I visualised Rose Marie's reception.

"No," I repeated lying my head in her lap.

"We can't stay here."

"Tell him to drive to Hampstead Heath," I slurred, with the taxi spinning round the girl who cradled me.

I know why I said Hampstead Heath. It was because it represented the country to me. Whenever I am ill my instinct is to crawl to grass somehow. Only the smell of wet leaves could act as antidote to the fumes of this foul brandy.

"Hampstead Heath," I drawled, then passed out.

I remember getting out of the taxi; I remember her holding me up and staggering down a path towards a large laurel. That's all I do recall. Though God knows I've tried. The only thing I'm certain of is that something there died. Perhaps I slept? Perhaps I did nothing but sleep? Perhaps nothing was the crime I committed? I do not know. Something there died.

I have no recollection of how I got from the Heath or even of entering Boosey & Hawkes' office in Regent Street. She must have held me or I must have walked like a sleep-walker.

I came to as I heard the music on the wire that Boosey & Hawkes were developing. The tape ultimately supplanted their invention. I managed to make some appreciative comments. Then

Petra put me in another taxi and I went home alone to Rose Marie who put me to bed for an hour in an effort to sober me up sufficiently for dinner.

It was not ordinary drunkenness: I had been poisoned. It took me two days to recover from it. In a sense I never have.

After leaving St John's Wood High Street, Peter Pears rented a house in Oxford Square. It had the advantage of a large music room and the house was sufficiently big to enable Peter to give his parents a flat on the ground floor. Ben, Marion, Erwin and Sophie Stein accompanied him: I was a frequent guest there. I have many vivid memories of that house but two stand out in my mind: the first occurred one winter's evening. Marion and I had been out to a cinema: Peter was away singing in a *Messiah* somewhere and Ben had gone to the Albert Hall. I believe Sir Thomas Beecham had grudgingly and unhappily included the *Interludes* from *Grimes* in the programme. At any rate, Ben had gone to this concert to sit in the audience to hear one of his own pieces. I can't think why neither Marion nor I had accompanied him as we usually did, nor why the Steins did not either. However, we got back from our film before him and were having a cold supper which Sophie had prepared when Ben came in. I don't know why, but the fact that I was eating beetroot stays in my mind as an important detail whereas it has no relevance at all. I noticed that he looked disturbed and a little depressed but assumed that was because he'd heard Sir Thomas doing his worst to prove that there was no modern English composer worthy of his notice. But when we were alone, Ben said he'd had an odd experience. Apparently when sitting in the auditorium, he had happened to notice that a young man seated beside him was following his composition from a printed score. Ben was naturally gratified: he was immensely proud of his first published scores. He felt he had to say something to his neighbour.

"I see you're interested in Benjamin Britten," he remarked casually.

"Of course I am," the young man said.

Ben smiled and then, after a few moments, asked:

"Why of course?"

"Because I am Benjamin Britten," the man said as though his identity should have been recognised.

"And what did you say then?" I asked Ben.

"Oh are you? I couldn't think of anything else to say. But I wonder who he was?"

"Maybe he was Benjamin Britten," I said, teasing him more than I intended.

Ben looked confused. I believe my remark worried him for days.

I had an impulse one day to buy Petra a small present. I had realised that there could be only a sad future for our relationship. But I knew that the feeling between us was of the type that neither morality, convention, nor even time could entirely destroy. Perhaps it could only be destroyed by being fulfilled? There was little chance of that. In this mood, I went into a small jewellers' shop in Grosvenor Street. Bracelets, rings and other things I was shown, didn't interest me. Then on a tray of odd trinkets, I noticed a gold watch key with an amethyst in the centre. With due acknowledgements to Freud, I bought it and a gold chain too, so that the girl could wear it as a pendant.

"It looks as if we shan't be seeing much of each other in future... plenty will happen to you, a good deal will run over me, and I dare say we shan't always be able to talk to each other; but whatever happens, wear this key whenever you want rescuing. No, don't put it on now, now there is no need."

After taking Rose Marie to Switzerland I returned with her to Devon. We stayed with my mother and sister for a time, and then moved to a guest house nearby. Rose Marie was not strong enough to undertake running the house at Mead. The children were still boarding at a kindergarten. I continued to write *Stratton*. We lacked privacy in the guest house: I could not bear the communal meals or the conversation in the evenings with hypochondriacs, spiritualists and be-dentured gnomes. Rose Marie too longed to get home. Eventually my sister persuaded her gardener and his wife to come to Mead: he, to bailiff the farm; his wife, to run the house for Rose Marie. These arrangements were far from satisfactory: the woman was willing; her husband wholly inexperienced. But we bore with them; I watched the farm going from bad to worse and did nothing but bite my pen. It was so good to be home again in Welcombe. Rose Marie's strength improved. Within a few weeks we had almost forgotten she had been ill. Her cough had entirely disappeared: only the regular X-ray reminded us. The children could come home for their holidays.

As a treat we took them up to London and stayed for a few days at Durrant's Hotel. Petra volunteered to come along and baby-sit so that I could take Rose Marie to a theatre or two. Seeing her again was painful. My feeling for her had not changed. But there was nothing I could do except to continue to write my play, pouring my feeling for Petra into Stratton's for Katherine. I was not unaware of what I was doing. Nor was I proud of it. It is wrong to misuse literature. The sublimation neither fooled nor satisfied me. But there was nothing I could do but waste what I wanted or hurt what I loved. And Rose Marie was not unaware of my attraction to Petra: I feared her jealousy; at each hysterical scene, I feared another haemorrhage. I began to placate, to sell myself short, to make any sacrifice to avoid these scenes. Petra was the first to burn. We decided not to see each other. She accepted this hopelessly. But before we parted, she agreed she would not write or telephone me if I would make one promise: to see her on her twenty-first birthday. I agreed: it was several months away.

I returned to Devon, supervising the farm, indulging in my passion for repairing cottages and writing *Stratton*. By a painful accident or an unconscious design, I found myself in London in the last week in October. I had heard that there was to be small party to celebrate Petra's birthday. In the circumstances I was not surprised to be uninvited: I made careful arrangements to distract myself that evening. But just as I was leaving my hotel I received a phone call from Marion to remind me to keep my promise to be there.

"It's the one present she wants," she said. "So you mustn't disappoint her. The party begins at seven. So come at ten even if it's only for five minutes."

When I entered the room, it was crowded. Petra, who was

seated on the floor wearing a red velvet dress, got to her feet and instantly took my hand and led me out of the room.

"This is my present," she said running ahead up the stairs, "five minutes alone with you in my room. Here are my other presents," she said, shutting the door and again flinging herself on to the floor. "Well, say something. Say you like my dress. It was especially for you."

She sat there on the floor: a ring of scarlet velvet, one hand supporting herself, the other playing with the back of her hair as usual. While looking down at her then, I knew I would never forget the image. Her face radiant, "running down the garden of eyes," her lips waiting. We clung together as though on a raft. I got to my feet and pulled her up.

"I'm going now," I said.

She led me down the stairs to the front door.

"Remember to keep your other promise," she said through her tears.

I closed the door.

That evening Rose Marie asked me if I'd seen Petra.

"For five minutes," I replied.

"So you've got a good conscience for once."

"Yes," I lied, knowing that I had seen a girl die as I closed a door, and that murder is a crime most of us get away with.

After Petra's twenty-first birthday, I did not see her again that year. She rang me a few times in Devon. After Christmas I braved London once or twice, and was asked to go there by Ben, who wanted to play *Albert Herring* to me. Petra and I managed to meet a couple of times on a buffet on Waterloo Station. During the winter the tryst I had made with her a year before came to my mind.

"If you still want me a year from now I will meet you somewhere."

"Where?"

"In Rapallo."

"When?"

"May 1st."

I wondered if she had remembered that. I had let her down so many times since then. We had hardly seen anything of each other for months. When May came, I assumed that my promise had been forgotten, trodden into her teens. But I thought of it. In that sense I suppose I kept it. I doubted if she had done even that.

But on May 3rd I received a postcard from Rapallo. For once it wasn't from Ezra. It was from Petra. There was not a word on it, just the address: a postcard of the bay with the postmark May 1st.

These are the little deaths I died.

A few weeks later, I went to London, to one of Ben's concerts. I hoped Petra would be there. But she wasn't. Audrey Christie came up to me in the interval. I felt shifty.

"Where is she?" I asked her.

"Abroad...she went to Rapallo to meet you. She waited for you ...then some cousin took her motoring through Austria and..."

"And?"

Audrey looked at me. She thought me both pitiful and despicable.

"You want to know? She gave herself to him."

"That's happened before."

"She gave herself to him because she says he meant nothing to her."

She turned and walked away. I left the hall.

Most people feel shame for the sins they committed; but I for the temptations I overcame.

It is when we try to preserve the good opinion of ourselves, that we lose that altogether.

I had grown very fond of Kathleen Ferrier during the rehearsals of *Lucretia*. She was perfect in the part, but that was not the reason. I liked her because she was so modest and vulnerable. And I enjoyed her bawdy Lancashire humour and rushing round antique shops as we did on tour in Edinburgh. Her greatest gift was the way she enjoyed doing simple things. She was the ideal person to have down at Mead, and as soon as Rose Marie and I opened the house again, Kathleen was one of our first guests. She did not ride, but loved the horses; and, as she had had no children of her own, she would spend hours in the evening singing to Briony and Roger, who naturally refused to go to sleep. Ben and I had originally planned to write two works especially for her, *Letters to William*, and a Cantata on the theme of Hylas. I sketched both works. And actually completed "Hylas", which Ben was then to set. He never did.

Living at the top of the hill at Mead made us more accessible than when we were down in the valley at West Mill. This was not always an advantage.

One winter's night there was a knock on the door about eleven o'clock. Rose Marie and I were going to bed. Cursing I went into the hall to find an unknown middle-aged visitor.

He introduced himself and mentioned the name of a friend of mine called Jimmy Bomford who lived surrounded by his collection of Impressionist paintings in Wiltshire. I thought it was a very odd time for this man to call but could do nothing but invite him in and take his coat. When he was by the fire I offered him a whisky.

He was very grateful for the drink.

"You'll stay the night, of course," I said.

He was very grateful for the bed.

"By the way," he said, "I've got my butler with me."

"Your butler?" I exclaimed, thinking this was rather eccentric. "Where?"

"I left him outside," he said casually. From which I assumed he meant in his car. But I had, now I came to think of it, seen no car in the farmyard when I had opened the door. Perhaps he had left it on the road?

I glanced at my visitor as I got up to go to the front door again. He didn't offer to move himself, but sat sprawled before the fire with the decanter and siphon by his side. He looked shabby, but not shabby enough to be the rich eccentric who would go on a midnight hike with his butler.

I went to the front door and peered out into the yard. I had been right: there was no limousine parked there. But in the shelter of the tractor house I saw a figure beating his arms to keep himself warm. I called him in. He was a little older than his master and if anything better spoken. This didn't surprise me. It's often the case.

I apologised for his having been left outside like a dog or a bicycle and steered him into the kitchen where he was given a hot meal.

I told Rose Marie that two rooms would be needed for our guests. She said they would have to sleep in rooms adjoining the nursery. Then I returned to my guest who was very comfortable.

"You looked cold," he said, "standing out there in the yard. Let me pour you a drink."

"Thanks very much." I watched him pour one finger for me, two fingers for himself.

"Can you tell me the time?" he asked, setting the decanter down beside him.

"Eleven thirty-five," I replied glancing at my wrist watch.

"Not long now," he said.

"No," I replied, grateful that it would be soon time for bed. As he sipped his whisky I wondered how he and his servant had reached the farm without a car. I had heard no taxi. There are no buses. The farm is eighteen miles from Bideford station. And there are no trains at that time of night.

"I think you'd better ask your man to drive your car into the yard," I suggested, thinking it must be still out in the road.

"I didn't come by car," he said proudly, "we hitch-hiked."

This piece of eccentricity silenced even me.

"What's the time now?" he asked again rather more anxiously.

"Ten to twelve," I said, getting to my feet and feigning a yawn. But he didn't move.

"Only ten minutes more," he said enigmatically, "and then we'll celebrate."

I sat down again. Could it be Christmas Eve, I wondered? No, I wasn't getting that absent-minded. The children would have told me. It wasn't even December.

"Celebrate what?"

My visitor smiled to himself but didn't reply, first eyeing the telephone beside me and then fingering the decanter in anticipation. Just then a clock in the dining-room struck midnight.

My visitor listened to every stroke and sighed audibly with a mixture of relief and pleasure. Was I going to witness some metamorphosis and see him suddenly turn into a fairy Princess on the last stroke? Was a coach made out of a pumpkin and drawn by four white mice going to appear in the farm yard and would my visitor and his butler, who was obviously the ugly sister, step into it and glide up over the Dutch barn?

But his wellingtons didn't turn into silver slippers. And he looked even more solid than ever deep in the armchair.

"Well, now we can celebrate properly," he said taking the stopper out of the decanter.

"By all means." Two fingers for me, a fist for him.

"But what are we celebrating exactly?" I had the temerity to ask.

"The time," he replied. "It means we've been out precisely three weeks. They can't put you inside again if you stay out for three weeks, at least not without certifying you again.

"Doing what?" I stammered.

"My butler and I escaped from the Asylum three weeks ago," he boasted, "but they can't put us inside again now – not till we want to go back, that is."

"And will you?"

"Sure, when we've had enough of bumming it around," he said, "but we're quite comfortable for the time being."

"I'm so glad," I said faintly.

"Yes," he went on expansively, "my butler and I usually winter in some asylum and keep out for the summer."

"What d'you do then?"

"Sponge," he replied, helping himself to another. "But this year, we broke out before we usually do because I couldn't stand the Colonel any more. He sat next to me in the dining room. I couldn't stand him – not because he was as mad as a hatter, but because he had the nasty habit of putting milk in his tea."

"And what d'you put in it?"

For answer he picked up the decanter.

But I didn't feel like celebrating. And as I showed these two maniacs up to their rooms adjoining the nursery I felt apprehensive. Rose Marie and I kept watches through the night.

In the morning she rightly insisted that I should indicate that our non-paying guests should terminate their stay.

"You could offer to drive them to the station."

"They don't travel by train."

"Or take them part of the way."

"I'll do that immediately they come down and have had their breakfast."

"Lunch will be in ten minutes," she said.

After the meal I turned to my guest and bravely suggested that he and his butler, who was then tucking in in the kitchen, might like a lift as I was driving to Bideford.

"No, thank you," he said, "we prefer to walk; you never know what company you might run into hitch-hiking, meaning no offence, of course."

The first maniac then collected the second maniac and thanked Rose Marie profusely for her hospitality.

I walked across the farmyard with them. They had, of course, no luggage. As we reached the front gate, my guest imperiously asked his 'butler' for the chalk. I observed the man fish in his coat pocket and produce a piece of ordinary chalk such as is used on a blackboard which he handed to his 'master'.

"We've enjoyed staying with you," the latter said to me, "and to mark our gratitude, I intend to mark your gatepost in no uncertain way."

So saying he went to it and drew Ø on the base of the post.

"And what's the significance of that?" I asked wondering if I were on the verge of voodoo.

"That sign means you won't be troubled with such as us any more. To any tramp on the road, that sign means 'Don't go in there, they keep a dog and will phone the police'!"

"Thank you very much," I murmured.

"Not at all. But you see," he went on, taking the chalk and drawing /// on the road, "if I had put that on your gate post, it would have indicated 'here lives a sucker who's good for a square meal and an old suit'." He then erased the sign with his foot.

"Are there other signs besides these?" I asked walking along the road with them.

"A whole language," he told me. "We people of the road mark every house we go to so that those behind us don't get misled."

Just then we passed a neighbour's gate. My guests glanced at this gate and then drew my attention to ∠ carved on the side of it.

"That means 'as mean as sin'," I was informed. When we

reached the main road I decided to turn back. Before I did so we sat in the hedge and smoked a cigarette while they copied out the tramps' alphabet.

"Who knows, one day you may need this, sir," the butler said handing it to me.

I thanked them and as I walked back I pondered how inconsequential and seemingly unrelated events can be. There I was holding a tramps' alphabet as a possible consequence of refusing to play along with Jimmy Bomford when he had offered Ben and me £5,000 towards the production cost of the *Rape of Lucretia* and then later announcing that that offer was conditional on his doing the décor. Peeved over that disappointment, I wondered, had he sent these maniacs on to me as a sort of revenge? If that was his intention, it had misfired: I was quite sorry to see them go.

As if I had not enough distractions, tobacco became another; not content with smoking it to excess, I began to grow it.

I started doing this in the war when cigarettes were scarce. I had guessed that it must be possible to grow tobacco in England since I knew it grew in Germany and Ireland. Then one day, when motoring to London, I had found a small tobacconists' in Salisbury that was selling some cigarettes made from tobacco which had been grown in the New Forest. Later, I wrote to Kew Gardens and asked if they could let me have any information on how tobacco could be grown in England. They replied that it was not possible. Similar enquiries made to the Imperial Tobacco Company produced similar discouragement. But I eventually traced the tobacconist in Salisbury, who had retired. He told me of the successful experiments in the New Forest, provided me with some seed, and the methods of cultivation.

I did some research and discovered that not only had this country grown tobacco, but in sufficient quantities to export it. Apparently the English cultivation had been made illegal when the colonists in Virginia had found home produce competing with the tobacco grown in America. The Redcoats of James I had gone round the Vales of Pickering and York and many other districts where tobacco was grown, and burned the crops. By 1942 I was growing half an acre on the farm without difficulty: the only pest was slugs. The tobacco itself ripened, even in an average summer. I used to cure it in a small barn and then send it up to Salisbury to be made into cigarettes. I tried to get the law altered so that English tobacco could compete with the leaf that was imported. At that time Hugh Dalton was Chancellor of the Exchequer. He dismissed my arguments, and when questioned in the House, stated that there was no need to alter the law since it was impossible to grow tobacco in England anyhow. I offered to give one hundred guineas to charity if Hugh Dalton could tell which of two cigarettes was home-grown. He refused the challenge.

When I was not trying to keep the slugs down or topping the plants, I was busily writing a book on tobacco cultivation and organising the co-operative which would cure growers' leaf and manufacture it for them. We soon had several thousand members.

During this winter, Martin Browne, who had produced *This Way to the Tomb* and Eliot's plays *Murder in the Cathedral* and *Family Reunion*, asked me to lunch one day. He told me that C. B. Cochran had approached him with the idea that he should produce a revue which Cochran had suggested should be written by T. S. Eliot, Christopher Fry and myself. He wanted Ben to compose the music.

"It's a brave, imaginative and typically Cochran idea," Martin said, "but the question is how will any of you so-called highbrows respond to it?"

"You can count on me," I said, "it'll be fun to write but I can't imagine Possum unbending that much, though *Sweeney* proves he could write it."

"What about Britten?"

"He'll play along. Your best plan is to get us all together and see what ideas come out of the meeting."

Accordingly, Martin Browne asked Eliot, Fry and myself to lunch with him at the Étoile. Martin outlined the proposal and to everybody's surprise Eliot was enthusiastic about it. He said he would enjoy trying his hand writing contemporary satire, or light lyrics or sketches. The problem was how our various contributions could be integrated into some whole.

"What we need," Eliot suggested, "is for somebody to have an idea for a theme and then delegate various parts or sketches to the other two to write."

I agreed with this. Martin Browne turned to Fry and asked him if he would be willing to do this and then tell Eliot and me what he wanted us to write. Fry accepted. Cochran was delighted. Eliot and I waited; after waiting a couple of years we forgot the idea.

About a year after Rose Marie and I got back to Devonshire, the *Evening Standard* asked me whether I could possibly take over their film criticism. I told them I couldn't do this as I had my farm to manage, and anyhow had nowhere to live in London. Beaverbrook stepped in, and the next thing I heard was that a large service flat in Kensington Palace Gardens had been taken for me and all expenses including meals would be paid. Rose Marie needed a change: I was getting short of it. And having been treated so well by the *Standard* I felt I ought to respond. So for the next month or so Jan wrote his Journal in the foyers of every London cinema. It was a terrible chore. No wonder critics are moronic; their routine would reduce anybody to idiocy. Generally I had two but sometimes three terrible films to see in a day. The first at ten-thirty, one after lunch and often another in the evening. When an American company had a première, they used to provide me with a hostess, as they called it. She was generally a brassy blonde and her duty was to keep me awake through the showing and then attempt to souse me in whisky before my expletives could solidify. After a week or two of this terrible travail, I suffered from a permanent headache and acute nausea. My criticisms became increasingly violent. Film companies threatened to withdraw their advertisements from the paper. The blondes snuggled closer: undrunk whiskies were slipped to me in the dark. I begged the Editor to hurry with finding somebody to relieve me.

"If I have to sit through another Hollywood musical," I threatened, "I shall fling my shoes through the screen."

At last the relief came. I was at the Tivoli cinema in the Strand. The film had been as appetising as a dromedary's diarrhoea, the hostess had been brassy, the smoked salmon sandwiches in the interval had been insipid without any lemon. But I was happy: that was my last film.

"Thank God I don't ever have to see another," I announced as the lights went up, to a critic from another paper sitting beside me whom I did not know.

"Why, where are you going?" he asked.

"Devonshire;" I replied briefly. "I've finished this job. Devonshire is where I live."

"Lived there long?" he asked.

"Years."

"Ah," he said; "I suppose you don't happen to know that fellow Ronald Duncan? He lives down there."

Something in his expression put me on my guard.

"No," I replied, "I haven't run across him."

"If you do, punch his face, the bloody homosexual fascist."

"It'll give me pleasure," I said, looking closely at my colleague. I am certain I had never seen him in my life before. And clearly he'd never seen me.

As I left the cinema I felt I had been punished for teasing Ben so cruelly when somebody in the Albert Hall had introduced himself to Ben as Benjamin Britten. Now I, too, scuttled home not wholly certain of my identity.

Critics and literary detectives have sometimes speculated whether or not some part of my plays had an autobiographical source. But none have suspected that I took the final curtain of *Saint Spiv* straight from my own experience.

After Rose Marie and I returned to Devon, I had to go up to London two or three times a month to see my agents or publishers. I had no flat or pied-à-terre there then. I could not stay with Petra because she lived with her parents. Sometimes I managed to find a camp bed in Richard March's flat in Hill Street. But when his wife was there I used to ring Sophie who always responded with a supper and a sofa. I began to rely on her hospitality.

But one night, having found that Richard couldn't put me up, I phoned Sophie and she told me she could not let me have a bed.

It was then about eleven o'clock. I spent the next hour or two wandering from one hotel to another. None had a bed. London had been bombed: many hotels were still in shambles: few had been rebuilt. It was difficult to book a room even weeks ahead.

Knowing Kensington is full of small hotels, I set off to that area and tramped up and down Queens Gate and the Cromwell Road. I must have drawn a dozen complaining porters from their beds. I trudged on now feeling cold, tired and miserable and very unwanted. At three a.m. I found myself at South Kensington tube station. A phone box stands outside. I went in and made another three calls. They were unsuccessful. I had no more pennies. I went to leave the phone box. It was raining hard. I returned to the phone box, and using my brief case as a pillow, I curled up on the concrete floor. I took my shoes off and found myself automatically putting them outside the door. A passing policeman paused on his beat.

"I'm just snatching a couple of hours sleep," I said.

"O.K., but don't expect me to clean your shoes."

I took them in again.

There must, I thought, be some way of turning my predicament to my advantage. Then I glanced up at the phone.

"Will you make an alarm call to this number in a couple of hours' time?" I asked.

"But it's a call box;" the operator said.

"And there's no hot water bottle here either," I added testily.

I curled up on the floor again. A few months before, I had been in the Savoy. I still had two plays running in London. I was down but not yet out.

I returned to Devon. A second night spent in a phone box had few attractions.

When Marion returned to England from Brussels where she had had a temporary job as governess at the Rothschilds', she and her parents had moved to a flat in Melbury Road which they shared with Ben and Peter. Pears had sold Oxford Square when his parents died. Marion continued with her piano, working hard to reach a concert standard. I heard all this in Devon. I also heard that Marion had a boy friend who was young, musical, tall, handsome and rich.

"What's more," Sophie confided in me when I called to see Ben about something or other, "he's a member of the Royal Family."

I gathered that George Harewood and Marion had met at a performance of *The Beggar's Opera*. He had known Joan Cross for some time and had met Ben too.

A few months later, when I was staying in London at Richard March's flat in Hill Street, Marion phoned to ask me if I was going to the party which Ben and Peter were giving at Melbury Road. I said I had not heard about it. She told me that Petra would be there. I did not promise. Seeing her again would be painful. Fourteen years separated us, but that was not the only thing that did. She lived with her parents: we were never alone together except in taxis. It was a joke between us, and painful to us both. It was one of those relationships which started on the last page as soon as we met. Nothing had to be said: nothing can be forgotten.

I debated the issue with Richard; intrigued by the possibilities of the evening, he urged me to go and said he would accompany me.

The small flat was crowded with musicians and singers. George Harewood and I took our drinks and went and sat on the stairs. We sat there gossiping and forgot the party going on beneath us. After a time Sophie came up to me. I could see she was bursting to tell me all about Marion and George whose engagement was imminent, but as she spoke I saw Petra enter the room. I muttered some excuse and crossed the room towards her. For the rest of the evening I kept close to her.

I left the party with Petra. I had not forgiven myself for not going to Rapallo, and it did not help that she had forgiven me.

I am not unaware as I write this that my motives might be easily misinterpreted. I am not trying to parade myself as a philanderer. *The Lives and Loves* nauseated me. I was incapable of having a casual affair. Perhaps that's more the pity, for by becoming so deeply involved, I only caused the greater damage. But perhaps pain is the only real gift a man can give to a woman? By that token I see I was generous.

The next day I lunched with Petra at the Écu de France, and

somehow persuaded her to come down to Devonshire with me for the weekend. I telephoned Rose Marie from the restaurant and told her that I was bringing a girl down for the weekend.

"Who?"

"Petra."

"Why?"

"She's not been well, a weekend in Devon will do her good."

"Very thoughtful of you," she replied acidly. "You really are a good Samaritan, especially with pretty girls."

(Pause).

"Then you don't want me to bring her down?"

"That's where you're wrong. I do."

Now it was my turn to ask why.

"Female spite."

"Ah..."

(Pause).

"All right, darling. I won't bring her down."

"Why not? You obviously want to."

"I don't think it's such a good idea any more."

"You mean you want to be loyal and faithful?"

"Perhaps."

"You bring her down. It's about time you got some proper experience instead of wasting your time with a schoolgirl crush."

This sort of conversation with Rose Marie was typical. At the time I sometimes felt I had wandered into a French farce. Or that life was becoming like a novelette which I would certainly not have read. When I complained of this, Rose Marie would point out pertinently that it was I who was writing it. This was not wholly true. We were very much joint authors.

I don't know whether insensitivity explains my courage, or whether gargantuan naïvety accounts for it. It could be both. But I bravely entered the farm with Petra and was very much surprised, and hurt, to find Rose Marie had defended herself against this intrusion, which she herself had insisted upon, by drinking half a bottle of Chartreuse and persuading the vet and the French *au pair* girl to support her in some kind of a party. Rose Marie was determined not to give Petra the impression of being the dull little wife who sat quietly at home.

The party being bibulous, Petra joined in. As usual I remained coldly sober and disapproving, sensing that the forced gaiety was Rose Marie's way of making a protest.

Even so, the next morning I was surprised by Rose Marie's angry resentment. She protested that I had humiliated her by bringing another of my girl friends into the house. I reminded her of the phone conversation when she had insisted I brought Petra to Devon.

"Only to see if you would," she cried.

"Then I'll tell her to go."

This was awkward but I did it. I explained to Petra that Rose Marie was jealous of her and to my guileless surprise, I found the girl was now delighted at being kicked out. As I drove her to the station, I realised sadly that there is nothing a woman values more than the jealousy she receives from another. It was much more precious to her than if I had presented her with myself. I disliked her for this. Then in the station, Petra began to weep. I didn't believe these tears were for me. They were not.

"I'm upset," she said, "because I can't help thinking of the brave way Rose Marie tried to behave and how miserable she must be feeling because she couldn't carry it off."

I liked her for that. The unpredictability of women fascinated me. I wanted them to be consistent but was grateful when they were not. In the centre of my childish soul I wanted them all to love me and adore one another. And of course with me as a common denominator between them, as proof of their mutual good taste. I could never understand why they could not be the best of friends. This was my ideal. Half my life, I perceive, was dedicated to this crusade...

"Shan't I see you again?" Petra asked over the window of her compartment.

"I'll ring you when I'm next in town. We could go to a play or something."

"I prefer opera."

"More reliable."

"They're giving a new *Tristan* the week after next," she said.

"All right. I'll try and get up. We'll go to that."

For the next week I buried myelf in writing as a protest for having to send Petra off. When, of course, I should not have taken her to Mead in the first place. But Rose Marie was not content to let things lie there: she could tolerate any of my sins but one—injured innocence.

"The phone doesn't ring much nowadays, does it?" Rose Marie announced one evening a few days later. She was bored.

"No. It doesn't."

"Why's that?"

"I don't know."

"Has Petra given up?"

"What?"

"Pursuing you."

I had, of course, not told her about Rapallo. Shame, which she mistook for anguish, was visible on my face as I thought of it.

"Is that why you now look so miserable? Anyhow I don't blame you."

I picked up my pen again. I was not in a position to pursue an argument on the technical definitions of adultery or unfaithfulness.

"I suppose you ring Petra up from the call box?"

"No."

"Don't tell me you're not in touch with her?"

"No."

Rose Marie looked infuriated. She loved pulling my hair. It was as if I had now suddenly gone bald.

"I suppose you've arranged to meet her in London?"

"No."

"Now I know you're lying."

"She did ask me if I would take her to Covent Garden when I was next in London," I admitted; "but I don't think I will."

"Why?"

"It might lead..."

"Don't you find her attractive?"

"Very."

"Then why don't you sleep with her?"

"What did you say?"

"I said: why don't you sleep with Petra?"

178

"After the brawl we had last weekend, I think I'd rather be castrated."

"I was upset then only because you brought her here. I don't care if you go to bed with her in London. In fact, I think you should."

"Why?"

"You owe it to me."

By now I had lost my pen completely. This line of reasoning which I didn't follow had promising possibilities.

"You were a bloody virgin when you married me," she said. "And if you don't sleep with Petra or somebody I shall never know what other women experience."

This was frank. This was true. I knew of her fear of being inadequate to herself and to me. A feeling of immense tenderness flooded over me for her. I went and embraced her.

"All right, love, I'll sleep with her," I said nobly, as if undertaking some sacrifice.

"And don't pretend you don't want to. And remember, you don't have to fall in love with her either."

We were both very gay and affectionate for the next week. I found the new play for Salisbury Cathedral, *Our Lady's Tumbler*, ran easily from my pen.

It was June. There was a heatwave. I stood in the corridor of the train in my shirt sleeves pondering the evening before me. It never occurred to me that Petra would not comply. The only thing that worried me was the irritating possibility that Richard March might be using his flat. But the weather made it probable he'd be down at his cottage in Newbury writing his book on Kleist. This proved the case. I bathed and dressed in the flat, then called for Petra in Kensington. She looked even prettier than the image I carried in my mind.

After giving her the conventional seducer's supper at the Caprice we went back to Hill Street. Her parents were happily away. I made some coffee. We didn't drink it.

Next morning Petra was still wearing her long black evening dress as we walked up Park Lane looking for a taxi. It was a lovely June morning. Girls in their gay printed summer frocks turned and stared at her on their way to work. She was too late for one party, too early for another. We didn't care. She had made me very

179

happy: I bought her an armful of flowers, put her in the taxi and then hurried back to the barrow. One end of it was heaped with White Heart cherries. I can never resist buying cherries especially when I am happy. And I know why this is; shooting cherry stones from my fingers was one of my delights when I was a child. It still is. I bought Rose Marie a basket of the fruit and presented it to her when I returned to Devon that afternoon. But she didn't seem very interested in it. After we'd driven a couple of miles from the station, she could contain her curiosity no longer.

"Well, did you see Petra?"

"Yes."

"What did you do?"

"Took her to the opera."

"And after?"

"Gave her supper."

"And?"

"It was quite a good supper. Mario looks after me well."

"I am not interested in what you had to eat."

"And we had a particularly good Moselle."

"Did you sleep with her?"

"Yes."

"You did?"

"Yes...I owe you an apology."

"Don't be silly. I wanted you to."

"I mean I see that many things are entirely my fault. She taught me that women are like violins, there's little music if you don't know how to play them."

"And did she show you?"

"Patiently. As you know, she's quite a musician."

"Good for her."

I suppose this tolerant or conniving attitude to my first adultery could be presented as mitigating circumstances for those, or some of those, which followed. I have always taken music most seriously.

During the next month or two, I went to London on several occasions over the casting of *Stratton*. Petra was away.

It was then I learned from Marion's father, Erwin, and also

from Ben, that though the King had given his permission for her marriage to George Harewood, the engagement could not be officially announced until Queen Mary approved. The entire Royal Family was terrified of Marlborough House. I was told that only two people had any influence on Queen Mary: the Spanish Ambassador, the Duke of San Lucar, and her Mistress of the Robes, the Duchess of Devonshire. I decided to help Marion with a pincer movement. I knew Pamela Hope-Johnstone, who was the Duchess of Devonshire's grand-daughter. She was a friend of Ben's too. I spoke to her and asked her to talk to her grandmother. And I knew too that San Lucar was a friend of Robert Speaight, who had played Antony in *This Way to the Tomb*. I confided in Speaight who promised to get his friend to exert his influence at Marlborough House. Then I returned to Devon.

A few weeks later, Pamela Hope-Johnstone, whose husband was the British Council's representative in Holland, arranged a house party to coincide with the Holland Festival at which the first performance of Ben's *Spring Symphony* was to be given. The house was an old shooting lodge about ten miles outside Amsterdam. The guests were Ben, Peter, Kathleen Ferrier, George, Marion, her father and mother, Rose Marie and me.

None of us knew our host, but he charmed us all, particularly Sophie Stein who was captivated by his good looks. The Hope-Johnstones had been married about five years and had two children. They seemed a happy family.

To get into Amsterdam easily I hired a small Volkswagen car. Ben and Peter had their own. Kathleen Ferrier was driven by her agent. So George and Marion used to squeeze into the back of the Volkswagen.

In the car there was much hilarity coming from George at Rose Marie's stream of unconscious malapropisms—such as when she referred to the car as a wretched Feuchtwangler. It was a most successful house party. There was even laughter at breakfast, especially the morning Ben came and sat down and then said solemnly:

"I've been pondering something during the night. It's this: can you tell me, Ronnie, why you don't get struck by lightning in an aeroplane?"

"Do you want me to?" I asked.

This kind of schoolboy humour always delighted Ben. While no Festival event gave George so much glee as the sight of me wandering round the Volkswagen with a watering can looking in vain for some hole to fill the non-existent radiator. It was as if we all had an epidemic of giggles. Nothing, not even Lord Montgomery's unhappy remarks to Ben after the first performance of the *Spring Symphony*, stopped them.

But behind this gaiety there was a feeling of apprehension about Marlborough House. Marion's parents were far from confident that Queen Mary would consent. Official permission for the marriage would not be given unless she did. George masked his concern with hilarity. Sophie Stein confided her fears to me and asked what I thought Marion should do if the marriage was forbidden.

"Sin," I replied.

Just then George received a message that Queen Mary would see him and Marion at Marlborough House the next morning. Rose Marie and I flew home to London with them early in the morning.

A car had been sent to London Airport to take them straight to Marlborough House. George offered us a lift. But a customs officer delayed me. I declared a box of cigars. For some strange reason he must have suspected me for a smuggler of diamonds and proceeded to weigh each cigar. It was a large box. George and Marion had to hurry off leaving me to protest my innocence. Though may be that is not the right word when lack of courage, not moral scruple, alone stood between me and the crime.

"And I would just like to see the cigar," Rose Marie commented, "if you had inserted a diamond inside it! You can't even do up a parcel of books without tying yourself up with the string."

The engagement was announced a day or two later. George told me that the only remark his mother had addressed to Marion was the somewhat irrelevant question "Can you cook?"

A week or two later I went up to Aldeburgh to spend the weekend with Ben. He was very pleased about the wedding. He liked George.

"I think you should do something about it," he said. "You could write something. And we'll make a cantata to be performed at the wedding."

I agreed.

"We've only a few weeks to do it in, so try and let me have it in a few days. I'm sure Marion will be touched, if you were to make this gesture."

I went home to Devon, and abandoning *Our Lady's Tumbler* again, sat down and wrote the words of *Amo Ergo Sum* which I telephoned to Ben. I took the title out of a line of Ezra's.

For both George and Marion the cantata now became almost the principal reason for their wedding. He began rushing round to find a church willing to stage the first performance which Ben was to conduct, and Peter and Joan Cross to sing the solos, in the middle of the ceremony. Several vicars refused him. Finally St Mark's in North Audley Street agreed.

The engagement provided a field day for the Press; a handsome member of the Royal Family marrying a commoner was sufficient to wet their lips; that Marion was a pianist born in Vienna of a Jewish father fitted into all their most sentimental democratic slush. And when they discovered that she was not only pretty, but photogenic too, saliva drooled down Fleet Street. Gossip columnists became levitated: here was an event where the snobbish concern in the Royal family and so-called forward-looking democratic interests were happily identified in one glorious beano. The *New Statesman* and the *Daily Express* found common ground to enthuse. The public became as excited about the wedding as if it were the Boat Race.

One newspaper got hold of the libretto of *Amo Ergo Sum* and printed it about a week before the wedding. I immediately received several telegrams of protest against the text sent by societies whose purpose was to uphold the Church of England. For the life of me, I couldn't see how I had offended them. I dismissed these petulant missives from my mind. But a day or two later, Ben phoned me in Devon to say that it looked as if the cantata would be banned from the ceremony unless I agreed to alter it. Apparently the society for the upholding of the Church of England had petitioned the Prime Minister on the grounds that a line in the libretto was tantamount to Romanism. They accused me of seducing the Royal family to the Catholic Church and offending against the Thirty-nine articles.

"I haven't a clue what everybody's worrying about," I said.

"The lines which they object to," Ben informed me, "is the verse for the choir which starts the piece:

> *Now let us sing gaily*
> *Ave Maria!*
> *And may the Holy Virgin*
> *Who was the Mother of Jesus*
> *Grant that these two children*
> *May live together happily*
> *For faith releases gaiety*
> *As marriage does true chastity*
> *Ave Maria!*

"It doesn't seem to improve by being repeated on the phone," I said. "But I still don't see how it offends the Church of England or can worry the Prime Minister. Is it the line about chastity?"

"They say that only the Roman Catholics believe that Mary can grant. Whereas we are supposed to believe that she can only intercede with God."

Ben sounded miserable and confused. He'd set the verse: the choir had learnt it and now, as usual, I had put my foot in it.

"Then, if that's all the trouble is," I said, "it's easily dealt with. Just change the word 'grant' to 'pray' and see if that will quieten the fools down."

It did.

We went up to London for the wedding a few days early so as to attend rehearsals of the cantata. The wedding had become very much a musical first night. George arranged for a private recording to be made. Music critics began to rush along to Moss Bros to hire morning suits and try to wangle an invitation.

This time I stayed with Richard. When I arrived I found him unusually attentive and sympathetic, anxious that I should not be left alone. I could not understand this: he was generally self-absorbed. We went out to dinner. Quite casually he asked me if I would be going to the funeral.

"What funeral?" I asked.

The poor fellow had thought I knew. It seemed that everybody in London knew. Nobody had dared say anything to me, fearing to put a finger in a wound. But I did not know. Petra had been killed in a motor accident two days before.

He followed me out of the restaurant. We walked. I do not know where we walked. My grief was not like sorrow: it was like rage; rage at the waste.

I have never worn a hat in my life. But for George's wedding I went to Lock's. I sat pensively in the car driving to the church, recalling that I had denied a white wedding to Rose Marie but had somehow found myself contributing a good deal to Marion's.

"Cheer up, ducks," a dear old char yelled at me.

The crowds were thick on the pavement. It was just like the Lord Mayor's Show.

As we were ushered to our pew, I observed that the libretto of the cantata had been printed on the order of service. At least it was an improvement on Hymns Ancient and Modern. I observed Winston Churchill reading it over his glasses. Marion was late. George looked nervous waiting by the altar. She must have been delayed by the crowds.

Half-way through the service, George and Marion moved from the altar and sat each side of it on two plain deal kitchen chairs. Then Ben appeared, looking like the Wizard of Oz wearing a gown too big for him. He conducted the cantata. I could see that George was visibly moved. I hoped he would not applaud and rush round out of habit to the artists' dressing room.

Then we all trailed to the reception at St James' Palace. The crush of people on the staircase waiting to be announced looked as if Gower Street had stormed the Bastille: a field day for Moss Bros. Not since Charles II had so many artists invaded these precincts. And they all looked so much better dressed, with Flash Harry leading the contingent, than George's county guests from Yorkshire.

There was Queen Mary, who had not been well enough to be at the service, sitting bolt upright by a pillar. I failed to reach the buffet. She always reminded me of my aunt Henrietta. They belonged to the same school.

"I'm sorry I did not hear your poem," she said sincerely. "I hope it was sung to your satisfaction."

I told her that George had had it recorded.

"Then please send it to me," she said, "I would like to hear it."

I sidled towards the buffet. She remained at her pillar. E. M. Forster, always short-sighted, later mistook Her Majesty for the wedding cake.

Soon after George and Marion returned from their honeymoon they invited me to lunch at George's old flat in Friary Court where they had to live till they could find a house. They had seen one in Orme Square. Marion asked me if I would like to go and look at it with her after the meal.

We walked round the empty house and she then showed me over the mews cottage which was attached to the house.

"I thought you might like this as a pied-à-terre," she said. "I know you've nowhere to stay when you come up to London. George thinks it a good idea," she went on, "if you like it you can work out the rent with him."

The cottage was precisely what Rose Marie and I required.

"The only disadvantage to the place is it lacks a telephone. But you can share ours, and the garage underneath."

I thought I had better check that George also approved this offer.

He did. I gathered it had been his idea.

"We don't need the place," he said, "and we'd much rather you and Rose Marie were there than anybody else."

I accepted gratefully. It was what I had needed for years. I hurried back to Devonshire to tell Rose Marie that she had a flat in London at last.

For the next few weeks we were happy planning the furniture, going to sales, painting and making curtains. I loved the place. It was a cottage, not a dreary box of a flat. We extracted more fun from getting it straight than our neighbours did furnishing their place across the garden. I brought all my Gaudier drawings up from Devonshire and hung them up the stairs.

Part Four

Learn of the green world what can be thy place
Pull down thy vanity
        Pacquin pull down

THE outbreak of war interrupted my correspondence with Gandhi. Though my stay with him at his Ashram *Segoan*, outside Wardha, had continued to influence me. You can define a great man as a person who leaves an indelible imprint. Even though we had disagreed, and I had refused his invitation to return to India to live with him for a year because he had thought it wrong to indulge one's senses by listening to Mozart, yet I still conversed with him. He was one of the three serious men I ever met and the only honest one. Consequently though we couldn't meet or even correspond, I had often found myself writing a poem or a part of the play—most of *This Way to the Tomb*—as if to convince him of my point of view. He became the reader I wrote for though I knew he would not often approve of it.

Naturally I followed all the events in India closely, especially after Lord Mountbatten had been appointed Viceroy. And, as Gandhi achieved *Swaraj*, I saw that the resultant violence between Hindu and Moslem must have been turning his triumph to ashes and alum.

My worst fears were confirmed by letters I received from India from Pyrarlal, Gandhi's secretary, from Mahadev Desai, and from Princess Amrit Kaur, who became the first Minister of Education. I felt more sympathy for him when he was living then in the Aga Khan's palace in Delhi as virtual ruler of free India than I did when he had been a prisoner with his ideals intact and his faith in his purpose unshaken. Knowing him as well as I did, I was certain that the persecution of the Moslems would ultimately drive him to fast to death. His assassination — an event he had often talked about to me – only prevented him from terminating his life voluntarily. The news of his assassination came as no surprise: I did not grieve. I knew how much he must have suffered by blaming himself for achieving an independence which had become an excuse for violence and the abuse of power. I was grateful that the bullet had left Gandhi enough life to forgive the assassin. His whole existence had been a pilgrimage towards this appointment.

Soon after his assassination I was sent a copy of the Diary which Gandhi had kept after Independence. It was one of the saddest documents I ever read. I told Eliot about it: it was he who then urged me to make a selection of Gandhi's writings and write an introduction to them. I agreed reluctantly: I am too unmethodical to make a good editor. But I now set myself the task of reading everything Gandhi had written. It was a formidable assignment: he must have been more prolific than even Tolstoi. But I cut him down ruthlessly to one volume, yet insisted on quoting the Delhi Diary almost in full.

Some years after the editing of this Selection, Messrs Hutchinson asked if I would write a definitive Life of the Mahatma. I agreed in principle but before signing the contract, which was a commission for £600, I spent a couple of months estimating the amount of work such a biography would entail. I soon realised from correspondence I had with Durban that I would have to visit Natal if I were to cover Gandhi's South African years adequately. I discussed the biography with Lord Mountbatten, who offered me all of his invaluable material. But he convinced me that I would have to spend at least six months in Delhi if I were to examine all the documents which he mentioned. Accordingly I told my agent, David Higham, to ask the publishers to guarantee me a further £600 to cover the expense of my visits. They refused, informing him that my expenses would have to come out of their advance. This seemed to me to be asking me to work for at least two years and to pay myself for the privilege of doing so. I consequently refused the commission and abandoned all the notes I had made. I did this with some relief: it was more to my inclination to live my own life badly than misspend it writing about others.

But now I got lost in something else. That is something which can easily happen to a writer. Our living is so precarious we tend sometimes to accept the jobs we are offered without due scrutiny. The Falcon Press wrote and asked me if I would edit Alexander

Pope's Letters and write an introduction. I had, a year before, made a selection of Ben Jonson's poems for a subsidiary of this firm. They now offered me a fee of fifty guineas. I accepted, thinking it was the sort of job I could do in the train during my frequent journeys to London. Having signed the contract, I wrote to the London Library and asked them to send me Pope's Letters. To my horror nine enormous volumes appeared, each in tiny print containing several hundred thousand words. I cursed the invention of the penny post and wished Bell had invented the telephone a little earlier. Even a dozen journeys across the Trans-Siberian railway would have been insufficient to get me through this. I looked for a loophole in the contract: there was none. I had already spent my fee. I began to read casually. I became absorbed: for the entire winter I hibernated in Pope's mail-bag. His prose was magnificent; not even Swift excelled him.

When I eventually emerged triumphantly holding a slim volume of my selection, I learned that the Falcon Press had gone bankrupt and their chairman had been hurried off to gaol for fraud.

Having spent six months earning £50 I now had even less incentive to examine my next commission. This looked much more promising. A firm of Poultry Breeders, near Kettering, wrote and offered me £100 if I would write an article for an American magazine on some "infallible Sexing Process" which they had invented. I assumed this was with chickens but nevertheless was intrigued. With my usual difficulty I eventually reached my destination, having thought that Kettering was near Oxford. A director met me at the station: gave me an expense-account lunch at a *table d'hôte* tavern. And then hustled me to his factory where I was shown a Japanese gentleman who was busily raising the anus of newly hatched chicks to his mouth, running this part of the bird across his lips, and sorting them into two trays before him. There is a slight protruberance on the anus of male chicks (or vice versa) which for some odd reason only the lips of Japanese are sufficiently sensitive to spot without error. These gentlemen are highly paid. But I heard about this process before and wondered why I had been dragged to Kettering. The director now informed me that his firm had invented a new process of sexing which was 100 per cent. certain, whereas the method I had just observed had a five per cent. error and was expensive.

He showed me dozens of trays of eggs in the incubator room. "All these eggs will hatch females," he informed me. "We merely immerse the eggs in a solution containing hormones before incubation and sufficient is absorbed through the shell to determine the sex."

"Has this any human application?" I asked.

"Indubitably."

Within an hour I was on my way back to London. I thought I had earned an easy fee and began to draft the article. It was complete by the time I reached London. But I had counted my chicks a little too soon. In fact I had to spend the next month writing and rewriting this article. Let every young writer be warned about American magazines. It is fairly easy to satisfy an editor of any magazine once he decides what it is he wants. But this is not possible with these. They have as many editors as an oil distillery has filters. It is not possible to satisfy all of them. You try, you go from draft to draft incorporating their memos and minutes, you regurgitate, revise, reshape and rehash. After six attempts to please their committee of the Lowest Common Multiple of Intelligence you are advised to recast your article about the arse holes of chickens along the lines of your original draft. The sub-editors have proved their point: which is that they have a job to do. Now crazed with drafts you begin to write gibberish...

I mention these two commissions as a fair glimpse of what a poet has to do unless he is to sink into the maw of the BBC or into some advertising agency. I suppose half of my time and two-thirds of my energy has been wasted in this way. My conclusion is that it is preferable to become a wolf than dissipate your time keeping one from the door.

My reaction to having written *Stratton* was to decide to write a comedy: the most fitting medium in which to express despair. And I was angry that just because I had written *This Way to the Tomb* I now had the epithet "highbrow religious poet"

192

The author at West Mill

Kathleen Ferrier at Mead Farm

tied to my tail, apparently for ever. This label, like any other, was not a description but a restriction: in the commercial theatre, it amounted to the sentence of death. Consequently I made up my mind to write a play set in contemporary London peopled with spivs, barrow boys, costers, in which I could draw on the Clapham and Brixton which I'd known so well as a child, and in which the language would be in keeping with the idiom of Wandsworth Road and the Elephant and Castle. I knew that this idiom was as lively now as it had been in Elizabethan days. I was determined to lift poetry out of the deadening associations of Kensington Gore, the effete and polite dust of the Religious Drama League, and give it back the immediacy of a coster's sharp tongue without any Empsonian ambiguities bedevilling the text or beclouding the action. I planned to contrast the vitality of the costers with the effete culture-mongers of Bloomsbury whom I wished to satirise as Jonson had done in *Volpone* and Pope in the *Dunciad*.

For my hero, I invented a spiv called Horace or 'Orace, in whom I tried to personify the universal human condition of naïve hopes foredoomed to complete failure. I made him down at heel, a jailbird, pickpocket and drunk, but with hopes, plans and schemes of success in inverse proportion to his possibilities of realising them. I became very fond of this character: it was partially autobiographical. And I also drew on the image of my son who had at that time worn a tall chef's hat when he played at being butler, and who sold packets of cigarettes at an ex-horbitant profit to guests at Mead. I too had had my hopes of making a pretty penny dishonestly: and had sold chive plants via an advertisement in *The Times* personal column at 2s. 6d. a clump (making 1,000 per cent.); milking goats during the war at twelve guineas each; tobacco seed at five bob a packet, and only a year before had invested in Vortax and believed this invention would pay off my overdraft.

It was Gerald Brenan who put me on the Vortax path. When Rose Marie and I had been staying with him at Aldbourne some years before, he had told me that if Borax was dissolved in water, iron or steel wouldn't rust in it. I can't recall how this matter arose in our usually literary conversation, but I immediately saw commercial possibilities in this scientific fact. Later, I bought some borax, dissolved it in a tumbler of water and then left my razor in it. Brenan had been right: the razor did not rust. I saw a fortune in this, or, at least a most profitable side-line to subsidise my poetry. My next ridiculous move was to register a trade mark —*Vortax*—and I had thousands and thousands of paper packets printed, each depicting a razor held in a tumbler of water marked price 1s. A quick calculation with a slide-rule showed me that if I put ½oz. of borax into each packet, coloured with copper sulphate to camouflage it and confuse my competitors who would doubtless analyse it, I would make 11d. per packet. On the assumption that there were 20,000,000 males in the country who had to shave (and dry their razor afterwards) and, if only one in twenty bought a packet of Vortax once every two months, I saw that I had a clear profit of

$$\frac{20,000,000}{20} \times 11\text{d.} \times 6 \text{ p.a.}$$

$$\text{or} \quad £\frac{20,000,000 \times 11\text{d.} \times 6 \text{ p.a.}}{20 \times 240}$$

$$= £5,288 \text{ 10s. 0d. per week.}$$

I meditated gaily on this figure for days. It didn't seem beyond my reach; after all, a Mr Kellogg presumably made money by putting very little into a packet, and several articles in the kitchen contained Vim and soapflakes, and reinforced my conclusions that this additional sideline could, if energetically exploited, pay the production costs of some of the plays I threatened to write. With these irrefutable figures before me I decided to invest a few hundred pounds on advertising Vortax in the National press. I even persuaded my friend Spottiswoode to become a partner in this enterprise. I myself took specimen packets to Woolworths, expecting a large and regular order. Meanwhile at Fenton Laboratories (a barn at Mead) the scientist fed spoonfuls of his mysterious formula into thousands of garish packets and wore his tongue out sticking the wretched things up. Woolworths did order two dozen: two local hairdressers in Bideford were cajoled into taking another dozen and the advertisements in the *Daily Express* sold three dozen more. I was left with 10,000 packets which, if I lived for a century and shaved henceforth three times a day, could not be turned into a useful asset...Such actual and utterly ridiculous dreams of mine lay behind 'Orace and the other spivs.

Reece Pemberton, who was doing some designs for *Stratton* asked me if he could read my new play. I gave him *Saint Spiv*. A week or so later, he told me that a friend of his, a young producer just down from Oxford called Kenneth Tynan, had read the play and was keen to produce it. I agreed to meet him. And was immediately impressed by his enthusiasm and quick mind. A few days later he phoned me in Devon and asked if he could come down to the farm. For the next five days we talked Theatre round the clock. It was while he was at Mead that I received a letter from Eliot saying that a young poet, whom he thought very promising, was lying in hospital in Penzance having broken his knee in a fall. Eliot hoped I would be able to visit him and possibly let him recuperate on the farm. He added some postscript warning me not to give him much to drink. He was suspicious what had caused his fall...I cursed Possum for not realising that Cornwall was larger than Chelsea but the next morning Tynan and I drove to Penzance planning productions by the mile. I enjoyed his enthusiasm.

I went into the hospital alone and found Eliot's young friend clutching a bottle of White Horse under the bed-clothes. He told me he'd broken his knee when he was drunk and had tried to climb into a girl's room and had fallen down through a green-house. He too didn't seem sure about the story. I suspected that he had, in fact, been pitched from a bus or fallen over a foot-stool. From the exhibition he put on for me flirting with all the nurses, I could see he was trying to convince himself about something. He had no need: he gave me his poem to read. Eliot was right: only it was more than promising.

A few days later I drove down to Penzance again and brought him back to the farm. His knee was in plaster: he sat for a week by the fire reading my books and using my typewriter. I didn't offer him any whisky: but told him to help himself from a crate of beer. After three or four crates he asked if he could borrow my typewriter and the fare to London. I drove him to the station, bought his ticket and thanked him for his company.

A week or two later I went to London and heard through a mutual friend his account of his visit to Mead.

"Duncan took me to his farm and kept me without a drink for a week. And all that time he made me saw logs in his farmyard while he sat with a crate of beer in his study: the bugger."

I have often wondered how many accounts like this I have believed. I suspect such people wrote most of history and a good deal of literary biography.

After my last secretary had married in her film-star robes which I had procured from Pascal, I began to sink in chaos. Kitty Black eventually recommended a girl called Maria. I interviewed her briefly in London. I have a vivid recollection of her arrival. I was sitting on the beach at Welcombe one evening with Rose Marie. We had bathed. It must have been extremely hot. A girl came running down the beach towards us.

"I'm Maria Thomas. Your sister picked me up from the station and told me I'd find you here."

"We've just had a bathe," Rose Marie said, needlessly as we both still had our costumes on.

"I think I'd like one too," the girl said, unzipping her skirt. "It was hot in the train."

"Yes, do," Rose Marie urged unnecessarily.

"I haven't got a costume," the girl announced; "but fortunately there's nobody on the beach."

She ran naked into the waves.

"And who is Maria Thomas?" Rose Marie asked.

"My new secretary," I replied, gazing reverently after her pretty figure. "You met her for a moment in London."

"Of course I recognise her now," Rose Marie said. "I'd know that bottom anywhere."

But Maria's subsequent behaviour was most unlike the impression she'd created on her arrival. She was not flirtatious and made it abundantly clear to me that she had not only left her husband but the whole male sex. She was a very intelligent girl with an Oxford degree and two languages. She bristled with progressive opinions and advanced prejudices. She was, I discovered, a Communist, and consequently she looked down on me from her proletarian heights as an untouchable, a landlord. But she would have been deeply shocked if I had called her a snob. I didn't know anything about her family background or her marriage but both had left her with an extraordinary independence and a need to belittle the male sex. She was so efficient that I was intimidated by her: she would correct my English, inform me my facts were inaccurate and, when I dictated an article, she would type it in silence, disapproving at the heresies I expressed. But slowly she began to unbend and her energy made her enjoy the farm: she rode well, and in the afternoon would help me do odd jobs, whether I was white-washing the shippon or weeding my vegetable garden.

But in spite of her attractive figure and her vitality no sexual intrigue developed between us. I suppose this was partially due to the fact that I was still mourning for Petra and perhaps because she had been so insistent on sex equality that she had succeeded in making me feel completely inferior. Consequently, though we worked together for almost a year, I had no conscious temptations in her direction. Rose Marie perceived this and had no qualms in leaving us alone together by day or by night. This trust must have eventually piqued the girl. When Rose Marie went away for a long week-end she was confident that all would be well and that Maria could look after everything with her usual efficiency, including Ken Tynan who was down again to talk about casting *Saint Spiv*.

Observing my secretary cooking our meals, making beds, Tynan made some comment to the effect that the situation reminded him of a story by Somerset Maugham. This didn't help. Maria decided to give Rose Marie a jolt, though the poor girl had had enough. Without any encouragement from me she announced just before Rose Marie returned that she had laid the scene.

"What have you done?"

"Put my black nylon nightie under her pillow in your bed, left half a bottle of wine on the bedside table and littered the room with my lipstick, perfume and cigarette ends."

I looked apprehensively at Tynan, observing later that it is sometimes safer to go to the dogs than risk the punishment for not going there.

There was no way for me to alert Rose Marie to the set she was going to walk into.

She arrived just before dinner and went straight to her room to wash. Meanwhile I carved even more clumsily than usual. I thought it a dangerous joke.

But to Maria's disappointment Rose Marie showed no tension or jealousy during the meal. After it, I tried to get to my room to tidy it up but Maria managed to trap me with Tynan and then suggest that Rose Marie, who'd had a long train journey, might go to bed. Maria now waited for some reaction when her night-gown was revealed under Rose Marie's pillow. But none came. We heard her light switched off. The French farce wouldn't get off the ground. I went to bed with some trepidation, realising that Maria wouldn't be there to admit that the scene had been laid as a joke and knowing only too well that I was unlikely to be believed when I produced that as an explanation. With that courage which in other spheres is rewarded by a D.S.O., I eventually got into bed. Rose Marie appeared to be asleep. But I knew that sleep. I lay rigid expecting the panther to pounce. But she did not move. I rose early and removed some of the "evidence" in-cluding the wine and the lipstick-covered cigarette ends. But I couldn't manage to get hold of the "proof" since it still lay beneath Rose Marie's pillow. I tried for a moment and then gave up, realising that it was dangerous to wake one woman by taking the nightdress of another from beneath her.

Tynan and my errant secretary were already at breakfast when I got down. They looked at me quizzically.

"No, she hasn't said a word," I said, gulping at black coffee.

Maria looked annoyed. Such indifference amounted to slight.

"Well?" she asked Rose Marie as soon as she came down. "Don't you want to ask me a few questions?"

"Should I?" Rose Marie replied.

"You're very difficult to play a joke on," Maria complained, "you're too unobservant. Didn't you notice my scent in your room?"

"Yes, I meant to tell you you shouldn't let Ronnie steal it."

"And didn't you see my lipstick-covered cigarette ends by your bed?"

"I saw those and thought he'd been dictating to you while he lay in bed."

"And my nightdress under your pillow. What did you think when you saw that?"

"I didn't see it," she replied. "I'm sorry. But if I had seen it I shouldn't have assumed what you hoped I would."

"Why?" Maria demanded almost aggressively.

"Because, duckie, in those circumstances you wouldn't have needed a nightie at all."

Tynan and I had said nothing. Now Maria was silent too. Rose Marie was so beautiful that other women inevitably wanted to bring her down a peg. I was that peg.

Because *This Way to the Tomb* and *The Eagle has Two Heads* had both run for over a year, I thought that the prejudice against poetry in the theatre had been lessened, if not overcome. I was naïve enough to believe that I would have little difficulty in finding a management for *Stratton*, especially since it was a play in a modern setting, whereas the other two had not had that appeal. And in addition the play contained both a murder and trial scene which on one level made it sure of some commercial approval. I could not have been more mistaken.

I first submitted the play to H. M. Tennants Ltd, since they had presented *The Eagle*, and made many thousands of pounds from it. Mr John Perry in their office eventually read it and announced that personally he didn't like any poetry and thought it had no place on the modern stage. Perhaps he had never read *The Eagle*, and had mistaken the flexible verse for prose. The average Englishman who is supposed to be so fond of poetry, I find, fails to recognise two lines of it together, unless they rime with a bump and have the metre of a metronome. No wonder they have a prejudice against it: but they should blame their illiteracy, not the language.

My agent, Margery Vosper, posted the play around and filed the rejections. A year passed, I had overdrawn my fund of impatience, and was now angry and depressed. Kitty Black, who had been instrumental in persuading me to write *The Eagle*, was sympathetic. She believed in *Stratton* and eventually came down to Devonshire to tell me that she was certain the play would be snapped up, if only I would allow her to retype it all as prose.

"As you've written it," she said, "it looks so awe-inspiring and so bloody intellectual."

She feared I would refuse her suggestion. But of course I readily agreed. I didn't care a damn how it was typed or whether it was called a verse play or a thriller in prose. All I wanted was to get it acted. I knew it would work as a play if only I could overcome the prejudices against me as a poet. I discovered that in the theatre to be known as a poet is to have a bad name. Kitty typed the play out again and resubmitted it to managements who had previously rejected it. Their interest was of an entirely different order: she knew her Shaftesbury Avenue.

Eventually Anthony Quayle, who was then director of the Memorial Theatre at Stratford, wrote to me saying he'd read the play and would like to meet me for luncheon. I thought he was going to present it but found that he wanted me to rewrite it.

"You've written two plays in one," he said, "simplify it and let me see it again."

I refrained from telling him how to act. It's odd but people think they have a right to their opinions. They have, so long as they keep them to themselves. I have no right to an opinion about electronics: I am not a physicist. Unfortunately I believe I expressed some of this at the time. This was both tactless and boorish of me, for at least Quayle had bothered to see me. Whereas neither John Gielgud nor Laurence Olivier to whom I had sent the script could find sufficient manners to acknowledge its receipt. Let me record that these two knights of the theatre discouraged me over and over again. The majority of stars are not really interested in looking for new plays: they are concerned with following fashion and jumping on the bandwagon. If I had shown any promise at all as a playwright in my thirties, these two, by their repeated snubs, did much to try to kill it. I was angry. I am still angry. Anger consumes me. There is one word which describes my experience, indeed my life. It is: "waste". An artist in this country, in this age, is "wasted"; his energies are dissipated, his vision is blurred, his intentions frustrated. Only mediocrity can possibly survive where mediocrity alone flourishes, where fashion parades as taste and cynicism and indifference covers all.

With this fury inside me because I could not find a management to present *Stratton*, how was I to know that I would be almost driven mad when I did?

The manager's name was Jack de Leon. He ran the theatre at Kew and occasionally presented plays in the West End. He had a split personality; part of him lived in the Renaissance; his little villa at Richmond was filled with reprints of the Madonna. He was also a Baconian, and had translated Goethe's *Faust*. He was, down one side, a mystic with a leaning towards the Vedas and Alchemy. But there was another side: he was one of the sharpest managers in the West End theatre who would pick up the *Gita* again unruffled after spending an hour on the telephone knocking ½ per cent off an actor's salary. *Stratton* had made an instant appeal to the metaphysical side of his nature; he thought he spotted an overt reference to the *Upanishads* in Act Two. When he interviewed me in his tiny office off the Charing Cross Road, he was as excited as a Medici in mufti who'd just found Donatello amongst his bricklayers. A joss-stick burned beside a dictaphone. For an hour, while he sipped orange juice, occasionally breaking off to squeeze an agent on the telephone, he told me of the deep philosophical meanings within my play. Like a pickpocket who'd been grilled in the police station for hours, I was in the mood to confess to anything. I didn't argue with his interpretations. Experience had taught me that it is a waste of time to do so. For if a writer refutes the statement that he has put a certain meaning into his work, he is soon to hear that he has done so *unconsciously*. A poet is like an old lag with a long record: he has no hope of proving his innocence. And of course I was by now pathetically grateful to anybody who had read my play, even if I didn't recognise their interpretation of it. I thought I could set those matters right with the producer. *Stratton* not only fired the mystic in de Leon, it appealed to the Shaftesbury Avenue foot-pad in him as well.

"You've written a part for a great star," he told me, fingering the bank of telephones. "Olivier will be a fool if he misses the chance. It's the biggest part since King Lear."

I said nothing and waited for him 'to talk turkey.'

"I will take a year's option on your play," he announced

resuming the mantle of the Medicis, "and will arrange the contract with your agent immediately."

He didn't notice me leave. He was in a trance in which he perceived a vision of Buddha riding up on a white charger with a sheaf of box office returns in one hand and a film contract in another. *Stratton* had integrated the two halves of the impresario's personality.

Months elapsed after de Leon took his option and nothing happened. Margery Vosper informed me that he had so far failed to find a star. What became the usual round now began. I trundled up to de Leon's sanctum. He told me that Olivier was not available because he was making a film; Gielgud was in another play; and Orson Welles didn't answer the telephone.

"The part demands a great star," he said truthfully, "it requires a 'heavy' and there are not many. It's a pity Godfrey Tearle is dead."

As usual, copies of *Spotlight* were produced. Lists of improbable names compiled, which somehow or other, whatever the part or the play, inevitably included Guinness.

The list was short: glancing at it I felt convinced that *Stratton* wouldn't be produced until Sir Henry Irving staged a resurrection.

At this moment de Leon suffered an inspiration.

"I have it!" he cried high above Wyndham's. "The very man... a great star who's looking for a great part..."

"Who?" I asked in a whisper.

"Clive Brook," he bellowed. "I'll ring Clive immediately."

"But isn't he a film star?" I remembered vaguely seeing him play Sherlock Homes when I was a child.

"He was," de Leon snapped. "He fetched them into Huxley's play *Gioconda Smile* over the road for a year. Brook's just the right age and weight and is the one star in that class who could play the love scenes with Katherine convincingly. He's not queer."

I returned to my Devon burrow.

A few days later de Leon rang me. He assumed the voice of an oracle.

"Brook likes it," he announced simply. I thought the phone had then gone dead but discovered that de Leon had merely made a prolonged pause—for prayer.

"Yes, he likes it. He says he's determined to play it. Can you come up to meet him tomorrow?"

"Are you sure he's all right for the part?" I was now more than doubtful myself, Rose Marie having confirmed my suspicions that Brook was a film star.

"Did you see the *Gioconda Smile*?"

"No."

"You should have. We'll meet in my office, then lunch in the Garrick Restaurant."

Clive Brook certainly had a good tailor. And I noticed that we went to the same shoemaker. He succeeded in patronising me with his compliments about the play. Then blandly admitted he wasn't sure what it was all about.

"I shall want you to make one or two alterations," he announced, as if I was giving him a fitting for a frock coat.

"Although you don't know what it's about?"

De Leon tactfully suggested we went to lunch.

Now began one of those relationships of which there have been several in my life, in which I have been held by an inexplicable fascination. Repelled by everything I saw but somehow unable to remove myself from it. Nothing less than masochism can account for my close acquaintance with such megalomaniacs as Beaverbrook, and Pascal. They must have had something in common to attract me. I think the truth was that each needed a priest or a psychiatrist and lacking either, clung to a poet instead who often has some of those attributes—at least a capacity to listen with tolerance. I suppose we all need to be needed—until we die of an excess of it.

After the meal, we returned to de Leon's office to start casting and to agree on a producer. A brief list was optimistically drawn up—in which every name was either Peter or Tony. Then *Spotlight* was again produced and as de Leon flicked the pages of photographs, he commented:

"No, not X, she's put on pounds round her hips."

"Don't mention Y to me. Her breath smells."

"No, you can't play with that bag, she will fidget behind your back and upstage you."

Eventually, of course, they put Vivien Leigh at the top of their list with Deborah Kerr beneath it. Both were referred to by their nicknames. I waited, expecting either Brook or de Leon to have the usual and sudden inspiration which always intrudes such casting sessions.

"I have it," somebody says looking through a glass darkly. "Though you might think it a long shot...we could send the script to Greta Garbo."

Generally nobody comments, whereupon the person defends his inspiration with the remark:

"But she could play it...she'd be magnificent."

This suggestion, however, was not made on this occasion. But de Leon came near to it.

"I suppose Marlene is a bit too old," he mused sadly, forgetting his own vintage. "But I would love to see you play it with Marlene. I'm sure she'd do it for me."

But he'd made his point. He was on Christian name terms with Dietrich. The two of us were suitably impressed.

The name values of the stars were weighed as though each was fatstock at grading. Their suitability for the part was hardly considered.

"With you and Viv in it," de Leon announced, "the libraries would do a £20,000 advance deal." He went into a trance listening to a full choir of cash registers.

But Brook looked annoyed.

"Perhaps you'd like to offer *Stratton* to Larry. I'll withdraw, if you like," he offered.

Eventually a list of improbable starters of the fillies, or rather mares, was drawn up and the three of us congratulated each other on the ideas we knew would never be realised. It was a typical casting session. How typical, I unfortunately did not know at the time or I would have abandoned playwrighting for some stable and sensible profession such as deep sea diving.

After several weeks had elapsed in which my telephone bill devoured the advance I had been paid and I had heard that none of the Tonys were free and all the Peters were making films, we settled on John Fernald to produce the play. He and his wife came down to Devon to discuss it.

He was enthusiastic about the play but depressed that it had been cast. While I continued my beachcombing he gamely slithered over the rocks behind me discussing the play and the rest of the casting. His ideas were sound: without the mystic to bedevil them we even began to feel optimistic and to look forward to the production.

Unfortunately de Leon had not been idle meanwhile and he had gone through the script and had marked certain passages which he considered might be cut and others which he hoped I would clarify. He urged me to accept Brook's invitation to stay with him at his farm in Sussex.

Brook didn't farm the land himself but let it to a tenant. Every field was a rabbit warren: it is fair to say he was unhappy about the condition of his land.

I discovered that for the six weeks while we had been trying to settle on a producer, Brook had done more than study the script: he almost knew his part and his wife told me that he had worked unceasingly on the play. I had not met this kind of enthusiasm in an actor before and assumed that he was worrying about the part because it was large, and extremely exposed. But after a couple of days with Brook I discovered that his involvement with *Stratton* was deeper.

In the play, Stratton is a famous Judge whose son, a physical replica of himself, has followed in his father's footsteps by becoming a barrister. Brook's son was a young actor. That was as far as the parallel went, but it was sufficient. It was clear that Brook had identified himself with the part. He had no choice but to play it.

During the next few weeks while we cast the other parts, Brook commissioned a Royal Academician to paint the portrait of himself in Judge's robes which was required as a prop in the play. When talking about the character he would slip into the first person. De Leon assured me that Brook's involvement with his part would mean he would give a great performance.

The rest of the cast got little production. They sat around in the stalls doing *The Times* crossword puzzle, busying themselves with innumerable trays of tea. They were an admirable lot, a highly trained professional cast: Michael Hordern, who played Courtenay so well that I wished I had centred the play around him; Elspeth March, and the late Betty Ann Davies.

While the rehearsals proceeded I suffered more than I endured. Only a part of me survived them. And there were difficulties, too, with the gigantic set which proved more expensive to build than the mansion itself which it was supposed to represent; and on top of this there were, surprisingly, troubles with the music. I had, of course, asked Ben to write it. He had readily agreed and had promised the score within a few weeks. Knowing his ability to produce what was required I put that side of the production out of my mind. At least he wouldn't let me down. I snatched a weekend in Devon to see how the corn was coming in and while there received an angry telegram from Ben to the effect that as the management had refused to give him a contract he was going to stop writing any more music. To my horror the telegram read as though Ben had come to the conclusion that I had been trying to get something for nothing out of him. This was not what he'd thought; what he was doing was to alert me to the management's cheese-paring tricks which were going on behind my back. It appeared that de Leon had negotiated Ben's fee with his publishers, Boosey and Hawkes, where he had run into Dr Roth. There had been tortuous and trivial games of badminton along Regent Street with $\frac{1}{2}$ a per cent; de Leon, abandoning his role of the Medici, had treated Ben like any Charing Cross Road composer. Furthermore, no contract had been signed or fee paid. Ben, exasperated by this bazaar method of bargaining, had sent this telegram to me. It made me ill for a week. But fortunately, after a dozen trunk calls from Devon, I managed to uncross some of the lines, to acquaint de Leon with the original homily that it was not good business to look a gift horse in the dentures, and that if he didn't send Ben a hundred guineas that day I would do so myself.

After I had untied this typical Shaftesbury Avenue tangle the music arrived within three days; either proving that Ben had finished composing it very quickly, or that his telegram had been a protest, but that, as I guessed, he hadn't stopped composing as he had threatened. I was delighted with the score: it was precisely what I had wished. I now feared that de Leon would save money by having the music performed by some *ad hoc* ensemble he'd scrape together in the Charing Cross Road or from beneath some potted evergreen plants in the Grand Hotels along the South coast.

I forestalled this danger by cunningly telling him that the English Opera Group would be the cheapest ensemble as they would need less rehearsal because they were used to playing Britten.

Meanwhile the rehearsals continued to be waged. Brook's moods alternating between confidence and despair; the rest of the cast continuing to gulp tea in the stalls; they sympathised with me for my agony in the Winter Garden. Betty Ann Davies, who had a smallholding in Kent, used to try and take my mind off the rehearsals by asking my advice about how to rear Khaki Campbell ducks. Meanwhile de Leon would look in occasionally to make our experience all the more bitter by announcing that the house at Brighton, Manchester, or somewhere, was already sold out on Brook's name alone. There was no doubt Brook was a star. After each rehearsal de Leon would cling to me and drag me off to talk about Brook's part: this inevitably led to a plea that I should clarify some motivation by writing a few lines into the script. He didn't believe in subtlety. And consequently any lines obscured by intelligence were called upon to be cut. The producer was not consulted. I stupidly agreed to make these messy alterations.

Eliot had performed some miracle at Fabers and had managed to get *Stratton* already into page proof, intending to publish it by the time it opened in London. He had, as usual, pointed out to me that it was better to delay publication until the text was finalised to a prompt copy. But I had told him there would be no alterations and I wanted the text out soon after the play was produced. Now, after only a fortnight, these page proofs were sellotaped with insertions, deletions and confusions. I had been paid £50 advance for the book rights and realised the corrections to the proofs would cost much more. Guilty, I took the tattered remnants to Russell Square and laid them before Tom. He looked sadly at the muddle and confirmed my suspicions about the costs. What he didn't tell me was that the play would now have to be entirely reset at the printers and that he would personally, pay the bill. But this, I discovered sometime later, is what he did.

As the play was to open at the Theatre Royal, Brighton, John and Audrey Christie had asked Rose Marie and me to stay the previous weekend at Glyndebourne. It was near enough for me to drive over to the Sunday dress rehearsal. And as George and

Marion were returning from their honeymoon that day, they immediately drove down there too, so that we could go to the opening of the play together. I was a little apprehensive about this house party. I knew that George Harewood and John Christie were suspicious of each other: on the one hand, John had always maintained that, from his experience as an ex-schoolmaster, he could tell that George was a homosexual. He had told me loudly in St James's Palace at the Harewood wedding reception that George's marriage only confirmed this opinion—"people like him take a wife to cover up," he had said. These suspicions of John's were without the slightest foundation. On the other hand George was suspicious that John Christie knew nothing much about music and less about singing: and this was, of course, true.

Fortunately these mutual suspicions never came to the surface. Manners are useful. Audrey Christie was a clever hostess who had learned to steer John from one unpardonable gaffe to another unforgivable indiscretion. Considering the number of bricks John dropped, it was surprising he had not built a bigger opera house.

De Leon and his publicity agent had been delighted that the Harewoods had agreed to attend the First Night of *Stratton*. It was their first public appearance since their marriage. But it was a coup that badly misfired. To begin with, our over-zealous Superintendent of Police had decided to protect the Royal newly-weds by laying on a police escort in traditional American fashion. As we entered the outskirts of Brighton, the car was suddenly flanked by policemen on motorbikes. At first George thought they were speed cops. We drove up to the theatre in this fashion, only to find the corps of beefy coppers keeping the gaping crowds at bay. De Leon rubbed his podgy hands gleefully; the publicity agent beamed like a gold prospector who'd tripped over Fort Knox.

The first performance went off better than my enemies hoped. Betty Ann Davies and Michael Hordern gave excellent performances: Clive was at his best and there were none of those disasters which every playwright anticipates from the lighting board or from the use of tapes. At the champagne party afterwards to which the dei Medici had invited a hundred, and double that number had appeared, even I began to feel confident until I realised that the jamboree was composed largely of gossip writers who were interested, not in my play, but Marion's dress. She was the focus of the flashlights: Brook stood unnoticed in the shadow. This was to have been his evening. I felt something not unlike sympathy for him.

The next morning we found the London Press had broken their rule not to review plays on tour before they reached the West End. There were double columns and photos in every national paper. But it was the Harewoods who were the headlines, the play itself was reviewed with confusion. Brook's name only was listed amongst the cast. The disintegration of *Stratton* had set in.

John Fernald called a rehearsal the next afternoon. Everybody blamed everybody else and, as usually happens on these post-mortems, the text finally received the sentence, whoever had been condemned. I was found guilty of being a poet and hurriedly left Brighton before I could be put in the stocks. Only de Leon was happy: he had over £3,000 advance bookings for the week.

After Brighton, the play's tour took it to Southsea and Bournemouth. It was then to go on to Stratford and Birmingham before opening at Wyndhams Theatre. I had returned to Devon after the first night and decided to let the play settle down on the road before seeing it again. I had also to digest the disappointment of the notices. This took some doing. It was only my second play: I was vulnerable to spite, not insulated against insult. I had spent a year writing it, two years getting it on: now I felt hurt like a woman might who cooks the best dinner she can, serves it as well as possible, and then learns that her guests have preferred biscuits. It was not merely a question of my believing in my play: it was me. I was very personally involved. If it is the function of critics to discourage creative writers, I admit with *Stratton* they nearly succeeded.

I learned from Fernald that the business at Southsea had fallen off, and that he had decided to put back some of the cuts which had been made. I was warned the process would prove difficult and advised not to reappear until late in the week at Bournemouth.

I bought a seat in the theatre during a Saturday matinee. Nobody knew I was in the house. The first act went off without a hitch and the curtain fell to Britten's music on cue. Then to my utter amazement I heard the overture to *William Tell* being played.

I thought I had gone out of my mind. But the fearful strains were unmistakable, and peering over the orchestral pit I observed three terrible females scraping away regardless beneath my glare. I complained bitterly to somebody on the theatre staff, pointing out that their intrusion ruined the effect that Britten's music created. He informed me they always played in the interval and invariably *William Tell*. He then began to pick his teeth with a nail file.

I returned to my stall to hear these dreadful harpies banging out *Ole Man River* as the curtain rose to the last act of *Stratton*. As these strains died away I began to smell fish. Of course the theatre was on the front, but surely the tide doesn't sweep beneath the stalls? As the big scene between Stratton and Katherine began, so my neighbour continued with her fish and chips. But if she had been enjoying a cannibalistic orgy I would not have noticed her, for my attention had now been taken by some extraordinary events on the stage. It was precisely as if some drunk had shuffled the pages of my play like a pack of cards, had then recorded it, and played it backwards at the wrong speed. My mind began to skid as I listened to the piffle on the stage. It sounded like an adaptation of *Hamlet* and *The Merry Wives of Windsor* made by Joan Littlewood. The curtain fell gratefully.

Shaking with indignation, I found the pass door. It was Michael Hordern who told me what had happened. Apparently, Fernald had been banned from the theatre, whereupon de Leon had not only reproduced the last act, but had rewritten a final scene which I had just endured. I marched to de Leon's lair. He began to bluster, then to insult. I ran to the station to catch any train to go anywhere. Indeed I do not know where I went. I have a hunch I ran to Ben's and then eventually found my way back to my farm to cleanse myself in pig dung.

During the next ten days I lived on the telephone, with de Leon trying to mollify me to prevent my issuing writs against himself, and even the three fearful spinsters in the stalls. He agreed to cut the scene he had written if I would write a new one. Along what lines? I asked. He said he would let me know. Two days later I received a synopsis for a new last scene. It did not take me any time to write: it was precisely the scene I had written in the original script. I did not comment on this. I sent them a copy of this scene. They did not recognise it and thought it made a great improvement.

When two or three other cuts had been rehearsed at Stratford, I decided to look at the play again at Birmingham. What I saw there was a successful Whitehall farce. It could have been called *Stratton in the Thark* or *Rookery Pook*. The citizens of Birmingham were enjoying themselves. I phoned my agent, Margery Vosper.

"It mustn't come in," I cried. "Sink it, sink me, abandon ship. Let it be known I was torpedoed by a shark."

As soon as we had some furniture in Orme Lane, we decided to entertain. Meals were eaten in the kitchen which we'd divided so that part could pretend to be a dining room. Rose Marie excelled at this kind of improvisation, and was at her happiest playing with the cottage. Tom Eliot was her first guest. George and Marion also came over from the house. But neither poetry nor music were mentioned at the meal. Eliot talked the whole time about his bowels which had become an obsession of his. As he left, he suggested I should join the Garrick Club of which he had recently become a member. He offered to propose or second me. Rose Marie took this suggestion as a poor compliment to her meal.

My agent, Margery Vosper, telephoned me to say that Jack Warner had offered her £40,000 for the film rights of *The Eagle has Two Heads*, and she could not see any reason why the deal should not be completed within a week. During the next twenty-four hours Rose Marie and I amused ourselves by spending the money. This did not call for much imaginative effort. The next morning Margery Vosper phoned again to say that Warner had asked if I would cable to Bette Davis, who was going to play Eileen Herlie's part in the film, a synopsis of the play so he could be certain of her agreeing to play the film before he bought it. I was assured it was a mere formality and urged to get the cable off within twenty-four hours. It is never easy for me to write a synopsis anyhow, but to try and condense it into a cable produced another pressure, especially when half my mind was on spending the booty. If I condensed it too much, I thought, she would not understand her part. If I make the synopsis adequate the cost of the cable will bankrupt me. But with the bait of £40,000 dangled before me I found an extravagant compromise. I learned by the end of the week that the cable had arrived: that the star had been so intrigued by the synopsis that she had actually read the full text and "would have played it if she had not discovered that same week that she was pregnant". My £40,000 dissolved and I was left holding a bill for £15 for the cable.

Soon after *The Eagle has Two Heads* was published, Denis Dobson asked me if I would translate the diary which Cocteau had kept while he was making the film of *La Belle et le Bête*. I had seen the film with Jean Marais playing the Beast and had enjoyed Bérard's décor. I agreed, thinking it would be a fairly easy way to earn a hundred guineas, and thought that I could do most of the work in the long evenings at the farm. This was the sort of mistake I was always making. I found this diary twice as difficult to translate as *Machine à Écrire*, which I had done a year before. As it was a diary, the language was, of course, more colloquial, and full of difficult slang. In addition, there were passages which Cocteau had obviously written when he had been suffering from the carbuncles which he had shown me. These were very involved: particularly the passage in which he had recounted the film sequence where Le Bête had been shot against a scene of sheets hung out to dry on a line. I ploughed in a whole winter on this work, but enjoyed making a translation of the original fairy story of *Beauty and the Beast*, which was published with the diary.

Many farmhouses in Devonshire, especially those near the coast, display little notices: *Visitors taken in*. This is a highly ambiguous statement. But I didn't know the degree of duplicity which was involved in it until I embarked on the visitors trade myself. It was an inevitable step. Farmers have to plant a cash crop. That is what Devonians call the tourists. They pay ready money for cream teas and a bed. Of course, little of this pin money shows in their income tax returns.

One Sunday afternoon while I was sitting by the fire in the sitting room reading the papers, I heard a car drive into the farm, then a couple with two children marched into the house and sat down around me. I rose to my feet expecting Rose Marie to follow them in to introduce me. I assumed they were friends of hers. I was mistaken.

"Tea for four," the man said curtly, still sitting in the armchair opposite me, while his two brats picked up the paper I had been reading.

"Very good," I replied, and went straight into the kitchen and prepared a cream tea which I carried back into the sitting room and placed in front of my uninvited guests. I did not make the mistake of sitting down and continuing to read my paper, nor could I have done so, as my chair was occupied and my paper was now scattered in sheets on the floor. I retired to the kitchen where it was obvious I belonged. There I meditated on the fact that an Englishman's home is no longer his castle. Half an hour later I heard these tourists departing. I thought it would be polite to see them out.

"How much do we owe you for the teas?" the man said, adjusting his hat in the hall mirror.

"Nothing," I replied.

"How's that?" the woman asked aggressively.

"We don't do teas," I murmured.

"Then why the hell didn't you say so?" the man demanded angrily.

"You didn't ask me," I said. "You just stalked into my sitting room and told me to get you some tea."

"Doesn't everyone do teas?" the woman said. "How were we to know? You should put a notice up if you don't."

Later that afternoon when Rose Marie returned from her walk, I reported this conversation to her.

"You were a fool not to charge them 6s. a head," she said. "You made an expensive gesture."

This thought grew like a seed in my mind. The harvest was a loss of more than four cream teas.

After we moved up to Mead we eventually decided to let West Mill. Our first tenant was an Austrian refugee called Flügel. He was a playwright. Capitalising on this affinity to his landlord, he used to omit paying his rent. Whenever I called upon him to try and obtain it, he would start to read his latest Viennese comedy at me. Eventually I decided it was preferable to regard this tenancy as a "Grace-and-Favour." Mr Flügel kept goats. They devoured my precious fig trees, and the olives which I had carried back all the way from Var. One day, peering over the valley, I noticed that there was no smoke coming from the cottage chimney. I discovered that Mr Flügel had done a moonlight flit.

My next tenant was even less fortunate. She was an enthusiastic nuclear disarmer. But I never understood what principle motivated her when she smashed the sewage pipes with an axe, and demolished chairs and tables by hurling them against the wall. I sued her, but could not enforce judgement.

Mead was much bigger than West Mill. With two small children, Rose Marie found it necessary to get help. None of the locals wanted to go charring. Eventually an agency sent us a girl from Germany. She could not cook: but she was an enthusiastic potato peeler. She also had the habit of addressing me as "Herr General." The title seemed more than inappropriate as I was a conscientious objector. I thought she was being sarcastic. But the respect in her voice belied that. The girl settled down. One morning a few weeks later, I noticed a young man sitting in my study, reading the newspapers. I did not know who he was, but assumed he was one of Rose Marie's friends whom she had asked down for the weekend. I merely passed the time of day with him. I noticed at lunch that his conversation was not as adequate as his appetite. Subsequent meals reinforced this impression. After he had been in the house for about three days, Rose Marie asked me one evening where my friend was.

"My friend?" I asked. "Not only do I not know who he is, but you failed to introduce me."

"I thought you had asked him down," she replied. Neither of us had the faintest idea who our guest was. I went in search of him. He was not in any of the rooms downstairs. I looked upstairs. There was nobody in the guest room. I heard murmuring from the room in which the German girl slept.

"Though we don't know who he is, it seems that Gerda does," I reported. When we tackled her the next morning, she admitted that she had asked her husband to spend the weekend with her. She had, in fact, only taken the job with us in order to get a free passage to this country to marry him, and to have her child, which already showed beneath her apron, on the National Health. This explanation cleared up a good deal, but I was still intrigued to discover whether there was any sarcasm in the way she addressed me.

"Your advertisement," she explained, "asked for a cook general; therefore I naturally thought you were a high officer."

At this time my farm bailiff and his wife, who had helped Rose Marie, gave me my son. By which I mean that up to that time I had always favoured Briony who had charmed me since her birth, but Roger had never moved into my affections in the same way. He did so at the age of four. Seeing we were without servants, Roger decided to appoint himself butler. He found a white coat from somewhere and used to wear a chain with a silver wine label attached to it round his neck as his insignia of office. Thus attired he would wait at table, especially if we had guests. At that time I would have shot anybody who had laughed at him. He really believed he was helping: a child's seriousness is the most serious thing in the world. Not even Chaplin at his most pathetic ever touched me as Roger did at this time, especially when he told me that what he wanted for his Christmas present was a tall chef's hat "because it would give him height when he waited at table." I searched London for such a hat and eventually found a shop that sold them in Wardour Street.

Another trick he had which I found most endearing was to go to buy packets of cigarettes from a neighbouring farm, and then wait till somebody in the house ran out of them. Robert Speaight was always doing this, whereupon Roger would run upstairs to produce a packet which he sold at a profit. I used to smoke myself into a stupor so as to have to buy from his black market. One day I found him toddling round the house wearing his tall white hat and his badge of office, collecting shoes to be cleaned in his pantry.

These are the things I found precious. I could never resist and was entirely vulnerable to this quality of pathetic childlike seriousness. Each time I found it my life was bent round it, till finally it was nearly destroyed on it.

The quickest way of losing your friends is to do them a favour. This friend must be nameless: he was a neighbour in Devonshire. He had been married for many years but was childless. His wife became pregnant: the village rejoiced for her. Unhappily, the child was born dead. After this the woman became hysterically depressed, especially as the surgeon had told her that she could not have another child. Her husband told me that he feared she might go out of her mind. I suggested that they adopt a child. He thought this a good idea, as did his wife, and applied through the usual channels, only to discover that, because he was over forty, he could get no help from the Adoption Societies. This depressed his wife even further, as she felt the one solution had been taken from her.

I was in London a few weeks later when I heard of a girl who, having got drunk at a party, found herself pregnant. Hating the man who had taken advantage of her, she was determined not to have anything to do with his child, though she was afraid of having an abortion. I thought I was doing a favour to two parties by acquainting each with the other's difficulty, but in keeping their names to myself. Eventually everything was arranged. The girl went into hospital in London to have her child and my friends in Devonshire went up to receive it, though their identity was kept secret from the mother. The child flourished. The mother recovered. For a couple of years I felt I had done some good. Suddenly the man turned against me violently and actually moved from my district rather than suffer from seeing me occasionally. As usual, I was not only hurt, but completely bewildered. I suppose gratitude is an intolerable burden, or maybe the suspicion had passed through my friend's head that he was fathering my child.

After the de Leon production of *Stratton* had sunk on the road, I tried to forget everything concerned with that play. Once again I returned to Devon to revise *Saint Spiv*. But Ashley Dukes urged me to let him stage *Stratton* at the Mercury Theatre. I was grateful for that theatre: its size was almost a comfort to me. All I wanted was to see the play produced as I had written it. I discussed the matter with Eliot; he advised me to let Ashley go ahead.

This play was ill-fated, but this time it was not the cast, the production, or the management that went wrong. It was the weather. The play opened in mid-June in a heatwave. The critics, sweating in the small theatre, were more spiteful than ever. When Ben went to the play, he told me there were only a dozen in the auditorium. The theatre was half-empty a few days later when Eliot pushed John Hayward's wheelchair into it.

The smallness of the audiences surprised me: my last play there had run for over a year. I had worked twice as hard writing this one. It was a far better play. Knowing this, I felt more than depressed: the public have no discrimination of their own. Fashion is all of taste.

A few weeks after the *Stratton* débâcle at the Mercury Theatre, Ashley Dukes came down to Mead for the weekend. I enjoyed his company; his anecdotes amused me and it was my ambition to beat him one day at chess, or fool him with a wine. But they both remained unfulfilled. I usually had to lay my Queen down; even blindfolded he could tell one vintage from another.

I took him for a walk across the cliffs. I felt I had to do more than thank him for staging *Stratton*. Indeed, realising that he must have lost at least £1,000, I felt I could do nothing less than offer to share some of the deficit. Very embarrassed I put this to him. He refused. I pressed my offer.

"Since you insist, I must tell you that I haven't lost a penny on the production."

"Don't be absurd," I said, "the Arts Council didn't guarantee it and it was playing to nothing in that heatwave."

"True, the play lost nearly £1,500 — but I didn't. The production was underwritten by a friend of yours who offered to guarantee it so long as you were never told."

"I must know who it was," I said, "I can't think who it can be. I haven't a friend who could bear that sort of loss." We walked on in silence while Ashley considered his dilemma.

"Very well," he said eventually, "I will tell you who it was, if you will promise never to let him know I've told you."

"That means I can't thank him."

"Precisely. But you can still be grateful."

I agreed.

"It was Tom Eliot. He paid your losses out of his royalties from *The Cocktail Party*."

I learned a good deal from Leavis at Cambridge about textual criticism. But Leavis kept closely to the known names of literature; whereas Ezra introduced me to many poets such as Cavalcanti and Golding, whom Leavis had never mentioned. With the examination syllabus before him, he had, of course, an excuse. But in fact the syllabus seldom bothered him or distracted his supervisions. The list of poets he advised me to read had, I discovered later, many serious omissions, especially since he advocated "minority culture": it was strange to find that he had concentrated wholly on names canonised by majority respect.

One of these omissions was Rochester. I was first pulled up by the quality of this poet by:

Love a woman you're an ass

and immediately read as many poems of his I could find in the anthologies. There were few. I told Ezra of my enthusiasm for Rochester and he suggested I read Dorset too. I did so, but was not equally impressed.

I had decided to see what of Rochester's work I could find in the British Museum. I remember the morning very well: for setting out to seek the past, I found both the present and the future most precarious. An air raid had been in progress. I had stepped over much plate glass as I walked towards Great Russell Street. But by the time I had emerged the All Clear had sounded and I had unearthed a vast amount of Rochester's poetry which, as far as I could see, had never been published. The librarian allowed me to arrange to have photostat copies made of all the manuscripts so that I could work on them at leisure in Devonshire. As I did this over the next year or two I soon realised that not all the manuscripts were authentic Rochester. I compared these poems with the texts published in the Nonesuch edition of his poems, which had been edited by John Hayward. This comparison shocked me. I eventually decided to re-edit Rochester and wrote to Eliot to offer the book to Faber's. He suggested that we discussed the matter the next time we met.

"I've compared the manuscript texts with the Nonesuch edition," I said, "and this illiterate tout, Hayward, has not only buggered up the sense of the poems by punctuation which looks as if it emerged from a pepper pot, but he has actually censored verses, either by omitting lines or altering a phrase or two. It really is the worst piece of editing I've seen, and reinforces the suspicions I've always had over his Donne."

Eliot studied the floor. But this was a habit of his and didn't caution me.

I weighed in against Hayward for another ten minutes.

"This is all very embarrassing," Tom said sadly. "I don't know what to do."

I misunderstood him.

"You don't have to tell me now whether you'll publish it or not. I'll do the work anyhow and let you see it when it's finished. I'm no scholar but I can't muff the job as badly as Hayward has done."

"Most embarrassing," Tom murmured, and I left him still studying the carpet.

An hour later, I met Ashley Dukes at the Garrick and told him that Tom had upset me by saying that my discovery of some marvellous bawdy poems of Rochester was most embarrassing.

"Didn't you know that Tom had moved into John Hayward's flat?" Ashley asked.

It was my turn to be embarrassed. I eventually allowed the Forge Press to publish my edition but naturally sent Tom a copy. He wrote an unhappy little note to thank me, then took up a position of neutrality while Hayward wrote rude letters to me and my publishers accusing me of libel and threatening an action.

"I don't think we'd better lunch at Carlisle Mansions," Tom said the next time we met. "John is so spiteful."

During the summer of 1950, I was asked by the Festival of Britain Committee if I would accept a commission to write a play to be performed in Salisbury Cathedral. I went to Salisbury and stayed with Sir Reginald Kennedy-Cox in the Canonry. I had known him since I was a child; he and my uncle had founded the Dockland Settlement. He and the Dean took me into the Cathedral and told me that they wanted a new play which could be performed before the altar and which required no scenery of any kind. I accepted the commission, not because I had anything in my mind I wanted to write about, but because the challenge of writing something for those conditions, without any scenery or set, imposed the kind of limitations which I enjoyed. I told them that I would think of some subject and submit it to their Chapter.

I then returned to Devon, and while messing about the farm occasionally tried to think of something to go into the Cathedral. But every time I did this I found myself thinking of a clown. I told Rose Marie of this.

"You're supposed to be writing a play for a Cathedral, and not for a circus," she said. But it was no use. The clown stayed in my mind. I saw him performing somersaults up the aisle and standing on his head on the altar. It looked to me as if I would have to abandon any idea of writing this play altogether. Then suddenly the bizarre filing system in my mind got reshuffled and I remembered that some years ago, I had received through the post, from a girl I had not met, a suggestion that I should write a ballet on the theme of a French legend called *Le Jongleur de Notre Dame*. She had enclosed a brief synopsis.

"I've found out who my clown is," I told Rose Marie. The same day I sketched out a play based on this theme, inventing three other characters who each made an offering to the statue of the Virgin which did not move until the clown danced and stood on his head before her. The Dean and Chapter received my idea enthusiastically, even when I told them that the music would be modern, and saxophones and percussion would be used to accompany the the clown's acrobatics. And strangely enough, it was not the somersaults that worried them, but my request that a large statue of Our Lady should be placed before the altar. They feared Catholicism more than the circus. But the Dean managed to allay their fears of any Popish plot and I was eventually given an entirely free hand.

Sir Reginald told me that as Cecil Beaton lived outside Salisbury, it might be appropriate if he were asked to do the décor. So I went to see him in his elegant cottage where he lived surrounded by roses and leather bound volumes of news cuttings. I asked him if he could design a statue of Our Lady from which a rose could drop. We thought of several ridiculous mechanical devices which were sure to go wrong in performance and, of course, finally decided that the safest and simplest solution was to make a statue behind which a girl could stand and drop the rose, only the live hand being visible. Beaton said he would undertake all the costumes, and looked forward to doing them because the Cathedral would carry formalised design, larger than life. We agreed to set the play in the Twelfth Century.

I decided to make the most of the opportunities of the setting and use as much music as possible. And though I only needed a small orchestra to accompany Brother Andrew's acrobatics, I sketched out two hymns to be sung by a full choir to open and end the play. The first hymn I called *Hymn for a Festival* and the last was to be a *Hymn to the Dead*, a sort of *Dies Irae* to be sung while the body of the clown was picked up at the foot of the statue of Our Lady and then carried down the length of the main aisle. In addition to these needs for music, I had invented the idea that there was a myth that the statue of Our Lady would make a sign when the perfect offering was made to her on her Feast Day. The Abbot of the Monastery, where the statue stands, chooses three monks to prepare their individual gifts: a poet who writes a poem: a gardener who grows a rose, and a musician who composes a song. It is because Brother Andrew has nothing comparable to offer the statue that he tries to dance and turn somersaults before it, failing to find the agility he had as a clown before he had had to retire from the ring and become a lay brother as a means of existence. It was important to the play that these other offerings should be serious in order to heighten the contrast with what the clown himself had to offer. I asked Ben to write the music. He said he would like to do so, but would prefer that I gave the opportunity to Arthur Oldham who, at Ben's suggestion, had been music director of *This Way to the Tomb*. Oldham was then Ben's pupil and protègè.

Gabriel Pascal had abandoned his plans to produce *This Way to the Tomb* in Florence and sold the Italian rights of my play to a Signor Berano. I don't know for how much—he had originally acquired the rights from me for £50. This Signor Berano wrote and urged me to go to Rome to discuss a production of the play there. Impressed by the fact that he said he owned his own theatre, I agreed. But I had delayed my visit until *The Rape of Lucretia* was being given at the Rome Opera House. Naïvely I thought that would be a production worth seeing.

My first shock was when I was met at Rome Airport by Signor Berano. He was loud: his mother-of-pearl shoes and diamond ring spoke in headlines: he had, he informed me, as he hustled me into his fat limousine, made a fortune in scrap iron and intended to devote it to culture. "Which means you," he leered. "Now I've bought you, I intend to put you over big." He made me feel like a commodity, a sort of Hair Lotion which the public was going to be bullied into buying. His A.D.C., an obsequious amanuensis called Schmidt, informed me that my first press conference was due to start in half an hour. I became very morose and then noticed that the car was not heading for Rome but out to the country.

"Where are we going?" I asked listlessly.

"To make you feel at home," Berano said consolingly, "to my farm. I know everything about you, and as you're a farmer as well as a poet, I thought the press should see you first in your own element."

The car stopped in the courtyard of a typical tycoon's farm— large dogs, tarred tubs and no dung-heap. I was frog-marched to the nearest field and a single furrow plough drawn by a couple of oxen was thrust into my hand. In this ridiculous position, the cameras clicked.

We then returned to Rome, where Berano showed me his theatre, and announced that his wife was expecting me for dinner.

Their flat was a sort of opulent American penthouse with a balcony overlooking the Via Veneto. After the meal while my host was fetching his cigars, his wife led me on to the balcony to admire the city lights.

Exhausted by the journey, the company and the meal, I fell into a sort of daze looking at the view. Dimly I heard my hostess offer me some fruit.

"No, thank you," I replied.

Perhaps a few minutes may have elapsed. My hostess, a fat, besequinned woman of forty, stood beside me. She took my hand. The next thing I knew was I was clasping something which I thought was a melon.

"But I really don't want any fruit, thank you," I said, turning to see that she had not led my hand to the fruit bowl but thrust it inside her dress.

Standing in this hideous predicament I could hear my host putting liqueurs and glasses on a tray in the room just behind me.

With her other hand she held mine to her, releasing it only when her husband approached the door.

"A cognac?" he asked affably. "I hope you've enjoyed the view."

I drank my brandy gratefully, not unaware of the rigours I had escaped by taking the precaution of booking a room at the Quirinale.

The next morning I went to the Opera House to secure my seat for the evening's performance. It occurred to me that I had never authorised an Italian translation of *The Rape of Lucretia*, and had never been consulted by the publishers on the matter. But I assumed Ben had looked after that. Outside the Opera House I saw copies of the Italian text of my libretto being sold in the streets. I bought one and, over a cup of coffee, began to glance idly at the book—my Italian is almost non-existent. But even this sufficed to send me hurtling from the café. I went straight to the Opera House and asked to see the Director. Waving the sheaf of illiterate howlers in his face I demanded a meeting with the translator.

"You can't perform this piffle tonight." I warned him some of the lines would cause a laugh. "At least the most ridiculous must be changed."

The silly man thought I was being pedantic.

"Look," I went on, "I know a libretto is only a libretto and a lot of the words in an aria can't be understood anyhow. But in this piece there is a lot of *recitative secco* and that will be heard and it's not meant to be as funny as this is."

He eventually went to the phone and returned to tell me that the translator had been called out of Rome.

223

"You know, he should have made a good job of it," the Director went on reassuringly, "he's a Professor of Literature and one of out best translators."

"Then he must have been drunk," I replied. "Look at my line *In the forest of my dreams*. It's hardly rendered correctly by *I sleep in the trees* nor is..."

Just then the Director was called out of his office. I decided to make some enquiries of my own, and when his secretary came in to answer the telephone on his desk, I asked her if she happened to know who had translated the opera which was being given that night. She was a girl of about nineteen. I could see she didn't understand English, so I repeated my question in French. She beamed, and proudly pointed to herself.

"You? A Professor of Literature?"

She shook her head pointing to a small dictionary.

"There must be a thousand washerwomen in Rome who would have made a better job of this than you."

She smiled self-deprecatingly, not understanding a word I'd said.

If I hadn't already promised to take a friend to the performance I would not have gone. But as I had, I was forced to endure the first act: the tempo was slow, the singing was ragged and the décor tatty. And this was Rome...I fumed with indignation as the secretary's gaffes were bellowed across the stage. But there was worse to come. In the second act of the opera, Prince Tarquinius is supposed to steal through the sleeping house towards Lucretia's bed. The Male Chorus describes his stealthy progression:

> *Panther agile and panther virile*
> *The Prince steals through the silent hall.*
> *And with all the alacrity of thought*
> *He crosses the unlit gallery,*
> *Where a bust of Collatinus*
> *Stares at him with impotent blind eyes.*
> *Now he is passing Bianca's door.*
> *Wake up, old woman! Warn your mistress!*

The description of Tarquinius's slow approach to the bed usually takes a couple of minutes and his stealthy movements towards

The author and Benjamin Britten at Glyndebourne 1946, preparing *The Rape of Lucretia*

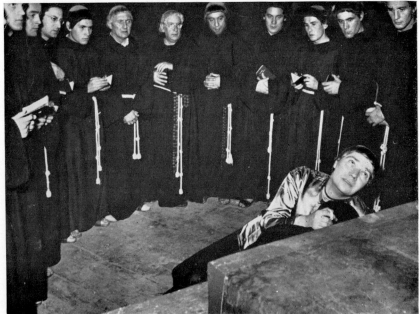

Our Lady's Tumbler, Salisbury Cathedral, 1953

the sleeping Lucretia usually produces a certain degree of tension. But Rome Opera had other ideas. They owned a revolving stage. And had decided that Tarquinius should stand by Lucretia's bed on the revolve and that it should move towards him—but, the imbecile producer must have argued, to suggest that it is Tarquinius who is stealing towards Lucretia, he must move his knees up and down to give the impression he is walking...So the scene was played with the chaste Lucretia revolving rapidly feet first towards her raper who merely waited for her approach.

But the following evening was more pleasurable. I had spent a tiresome day with Berano, whom I began to suspect was using the secretary at the Opera House to translate my plays too. John Drummond, who a year or two before had lived near Pound in Rapallo, but was then working in the British Embassy, asked me to go to a party which the philosopher Croce was giving. It was a very informal gathering. There must have been fifty people in the room. But none made any impression on me. Nor did Signor Croce either. For as I entered the room I saw a girl of arresting beauty sitting on a divan in the middle of the room. I think I would have admired her raven black hair even if her face had been ugly: but it was not: her features were so regular and finely shaped that not one was conspicuous. She was in her early twenties. What held my eyes was the graceful way she sat on the sofa and how she seemed to be apart and oblivious of her surroundings. It was as though she was a statue in the room. Somebody offered her a drink. She refused. I was relieved; a cocktail in her hand would have looked incongruous and spoiled the image. Croce talked to me, but I did not listen. All my attention was held by this girl who seemed entirely oblivious of the rude way I stared at her. But she appeared so poised, so much like a statue, there to be admired, that I did not feel that I might be embarrassing a person. Though I had not seen her before, this was not the first time I had seen her. For me she was the embodiment of the girl I had imagined as Katherine when I had been writing *Stratton*. It was as though my mind had projected her, my fantasy taken on a life of its own. And now I found myself cutting Croce short to ask him to introduce me.

"La Proclemer," he said, presenting her.

"Your first name?"

"Anna."

"It should be Katherine."

"Why?"

I told her. She did not seem surprised.

"Send me the play. I'm an actress."

"Of course you are," I said, "I wrote you." She smiled proudly, not denying it.

Just then an unknown Italian came and sat beside her. She introduced me. As usual I didn't listen to the name. This man struck me as being offensively friendly towards my creation. And by ignoring his remarks I tried to indicate that he was intruding. But he was thick-skinned and didn't budge. It was immediately apparent that Anna liked him. I managed to escape across the room to where my friend John Drummond was standing.

"Tell me about Anna Proclemer," I demanded.

"She's the best actress in Italy," he said, "plays mostly classics. They've always tried to make her go on the films but she refuses because she says Italian film actresses are judged by their busts and not their talent."

"She speaks English perfectly?"

"Yes."

"And who's that man beside her?"

"The famous novelist, Vittaliano Brancati."

"Never heard of him."

"You will," Drummond said, "he's her husband."

I left the party instantly, furious that somebody I had created had dared to saddle herself with a husband and a writer at that—without my permission. After I'd walked about a mile I realised I was not only thinking insanely but had behaved more rudely than usual. Not only had I failed to pay my respects to my host but also to Anna Proclemer too. I decided I would send her some flowers. But when I sent to do this the next morning from the airport I realised that I had also forgotten to obtain her address. I had omitted to do this, I suppose, because I felt so certain that she lived in my mind.

That autumn I took Rose Marie to Majorca for a holiday. Soon after we reached Palma, Robert Graves invited us up to where he lived. We had not met before. And due to Leavis' influence on me, I had not read much of his poetry and had been prejudiced against what I had read.

As soon as we reached his eyrie, he sat me down in his study while Rose Marie was entertained on the terrace by his wife. Graves was a swarthy figure, not unlike Pound in appearance or manner. Oddly enough, he immediately waded into an attack on Pound's lack of scholarship. I tried occasionally to deflect his animus against this or that literary figure, but found it difficult to stem the flow. I could see that Graves was not interested in me, but had got me up there only to arouse my interest in him. After a very exhausting day sitting rather unwillingly at his feet, Rose Marie and I trailed back to Palma by bus. We resolved to make certain that the remains of our holiday was not interrupted by "literature". To our amazement, when we woke up the next morning in our hotel, we were told that Graves was already downstairs waiting for me to get up. He must have risen at dawn to make the journey.

The reason for his visit was soon apparent. He had told me the day before that he had completed a book which dealt with the subject of pagan myths within Christianity and how he had found difficulty in getting the work published. He now told me that he had sent the book to Fabers and asked me to put in a word for him with Eliot, to persuade that firm to publish it. He was genuinely anxious and somehow believed that my help would make all the difference. I was amazed at the turn round: yesterday he had patronised me, today he was seeking my assistance. I promised to write to Eliot about the book, and when Graves had this assurance and had thanked me, he left to make the trip back.

All of which is very trivial no doubt. Except that it leads me to confess to an act of which I am most ashamed. A week later, I wrote to Eliot from Spain telling him about Graves' book and urged him not to publish it. I argued that it weakened the Christian belief and was essentially destructive. No doubt my letter still exists somewhere. It was a piece of perfidy. I suppose, I hope, I believed in my own arguments when I wrote them. Whatever they were, they came home to roost.

The justice of this does nothing to expiate the sense of shame. The memory is uncomfortable. I can't understand what my real motives were in writing that letter. Had I resented Graves' patronising me, talking at rather than with me? Did I dislike him because of his attitude to Ezra, whom I considered both a friend and a superior poet? Was I tired of people using me as a mat in front of Possum's door? None of these possibilities explain the incident. Perhaps my motive was that my unconsciousness was already meditating on the Judas poem and impelled me to a small act of betrayal so that I might experience what I was to write about?

When Rose Marie and I arrived in Madrid after an abortive call at Malaga to see the Brenans who were away, Walter Starkie, the British Council representative in Spain gave a small party for us. Several producers, including Luis Escobar, had been invited. We sat around being grimly polite and bored. Then just as I was wondering how soon I could make my excuses to go, a woman of about thirty swept into the room. She apologised for being late. Starkie introduced her as Conchita Montes. Her name meant nothing to me: I did not know anything about the Spanish stage. It was she who insisted I went to see Zorilla's *Don Juan*.

After leaving Madrid we flew to Bordeaux. I found, when we reached there, that I had changed all my travellers' cheques and had nothing but a £5 note. It was Sunday: no bank was open and we discovered that nobody in the city would change a fiver since many of these notes had been counterfeited by the Germans in the war. We had arrived at ten o'clock in the morning. We left the airport on foot, having no money for the bus. I called at the Consulate. It was closed. I telephoned the Consul and was told he was playing golf. By this time I needed my coffee and Rose Marie was hungry. We walked around the city like a couple of waifs, staring into the shop windows, greedily eyeing rolls of bread. By lunch-time the smells emanating from the meanest restaurant cut like a knife into us. I, too, was now ravenous and Rose Marie was foot-sore. Then I remembered that I had the habit of keeping a few English coins in my waistcoat pocket which was in a suit in my bag—change which I did not want muddled up with the foreign coins in my trouser pocket. We went back to the airport, found the suitcase, and a precious 2s. piece. This I was able to change. Feeling wealthy, we went back to the city and sat sharing one cup of coffee while I wrote *Jan's Journal* which had to be posted that afternoon. After paying for the cup of coffee and a stamp, we were left with 1s. 3d. for dinner and a night's lodgings. Eventually we could bear our hunger no longer and went into a rather flash restaurant with our few coins. Rose Marie ordered a plate of soup and some rolls. She had a rush carrier bag with her which she had bought in Spain. It was not simply our predicament which made us see the waiter as a menacing figure: he had, in fact, a black patch over one eye and a wooden leg. This appearance did not help me during the next few minutes, while I tried to secrete one roll after another from the table into the carrier bag. We paid the bill, and gave the man a five-centime tip. He eyed the empty bread basket suspiciously. We scurried out of the restaurant and ate the proceeds in the park. It grew dark. It was cold. The prospect of cuddling up to my fiver in the gutter became less amusing. I went into one or two hotels and explained my predicament. Their way of dealing with our situation was to say that they were fully booked anyhow. We decided that we might get more sympathy in a less prosperous area, and eventually found a very decrepit pension called *Les Trois Ours*. We decided to walk in boldly, take a room, and then face the proprietress with the fiver after we had had a good night's sleep. The room we were given was so damp that the wallpaper peeled in coils over the bed, which itself was too dank to sleep in. Apparently the rooms in this establishment were not taken for the purpose of repose: nobody ever bothered to get into the beds there. The proprietress seemed surprised that we had stayed so long. We had slept hardly at all. We handed her the fiver, ran to the airport and caught a plane to Paris.

In Paris I went to see my agent there, Madame Sciatal. I had not met her before, and when we did neither of us was impressed. I thought she looked like one of Louis XIV's mistresses' lovers. And it was obvious that Cocteau had poisoned her mind against me. We wasted each other's time and patience for half-an-hour. But as I was leaving her office, Peter Brook appeared. I happened to tell him that I had just been to Madrid. He asked me if I had seen any plays there.

"Only one, Zorilla's *Don Juan*."

"You ought to write a Don Juan. I'll produce."

It was a suggestion which took immediate root. Within forty-eight hours it had become an obsession. I walked Rose Marie round and round Paris, working out the structure of the play so that it could carry my "certainties". Every play I write has its certainties, by which I mean a point of view or scenes I know I want to write, and to which every other consideration has to bend. In this case the certainty was unfulfilled love. I was, of course, sill thinking of Petra.

"I don't want to write about an ordinary philanderer," I emphasised.

"You mean it's not going to be autobiographical? Or perhaps you mean it is?"

I was caught either way.

In the plane to London I sketched the sepulchre speech, using various prepositions: "within this sepulchre": to "to this sepulchre", "outside this sepulchre", etc., as a means to emphasise Don Juan's tension and as verbal points on each of which he could rap the tomb with his knuckles.

My mind was filled with the play. I was not writing it: it again seemed to be writing me. I was anxious to get back to Devon to begin putting pen to paper. But a day or two after reaching London, I received a note from Olivier suggesting that I went to tea with him in his dressing room at the Haymarket where he was playing Richard III. I had not met him, and naturally assumed that this invitation had been made at Peter Brook's suggestion.

Olivier sat in chain armour and through his visor, as it were, nibbled anchovy toast. He said how much he'd enjoyed *The Eagle has Two Heads*, and for the next fifteen minutes we talked animatedly but not about the theatre: we discussed tuberculosis. His wife, Vivien Leigh, was then in a sanatorium: he'd heard that Rose Marie had been in one too. I told him how I had made her eat raw garlic. We discussed the effect the disease had on the temperament of the patient. An unspoken sympathy was articulate between us. But I felt I had already stayed too long and rose to go.

"No, I'm not on for another fifteen minutes," he said. "What I really wanted to ask you is if you'd think of writing a play for my wife and me. Have you got any ideas?"

I told him I was mulling over a Don Juan, and obviously Vivien Leigh would be ideal for Doña Aña.

"Splendid," he exclaimed, "do go on thinking about it. I'm definitely interested, on one condition..."

"What's that?"

"That you turn the play on the theme of unfulfilled love," he said, "otherwise I couldn't play it."

This was uncanny. "But that's my condition too for writing it," I exclaimed.

"Otherwise Don Juan's an adolescent and a cad," Olivier said.

"Precisely."

Our accord was complete.

"I'll bring you the first draft within three or four months. No, I don't need any contract."

I couldn't get home to Orme Lane fast enough to tell Rose Marie of this. After the *Stratton* débâcle, this was precisely the encouragement I needed.

I changed my plans and insisted on driving to Devon that same evening. I knew that all I had to do was go for a ride on Dil Fareb to find most of the play in her mane or on her saddle. As we drove through the night I began mumbling bits of speeches involuntarily. I shall always remember this journey because after we'd been on the road for about four hours, and had just passed through Exeter, I turned to Rose Marie and said:

"Tell me when you're tired and I'll drive."

"But you are driving," she replied dryly and a little fearfully.

No play possessed me so completely as this one did...

A gallop or two on Dil told me that what I also had to do was to write a contemporary Don Juan too, but I decided to write the traditional costume play first, and then perhaps add the other as a sequel to it later.

Before leaving for Spain I had told Kenneth Tynan that I would agree to his producing *Saint Spiv* if he could cast it. I didn't expect he would or could. I had met his kind of enthusiasm before. But I had misjudged him. Within a week of my return he announced he was ready to start rehearsals. His cast list was so good I could only agree. This left no time to arrange finance for the play. To my horror, and my friends' dismay, I found myself underwriting the production. And although it was a modest one at the Watergate Theatre and Tynan had somehow persuaded the cast to take less than the Equity minimum, I stood to lose £300 per week. My income then from all sources was under £30 a week. But Tynan's enthusiasm for the play was infectious and the author had not been inoculated.

For the next few weeks I had to put the manuscript of *Don Juan* aside and rehearse *Saint Spiv*.

My first worry here was over the title. I had submitted the text to Eliot. He had written to me to say that Fabers would publish the play if it were produced, but he urged me to change the title. It was clear that it offended his theological sensibilities. With some regret I altered it to *Nothing up my Sleeve*.

Tynan showed considerable ingenuity in his production, especially as the stage at the Watergate Theatre was so tiny and considering the scenes were set in a market off Clapham High Street; Epsom Downs on Derby Day; and not least in the Albert Hall. But with a few suggestive props and cut-outs, Reece Pemberton, who had also designed the costly box set for *Stratton*, got over these limitations. Our main difficulties during reherasals were between Tynan and Arthur Oldham who had composed the music. Both were very talented: and this made one dislike the other all the more. When I was not trying to keep the peace between them, I was waging my own war with the actor, Harold Lang, who played the lead as the down-at-heel Spiv, Horace. I had conceived this figure as a Chaplinesque character. He was meant to be funny but, of course, never aware of it: a part to be played with deadpan seriousness if his pathos was to be realised. But Mr Lang played the comedy with a post-box grin on his face. If he thought a line was funny, he would wink the point home. Sadly, repeatedly, and even patiently I would explain to him that serious intention was the essence of comedy and the slightest sign that he found his situation funny would mean that nobody else would. I asked him when he had seen Chaplin, Harold Lloyd or Buster Keaton grin? But both Tynan and I could do nothing with him.

Fortunately, Harry Fowler and George Rose were in the cast too. When we opened, the play was well received by the critics. There was talk of a transfer but it remained only talk.

After we'd been playing a couple of weeks, I received a disastrous letter from Equity. Apparently one of the actresses who played a small part had, in spite of Tynan's arrangement with her, complained to the Actor's Union that we were paying less than the minimum wage. Tynan had, in fact, approached these out-of-work actors with an offer of £8 a week with the understanding that only if they accepted this could we afford to stage the show. It was an attempt to spread the risk or obtain a co-operative production. And the actors stood the chance of obtaining a better wage if the show transferred, or failing that, at least being noticed by the critics and commercial managements. This indeed proved the case: one obtained a film contract and another was signed up by the Old Vic. But British Equity was not interested in those benefits. Their letter demanded that we paid the basic wage in future and retrospectively or they would close the show. This meant our get-out was increased by another £150 a week over and above the possible takings if we played to full houses. I couldn't close the show because I was already committed to paying the rent of the theatre for a further three weeks. Tynan offered his producer's fee back: it had been only £25. I looked a little rueful when people congratulated me on having another play running in London: I knew I could not lose less than £1,000. Nor did I receive any sympathy for this loss, as friends who are always generous in this respect assumed I was carrying the loss against tax. This wasn't so. I had discovered that there's no advantage in having more losses than income:

and my farm already took care of that contingency. As it was, I was left with the only consolation of owning the props. These consisted of an old raincoat, a tray and a couple of cups. Rose Marie referred to them as her expensive tea set.

As soon as I had returned from Rome I had, of course, sent a copy of *Stratton* to Anna Proclemer. Not knowing her address I posted the book to Signor Berano and asked him to forward it to her. I was not optimistic that she would ever receive it; or if she did, that I should hear from her. Actresses often tell an author at a party that they'd like to read his last play and that is the last they think of it. How often had I seen these typescripts lining bottoms of their wardrobes, piled on top of an unused suitcase, stacked in the airing cupboard, or even propping up a sofa which had lost a leg. But about a week later I received a letter from Anna saying she had liked the piece and would play Katherine when it was produced in Rome. She went on to warn me against all Italian translators, telling me that even Professor Rosati, whom I had seen in Rome on Eliot's introduction, was too academic to convey the idiomatic verse I had attempted. She gave several instances of his failure. From which it was clear that not only did she speak English, but she even read it too.

I replied. We were soon corresponding regularly, writing to each other about Pound, Dante or Eliot. But both of us knew that literature was not what we were writing about. She had asked me what I was writing then. I had sent her some of *Don Juan*.

For the next few months I did not hear from her at all, then one day I received a note saying that she was coming to London and suggesting that I called at her hotel, the Green Park, for a drink.

"I suggest eleven o'clock in the morning," she wrote, "and then we can discuss *Stratton*." I thought the time a little odd and perhaps unnecessarily cautious.

A few days later I went to the hotel and found her waiting for me. She looked more beautiful than when I had first seen her.

"By drink,' she said, "I meant coffee. I know you drink gallons of it and seldom touch anything else.''

It was a pretty compliment, telling me that she'd taken the trouble of finding out something about me, however trivial.

For the next five minutes we talked volubly without either of us listening to what the other said. Her eyes were the only words I heard. I did not see Brancati come towards us nor notice him till he sat himself beside us.

"You remember my husband?''

"Yes,'' I replied ungraciously. But he did not evaporate with my glance. We exchanged greetings; the warmth of his I interpreted to mark his self-confidence. It was, I thought, as though he was saying: "I can afford to be friendly to you because my relationship with my wife is quite impregnable and beyond your reach!'' After a few minutes' conventional conversation, I left without the opportunity of making any arrangement to see her again. I could have asked them both to dine with me and Rose Marie. But social life was not precisely what I had in mind.

As I left the hotel, I doubted if I would ever see Anna again. She had told me, too, that she was only staying two days more in England. I felt miserable.

For something to do, I phoned my friend Nigel Spottiswoode and asked him to meet me. I needed sympathy or at least a pair of ears. And nobody was better trained: up at Cambridge, he had had to listen to my bleat about Laura; he had seen me through my abortive infatuation for Diana; and even listened attentively to my emotional travail over Rose Marie though she was his girlfriend. So naturally I phoned Nigel. Over a cup of coffee I told him about Anna, how I had only seen her twice, and had just left her and her husband together, knowing I would never see her again.

"Didn't you say Brancati was a Sicilian?'' he asked. "Then it might be just as well if you didn't try to see her again. Sicilians express their jealousy with knives.''

"Don't worry. I've decided to abandon the chase. She was the embodiment of a fantasy, she must go back to one.''

"In that case,'' he said, "let's leave her in bad company—in your mind. And go to the National Gallery.''

"Why the National Gallery?''

"They're exhibiting the Collection from Munich. There's a fabulous Botticelli I want to see. I was going there when you phoned me."

We walked through St James's, down Pall Mall and entered the Gallery.

"Well?" Spottiswoode asked after we'd been standing a few minutes in front of the picture, "what do you think of it?"

"You tell me what you think of her," I replied quietly.

"Of whom?"

"Anna."

"Pull yourself together," he said, "a fantasy is one thing, but illusions are..."

But he didn't finish his sentence, for at that moment Anna, who had been standing in front of us looking at the Botticelli, turned round. She smiled; it was as if the picture had reached through its frame and projected her. But there was a look of incredulity or apprehension behind her smile. Brancati, beside her, turned too. He nodded impassively. I introduced Spottiswoode and then, feeling embarrassed because it was obvious that Anna and her husband thought I had followed them to the Gallery, I instantly turned away and went to look at the pictures in an adjoining room. Spottiswoode followed.

"How's that for a coincidence?" I muttered. "Nine million people in London and I have to run into her again within an hour of parting with her for ever."

"It was I who suggested coming here," he admitted, "or I would have sworn it wasn't an accident. Now you'd better look out for that knife."

We left the Gallery. That evening I decided to drive with Rose Marie back to Devon. I could do nothing with the feelings Anna had aroused in me but write and exhaust myself by finishing my play. As we drove along Rose Marie understood my silence intuitively.

"And did you see your Roman actress?" she asked.

I told her the whole story. She enjoyed hearing it; she seemed incapable of jealousy and because of that I naïvely loved her all the more.

"Don't worry, darling," she said, genuinely sympathetic.

"Anna will be back, and next time without her husband."

"What makes you think so?"

"I don't think: I know," she said enigmatically.

We drove on, gaily gossiping without a trace of resentment... our intimacy was an identification – it was not that we tolerated one another: we had become one another.

A few days later, I was surprised to receive an open postcard from Anna. It said she was home but homesick. We now began to write to each other every day. But not about Pound, Eliot or Dante. Even so we'd met three times, exchanged no more than ten minutes' conversation and were separated by two thousand miles. In one letter I learned she had a daughter. In another that she was leaving Rome and going out on tour with a new play. This correspondence took for granted what neither of us had expressed: the attraction we felt for each other was such that neither of us had need to mention it. All we could do was to sympathise with each for being lamed with the other. Fortunately, we were both busy: she with her tour, a husband and a daughter. I, with my family, farm, and a play to finish.

While writing *Don Juan*, I was somewhat inappropriately interrupted by my second marriage. It was not bigamous, nor had Rose Marie died. What had happened was that she had become a practising Catholic again. With one avalanche of a confession, she had told her priest in Bude that she had gone through a marriage service at a Registry Office to a non-Catholic, and that she already had two children who had both been baptised in the Church of England. The poor astounded man gave her a penance and told her that she was, in the Church's eyes, unmarried, living in sin, and that her children were illegitimate. He urged her to mend her sinful ways forthwith and gave her precise details of how to do so. I was writing when she came back from church and didn't look up from the paper, until I realised that what she had said as she'd passed through the room was:

"I'm moving you into another room. You can sleep there until you marry me in a proper manner."

I put my pen down and went upstairs to check on my renewed bachelorhood; she was in earnest. My things were being moved.

"Poor little bastards," she said, looking down through the window at Roger and Briony playing on the lawn.

After enduring this chilly state of affairs for a few nights, I enquired what I had to do before normality could be resumed.

"Marry me."

"In a Catholic church?"

"In a mosque, if you like. Let's get on with it."

"It will take several weeks."

"Why? Why not today?"

"The banns have to be up for several Sundays. I will see Father Brown today. But it will be at least a month before we can be married and you needn't think I'm going to anticipate the honeymoon."

She looked too naïvely devout and childlike in her earnestness for me to argue with her. I remember venting my impatience with my unmarried state by taking our bastards for a ride.

At the end of the week I began to confuse Father Brown with Torquemada. Chastity was a region in which I did not like treading. I began to suffer from erotic hallucinations, vulnerability and a sense of being persecuted. After a few weeks of this Rose Marie and I drove into the tiny galvanised iron church in Bude. I had made the point that it would be inappropriate for Briony to be her bridesmaid. But knowing how serious the service was to Rose Marie, I conformed with her mood. I was determined not to spoil her second marriage day as I had the first. The service meant more to me, too, than the squalid Registrar's office. The only hitch came when after the service, Father Brown handed the register to Rose Marie to sign. Under the heading of "previous state or occupation", Rose Marie naïvely scrawled "housewife".

"You can't put that," the poor man said, "you weren't a wife till ten minutes ago. Oh dear, this is a kettle of fish..."

I wrote *Don Juan* in Devon, working on it for a couple of hours every morning before getting lost in the farm or in my mania for repairing derelict cottages. With Zorrilla's play as a guide to the structure of the scenes, the work came easily. Laurence Olivier's interest had stimulated me; his stipulation that I should turn the play on the theme of unfulfilled love was in line with my own emotional impulse at that time. As I completed each scene, I sent it off to Rome. Anna waited for it and commented on it page by page. She was determined to play the part of Doña Aña. I wrote the part for her and not for Vivien Leigh, whose Cleopatra had lacked the warmth and tenderness which this character requires.

It was encouraging and helpful to have this great actress looking over my shoulder, as it were, and commenting on each page. Her remarks in the letters which she wrote every other day taught me more about playwriting than any critic had done. I had sent her the scene between Don Juan and Doña Aña at the beginning of Act Two:

DOÑA AÑA: Well, why don't you say something?
  Don't tell me you feel ashamed.
DON JUAN: No.
DOÑA AÑA: Then why are you silent?
DON JUAN: From boredom.
DOÑA AÑA: You swine!
DON JUAN: For you know as well as I know
  That whatever we do when we're apart
  Makes no difference to us when we're together.
  I wish it did. It might give me some release
  From this world which has contracted
  To this prison of your eyes...
DOÑA AÑA: You don't deny...
DON JUAN: Not at all.
DOÑA AÑA: ...Your unfaithfulness?
DON JUAN: No. I admit the attempt, but cannot claim
  The achievement. My intentions were to destroy
  My memory of you. I was more faithful than I knew.
  You tried one way to forget me; I—another...
  You say you've succeeded: I confess, I failed.
DOÑA AÑA: Did none...console you?
DON JUAN: Before I had met you, I tried to find you.
  After I had known you, I tried to forget you.
  There have been many lips and many eyes
  But they've been your lips, they've been your eyes.
DOÑA AÑA: Your cloak is torn...
DON JUAN: Those who can be parted, never loved...

239

DOÑA AÑA: If you'll take it off, I'll mend it...

DON JUAN: For to love as we love is to be
Never separate, yet always lonely.
Aña, can you deny, you feel as I feel...

DOÑA AÑA: *(taking the cloak and sitting down)*
It's torn almost beyond repair.

DON JUAN: That you suffer as I suffer...
(He sits on the floor beside her)

DOÑA AÑA: ...But I'll try to mend it.

DON JUAN: You talk of faith. But it's you who are unfaithful:
Seeking a God outside you, betraying the God
Crying inside you.

DOÑA AÑA: Don't talk any more.
This moment becomes a memory even while we live it.
Too frail to be experienced except in retrospect
Even as I speak my voice sounds distant to me.
May this remoteness veil my immodesty
For I will tell you how I love:
    I love you as a river loves the sea,
      When I turn away from you, it is only to
                    flow back to you.
      When I am quiet lying in pools of stillness
      It is because I am content, knowing I shall
                    reach you,
      And when I am hurrying, I am hurrying
                    towards you.
    For I love you as a woman, and the mouth of
                    that river
    Is the lips of this woman.
    (she kisses him, then stands and moves away)

Anna's comments on this scene influenced the way I was to write other scenes in other plays. She said how much she liked Doña Aña's confession of love at the end of the scene with its extended river metaphor. But she most commended me for the essential feminity of the simple question half-fearful jealousy, half bitchy self-satisfaction.

Did none...console you?

240

"This is so genuinely feminine," she wrote, "and will be quite poignant as that woman has just become a nun. And the most poetic line you've written for Doña Aña is

Your cloak is torn...

There's a passage in *Anthony and Cleopatra* when Cleopatra buckles Anthony's sword on to him and comments on that, because she cannot bear to articulate what is in her mind...This kind of counterpoint will act well and I can't wait to play it. More."

And so with this kind of sensitive and really intelligent encouragement, I wrote rapidly. But though I sent every line to Anna I was not unaware that I was writing them from my feelings for Petra. I had written a letter to her:

> 'Let me ask you one question
> And I will never ask another.
> Do I walk through your dreams
> As you now run through mine...
> Answer this question, I will not ask another.'

As I could not post this letter, I put it into the play. Word for word, it became the letter which Doña Aña receives from Don Juan, just before he appears in the scene which I've quoted.

It was Anna who perceived the opportunity for an actress here.

"As Doña Aña refuses to open the letter at first, it can remain unopened on the floor stage centre, and while she talks about it and circles it, the letter can embody her lover. It will define his presence more than if he were on the stage himself."

As soon as *Don Juan* was complete, I sent it to Peter Brook, who had suggested that I wrote it. A few days later he came round to Orme Lane. To my astonishment he said he was surprised to see that I had not written it in couplets.

"If it's to be in verse," he said, "it should be in couplets; they would give it the right style."

I told him that it was not possible to write couplets today without making a pastiche of Pope and boring an audience as much as Racine did.

"Anyhow," Brook said, "I think its a mistake to write poetry for the stage today. It has no longer any function."

"Why not?"

"Because the producer no longer needs it. Lighting equipment and other effects at his disposal can do all those things which poetry once had to attempt. Shakespeare only wrote in verse to describe things he couldn't present. He had no revolving stage."

I smiled at this arrogant piffle, and remained silent.

About this time I received a note from Eliot asking if he could see me as he had a "special favour to ask of me." Naturally I offered to go up to London immediately. For the life of me I could think of no favour I could possibly do him: he was rich, he knew everybody; there could be nothing he could possibly want from me and there was nothing I could do for him but waste his time. The only thing that did cross my mind was that he wanted my advice where to buy the best Stilton. That seemed to me to be the only sort of thing where I knew more than he did.

We met at the Oxford and Cambridge Club during the early afternoon. During the tea and anchovy toast I could see that he was extremely nervous, behaving just like a man who was about to ask me for a loan of £50.

"I'm sorry to drag you up here, Ronnie," he said eventually, "especially as you must be busy with your harvest, but I have a particular favour to ask of you. They are going to revive a play of mine, The Rock. The producer has told me that the choruses have dated. I wrote it many years ago. I dare say he's right. Anyhow I agreed to rewrite them. I have tried but I find I can't. My drafts are as dated as my originals. I wonder if you would write these for me? You could do it very well."

I shook my head.

"You're too busy?"

"No," I said. "I was shaking my head because it's so difficult for me to take your request in. You've no idea how this play impressed me when I read it first. I'd just left school. I can hardly believe you want me to scribble over it."

"But that's just what I do want," he said.

He called for the bill and we walked over to the desk where he signed it. Watching the time he took to write even his signature it occurred to me that it must be a painful process for him to compose anything. Then I remembered that he, like Ezra, always wrote his poetry on a typewriter.

I went straight back to Devon, put everything else aside, and worked as hard as I could on these excerpts. But the production never took place so I never committed these drafts to paper. And now I can't remember more than an odd line or two.

My occasional fits of absent-mindedness generally have no consequences but inconvenience to myself, but one nearly cost me my life. I had been asked by the BBC to do a programme in Bristol called *Desert Island Discs*, in which I had to play the gramophone records I would like to take with me to a deserted island. This programme entailed motoring from London down to Bristol one morning. I was driving alone, and had gone about fifty miles when, to pass the time, I turned on the car radio. To my horror I heard one of those parlour games in which morons ask nonentities a lot of questions. Whenever I had heard this programme come on the radio at the farm I had rushed out of the room. I now did precisely the same thing, travelling at sixty miles an hour, the door half open, myself hanging out and nobody steering the car...And I have known other lapses.

It is quite untrue that once when I had to change trains at Salisbury I spent two days and two nights in the waiting-room there, because I had forgotten where I was going. The lapse lasted a mere five hours, and was easily rectified when I had the inspiration to look at the destination printed on my ticket.

On another occasion I had received an invitation to address the Byron Society at Cambridge. I had a couple of hours to spend in London before catching the train on to Cambridge at six o'clock. I had arranged to meet an editor at the Reform Club for tea, in order to discuss an article which I had promised to write. We had talked for some considerable time when I noticed that I had only twenty minutes to get to Liverpool Street station. I rushed out of the Club for a taxi. I was most agitated.

"Is this the train for Cambridge?" I asked the ticket man at the barrier.

"Straight on," he said.

And that part of my mind which was not worrying about what

I was going to say to the Byron Society took this official quite literally. A quarter of an hour later a plate-layer interrupted my reverie.

"Where are you off to?"

"Cambridge."

"Wouldn't a train be quicker?"

I looked down at the sleepers at my side. My bag was still in my hand. I had walked almost a mile beyond the end of the platform, over crossings and through tunnels. My own train must have passed me...but rehearsing my notes I'd been oblivious to my situation. It was now most humiliating turning round and walking back to Liverpool Street to catch a later train. It was also quite terrifying.

For all that I don't like to be thought absentminded; these lapses are only occasional. Even so they have landed me in some embarrassing situations and frequently make me appear foolish in public. As for instance when I got on a bus in Regent Street and handed tuppence to the conductor.

"Where to, mate?"

"Calcutta," I replied, not looking up from my evening paper.

"Blimey, you don't 'arf want your money's worth. You'll 'ave to change. We only go as far as Oxford Circus."

Even the two nuns sitting opposite could not refrain from laughing at me. I immediately got off the bus and went into a café, and sat wondering what could have possibly made me say Calcutta when I had meant Baker Street. Such aberrations were becoming more than embarrassing—after all, I pondered, only a few days before I had been made to look rather silly when I had gone to a cinema in Leicester Square, and bought two six shilling tickets. As I picked up the change, and was about to turn towards the stalls, the girl in the box-office leaned forward and whispered very kindly:

"I suppose you know there's nobody with you, sir?"

"Isn't there?" was all I could think of saying. I now sweated with embarrassment as I remembered the look of infinite indulgence on the cashier's face, as she'd given me the price of one ticket back, and had then called, teasingly, to the usher:

"Show these gentlemen to the stalls."

Things are expensive enough, I thought, without having Dr Jekyll paying for Mr Hyde as well.

I sat in the café, but for all my efforts I couldn't explain to myself why I had said Calcutta. As far as I was aware this was the last place on earth I wanted to go to. I knew nobody there. I couldn't trace any association in my mind with this wretched city. After half an hour's futile introspection, I gave the pursuit up, and because it was so cold outside, in spite of being June, I ordered some more hot water, and settled down to read my evening paper. Opening it I glanced at the headline: "HEAT-WAVE IN CALCUTTA." I thumped the table with relief. The explanation was simple: my subconscious mind had reacted promptly against the cold June day, and had articulated my resentment against the miserable English weather.

"Will you be wanting anything more, sir?" the waitress asked, placing the jug of hot water on the table.

"Yes, bring me some hot buttered monsoons," I said. The girl blinked.

"That is, I mean, mangoes, of course," I said.

"We haven't any mangoes, sir. Would you like crumpets?"

"No, thank you," I said, paying my bill and fleeing.

For the next two years I was entirely free of this failing and didn't even lose my umbrella. But the details of my next lapse are still fresh in the mouths of my friends.

I was travelling to Waterloo from Bideford, and since it is my habit to pass the time in trains by catching up with my correspondence, I sometimes take a first class ticket in the hope of getting a compartment to myself. This journey I was unlucky: two men got in at Barnstaple; one, a little mouse of a man, very tidy and spruce, sat down beside me; the other, opposite in the corner. After a few minutes I observed that the little man was going to nibble. He'd taken a small case down from the rack, and setting it squarely on his knees, had produced a large paper packet of sandwiches.

Now I am one of those fastidious people who are nauseated by the sight of mouths munching sandwiches, and fingers picking at hard-boiled eggs. One doesn't travel first class in order to listen to munching dentures. As the little man began to unwrap his packet,

I opened my paper with reproachful vigour. For the next half-hour I was lost in reading the fatuous reviews, quite oblivious to my irritating neighbour.

After we'd left Exeter, the restaurant car attendant came round for orders for luncheon.

"I think I'd better have the first sitting," said the little man. The attendant gave him a ticket.

I was shocked. Greed is always revolting. After all, he'd only just devoured an enormous packet of sandwiches. I couldn't refrain from commenting.

"These spring mornings give one quite an appetite, don't they?" I said sarcastically.

The Mouse smiled wanly.

"Will you be taking luncheon, sir?" the attendant asked me.

"The second sitting," I replied, emphatically.

"That's some relief to hear," the Mouse muttered, as the attendant withdrew and closed the door.

For a moment I wondered if I had heard my neighbour correctly.

"I beg your pardon, but did I hear you comment that it was some relief to you that I was going to the second sitting?"

"That is so," said the Mouse.

"Then do you mind explaining yourself?" I yapped indignantly.

"Not at all. I'm relieved to hear that we are not having to lunch together."

"Why? Do you mind telling me why?" I had never met such insolence.

"Because I was apprehensive that if we had gone to the Restaurant Car together you might have eaten my lunch too."

"The British Railways are probably able to serve lunch for two persons," I commented.

"Even so, that might not have prevented you from eating mine."

"Sir," I bellowed, "you're obsessed with food. You're the greediest little man I've ever had the discomfort of travelling with. First you wolf a great pile of sandwiches..."

"I haven't eaten anything," said the little man. "That's why I want the first luncheon. You ate them all."

"That's true," volunteered the man in the corner. "I saw this

246

gentleman unwrap his sandwiches, and just as he was about to take one, your hand shot out from your newspaper and you helped yourself..."

"Nonsense."

"...both of us watched you. Before you'd eaten one sandwich your hand had taken another..."

"I deny it."

"I was too amazed to stop you," said the Mouse.

"You didn't even leave him one."

"I don't believe it."

"It's true," moaned the Mouse, "and I'm very partial to smoked salmon."

"I don't believe..." but as I said that I was aware of the lingering flavour of this delicacy on my tongue.

I sat down, abject with shame. I swallowed.

"That explained it," I said, "smoked salmon is a weakness of mine too..."

I held out my hand.

"I do apologise," I said. "Perhaps you'll let me give you luncheon?"

And with that we went up the corridor.

"Lucky I didn't bring my wife with me today," the little man said over his shoulder.

I wondered what he meant by that. Perhaps no more than that she liked smoked salmon too?

I write about my distractions but that is not accurate: many were attractions: farming, building, tobacco-growing and so-on to me all aspects of poetry. They are, in fact, practical poetry. As I've admitted, I would always put my pen down for the immediate pleasure of, say, peeling and cutting beetroot. No image I coined could compare to that vividness. The poetry in things is the attraction, not the distraction. So too with horses: to me a horse is a poem on four legs. No language, either of words or music, can get near to the subtle rhythm they contain. And not in the whole of drama is there a tension to compare with the stallion's electric eye and alarmed nostril. The poem is not only on the page. Perhaps poetry has often died on the page by being limited to it?

247

My passion for poetry led me not into the library but into the stable, the carpenter's shop or the vegetable garden, where I would sit watching the miracle of the blind runner bean's tendril change direction as I moved the stick to which it reached; or I would drop even Donne or Pope gladly to thrust my arm up a cow's vagina, feel for the calf's position, then straighten the bent leg and pull the slippery lyric to the shippon floor and then watch the cow's rough tongue lick the bag away and nuzzle the wet, leggy metaphor to the udder. Often my friends, seeing how little I read, would thrust a book into my hands. But whatever the book it is dropped if a carpenter comes near the house, and I can watch the curl of shavings leave the sharpened plane, or observe with what careless skill he hones the blade. When Pound read the Canzone of Cavalcanti to me, *Donna mi Pregha*, I immediately went off to write a Canzone. Similarly, the poetry of wood, its grain and honesty of substance impels me to try my own clumsy hand at carpentry. So it is with building too. Of course I have felt satisfaction when I have managed to turn one verse so that it repeats the pattern of the previous one effortlessly, when no rhyme is conspicuous like a rib sticking out through the subject, and the metre is so contained within the idiomatic run of the language that it is unobtrusive, yet I have found it equally satisfying to find a stone in the bed of a river with a good quoin to it: one that has just fitted into the wall where I was putting a new window so that when placed, its position seems as inevitable as the right word in a sentence, needing the minimum of mortar to hold it in its syntax. Only the lees of poetry are on the page. Every thing is a poem if you look at it long enough.

Then why do I try to write at all if other activities hold the same pleasure? Because sometimes I cannot help myself; a word or a phrase will ring like a bell in my ear and I write it down only because I know that that is the only way to silence it. I go to my pen as one is impelled to answer a telephone. Sometimes it is a wrong number, sometimes there is nobody there at all. And I suppose I write because it is, in the last resort, the only thing I can do properly. Or shall we say: the failure is not immediately apparent. As I look up from this page now I can see a Clovelly fisherman tempting the Bristol Channel with his tiny boat. It is the season for autumn herrings. I know he is trawling his new red nylon net across a shelf of sand off Hartland Quay. He is only half a mile off shore, just beyond the white horses, 'the reckless cavalry of waves'. I watch him enviously. Now he has cut off the engine and turned to haul. Slowly the sleeve of the net appears over the side of the boat, glistening with wetness, laced with light and heavy to haul. The net falls in careful coils on the deck and without breaking the rhythm of hauling it in or coiling it on the deck, he is able to flick the occasional piece of flapping quicksilver into one of the wicker baskets at his side, sorting the herring from the flat-fish and deftly flinging the odd star-fish back into the sea. There is a poet if ever there was one. I would, I think, enjoy his job better than this scribbling: at least his catch is edible. But were I to change, my net would foul the bottom; when I came to coil it, it would fall into a tangled twist on the cluttered deck, and a fish in the net would so excite me I would probably fall overboard with glee. It is true, I have tried it. I write because it is the only thing I can do with any degree of skill. Of course sometimes I fall off the page, but nobody notices.

My friends are idiots; they say I am fearless because I will ride an unbroken horse or go up in an aeroplane with a pilot who hasn't got his licence. Horses and aeroplanes don't frighten me: other things do. Indeed, I am a born coward and spend my time running from things which are safe and still. But there are the things which put me to flight. For instance, I have frequently ordered a meal in a restaurant then, still hungry, have rushed from the place with my meal uneaten because I couldn't bear to go on sitting there opposite some harmless old man with a cup of coffee in front of him who had said nothing, done nothing, to offend me, but who had savaged my mind with the image of his own gentle loneliness. Or how often have I, hurrying to an appointment, had to jump off a bus before I reached my destination to walk or run the rest of the way because I could no longer suffer the friendlessness which seemed to me to surround some woman sitting near me with her shopping basket. The lonely, the pathetic and the lost: these are the things I fear. I remember one day hurrying over the pages of some book on Oscar Wilde, and coming across a photo of him sitting alone at a café table in Paris some time after he'd been released from gaol. My friends who think I am brave often wonder why I read so little: it is I dare not open a book. For books are bled from loneliness and I see the blood on each page.

I have often thought I would like to pass a law forbidding any old man or lonely woman to sit alone at a café table; if they were to hang themselves in front of me they would not distress me so much. That, at least, would put an end to their predicament. It is the monotonous waiting for the next day and the next cup of coffee at the next café which I cannot face for them. Fools try to console me by saying such people are not lonely though they are alone, that though they speak to nobody they sit with their memories, and take comfort in them. What nonsense this is: if memories are pleasant they are unbearable; they fill us with nostalgia and regret; if they are unpleasant, they punish us with shame or remorse. Memories are bad company. But perhaps these figures I flee from sit stirring their coffee with hopes? That is possible. It is their hopes which make them so hopeless to me. What we fear is our fear. Clearly one day I shall walk into this nightmare and find myself an old man sitting alone at a café table. Do not, whatever the expression on my face, think I am enjoying my memories, just pity me and shoot me in the back of the head. I shall be grateful. We are often most merciful when we seem to show none.

Cromwell had once used Salisbury Cathedral to stable his horses; since then the Close had shown some peace until the production of *Our Lady's Tumbler* moved in. Rose Marie and I stayed with Sir Reginald Kennedy-Cox at the Canonry. It was he who had persuaded the Chapter of the Cathedral who had commissioned me to write the play. He had been interested in the theatre all his life and had written several plays himself. He was a staunch Churchman too, and this production in the Cathedral brought the two halves of his world together. Through his diplomacy the Dean and Chapter were most accommodating. They even allowed the pews to be removed and a raked auditorium installed each side of the nave. In one transept Arthur Oldham set up his drums and the jazz accompaniment for the Tumbler's dances.

In another part of the Cathedral, Cecil Beaton seemed to be holding the endless fashion parade of his costumes. And in front of the altar a choreographer took Merry Andrew through his steps. Nobody raised an eyebrow seeing him standing on his head or somersaulting by the altar.

The production went smoothly. George and Marion came down for the first night and stayed with us at Sir Reginald's.

After this production, Ben asked me if I would write an opera libretto for Arthur Oldham. Oldham was still his pupil and worked with him at Aldeburgh. Ben told me that he was impressed with his talent, and that the English Opera Group would commission the work. I agreed. Oldham wanted to write a comedy and had already considered the idea of the *Taming of The Shrew*. As I had done with the *Rape of Lucretia*, I again went straight to the original poem from which Shakespeare had drawn. In this case it was an anonymous poem called *The Taming of a Shrew*. I found it much more suitable a basis for a libretto than the Shakespeare play, because in the poem the character of Christopher Sly was a central feature, whereas Shakespeare casts the character in a very minor role. Oldham was impatient to start composition. It was his first commission for an opera.

He had just completed a ballet for Covent Garden. He came down to the farm, and we worked out a musical synopsis, keeping in mind that the work was for the English Opera Group. We therefore dispensed with a chorus and restricted it to eight characters.

The work was tentatively scheduled for production at Aldeburgh. Oldham was pleased with the libretto, but before starting to set it, he showed it to Ben, and to Erwin Stein who was also giving him lessons. Ben suggested several revisions which I made. After six months the finished script was in Oldham's hands.

But by this time a change had come over him. His bumptious confidence disappeared. When I met him in London he was on the verge of a nervous breakdown. Whereas he had previously written with facility, he now found it impossible to compose a single bar. This aggravated his condition. It may have been the original cause. He left his wife. A complete breakdown occurred which his friends were unable to arrest. The opera remained unwritten; after failing to obtain psychological help, he took refuge in the Catholic Church.

After Arthur Oldham's nervous collapse, he took a job as a sweeper at Broadcasting House. Rose Marie visited him there; she had become his Godmother since his conversion to Catholicism. He was happy doing this manual work and agreed that some other composer should set my libretto. When I met Gottfried von Einem in Salzburg with George, for the première of *Der Prozess*, he had asked me if I would write a comedy with him, so naturally I sent him the libretto of *Christopher Sly*. But nothing came of that. I next turned to Lennox Berkeley, who did not want to write an opera at that time. It was then that George suggested that I should meet Thomas Eastwood, a pupil of Blacher, who had recently retired from the British Council in Berlin to take up full-time composition. We met at Orme Square. I was immediately struck by his diffidence. It seemed too deliberate to be genuine. He decided to set *Christopher Sly*. This was the first of a long list of operas for which George had played midwife.

I ran into Roy Campbell in a pub near where Wyndham Lewis lived. We had not met before, though we had had some correspondence at the time I had edited *Townsman*. I liked his verse, especially the South African lyrics and though I didn't subscribe to his political views, I admired his independence and the way he refused to mount the left-wing bandwaggon which rolled so remorselessly through the so-called intellectual life of London in the forties. Campbell was a large man and aggressively aware of his masculinity. It was almost as if he had invented it, though I dare say he had to pay some royalties to Ernest Hemingway.

After we'd drunk a few highballs in the Notting Hill Gate saloon, he took me off to his flat nearby. He strode down Church Street like a figure from a wild Western film. I expected to see his bronco tethered waiting for him. His flat was in a sedate terrace house. He led me upstairs to his room, which overlooked the street. He had a trestle table by the window, but there was only one kitchen chair. I sat on it, he stood. The floor was bare without linoleum or carpet. On the floor was a sleeping bag and one or two pieces of camping equipment.

252

"Yes, that's where I sleep," Campbell told me. "I'm used to roughing it on the Veldt. I sleep better on the boards."

I was reminded of the games of make-believe I had played as a child with the old man who had lived next door.

It was easy to laugh at Campbell's open-air romanticism until one pondered how many illusions one carried around oneself. I once met a London bus driver who endured the tedium of driving a No. 11 to Liverpool Street by believing he was in control of a chariot drawn by ten Arabs. Most of us are as far from reality as we can get.

At this time Hans Keuls, my agent in Amsterdam, arranged a broadcast from Radio Hilversum of *This Way to the Tomb*. When we met to discuss this, he asked me if I would adapt a German play that had been written around the trial of Cardinal Mindszenti. He gave me a literal translation of the original. I found myself fascinated by two things in it. Firstly, by a minor character in the play, a spiv; I was also intrigued by the scene in which the Cardinal was brainwashed by the Russian Commissar before his trial. This scene struck me as strangely authentic. The actual name of the drug used on the Cardinal was given: sodium pentathol. I told Keuls that I would be willing to adapt the play if the author of the original would allow me to enlarge the character of the spiv. Keuls liked my idea, and asked me to accompany him to Amsterdam to meet the author. He was apparently a refugee from Germany. We found him living in a suburb of Amsterdam. He agreed to my suggestion of enlarging the character of the spiv. I then asked him why he had made the mistake of naming an actual chemical in the brain-washing scene when some critic would be sure to seize on it as an inaccuracy.

"But it is this chemical that was used," he said.

"How do you know?"

"I was a chemist."

As soon as I returned home, I wrote to the Press, to state that sodium pentathol, which could be bought at any chemists' shop without prescription, had these dangerous effects. The newspaper did not print my letter. I phoned the editor. He told me that if they did so, they would be breaking the law which makes it an offence to give knowledge which might lead to a criminal act.

I returned to Devon and wrote the play, but while Keuls was trying to get a star for the part of Mindszenti, another play also called *The Cardinal* and based on Mindzsenti, was produced; consequently my adaptation remained unstaged for several years. Eventually a production took to the roads. We opened in Leeds. The tour wandered round the provinces for a few weeks, but failed to find a West End theatre. Meanwhile, Keuls, in his enthusiasm, had sent my script to the Pope. He returned it with his Papal blessing. We still did not find a theatre.

Anna and I had written to each other two or three times a week throughout the winter. However my letters began, they always ended by my trying to persuade her to come over to England for a holiday. But she had a husband, a child and her career: she was either rehearsing a play or taking one out on tour. Her letters urged me to find some excuse to get myself to Italy: but I had none: no play of mine was being presented there. I could have manufactured some need to go, but thinking a genuine reason would shortly arise, I waited for this opportunity. I wrote and told her I couldn't afford the fare: she sent me a money box. Our letters continued: a feeling that was based only on a brief look between us, not that it ever resides on anything more durable or substantial.

Then one day in the late spring, I received a note from her saying that it was no use my pleading with her to come over because she could not, but she was sending a present over to me which she'd asked a girl friend to deliver. She told me her name and said she was a schoolteacher.

"Do please go up to London and meet her," she wrote. "She's an old friend of mine, quite pretty and you'll find her most interesting. I've told her to call you at Orme Lane next Tuesday afternoon about five o'clock. I hope that's convenient? You'll be able to give her tea. At any rate, I hope you'll enjoy the present."

I was annoyed. The idea of rushing up to London to give tea to an Italian schoolteacher who was quite pretty and whom I might find interesting, didn't please me. But to do less would have been discourteous to Anna. I assumed her present was some books of Italian poetry. It must have been June because I remember sweating in the train going up to London, and buying cherries at the station.

The cottage was dusty and untidy. Neither Rose Marie nor I had been up to London for several weeks. I found myself dusting, then going across to the house to borrow some milk and bread from Marion. George asked me what had dragged me to London in this heat. I replied testily that I had come to London to give tea to some schoolmistress from Italy.

"She must be very beautiful," he said.

"I've never met her."

"There's something fishy in this," he commented. "I've never known you so hospitable to foreign tourists."

"She's a friend of a friend of mine," I snorted, "but I shall need rescuing after an hour, so come over for a drink and then we'll go to a play or something."

This was agreed. With my line of escape secure, I continued to tidy up the cottage and put a kettle on. Then I went up to the landing on the stairs and amused myself by seeing if I could spot a typical Italian schoolteacher coming along round the corner from Bark Place.

I noticed a very plain girl with mousy hair and a large handbag approaching and fearfully waited for her to ring the bell. But fortunately she passed by. Then at about ten to five I saw a very beautiful girl with black hair and a scarlet dress approaching some distance off on the other side of the road. If only this were her, I thought, but I could hardly have expected Anna to be so generous or foolish as that. As the girl approached nearer the cottage I saw her put on a pair of dark glasses. But there was no hope that this would be her. And as she approached the door she seemed to lower her glasses down and glance towards it. But I must have imagined that. For no bell rang and she passed by. I continued to peer up the road in the direction of Bark Place, trying to pick out a schoolteacher, when suddenly the bell rang. I had seen nobody approach. They must have come from the opposite direction. I ran down the few stairs and opened the door. The girl with the scarlet dress stood there. She smiled. I was speechless. She took off her dark glasses. It was Anna.

"Aren't you going to ask me in?" she said.

"Didn't you walk by a minute or so ago?"

"Yes, I wasn't sure which was your house. So I came a few minutes early. I wanted to arrive at the stroke of five. Now I want my tea."

I took her hands. Her eyes danced gaily.

"Are you pleased with my present?" she asked.

"It's the best I've ever had in my life," I said. "I was completely surprised. I was really expecting a schoolteacher."

"Oh, I've several lessons to give you," she laughed. "To begin with, you shouldn't leave dustpans on the table you're going to serve tea on."

"And any others?"

"Plenty."

Then suddenly we both felt riveted with shyness, both wanting to embrace yet neither daring to indicate it. After all, apart from our letters, we'd only met three times: once at a party in Rome, then in an hotel, and another time as she stood beneath a Botticelli. And each time with her husband present. For five minutes we stirred tea and teased each other's eyes. She told me she'd arrived the day before and had gone to an hotel where she'd asked the porter the way to Orme Square, only to find that by some coincidence she'd been sent to an hotel only twenty yards from the square itself.

"So you're just around the corner?" I said, thinking that it wouldn't be far to carry her suitcase round.

She'd read my thoughts easily for they were her own.

"Yes, I shall be quite comfortable there." She puckered her nose in a tease.

This day was one of the happiest days of my life. I indulge myself remembering every detail of it: our shyness, my awkwardness: it is all precious to me. Even the incident of my hair...

After a few minutes of embarrassment, we abandoned our tea in the dining room. I had suggested that we went to the sitting room. This entailed going upstairs. But we never got up them...The staircase carried some of my collection of Gaudier which I had started when Pound had given me four of his drawings. While going up the stairs, I had been unable to restrain my admiration for her. We had ended embraced on the stairs. When our lips and tongues had tired, I had lain with my head in her lap...forgetting

256

that because I had been bathing in the sea the day before, I had put some olive oil on my hair to counteract the salt. When I moved my head then, a great dark stain showed on her lovely scarlet silk dress. It was obviously a new and very expensive dress, bought especially for our meeting.

"It's ruined," I said hopelessly.

"No, it is stained by your head. I shan't let anybody clean that mark off."

I doubted that. But the average girl would have been justly annoyed and shown it too. Anna was exceptional. She made even that little memory endurable.

When we eventually reached the sitting room and she had, as women do, explored the other rooms and paused to observe a photo of Rose Marie in the bedroom, I remembered that I had arranged an escape by asking George to come over. It was now necessary to think of an escape from this escape. I suggested that we went out to dinner and a play. She seemed a little puzzled by my pressing that idea, especially as it appeared that I had been intent on getting her elsewhere. But she agreed.

"I'll have to go round to my hotel to change," she said, smiling fondly at the enormous dark stain.

I scribbled a note for George: "Extra Tutorial," then walked round to her hotel and waited downstairs while she went up to change.

I can't remember what was the play we saw. I don't remember where we had supper. But I do recall vividly the happiness of being with her. Nor have I any recollection of what we talked about. I'm sure neither of us listened. Words are wasted when eyes are as articulate as hers were. I have memorised every question and answer they gave. And if I could paint I could still quote them honestly.

After supper I took her back to Orme Lane in a taxi wondering whether she would spend the night with me. I have never been able to hide my feelings. My face is probably the most articulate thing about me. She knew that I wanted her and I could tell our desire was mutual. Indeed we were so aware of it we were both frightened by it. If we had been only casually interested in each other we would probably have been capable of a casual affair and jumped into bed there and then. When people feel something like indifference for each other it can act as an aphrodisiac; it drives them to the act to spite the feelings they resent because they no longer have them; but intense passion can have the opposite effect: imposing a restraint which looks almost like chastity. And so, after giving her a drink, I walked round to her hotel and left her in the foyer.

Immediately I got back to the cottage, I phoned Rose Marie in Devon. She asked me if the schoolteacher had delivered the present from Anna.

"Yes."

"And what was it?"

"Anna."

"Mind how you undo the string. Where is she now?"

"An hotel round the corner."

"Not very hospitable of you. I shouldn't like you for a boy-friend..."

With stupendous naïveté, I congratulated myself that Rose Marie wasn't jealous and appropriately fell into a deep, child-like and untroubled sleep.

If Anna or I had resolved to remain faithful, as the world knows faith, if would have been difficult enough. As it was, we had no resolution and even the weather conspired against us. There was a heatwave, the air was languid and sensuous. The cottage was empty, her hotel was available; my wife was in Devon, her husband in Sicily. It was desire which kept us apart. We both knew that once we succumbed we would be lost to it. So for three days we busied ourselves shopping, talking for three hours over lunch and going to plays, only to walk out of them and wander aimlessly through the Park, not even daring to hold hands. It was not that I had asked nor she refused. Our need was so articulate in our veins, we could not talk of it except in silence. And to avoid hearing the shout from each other's eyes, we both wore sunglasses. But I did not merely want her, I wanted to know her. I was happy discovering such things about her passion for Piccalilli pickle, her aversion for fish, her extravagance with shoes and her several fastidious habits.

One afternoon as we strolled through St James's Park after

258

she had been shopping, I was chiding her on the way she squandered money.

"Have you always spent money like this?" I asked her.

"Yes," she said, "I get rid of it quickly because I hate money. It once hurt me so badly."

She told me that as a child she'd been brought up in Milan. Her father was an engineer. She herself had been sent to a convent.

"The important thing about my childhood was that I spent most of it longing to own a gramophone. Every birthday and Christmas I hoped to be given one only to be disappointed. My father always said he couldn't afford it. But eventually he said he would buy me a gramophone for my seventeenth birthday. I spent a year counting the days. When the day arrived I went into the sitting room and there it was: with a big horn and records beside it. I was enraptured with it and played it all the morning, then I had to go out to see a relative. I hurried home to get back to my gramophone. But when I ran into the room, two men were there carrying it out into the hall. My father's cheque for it had not been met by the bank...Maybe it sounds silly, but I vowed to myself then, that I would earn a lot of money in order to throw it away to prove I despised it for hurting me so much. The reason I work so hard is to revenge my gramophone."

Her story touched me. This was something I could understand. And thinking of her gramophone we walked into the cottage and almost sadly went upstairs to the sitting room. We talked for a few minutes and then I went downstairs to make some tea. When I carried the tray in I noticed that while I'd been downstairs she'd found an old silk dressing-gown of mine and put it on. I put the tray down, and as I did so I saw her clothes on a chair.

"I put this on because undressing is such an awkward thing to do." I turned. She was standing near to me. "And you see how easy it is to take a dressing-gown off me."

I carried her nakedness into the bedroom.

"We're too out-of-breath to make love," she said, "but if we don't we will suffocate for the lack of it."

Anna had met Peter Ustinov in Rome. One evening soon after she arrived, he asked her to go to a play and have supper with him. I did not know Ustinov myself then, and so I said I would have dinner somewhere and then go back to the cottage in Orme Lane and wait for her in bed. She said she would try not to be too late and threatened to wake me as soon as she arrived "if you dare to be asleep".

My evening alone bored me. At midnight I was in bed petulantly waiting for Anna's return. By one o'clock I was impatiently listening for her taxi to stop at the corner, feigning sleep with each one only to find it had been a false alarm. By two o'clock tiredness must have doused both my ardour and my anxiety and I must have dozed for an hour with one ear cocked for the sound of her cab. But somehow I must have missed this or Ustinov may have dropped her and as I had not been listening for an ordinary car I had not heard it pull up. For I could hear her moving about downstairs. Then I heard her come up the stairs and open the bedroom door. The light didn't go on. She was always considerate. I listened to her moving about the room.

"Hurry up, love," I said drowsily from the depths of my pillow, "just get out of those clothes and jump in here."

And she made no reply, I leant back and reached out from the bed to try and grab her. Instead of clutching her silk undies I found I was holding a fistful of something thick. Her coat?

"Do hurry up and get undressed and get into bed," I cried, then, my hand still holding her coat, I identified the material. It was serge. Higher up my fingers ran into a brass button.

I opened my eyes. An enormous tubby policeman stood above me. Then his torch shone full in my face.

"Thank you for the invitation, sir," he said solemnly, "but tired as I am, I'm on duty."

"I was expecting a young lady," I blustered somewhat needlessly.

"Quite so, sir. I'm not here to deputise for her. I came in because your front door was wide open and we've had a few burglaries in this district recently."

"I'm sorry, constable," I said. "It's my fault. I left the door ajar because I'd forgotten to give my latchkey to my friend."

"I understand, sir," he said. "I'll get along now and I'll leave the door ajar—so she can get in."

About fifteen minutes later I heard Ustinov's sports car draw up at the cottage. And within a minute heard Anna undressing in the sitting room. She was always considerate. Then she pranced naked into the room and dived into bed.

"Wake up," she commanded.

"Yes, constable," I said, turning her towards me. Half an hour later she asked me why I kept calling her "constable".

"Do I make love like a policewoman?"

"No," I said. "I was thinking of a policeman." After this remark I had to do some reassuring.

As I have admitted, I am a coffee addict. Without it I become irritable. Anna knew of this, and soon after she returned to Rome she wrote and told me that she was sending over, by a friend, a small Espresso coffee machine so that I could make it for myself. Weeks elapsed, and I forgot the matter. But then one day, a girl telephoned me at Orme Lane to say that she had brought the coffee machine over, had called at the cottage, and finding no one there, had taken it away again.

When, she asked, could she call to hand over Anna's gift? I was returning that day to Devon, and asked her to ring the following week when I would be back. She did so, and arranged to call at the cottage the next day with the machine. I forgot the appointment. She had to post it to me. A week later I received a letter from Anna, saying that she hoped I liked one present, but was surprised I did not bother to acknowledge the other gift she had sent.

"It was Gina Lollobrigida I sent over with the coffee pot," she wrote. And she wasn't joking. Never have I been so careless.

Part Five

But to have done instead of not doing
this is not vanity

THE German poet, Rudolf Alexander Schroeder, had translated *This Way to the Tomb*, and it was his version I had seen staged in Berlin. He had also translated *Stratton* act by act as I had written, and then rewritten it. I had not met him myself: Eliot had found the German publisher for the play and had asked Schroeder to do the translation. He had told me that he was a considerable poet in his own right, and I had been grateful for the introduction. Peter Suhrkamp, the publisher of both plays, wrote to me and asked me to attend the opening of *Stratton* at Bochum. I refused: the English production had distressed me so much that I did not feel I could bear to see the play again in any language. But he wrote again saying that Schroeder, who was an old man, had agreed to attend in the hope of meeting me. As I was not unaware of the compliment a man of his reputation had done me by translating my work, I agreed to go on condition Rose Marie came too, to fortify me against the disasters I anticipated whenever this play was staged.

We flew to Düsseldorf. Herr Schalla, the Director of the Theatre, who had produced the play, and Herr Skopnik, the Chief Dramaturg, met us at the airport. Schalla apologised to me for having rehearsed *Stratton* for only seven weeks. I did not tell him it was our habit to throw a new play onto the stage after three weeks. I went to their dress rehearsal with some trepidation: the two English productions had undermined my own faith in the play. But I was surprised: the play worked. All it had needed was actors: Martin Held played Stratton convincingly; Eva-Katherina Schultz was brilliant as Katherine; Herr Schalla himself as Courtenay was almost as good as Michael Hordern had been in the original English production. The production itself was faithful without being fussy, and imaginative without gimmicks. The first night the play was very well received. The

Mayor gave a banquet. Germany treats English playwrights with extraordinary respect. Knowing how little you are regarded at home, you feel almost an impostor there.

We stayed on a few days in the Ruhr because I became interested in Holsteins and went round several farms looking at this splendid breed.

Some weeks after returning to England, I learned that *Stratton* was proving a great success in Germany. This fact had an incredible sequel. The following winter an English management, looking for successful Continental plays to bring to London, actually approached me with the suggestion that I should translate a play called *Stratton* into English. I suppose I should have accepted this commission and made an easy fee? But I foolishly sent them the translation by return post. And, by making somebody look a fool, made another enemy. Of course this company dropped the project when they learned that they had not discovered the new Continental playwright called Rudolf Alexander Schroeder and that his original was only me. But I was grateful to this management. The incident often helped me. I savoured it again whenever I was in danger of treating the English theatre seriously. This illusion became less frequent. *Stratton* had been a failure in England and a success in Germany. The failure had hurt me; I now had to try to become indifferent to its success. It was the same play: the success or failure of a play was something I could not control. I realised sadly that it had very little to do with the quality of the work. For an artist, this realisation comes as a kind of grief. For a salesman of mass-produced bras or Y-fronted briefs, this fact is a relief: they know anything will sell if it is pushed hard enough. The difference is the business man is interested in sales, the artist in responses.

I was at this time, as the world knows success, successful. But it became meaningless to me for I saw that the quality of my work had absolutely nothing to do with it. *This Way to the Tomb* had run for a year. But I knew that it had been about to be withdrawn after fourteen performances when Beverley Baxter wrote it up in the *Evening Standard* and then filled the theatre for a year. It was his article, not my play, that brought the audience to the theatre. Without this publicity, *This Way to the Tomb* would have been a commercial flop. I could not avoid the conclusion that, in the theatre, talent counts for 10 per cent. and publicity for 90 per cent. What is worse, publicity is more effective without there being any talent to inhibit it. *The Eagle has Two Heads* had run for eighteen months and earned over £40,000 for the backers. But here again, I saw that this was due not to any quality in the play itself, but to the accident of its obtaining sufficient hoo-ha in the Press. This occurred because we had had to cast an unknown comedienne in a tragic role. Consequently the critics had their copy written for them: they could discover a great new star: they did so. In fact, few liked the play or even commented intelligently about it either way. I saw stars created because they owned large dogs and a profile: I observed good actors ignored because they were too serious or modest to stick their arse into the Press. I reread the criticism when Schubert's *Songs* had first been performed in London. After which it is not possible to take bad notices seriously—or good notices either.

What does the theatre mean by success? The answer is it measures success or failure by the number of bums seated. A successful play is one which runs. Now that it costs about £6,000 to stage a play and £2,000 per week to pay the expenses, a play is considered a failure unless it can run for about six months. *Hamlet* ran for two performances. *Othello* had only one.

It seems unreasonable to expect good plays to compete with the values which are applied to the merchandising of refrigerators. After all, these measures are not applied to a composer. Nobody expects a new quartet or symphony to run for one hundred consecutive performances, or calls it a flop if it doesn't. But in this country, the dramatist has to measure to the criteria which are applied to the vending of cornflakes. And whether his play achieves this sales figure or not, has, he must realise, little or nothing to do with what's in the packet but how it has been wrapped up.

Voicing these sad conclusions at this time, some people tried to cheer me up by such silly bromides as "quality counts in the end"; "the public can't be fooled"; "in the end, it's the play that counts". I disagreed. I still do so. We live in an age where fashion counts for taste. There are not one hundred people in this country who will risk making an artistic judgement without reference to other people's. It used to amuse me to test this. I would go to a new play and ask a friend whether he or she had liked it.

"Well," they would say, waiting to see how the cat would jump, "quite...in some ways."

"I thought it was brilliant..." I would say.

"Yes, it was, wasn't it?"

"...for the first five minutes, after which it was putrid."

"Yes, it was, wasn't it?"

And so on. With perverse morbidity I would persist in this game of assessing people's critical faculties. I used to invent a new composer or a new novelist and go around London talking about Jarvis Raxton's masterpiece *The Late Bradbury*. Within four days this unwritten novel used to be recommended to me by starry-eyed readers of the *New Statesman* who assured me that "Raxton had something and that they'd found his prose very penetrating".

On other occasions, I would impress the musical élite with my favourite composer, Ralkinov, a pupil of Shostakovich. None of these sensitive ears noticed that Ralkinov's suite was, in fact, *Eine kleine Nachtmusik* recorded at $33\frac{1}{3}$ and played at 78.

I once read a new poem by Eliot to the Contemporary Arts Society in Dover Street. The poem was much praised. What I had read was the first two lines of each paragraph in the last year's leading articles from *The Times*. I found it increasingly difficult to take the artistic judgements around me with anything less than hilarity. My success seemed nothing but a joke. A pity that the same sense of humour cannot equally well diminish my sense of "failure" now that fashion has farted in my face...

At that time I used to spend many hours arguing with George about my conclusions concerning an artist's reputation being quite unrelated to his merit. We never agreed. He would always try to assure me that "genius always got through in the end". Naturally he could name those who had; but I, for similar obvious reasons, could not list those whose identity had been lost for ever. I would remind him that only the accident of Sullivan putting his hat on the top of a cupboard which, when he went to retrieve it, brought down a large chunk of unpublished Schubert, brought this composer through. And I would ask whether similar accidents could be relied upon to rescue genius from the obscurity which lack of publicity or commercial success would necessarily impress on them? He would argue that a man of genius always persisted until he emerged. My answer to this was that second-rate talents could perhaps tolerate the rat-race, but the first-rate would "sing high and aloof, free from the wolf's black maws and the dull ass's hoof". We never agreed on this. But to be more constructive, we both used to spend many hours trying to think up ways and means of staging one of Schubert's unperformed operas. He wrote fourteen.

One night dining with George at Orme Square, he had told me that he'd been to Marlborough House to see his grandmother who had a chill. I don't know why, but I was concerned. I had only had three or four brief encounters with her, and these had not gone exactly smoothly; but somehow or other, I had nothing less than an affection for her. Perhaps it was because I was grateful to her for having squeezed her well-corseted figure into the uncomfortable stalls of the barn-like Mercury Theatre to see *This Way to the Tomb*, and also for trundling out to the colonies of Hammersmith again to see *The Eagle has Two Heads* at the Lyric Theatre in the first week of its presentation. And like everybody else in the theatre, I knew of many occasions where her genuine interest and presence had helped to prop up a production, or revive interest in a flagging run. I would not have been touched if Her Majesty had only attended Gala performances, but this wasn't the case. There wasn't a try-out theatre or a converted garage anywhere in London at which, at sometime or other, the House Manager hadn't to bustle round awaiting her presence.

"We ought to do something for her," I said aloud, "before it's too late."

"Such as what?" George asked.

"I mean she's helped the theatre so much we ought to make some sort of gesture to her in return."

"Yes, she'd be touched by that."

A day or two later it occurred to me that it might be a good idea if Britten wrote an opera to be performed on her birthday. But I dropped this notion because it was not broad enough based to allow all facets of the theatre to contribute to it. At any rate, George agreed that she would appreciate some sort of Gala to be given on her next birthday. It was, of course, to be a surprise. It meant there was only a few months to organise it.

My first move was to ask Sir Bronson Albery to lunch. He was enthusiastic and immediately offered the New Theatre. With a date and a theatre fixed, I started to sketch a programme. I divided the evening into three parts: opera, plays and ballet. This I thought would allow everybody to contribute something, or at least make it representative of all types of theatre.

Of course, Ben agreed to write whatever I thought would be appropriate. "But do give me at least a month," he said.

Drama didn't seem too easy to fix. I couldn't think of a suitable contemporary one-act play, and obviously as I was organising the evening I couldn't sit down and write anything myself. I went round to the Globe Theatre to talk the problem over with John Gielgud.

"I'll do whatever you like," he said, "but for this occasion I don't think you should have me alone, but Olivier too."

"Think of a play where you could appear together," I said hopelessly, "and a one-act play at that."

There was a long pause.

"If you can persuade Larry to play Caesar," Gielgud said, "I'll play Cassius. We could do an act of that."

It was a good idea and, at the time, a generous one too. Gielgud was the first actor in the profession, Olivier was fast becoming it. So I wrote to Olivier and told him of Gielgud's offer. He replied by asking us both out to lunch. After a course during which we'd talked of nothing but jewellery because his wife had given him an extraordinary slim pocket watch, I could see that Gielgud himself wasn't going to broach Olivier.

"Will you agree to play Caesar to John's Cassius?" I asked him, very much aware that I, who'd never cast a play, had skidded into the deep end.

"If you say so," he said, "but I hope you realise you're going to make yourself the most hated man in the theatre."

"Why?" I was genuinely bewildered.

"Because you can't ask everybody," he said. "They'll never forgive you."

With everything agreed the rest of the meal passed gaily. Then as we were having our coffee, Olivier turned almost affectionately to me and said:

"But tell me, Ronnie, what are you writing now?"

"I'm getting on with that play."

"What play?"

"Don Juan..."

"Don Juan? Why pick that subject? Shaw's done it, and Arnold Bennett has too."

For a second I thought he must be joking. I looked at him incredulously. There was no tease there.

"But we discussed it. It was almost your idea. Don't you remember suggesting I should turn the play on unfulfilled love?"

Olivier glanced questioningly at Gielgud as if to say "is he often taken like this?"

Gielgud studied his coffee cup.

Embarrassed, Olivier leant back in his chair and gave a forced laugh.

"I must say that would be a joke, wouldn't it?" he said. "Think of it. Actor gives poet idea for a play. Would make quite a story."

Gielgud continued to stare fixedly at his cup. I stirred mine. I could think of nothing to say. Olivier alone enjoyed his joke. As I had been working on the play for three months, I didn't think he was particularly funny.

He was unaware of my distress and immediately went back to discussing the casting of Caesar.

Discouraged to the point of nausea, I went home. As usual I told Rose Marie what had torpedoed me. As usual she put on her diving suit to try and re-float the wreck. The play, three-quarters finished, lay on my desk. I closed the manuscript book.

The next day, realising that the New Theatre wasn't going to be big enough for the Gala, I asked David Webster to lunch. He immediately offered the Royal Opera House and his office, too, to do all the paper work.

With these arrangements made we returned to Devon. But I was too depressed by Olivier's behaviour to write. As usual I threw myself into building and renovating a cottage, increasing my debts by profligate use of cement. A few weeks later, Queen Mary died. I wrote an Horatian Ode on her death. Then realising that that was a gesture which belonged to an age which had passed even before she was born, I threw the poem on the fire.

I was very excited when I heard that Stravinsky was composing *The Rake's Progress* and, of course, envious of Auden for having written the libretto. For months I looked forward to hearing the work and followed with amusement Stravinsky's tortuous arrangements about where it would be performed. He had given the rights to two agents, both of whom thought they owned them exclusively. One was Boosey & Hawkes of London, who had published him for many years and who had been negotiating with Covent Garden, and the other was, I believe, Ricordi of Milan who had been trying to secure the work for La Scala. In both cases, the negotiations were near to signature and both opera houses were confident that they had secured the work. By some unhappy accident, the two representatives of these two firms met in Paris and compared notes. Astounded at Stravinsky's deception, they decided to go to Switzerland and confront him together. This they did.

"Maestro," said the representative of Boosey & Hawkes, "I have, on your instructions, been negotiating with Covent Garden."

"While I," said the representative of Ricordi, "have promised the work to La Scala."

"Well, gentlemen," said Stravinsky calmly, "you are in a mess."

He then informed them that he had just accepted an offer from the Fenice Theatre at Venice. I heard many stories of this type about him. He was very fond of money. Like Beethoven, he would never hesitate to sell a work twice. Indeed, I was told at this time that he once went to a music library in Switzerland and persuaded them to lend him one of his own precious manuscripts because, he said, he wished to consult the original and compare it to a later version. The librarian agreed. Stravinsky promised to return the score within a day or two. After several months had elapsed and many letters had been written, the library was forced to send a representative to America to try and retrieve their property. Stravinsky seemed slightly embarrassed at the request. The reason was that he was then in the habit of letting the manuscript out on hire and was making a few dollars on the side. No wonder it was said of him that he signed his name with two parallel strokes through the "S". No doubt the reason for this was that he had once been an emigré, coming out of Russia without even a suit of clothes, having to borrow one for the first performance of *Rite of Spring*.

Nothing would have stopped me from being at the Fenice for *The Rake*. The Harewoods and I flew out and went to rehearsals. I had not seen Stravinsky for fifteen years or so. He was still as dapper as ever, his eyes just corkscrews, giving you the impression that you were the cork. He was staying at the Grunewald, a flashy hotel, with an entourage of relatives. It was a Gala occasion. Everybody who knew nothing about music was there. I don't think more than a dozen were interested in the piece. There is nothing worse than an Italian gala audience. Stravinsky was obviously suffering from the heat as he conducted the piece. The response was enthusiastic. I went to a party at his hotel afterwards. Auden was there, surrounded by the usual first night sycophants. I decided, out of diffidence, not to intrude or go up to him. After all, it was years since we had met. Later I discovered that he had been very hurt that I didn't approach him. How often is it like that?

When I saw the criticisms the next day in the Italian press I decided that I would try to rectify some of it. I phoned London and asked the *Evening Standard* if they would accept an article. I warned them that I regarded the work as a masterpiece.

"You can have 800 words," the editor told me. I rushed into a café and wrote them on innumerable small cable forms which I muddled up, but eventually straightened out. Of course, the article was not printed. Hadn't Beaverbrook told me again and again that what he was interested in was attack?

"Praise makes poor news," he used to say.

I decided to stay on for the second performance. Stravinsky did not conduct. Consequently, at least ten minutes was clipped from the performance. The tempo was improved and a better reaction from the audience achieved. After the performance I went off with Stravinsky to the Fenice Restaurant. I commiserated with him about the notices.

"I think the criticisms were very good," he said, taking something from his pocket. It was his cheque for the first performance.

Rose Marie had never been to Rome. When Anna was in England she had invited us both to stay with her and her husband at their flat there. Rose Marie accepted the invitation. Of course, she knew that Anna was my mistress. But she accepted, not out of connivance at that relationship which didn't appear to distress her, nor as a gesture of confidence in the deep affection between herself and me, but because she wanted to get to Rome and she knew I hated staying in hotels. This was the reason she gave, and both Anna and I knew it to be true. Her lack of jealousy astounded us.

"It is not because she's indifferent to you," Anna used to say, "but because she's so supremely confident of your love. I am merely a gift from her to you. A sort of bunch of flowers on your desk."

"She seems to like you herself."

"I believe she does. My clothes and my career fascinate her. She thinks I have the sophistication and self-confidence which she believes she lacks herself."

Nevertheless when Rose Marie and I arrived in Rome I had some apprehensions. I had no reason to believe that Anna's husband would be as tolerant as Rose Marie. I had seen his rather sullen features in London and had been told that of all men, Sicilians were the most jealous and violent. But Anna had told me not to worry. She had looked forward to our visit. It would have been almost impossible to disappoint her.

Vitaliano Brancati was both a novelist and a playwright. He wrote in the morning and spent the rest of the day in a café in the Via Veneto talking to other writers. In Rome they had managed to hold together some semblance of the men-of-letters society long after it had disappeared in London and Paris. He had greeted our arrival with civility but without enthusiasm. The latter, Anna explained, could never be expected from him. Rose Marie noticed how fond he was of Anna and asked me if he knew of my relationship with his wife.

"I hope not," I said fervently. "I believe Sicilians throw daggers accurately when they feel a vague twinge of jealousy."

Anna's habit was to come in to the room every morning where Rose Marie and I slept and sit on the end of the bed in her dressing gown gossiping. With her husband next door, I was then profoundly grateful for Rose Marie's presence.

The three of us would spend the day showing Rose Marie the sights; picnicking at Frigene or visiting the Caetanis at Ninfa. Brancati kept to his literary cronies. He never gave a sign of resenting my presence or any of the affection Anna showed openly to me. As I'd never heard of a sophisticated Sicilian, I concluded he was a blind fool. But I reached that conclusion without much conviction. He was obviously both intelligent and sensitive. And his affection for, and generosity to, Anna was touching. He was almost paternal in the way he indulged her extravagances which must have been difficult for a writer, even one whose novels sometimes reached the films, to support. But my nervousness about him lessened after a week, and I had no apprehensions when he suggested one evening that he give supper to the three of us in the Piazza di Spagna.

We sat at a table outside watching the fountain. Rose Marie and Anna were very gay. Brancati was quiet. But he usually was. I had learned not to be worried at his reserved manner.

I had ordered some consommé. Floating about on it was some pasta or noodles. I left these on my plate. Brancati observed this.

"Don't you like those things?" he asked me.

"No," I said, turning one of the noodles over idly with my spoon. "I don't like them."

"Strange, I would have thought you would. I would have thought that they would have reminded you of my wife's navel," he remarked with a smile.

I waited for the knife under the table. Neither Rose Marie nor Anna had heard his comment. Brancati ordered some wine. We spent the rest of the meal discussing the novels of Henry James.

He never referred to my appreciation of any part of his wife again. But what he had done was to tell me that he knew and that I wasn't to mistake his tolerance for ignorance.

"I suppose I'm a gift from him to you," I told Anna, reporting his remark to her later. "A sort of bunch of weeds on your dressing table?"

"We're very lucky, darling," she'd said.

I agreed uncomprehendingly, expecting some axe to fall. But it didn't. When Rose Marie and I left Rome for Rapallo, Brancati was genuinely sorry to see us leave. I arranged to meet Anna in Paris a fortnight later where I was taking Rose Marie to see the Covent Garden production of *Peter Grimes*, which was being staged there.

I used to see Eliot frequently when I went up to London, either about my own work or about Ezra's predicament. We used to meet either in his office at Russell Square where we had tea, or for lunch, generally at the Étoile in Charlotte Street or at the Garrick Club. On one of these occasions I had gone up from Devon especially to meet him at the Étoile. Our appointment was for one o'clock. Eliot was always too polite to be unpunctual, so by 1.15 I began to worry. I telephoned his office and was told that Eliot had sent me a telegram that morning postponing our lunch. I had, of course, left Devon before the telegram arrived. So I phoned Rose Marie from the restaurant and asked her to read it to me.

"Sorry can't make today's lunch. Have got to bury a woman. Tom."

I made Rose Marie repeat the last sentence. It seemed odd and so out of character. While I lunched alone I pondered why Eliot hadn't phrased it "have to attend a funeral". The matter puzzled me.

When we did lunch together a day or two later, he apologised for not keeping the first appointment. But gave no explanation. This was too aggravating of him.

"Did you, er...bury the woman?" I asked.

"Yes," he said, "I buried her. Now what shall we have to eat? I think I'll try some smoked trout."

No further mention was made of her identity.

Eliot was unusually relaxed during the meal, almost gay at times. But while he chattered on, I had dark thoughts about the burial of the woman. I noticed that he was wearing a black tie. I would, of course, have pressed most of my friends. But even at his most relaxed, Eliot had some kind of reserve about him which forbade any intrusion into his privacy, unless he volunteered it. This he frequently did with me. But not on this occasion.

A week or two later, I was playing chess with Ashley Dukes, an old friend of Eliot's, in the Garrick, and I showed him the mysterious telegram.

"It was his wife," Ashley had said.

"We'll have to do something about poor Tom," Ashley said to me a month or two later. "I'm getting very worried about him." He went on to say that he thought that what Eliot needed was the "love of a good woman, twenty years younger, preferably French."

"He's over sixty," I said.

"So am I," Ashley had replied defensively, "but I go to my mistress once a week and still walk from Notting Hill Gate to the Garrick every day."

But I did not think Ashley's diagnosis was correct, though Possum's subsequent marriage and the happiness he achieved proved that he was. My own idea at that time was that Eliot's sadness was much more complicated than that. I had noticed it when I had met him first in 1937. On that occasion I had been impressed by three attributes of his. His sad eyes, which remained sad even when he smiled, and his immaculate white collar and carefully manicured hands. He was the very antithesis of a Bohemian poet, so much like a family solicitor that whenever I visited him at Faber's I had difficulty in overcoming my feeling that I was back in my youth visiting my Trustees.

I had, I realised, only seen Eliot let himself go on one occasion. That was when Ezra's father-in-law had died and his wife Dorothy had been reckless enough to ask Ezra to come over to London from Rapallo and dispose of her father's flat. Ezra's way of dealing with the contents was to give it away to his friends. I and Wyndham Lewis had done very well out of this and a great deal of the furniture that Rose Marie and I had at West Mill derived from this incongruous source.

One day I had gone to this Kensington flat to pick up the Gaudier drawings that Ezra had generously given me. I had passed an armchair going down the stairs which had Wyndham Lewis beneath it. When the maid opened the door of the flat I heard a fruity baritone coming from the dining room. I went in. Ezra and Eliot had been lunching together and the latter was singing a bawdy ballad most energetically. As I had interrupted him he started the song again. Ezra had found some bottles of Piesporter amongst his father-in-laws' effects. Eliot had drunk this sufficiently to release a part of himself which I had never seen. An evening or two before, Ezra had shown me a photograph of a night-club singer wearing little but whalebone corsets and had remarked that "this was the girl who sang somewhere in Chelsea to whose club I took Possum knowing that the occasion would probably bump some poem out of him. It did."

> ...whose uncorseted bust
> Gave promise of pneumatic bliss.

Somehow I had doubted the veracity of Ezra's story in spite of the evidence of the photograph, but the song I had heard made me realise that there was a side to Possum which made this story probable though now remote. We spent the afternoon going through the books belonging to Ezra which he had left in the flat and I had arranged to take Ezra that evening to the first performance of Stravinsky's *Jeu de Cartes* in the Queen's Hall. I had borrowed my sister's tiny Morris car and Eliot climbed into the back and Ezra and I drove off to meet Rose Marie. About fifteen minutes later we heard Eliot remark that "you have now taken me sufficiently far out of my way, perhaps you will let me out here."

Years later when editing Rochester's bawdy poems I had compared one of them to the ballad that I had heard Eliot sing. He not only denied knowing the ballad, but singing it, and even went so far as to say he had never had lunch with Ezra in the flat at all. He was so adamant and offended by my suggestion that I wondered whether I had dreamed up the whole incident. It was easy to check. I wrote and asked Ezra. He replied by sending the words of the ballad.

Eliot had repressed so much of himself that he had even erased the memory of this incident from his mind. I had thought the Nobel Prize would help. He did not need money, and his Puritan conscience prevented him from giving himself any luxury. But his chest was bad: every winter he suffered from it.

"You will be able to get away more now into the sun and escape the November fogs," I told him.

"Where?" he asked.

"Spain or the West Indies?" I suggested.

"I couldn't bear the company."

I sometimes get a malevolent pleasure in describing other people graphically and unkindly. Some of these epithets stick. When Rose Marie was in her graceful twenties I described her efforts to clamber over the rocks on Welcombe beach as a "blancmange negotiating a toastrack." It's only fair that I should apply the same descriptive aptitudes to myself.

I am an animated ink blob. At school, I was made to be very self-conscious about my height: I was called "titch". I feared I was a dwarf. I once complained to my mother about this teasing and her advice was typical. "Tell them that poison is always in small bottles." I did precisely that. This attitude helped me to appear less vulnerable. But when nobody was looking I did stretching exercises and used to hang by my arms from the top of a door till one day somebody came and shut it, flinging the diminutive yogi to the floor with damaged fingers. Consequently I abandoned such rigours and settled for 5' 2", consoling myself that this was taller than Schubert and Keats. Even so, as this paragraph reveals, I still think that my lack of height is my most predominant feature. And I avoid looking at my reflection in the shop windows when I hurry down a street.

As to my colouring: I am so dark that I can feel faint yet receive no sympathy. Many have suggested, not quite behind my back, that I have a touch of the tar brush. I have always been pleased when people have remarked that I don't look English. But have felt irritated when they have assumed that I have just returned from

Davos when I have in fact not left the reading lamp on my desk.

My hair is still black, though I'm now told that I am fifty-two. True, there are a few grey hairs here and there to be seen now that I have had to cease pulling them out, because my dislike of growing grey is countered by the greater terror of being bald. That would be an indignity I do not think I could endure.

As to my features, my face hides behind my nose which, like a rock, sticks out into the ocean of vacuity about me. The mouth is small, the lips are thin: a feeble barrier for the wild and virulent tongue within. The chin is weak, oh, very weak. The ears? What extraordinary things ears are. I'd never looked at mine before. A pity they don't house some succulent crustacean. It would seem appropriate if a prawn were to emerge from their crenellated coral. This head is heavy, its weight has rounded my shoulders. My hands are like paws: the fingers stubby: nothing artistic about them. I could never have been either a pianist or a pickpocket. My body is slim, wiry, hairless and agile: I still feel I could get into any bed or out of any gaol. The skin looks as if it had been in the sun when it hasn't. Not a single hair on my chest. Hemingway would have despised me. But it is smooth and without blemishes. I've never had to bear the embarrassment of a pimple. But clearly my best feature is my feet. They are so narrow: I have always had to wear handmade shoes. The toes are straight, not turned in: I can pick up a cigarette with them. But beautiful feet are no more of an asset nowadays than a beautiful tail.

Why have I forgotten to mention my eyes? Because I know they are me. They are sad eyes. When my tongue is cruel, my eyes show pity. When my lips laugh, my eyes are still unsmiling. They are not sad because of what they see but because of what they've seen. I've always felt that my eyes were lent to me; that they themselves had looked before at sights I was seeing for the first time. Perhaps I borrowed them from the Wandering Jew? I'm sure they had felt remorse before I had experienced regret. I'm sure they had loved before I had even admired. I know they had grieved before I had mourned. These eyes of mine seldom weep because they have few tears left to shed. But sometimes I have known them shed one or two inexplicably when this dwarf that encloses them temporarily was believing he was being gay.

Even so, in spite of my indulging in this self-portrait you still do not know what I look like. You could not identify me. I will make it easy for you. Take a look at the Spanish bullfighter, the late Manolete. I was mistaken for him many times in Madrid, even by his close friends. We were doubles except in courage and grace. The likeness was even to the eyes.

If I were a painter and was drawing a self-portrait I would just draw my eyes and leave the rest of the canvas blank. Nothing important would be missing.

What would become of me if I went blind? The fear shadows me. I almost shake when I think of the bravery of the blind. My concern for my sight and my obsession with my eyes makes it difficult for me to write a poem without some image or metaphor about them not appearing.

> *I dare not close my eyes for fear of seeing you,*
> *nor open them to know you are not there.*

I had not seen Anna for some months. Then she wrote to say she was coming to London for a few weeks in June and asked me to take a flat for her.

Anna had her own Company now, in which she played with Vittorio Gassman. She always refused to leave the stage for the films which, she maintained, reduced her abilities to mere measurements. We had corresponded regularly: discussing what play I was writing, or the one she was rehearsing. I had not been able to go to Italy to see a performance, but Peter Ustinov, who admired her work and was a frequent visitor to Rome, told me of her successes. I found a bachelor flat for her in Wimpole Street.

When I met her she told me in the taxi that she had brought me a present. I guessed it was another coffee pot.

"No, it's not that, but I hope it will please you." We were both nervous of each other. Twelve months or more had elapsed since we had met.

Impatiently I watched her unpack. I couldn't see any books, cigars, or a bottle of Amaretto. Then she took a large package from the bottom of the case, and hiding it behind her back, she mischievously went and locked herself in the bathroom. Five minutes later she emerged shyly, wearing a beautiful light blue nightdress. "Do you like your present?"

"And I've brought a present for Rose Marie too," she said later. "I do hope she likes coral."

I could understand Anna's generosity. But Rose Marie's to Anna defeated me. She seemed at this time to be above jealousy; she did not ask questions, knowing the answers. And instead of resenting the time, and particular times, I spent with Anna, she would, if she made any reference to them at all, merely sympathise with me for the demands being made upon me. The obvious explanation that Rose Marie could afford to be tolerant, because she was indifferent, was untrue. The truth was, I thought, that we were so close and so identified, nothing between us was at risk. Whatever the explanation, Rose Marie's handling of this situation was so adroit and appeared so mature that it appeared to both Anna and me that we were both presents from her to one another.

When Anna came to leave London under a flurry of television cameras and journalists, I realised dimly that distance, and her successful career, would eventually part us, at least in part. We whispered plans which neither of us believed would happen. But she made no demands nor tried to elicit any promise except that I should continue to write my poetry.

There were several. But only in my relationship with Anna was there no resentment or acrimony. She never asked, was never disappointed. Unlike any other woman I knew, she gave without some sort of unseen promissory note. I think this was probably because she was truly emancipated. She was the most dedicated actress I ever knew. Her part was more real to her than I was. We were, too, both equals: I, with a wife; she, married to her career. This balance assured an independence; we were able to belong without the necessity to possess.

It was Arthur Oldham who introduced me to Antonia. He had been composing the music for *Our Lady's Tumbler* and working with me on the libretto for *Christopher Sly*, the opera we were writing together at the time. Since Maria had married I had lacked a secretary. Oldham knew a girl who might be able to come to Orme Lane occasionally in the afternoons. I phoned her: that same day she came to Orme Lane pushing a dilapidated folding pram. She was a dark, pretty girl with a boyish figure; the child was incongruous. It would have been more in keeping with her gamin-like appearance if the pram had been filled with firewood. She was twenty-two and looked younger. It was June: I offered her some cherries. She was wearing a printed cotton dress and leather sandals. These artless touches were as jewels. I was glad I had some cherries. I told her I was in a jam: a play and an opera to write, besides *Jan's Journal*. She offered to try and park the child with her parents during the afternoons and come and work with me while I was in London. She went off pushing her pram before her. A string bag containing some onions dangled from the handle. I found I had watched her until she turned the corner. But I had no sense of foreboding.

Antonia came to the cottage every day. She was unusually intelligent: it was pleasant to work with her and even pleasanter not to work with her. Within a week I was dependent. Rose Marie, too, had come to enjoy gossipping with her and having her around. At the end of a week when I realised I was going back to Devon I found I was depressed. Rose Marie guessed the reason.

"Why don't you ask Antonia to come to work with you down there?" she suggested generously and almost to cue.

I promptly did my best to persuade her. She agreed, but I became depressed again, because I suspected anything I looked forward to never happened.

"I tell you she won't come," I told Rose Marie when I saw her cutting enough sandwiches for three the morning we were going to drive to Devon.

"Why won't she?"

"Because she happens to have a husband, a child, a home..."

"They won't stop her," Rose Marie replied, continuing to make the picnic.

A quarter of an hour later Antonia arrived at the cottage carrying a battered suitcase. Rose Marie didn't even turn round.

"Happy?" she asked, handing me a basket to carry out to the car. She could read me like a book.

Inspired by Ben's formidable achievement in forcing a Music

Festival on Aldeburgh, I pondered the possibilities of making a similar kind of graft on to the dead stump of North Devon. But naturally I wanted to found a Festival that would present drama as well as opera. As I surveyed the scene, I became less optimistic: Devon was, and is, a Depressed Area from an artistic point of view. An opera company had never entered the county or got nearer than Cardiff; there were only two theatres: one in Exeter, another in Plymouth, both dependent on third class touring companies playing fourth class West End successes; and, of course there was not only no Symphony Orchestra in the entire West Country but, as I discovered, not a single concert grand piano. With this affluent desert before me I felt like John the Baptist facing a well-populated wilderness. But I couldn't see, if Ben had coaxed a Festival to grow on the smug meres of Suffolk, why I couldn't get something to sprout from the complacent combes of Devon. And he egged me on. It's odd how our friends want us to suffer what they themselves have endured. Ben and Peter offered to give concerts in Bideford and donate their fees to the Devon funds.

That autumn I began to take a closer look at the possibilities. Clearly Bideford was a prettier and better equipped place for a Festival than Aldeburgh. Though it had no theatre, it did have two large cinemas, one of which had a deep stage, several halls and adequate hotel accommodation for visitors, while Barnstaple, which is only ten miles away, had just built itself the Queen's Hall large enough to stage opera or a symphony orchestra.

It was clear that the Festival would have to be based on these two towns. I decided to call it the *Taw and Torridge* after the rivers which flow past them. My first move was to approach their Town Clerks to see what co-operation the Town Councils would give. The Town Clerks passed me on to the Mayors: the Mayors referred me back to the Town Clerks. Both officers passed the buck backwards and forwards until their lethargic Councils impotently intervened.

During the next few months, I motored thousands of miles within a radius of thirty, lobbying Councillors whose only interest was in football pools and drinking shandies with their toothful wives. My determination, indistinguishable from idiotic obstinacy, hardened with the difficulties. I became evangelical before Chambers of Commerce and almost matey and lyrically enthusiastic at Rotary Clubs. I even ate their luncheons. After three months of this sort of garrulous St Vitus' Dance, I had collected two donations of five pounds each and seven Deeds of Covenant. Both cinemas had agreed to let their premises at an economic rent without specifying what that would be.

But fortunately I had met Edward Blacksell, the headmaster of the Barnstaple Secondary School. He and his wife, Joan, both threw their energy and perverse optimism behind my punctured hopes. With their methodical abilities and diplomatic guile to help, a Festival Committee was eventually formed. I was elected Chairman and George agreed to become a member. He, Blacksell and I constituted an artistic triumvirate. The office of President was filled by the Lord Lieutenant of the County, Lord Fortescue. The formation of this committee was an exercise in Balkan politics. For, since the proposed Festival was based on both Bideford and Barnstaple, it was necessary to elect an equal number of people from each as the rivalry between them had persisted since the days of Queen Elizabeth. They had quarrelled over which had sent more ships to repel the Armada. Added to which, neighbouring towns like Ilfracombe, Braunton, Instow, Torrington and South Molton wanted to be represented on it for no other reason than to spite the other. I had no idea before I succumbed to the disease of festivalitis that urban loyalties were as belligerent as among Congo tribesmen. The only reason why they agreed to co-operate together in this instance was because the initiative for the Festival had come from a person who did not live himself in any of these towns. If I had resided in Bideford, Barnstaple would have remained aloof. But my domicile in the backwoods of Welcombe gave me a sort of United Nations impartiality in their eyes. Also, at Edward Blacksell's shrewd suggestion, I had pandered to the Socialist elements in both councils by obtaining the support of the two landed families in the area which they feigned to despise, but enjoyed hobnobbing with. And fortunately in this case, both Sheila Stucley and Margaret Fortescue were genuinely enthusiastic for a Festival and were soon holding Balls in Castle Hill and Hartland Abbey to raise funds, and attending every Committee Meeting. These met alternatively in the Town Halls at Barnstaple and Bideford with the Mayors and Town Clerks in attendance. But luckily I found an enthusiastic member of each council, Muriel Cox from Bideford and Frank Molland in Barnstaple. Both of these badgered their respective bodies to make the Festival a grant. And though each could have given up to a sixpenny rate, nobody considered this as even a remote possibility. After weeks of lobbying unimaginative shopkeepers, Muriel Cox managed to persuade Bideford to grant a halfpenny rate towards the Festival for cultural purposes. It was a considerable achievement comparable to persuading a society of pork butchers to subscribe to a jamboree for vegetarians. Though the halfpenny rate produced under £200 it created a precedent.

At Barnstaple, Frank Molland had not found the going so easy. Though they were not going to be outdone by Bideford, they thought they could dispense with direct financial aid by making an indirect subsidy towards the Festival by letting it have the Queen's Hall at a reduced rate.

Meanwhile Marion, by running a Ladies' Festival Committee in London and organising a concert or two in Orme Square, had raised more funds than either town. Even so, counting the Deeds of Covenant and the donations I had bullied my friends and relatives into giving, we had less than £500 in the kitty. For the next few months I abandoned all work, ate my way through mountains of small cakes at ladies' committee bunfights and exhausted myself trying to obtain some support from the Arts Council. I felt, not without some justification, that George, Ben and myself were, in fact, doing their work for them. Even so, they made us feel like schoolboys who had overspent our pocket-money on some escapade. After innumerable sessions before Pooh-Bahs at St James' Square, they agreed to grant the Devon Festival £250 per annum on condition that their representative attended all executive meetings. With this gratuity to encourage us, George and I set off from London one bleak, cold and foggy morning for Barnstaple. Molland had persuaded Barnstaple Town Council to meet to reconsider a Festival Grant if George and I would ourselves present the case before it. There was too much snow on the road for us to motor: we went by rail, froze in the train and failed to thaw out in the hotel. With tepid Windsor soup before us, to be followed by old mutton and tinned apricots and rice, we tried to console ourselves that the rigours we were enduring would be, if not rewarded, at least worth while. The next morning we traipsed to the Town Hall to address our congregation of Councillors composed of members of the Ancient Order of Buffaloes, Rotarians, Plymouth Brethren, Nonconformists and a few comparatively enlightened Trades Unionists thrown in. I spoke about the necessity for Devonshire to continue its musical traditions, pointing out that the first School of Counterpoint in Europe had been attached to Exeter Cathedral. George reminded the town that it was John Gay's birthplace and that a first performance of his masterpiece, *The Beggar's Opera*, in this town, realised and conducted by Ben, would be a fitting opening to the Festival. It only remained, he begged, for them to support our funds. The moronic masons dug their heels in: George continued eloquently, gently reminding them that if education was a good thing, something at the end of it besides bingo and the pools was equally necessary, referring tactfully to the examples of subsidised theatres and opera houses in Germany, and finally pointing out that one of the side effects of a Festival of the Arts would be that it would attract tourists and trade into local hotels and shops. He presented this case so admirably and answered their questions so tactfully and patiently that I felt confident they would respond generously. They granted a penny rate which would amount to £200. Freezing in the train back to London, which was without a restaurant car, we considered that it would cost us less if we underwrote the Festival out of our own pockets rather than ruin our health trying to raise money from councils and bodies constituted to support such things.

I had not fully recovered from this journey when Blacksell phoned me to say that there was a wealthy man living outside Barnstaple who had promised to support the Festival. This tycoon had invited me to dinner at his house. Blacksell urged me to go and collect his cheque which he thought might solve many of our problems. Accordingly I reluctantly crossed the steppes again and drove over ice-bound roads to be severely punished with hospitality: martinis concocted from the sting of a conger eel, followed by a lethal meal of gargantuan proportions. I told myself that those who starved for art were more fortunate than I who was slowly eating myself to death for the sake of culture. But as I waded to the comparative security of the shallows of the coffee I consoled myself as I grabbed the enormous cigar I had been handed, clinging on to it as if it were a jetty, that if my hosts' cheque was in proportion to his hospitality, the Festival could not only underwrite the opera, but even afford some national publicity. But I was not on shore yet: something like a tumbler of Drambuie was yet to follow. During this dinner I had to maintain a flow of intelligent but inoffensive conversation and it's never easy for me to be both at once. There were no other guests to take the strain and my host was determined to have his money's worth. He talked about art as if it were some fashionable luxury he could now afford to give his wife. I felt like a pedlar in stolen mink or a kind of pimp for a pornographic side-show. But I clung on to my manners. Not every martyr has been burned. Some have just endured listening to the wife of a prosperous tradesman singing arias from Gilbert and Sullivan to the sabotage of her own accompaniment. During this terrible excess, my host asked me whether I could arrange to bring the Harewoods to a party if he gave one at his house in aid of the Festival. He didn't wink, but he did produce his cheque book. I mumbled something non-committal and watched him go to his desk. He handed his donation to me. I put it in my pocket without looking at it and thanked him for his generosity. I wasn't certain how many noughts it would carry but was confident of two and hopeful of three. With this booty secure, I bolted almost precipitantly for my car and drove erratically down the drive. Once out of sight of the house I glanced at the cheque. It was for £5. My journey down had cost me more than that. My impulse was to turn back and return the cheque. I clung on to my manners. It was a great sacrifice.

And there were many, so many. That dinner was no greater waste than similar evenings which anybody in this country has to endure who tries to collect money for cultural purposes. At least half my energy as a writer has been wasted begging in this sordid and expensive style.

Naturally, as John Christie had been so generous over *The Rape of*

Lucretia and was such an enthusiastic supporter of opera at Glyndebourne, I was confident that he and Audrey would support the Devon Festival since they owned Tapley Court, just outside Bideford, also the Saunton Sands Hotel and the Marine at Instow. Indeed, many people in North Devon resented the fact that John had done so little for the district from which many of his rents derived and resented the fact too that it was spent in Sussex. I didn't articulate any of this when Rose Marie and I visited him at Tapley but was sure, even if he didn't see this opportunity to rectify his reputation in the locality, he would support the Festival for musical reasons alone. I outlined the proposed programme; he approved of it enthusiastically.

"But I won't give a penny towards anything for Bideford," he shouted angrily, wrapping his handkerchief compulsively round and round his hand. "Do you know what they once did to me? The police charged me with exceeding the speed limit in the town. And the bloody bench had the insolence to fine me. They'll never get another penny out of me."

I didn't argue with him. He had the virtues of an eccentric too.

In spite of these difficulties of raising finance we had to proceed with the programme. Opera companies, soloists and even actors, are usually engaged a year ahead. This meant making contracts and entering into financial commitments beyond our resources in the vague hope that we would obtain more guarantees once people had seen the proposed programme. Consequently George, Edward Blacksell and I had to commit ourselves by signing personal guarantees.

Because the English Opera Group was contributing so largely to the programme by agreeing to produce Ben's version of *The Beggar's Opera* and his *Let's Make an Opera*, besides a choral orchestral concert which was to include the cantata *St Nicholas*, and because they had experience of running festivals, it was agreed that the Group should undertake Artistic Direction of the whole programme. This meant that Basil Douglas, the general manager of the Group, became in effect the Artistic Director of the Festival. When the appointment was made, I could not envisage any disadvantage to it. But only a week or two elapsed before I

K   289

discovered that Basil Douglas was appropriating practically all the expenditure for opera and leaving practically none for drama. I had agreed to allow *Don Juan* to have its première at the Festival. This entailed some sacrifice on my part as Edinburgh had also asked for the play. But to my surprise I found that Douglas was far from pleased to have a new play in the programme. He even suggested that the theme of the play, especially the bawdy overtones, made it inappropriate for the provinces and likely to shock them. The argument seemed unconvincing, especially as the Group were themselves presenting *The Beggar's Opera* which, in whatever version it is presented, can hardly be said to be free of bawdy overtones.

The Festival Council instructed Douglas to approach London theatre companies to present the play. He reported that none would undertake the production. This, we discovered, was not surprising since the financial guarantee they had been offered was only £400. It appeared that Drama would have to be excluded from the programme, until Edward Blacksell approached E. Martin Browne to produce *Don Juan*. He had produced the original production of *This Way to the Tomb* at the Mercury and he agreed. Even so, Douglas vetoed this because Martin's estimate for staging the play was £200 in excess of the meagre £400 which was now budgeted for it. Fortunately a donor, anonymous to all but me, agreed to guarantee the difference. I was forced to make this expensive gesture because I had already promised Anna that she could have the part of Doña Aña. As she had helped me write the part I could not disappoint her.

When Martin came down to the farm to discuss the production, he admitted that even his experience of working on a shoestring budget at the Mercury would be strained if he was to stage a new play for £600 and present it for a week. But once Martin is convinced of the artistic value of a play he's not the sort of man to let a budget prevent him. We decided to ask the Bideford Art School to make the costumes: this had the advantage of implicating the locals in their own Festival. Since Epstein had often complained to me that serious painters and sculptors were given so few opportunities to design for the theatre, Martin agreed that we should approach him. Unfortunately he was ill. But Feliks

Topolski readily agreed to do all the designs and once he heard of our shoestring budget he offered to come to the farm and paint all the scenery himself in the tithe barn. This he did and was happy enough doing all this himself so long as Rose Marie or Antonia occasionally looked in on him. Like myself, Feliks enjoyed the company of pretty women.

Martin told me that on that budget there was no chance of getting any stars or even well-known actors for the cast. I told him that Anna Proclemer, the greatest actress in Italy, had offered to play. He was dubious that she could play in English, especially in a verse play. But he agreed to give her an audition. My next problem was to persuade her to submit to one. Anna was, of course, not in the habit of having to give auditions. I found the letter difficult to write—she had already refused two plays in Rome in order to keep herself free to play the part for me. I had underestimated her. She flew straight over to London and sat with a dozen other actresses whom the agencies sent along, waiting to read the part. Several gave quite good auditions. In spite of her experience, I saw Anna was nervous. But when Martin called her she went on to the stage without a script and played a couple of scenes faultlessly. Martin and I sat silent: it was the other actresses who'd come to read the part who applauded.

"Now our only problem," Martin said, "is to find a Don Juan who won't look ridiculous beside her."

He was wrong. British Equity, the actors' organisation for the enhancement of mediocrity now stepped in and refused to give Anna a working permit on the ground that there was no justification for our employing an Italian while many English actresses were out of work. For days Martin and I pleaded with the Union, pointing out that Anna Proclemer was a great actress who had agreed to play in a Festival for one week and was not therefore competing with actresses on the commercial stage. Also, we argued, such restrictions might cause retaliation and prevent people like Laurence Olivier from giving a performance of *Hamlet* in Rome. But Equity refused to budge. I felt like a composer who, having written a cello concerto especially for Rostropovitch, had been told that he mustn't play the piece since there were several enthusiastic cellists in Luton. Anna herself was too disappointed to weep.

Trailing her wings she sadly returned to Rome. I complained to the press. But it was no story to them then—and ten years later, when she was fêted after her performance as Gertrude in Zeffirelli's *Hamlet* at the National Theatre, they doubted if such a slight had really been made to such an actress.

The next best thing, I suppose, to self-control, is the ability to control one's conscience. Generally I excelled at this. But my relationship with Anna left me with some qualms, not because Rose Marie had complained about it, but because she had not. Anna was still in London when I had to go to Bristol for a broadcast. I said good-bye to her, making silent resolutions to be faithful in future. It was a pity that Antonia should have been in the car. As we drove off, though, I consoled myself that it was Rose Marie, not I, who had in fact persuaded the girl to work for me in Devon.

After a few days there, I dimly perceived that when I begin to resist one temptation it is only because of another. I began to project on to Antonia the resentment I felt against myself. I almost hated her: not because she didn't work well: she did; not because, when we weren't working, she didn't run round me on the farm finding the paintbrush I'd mislaid, or running back to fetch the tool I'd forgotten; she did all that too. Rose Marie called her my shadow. I resented her because she attracted me. I became rude, uncouth, boorish and sullen. She must have guessed the reason for my behaviour to her and her way of responding to it was to tease me artlessly. It was summer: that, too, didn't help. We worked in the garden: Antonia asked me if her wearing shorts would distract me. When I said shortly that it could not possibly, she took me at my word. But I had not allowed for three buttons of her shirt to be undone.

I continued dictating.

I endured this unconscious provocation from Antonia for several weeks. I never thought of myself as a person with much self-control. But what I had I exercised. If virtue is related to temptations, then I was most virtuous. It must be comparatively easy to be chaste, if you are locked up in a monastery with a lot of monks or, if circumstances in the world outside surround you with ugly or unwilling women. But I was never so fortunate. It seemed to me at times that I was the object of some conspiracy to drag me down to the level of my own nature. But when I counted all the opportunities and temptations which I overcame, I almost canonised myself. It was a delicious martyrdom, not of the hair shirt, but of the silk petticoat. I was crucified by hatpins. I used to ponder the theme of Brecht's *Hofmeister* and often wondered whether I might not make life easier for myself if I emulated the tutor's solution. This would have not only solved a moral dilemma, but removed some pain too. This part of a man responds, whether we do so ourselves or not: and if it is not indulged, the pleasure it anticipates quickly turns to pain. There were times when I could scarcely walk. But the attraction was not only physical, fierce though this was: we enjoyed being together: she thought I was feminine, I thought she was boyish, consequently it was one way of explaining the fact that we could enjoy doing innumerable things together, such as mucking out a pigsty, or going into Bideford to choose material for her summer dress, which are not usually shared when men and women are conscious of their external sexual differences and unaware of their interior affinities.

Even so, these differences obtruded: restraint emphasised them, and since my consciousness had now shifted to two feet below my head, it was not surprising that it argued with rigid logic that the way to overcome a thirst was to drink. But the consciousness on my shoulders resented this. My temper worsened. I was sullen, I sulked. Finally I lost my temper, threw my script on the floor, and told Antonia I wasn't going to work any more.

"Where are you going?"

"To the beach."

"Why?"

"We can make love there."

"You don't have to be so bad-tempered about it. Why do you resent your own desires?"

"They get in the way. Like a rake left on a garden path. Suddenly you tread on it and it hits you in the face. You reduce me to a thing."

"Maybe it'll be better afterwards."

We walked to the beach in silence. And without saying a word we climbed over the rocks, I leading, she following, now as angry with me as I was with myself. We reached Gull Rock. We couldn't go any further. We were alone there.

"Well?" she said, "what now?"

"Take your clothes off. Both of them."

"Aren't you going to tell me you love me?"

"I don't. You've made me want you, that's all."

"I see."

She kicked off her shorts, peeled off her shirt, and as I approached her, she ran and dived into a pool and swam to the other side. She knew I was a bad swimmer.

"Come on," she called gaily, clambering out onto a rock. "I'm waiting."

The water was cold. I swam using my deliberate and ungainly breast-stroke, and eventually clambered out of the pool, pulling myself up on to the rock beside her. She opened her eyes and smiled mischievously.

"What's happened to him?"

"The water was cold, very cold."

She stood and embraced me to repair the damage. We were both wet. The touch of her nakedness was sufficient. I pulled her down to the rock again, then flung myself down beside her, landing in intimate and amorous contact with two large jelly-fish. My screams perforated the still air. He who had been so proud, though briefly, now emulated a tortoise. My belly was already red and swollen too.

In spite of the pain I began to laugh. A consummation of hilarity.

"I'm still waiting," she said. This time I swam across the pool first. We dressed, then walked back to the farm. I was no longer bad-tempered. Jelly-fish, I discovered, satisfy the fiercest desire.

But because of this lapse, I redoubled my efforts to overcome my attraction to Antonia. Though I have given the impression here that I was a philanderer, I was not. I made what is known as good resolutions and told Antonia about them. This is generally a risky thing to do. Women don't mind being informed they are a temptation so long as you make it clear that you have no intention of resisting them. But neither was Antonia a philanderer. She, I discovered, had made her own resolutions too. She agreed to co-operate. Like a couple of kids, we made a series of vows: not to go to Gull Rock together alone; not to be left alone in the house, on the farm or down at West Mill; and never on any account risk sunbathing, riding through the woods or working together where we could not be observed. With this Charter of continence established between us we found ourselves paradoxically closer together than in copulation: nothing joins people so closely as a shared conspiracy. Naturally we could not tell Rose Marie about our pact of non-aggression: and consequently we should not have been surprised when she did not adhere to it. The very next day she made a move which made our secret seem a piece of mutual sadism.

Rose Marie had been given a small second-hand car by her father. We had used it for a year and then she had decided to sell it as I had bought another car. The purchaser wanted the car delivered in London. Rose Marie asked me if I would drive it up for her as she was too busy getting the house ready for George, Marion, Ben and Peter who were coming to stay for the Devon Festival a week or so later.

"I have asked Antonia to drive up with you," she said. "You can spend the night in the cottage and then come down by train the next day. There's so much to be done down here."

"Then Antonia had better stay to help you. I can drive up alone."

"No," she insisted, "I'm not risking that. You'll fall into a daydream unless you've got somebody talking to you, and have an accident."

I protested.

She reminded me of the occasion when I had offered to drive when I was already doing so.

"No, I insist that Antonia goes up with you, otherwise you might end up in Edinburgh or a ditch."

There was no arguing. The next morning Antonia and I drove off with our Charter as our only luggage. We were silent for some miles, sharing each other's thoughts.

"It's as if Rose Marie knew," Antonia ventured, "and was testing us, or showing she doesn't care."

"It's just possible she trusts me," I remarked, "have you thought of that?"

"You mean she doesn't think I'm attractive? Don't be so insulting."

We continued to speculate on what motive had landed us in this predicament, failing to realise that innocence is motiveless. My own thoughts were that I had mistimed my vows and that it might be reasonable in the circumstances to postpone implementing them. But though I did not articulate these thoughts, Antonia heard them.

"No, I'm certainly not sleeping with you," she exclaimed. "Rose Marie trusted me and I respect that trust."

"I don't think she's given it a thought."

"She's not that insulting."

Our animated conversation had at least kept the car on the road. Perhaps Rose Marie had foreseen that too?

I drove straight to the house to get the key of the garage from Marion. The house was in a turmoil. Antonia and I in our rags did not seem welcome.

George appeared unusually distraught. Apparently they were giving a dinner party for the Queen and Prince Philip to which Ben, who'd just completed *Gloriana* to celebrate the Coronation, had been invited to play the opera through to them. Antonia and I stole a bottle of milk and appropriately took our problem over to the cottage.

As though carrying some sacred relics as fervently as converts, we placed our respective cases in separate rooms. We emerged to have a snack and some coffee. I telephoned Rose Marie to let her know that we'd arrived safely and that her car could be collected.

"Did Antonia chatter to you all the way up?"

"Yes."

"Thank her from me. And enjoy yourselves."

"What did you say?"

"I said enjoy yourselves. See you tomorrow."

She'd rung off.

The telephone was on the stairs.

"What was it you made her repeat?" Antonia asked.

"She said we were to enjoy ourselves."

"Well, we won't," she said vehemently and went up to her room. I heard the door slam. I too went to bed. I did not know what she expected of me; I did not know what I expected of myself. For a time we avoided the time, both sitting together on the edge of the bath listening to the first performance of *Gloriana* which Ben was playing through to the Queen across the garden. But I went to my own room. Gandhi had talked a lot to me about chastity and the need of being unattached to the senses. I now found that chastity itself can be a kind of perverse sensual gratification. It was a hot summer night. We both failed to sleep. I watched it get light. Then Antonia tapped on the wall.

"Can you sleep?" she called.

"No."

"Nor can I."

"Come in here then."

"But what about our beastly vows?"

"We could cuddle those too."

"Well, at least we could have a cigarette."

"Yes."

She came in and got into bed, carefully lying above the top sheet. That way we managed an hour's sleep.

The next morning in the train we were exhausted from lack of sleep and self-control, or abuse, whichever way you look at it. But gay as though having accomplished a difficult feat.

"I hope you get the full credit for this," Antonia said ruefully.

"I doubt it," I replied. "I suspect that we are most punished when we punish ourselves."

Self-restraint is the most potent aphrodisiac of all. It is probably the only one. After a couple of weeks Antonia left Devon. We arranged to meet at the cottage in London. Since Rose Marie did not know of this assignation we had no promises to break except those to ourselves.

I remember it was a sunny afternoon, and because it was an occasion she had, as it were, dressed for it. She looked pretty: she had washed her hair. When I let her in, I noticed a slight incongruous touch; she carried a brown paper carrier bag. She took this upstairs into the sitting-room, then sat on the edge of the chair. We were embarrassed: we made conversation. I went and got some tea. We nibbled biscuits. We made more conversation. Then, unobtrusively, without her noticing, I peered into the carrier bag and noticed that it contained nothing but a black nylon nightie. Even so, we continued to ask each other about films we had never seen.

Perhaps it is not strange that I cannot remember how we got to bed, or anything of that night, except that the carrier bag remained undisturbed. I suppose the reason for that is that we remember when life trips us up, and not when we live as easily and naturally as we breathe.

While George was staying at Mead for the Devon Festival, he suggested that he and I should go to Salzburg immediately after, where they were performing *Don Giovanni* in the Riding School. We stayed at the Goldener Hirsch and while we were there we also saw a performance of Gottfried von Einem's opera *Der Prozess*, which was based on Kafka's *The Trial*. I thought it was a dull piece. Von Einem asked me if I would write a libretto for him. He said he wanted a comedy. As Oldham had failed to complete *Christopher Sly*, I mentioned that I had already written this libretto and for a time he thought of composing it but evidently dropped the idea. From Salzburg we went to Munich for a performance of an opera which we found had been staged a week previously, and so we decided to go by train to Bayreuth.

We consulted the hotel porter about the time of our train and hurried to the station where we found a long queue of beefy Bavarian hikers beside the ticket office. Our train stood at the platform; there were five minutes to go. Our only hope was that the forty hikers in front of us should take a collective ticket. But to our dismay, we had to watch each one fumble for his money and even pass the time of day with the official behind the grille. Only half the queue of knees had gone when we saw the train for Bayreuth leave the station. It was the last train of the day. We were desperate and frustrated. Glancing at the hoardings, we saw that the only entertainment in Munich that evening was a bad film which we'd had the misfortune to see six months ago. It was a moment when one has either to lead fate by the forelock or become resigned to sitting in one café after another through a dull evening. We marched resolutely to a taxi in the station yard and casually ordered the driver to take us to Bayreuth.

"It can't be done," he said quietly.

"It can," we said.

He looked astounded and informed us that Bayreuth was at least 300 kilometres distant.

"We did not ask the distance," I said.

"You've got four hours to get us there," George commented.

"But I could never get there and back tonight," the driver complained.

"Stay at an hotel," I suggested, "that's what we'll have to do."

The driver could see that it was useless to argue further with two resolute Englishmen. "This is the spirit and determination which built the Empire," I said.

"I don't recall that Livingstone took a taxi," George remarked.

In a few moments we were hurtling down the Autobahn at a dangerous speed. "Odd that we should be doing this when neither of us really care for Wagner," George said.

"Not at all," I replied, "it was all those knees which did it."

For the next few miles we sat in a more sober mood, observing the frantic meter and counting up our foreign currency to see how we could foot the bill.

"And there'll be his hotel bill on top," I added. But our financial calculations were suddenly abandoned as a panic thought crossed my mind. My knowledge of European geography has never been very adequate; but passing a signpost which had Leipzig on it, it suddenly occurred to me that we might be heading for the Russian Zone. I voiced my alarm.

"Maybe that's why the driver said he couldn't take us there? I'm sure Leipzig is in the Russian Zone..."

"We can just show our papers," George said complacently.

"If we hadn't left them in the hotel in Munich," I observed sadly. "They will say we've done a Burgess and Maclean," I added, imagining the headlines at home...

My imagination, or my ignorance concerning the location of frontiers was such that I was genuinely surprised and not a little relieved to see the Bayreuth Opera House. *Götterdämmerung* was being given; Wieland Wagner, the composer's grandson, had produced.

"Worth coming for," George said, regaining his enthusiasm. But as we took our seats in the dress circle, we had second thoughts. The rows were so close together that even I was uncomfortable, while George had even less room for his legs. Every time we shifted our positions, two women in front turned to complain. Meanwhile the opera continued until I became truculent with boredom and discomfort. We hobbled out into the garden and ordered a beer, and sat for the rest of the opera with a glass of Pilsner. The most expensive bottle of beer we had ever drunk.

Soon after I returned from Germany, Rose Marie and I went up to Edinburgh to join George and Marion for the Festival. Several days went by without incident, then a casual and innocent remark by George kicked a hole through my world. The four of us were lunching at the George Hotel. We were all rather gay. Half-way through the meal, George noticed that Rose Marie was using the handbag which he had helped me to choose for her in Salzburg.

"Do you like the bag we chose?" he asked her.

"Immensely."

"And the other one?"

"What other one?"

My foot sought his shin under the table. It missed.

"Ronnie was very extravagant. He bought two." My foot found its mark too late.

"Yes, I liked the other immensely too. It's such a help to have things duplicated."

The temperature at the table dropped precipitately. Marion tried to change the conversation. George began to munch his tongue. Rose Marie wore her Martha expression. I emulated a tortoise in preparation for a prolonged hibernation. The meal collapsed, not in silence, but in that kind of forced hilarity which is infinitely more ominous.

The girls went off together.

"I'm sorry. Why the hell didn't you tell me you'd bought the other bag for Antonia? I suppose it was for her?"

"Of course. I thought you'd guessed. Anyhow, don't worry. I dare say some day I'll do the same thing for you."

"I could eat my tongue."

I passed him the mustard.

For the next forty-eight hours, I did my fakir act: sitting on knitting needles that nobody else could notice. During all this time, the incident of the luncheon was not referred to by Rose Marie directly. She said nothing. She merely put her new handbag away and used a very old one which had no duplicate. The point was well made. I would have preferred a row: tension was always more punishing to me. Though I don't think Rose Marie realised that. She was probably trying hard to treat the matter with contempt. Or, maybe, she realised that we couldn't have it out and then continue to go through all our Festival engagements together. More probably still, she waited for me to explain, knowing I could have no satisfactory explanation. Meanwhile I traipsed the round of concerts and operas, watching the tide of emotion mount to engulf me. But not a word was said until we were in the air half-way to London.

"I suppose you gave that other bag to Antonia?"

"Yes."

"Was it exactly like mine?"

"No."

"Liar. George said it was."

The aircraft was full. I glanced at the escape hatch.

"Were the two handbags identical or were they not? I've a right to know. It's important that I should know." She was raising her voice.

"Why? What difference can that make?"

"If they were identical, she will one day accuse me of stealing hers."

"They were identical in design, not in price. We had found the bag we thought you'd like in the shop window. The assistant had said that the sun had faded the leather but he had a duplicate in a show case. I bought it. And as he was packing it up he said I could have the one in the window at half-price as the design pleased me. So I decided to buy that too, as I had to buy Antonia something after she'd done so much for me..."

301

"Of course."

"...during the Devon Festival."

Rose Marie said nothing. The plane sped on. The stewardess passed us sandwiches. But I knew these silences. I fingered my safety belt.

"Are you in love with her?" she whispered. The whole aircraft seemed to wait for my reply.

"No."

"Liar."

"But I'm very fond of her."

"She'd be pleased to hear that.".

I studied the clouds. The plane seemed to be going very slowly and silently.

"Have you slept with her?"

"That must be Lincoln Cathedral." I glanced down at the hospitable-looking spire.

"I said, have you slept with her?" Passengers craned. The stewardess hovered. There must, I thought, be at least some chance of the plane being hit by lightning, especially with this positive charge inside it.

"Answer."

I said nothing.

"Now I know your answer." We began to lose height. The tears were flowing.

"Do up your safety belts."

And there must, I hoped, be many planes which land by simply burrowing into the tarmac.

Fom London we motored straight down to Devon: on the journey Rose Marie never mentioned the issue of the handbag. I hoped that she had come to realise that there was nothing particularly significant in her finding out that I had bought a small present from Salzburg for Antonia, especially after I had returned from there she had upbraided me for not buying the girl something. Obviously what had made her suspicious was that I had lied. I don't know why I had done this. I suppose I felt at the time that any woman resents receiving an identical present to another. And by giving this as an explanation for my deception I hoped vaguely that she would let the damn matter drop. I should have known that when a woman says nothing she is asking everything. It is when they are chatting that they are most silent. But I thought she was tired. My own conscience was not burdensome. It is annoying to find oneself having to lie about something of which you are not really ashamed. I knew that my affection for Antonia did nothing to lessen my feeling for Rose Marie. Whatever silly convention maintained I was not going to reduce myself to the ridiculously false position "if you love me, you can't love her", etc. And even if I was eventually driven to admit that I had made love to Antonia two or three times, I could not believe that Rose Marie would mind particularly. This may seem excessively naïve of me, but she had, I told myself, not been disturbed over Anna or Petra. Indeed, I almost convinced myself that tolerance was connivance and gave me a licence which I had used with restraint. At any rate, Antonia was not at Mead any more. She was no longer my secretary. Now I fell silent. The thought of not seeing her any more, of not having her to work with or play with was like an amputation. I worried about what she was doing, where she was and if she were as unhappy as I. I knew she had left her husband. Her marriage had been on the rocks before she had met me. With separate thoughts we drove to Devon together: I did not know what hers were.

When we reached Mead, Annaliese, a girl from Bochum who was staying with us for the summer to help Rose Marie with the house and the children, greeted us. But none of her description of what she'd been doing in the garden during our absence was heard. Rose Marie was now in a mood: a tension that was all-pervading, intimidating. After a few hours, as though biting on a bad tooth, she continued her inquisition.

"What else of mine has she got?"

"I bought her a blouse too."

"I'm not referring to things."

There was another long silence.

"Have you? I said, have you?"

"Yes."

"Often?"

"No, not very often."

"Where? I said, where?"

"At the cottage."

"Here?"

"No, never here."

"Don't lie."

Then suddenly Rose Marie broke. I had never seen anything like it before. It was anger that looked like grief: it was grief compounded of self-pity, hatred and sorrow.

"Why did it have to be her?" she cried. "Why did it have to be her?"

I was bewildered. I tried to reassure her. I failed to stop the tears or stem the hysterics. She was utterly out of control. Annaliese, hearing the screams, came running into the room. I was terrified at the thought that she would bring on another haemorrhage. This was my only thought at the time.

Later, I tried to understand why Rose Marie had treated my *affaires* with Anna and Petra with gay sophistication and tolerance and should be completely distraught by finding out that I had slept with Antonia. Why was she different? I couldn't find the answer. Was it the last straw that had broken her? Something told me it wasn't this. Days later when she had recovered, I asked her.

"The others weren't in my house," she told me. Her reason seemed simple. Its simplicity convinced me at the time. I was never very perspicacious.

Apart from writing *Jan's Journal* and a few articles for the *Standard* about the General Election, I had written no journalism for some time. I had covered this because I had had to be in London anyway at that time and I needed the money. But I felt that my articles were very poor: because I knew very little about party politics and was not interested in them since I could see that real power lay with the manipulators of credit and not with the puppets in Westminster. To cover up my ignorance on the issues of the Election I had concentrated more on writing about the people who were voting, attempting to give a sort of Hogarthian picture of the contemporary hustings. It amused me to ridicule the democratic method. I did not believe that all men are equal or all deserve one vote. The motion that the majority was right struck me as palpably false, disproved by history and observation. I found innumerable instances to support this contention: a woman voting for Attlee because she liked Conservatives, down to the Labour candidate whose reference to foreign policy revealed that he believed Bolivia was in the Balkans. The right to vote, I tried to indicate, is like the right to write a poem, or the right to mend a motor car, dependent on capability. It struck me as damnably silly that Winston Churchill himself had only the same voting strength as myself or that both of us were equated with my pigman who was convinced that the United States was still part of the Empire.

The editor was not too happy with my satirising democracy or debunking the *vox populi*—"the general election is hardly the time to say that the people shouldn't have the right to vote," he said, "besides, some fools will think you're a fascist. Try and give a more general picture." Consequently I did this, but as I'd lost interest I thought the articles were facetious, trivial and poor.

Apparently Beaverbrook thought otherwise. A few weeks later the editor of the *Evening Standard* asked me to lunch with him at the Étoile.

"Lord Beaverbrook has gone to the States," he said, "and wants you to fly over to join him to cover the Eisenhower-Stevenson Election for us."

"That's a ridiculous idea. I know little enough about the English election; I know absolutely nothing about American politics."

"That's what I told him," Elland said, "indeed, I suggested Randolph Churchill. But he insisted I should persuade you to go because he wants you to write, not political articles, but more your impression of the States at the time of the Election."

"You mean I needn't even sit through those boring political meetings?"

"It appears you can do whatever you like," Elland admitted sadly, "as long as you agree to write a piece for us every day."

"Won't that cost a lot in cables?" I asked anxiously.

"Can you fly out in a couple of days?" he asked. "The office will arrange your visa, your flight, and give you a few hundred dollars for pocket money. Charge all your American expenses to our New York office whom I'll instruct to look after you."

I said I'd phone my decision that evening. I was tempted: it sounded like a party at somebody else's expense.

I was seeing Eliot that afternoon and so I asked him if he thought I should go.

"You won't like New York," he said, "but I think you should go there once."

He gave me several letters of introduction to friends there and the avuncular advice to avoid their cocktails.

"New Yorkers think that being hospitable is to make you drunk. Remember their gin is stronger than ours. It's a full time occupation staying sober over there, I can tell you."

Knowing his abstemious habits and my horror of hangovers I felt less enthusiastic about going. That evening I returned to Devon to see that the farm would tick over in my absence. Rose Marie convinced me I should go because she wanted me to bring back an American Food Mixer.

Whatever Jekyll and Hyde was, I was at that time the square root of it. In the morning I was in my rags helping to plaster out an old cob wall in a cottage where we were putting in a bathroom, and late that same evening, I was sitting above the Atlantic on a champagne and caviar flight.

Rose Marie saw me off in the train from Bideford. Antonia met me at Waterloo. I had, she knew, a few hours in London before catching my plane. She had learned to expect nothing more than a cup of coffee on the station. Then she offered to come to the cottage. I made her pack for me. I heard her in the bedroom wrapping my shirts in tissue paper. I dared not go in to watch her. But I could tell by the use of the tissue paper that she was being conscientious; she was not normally a tidy or methodical girl. I felt that she was taking such pains because she was grateful even to be allowed to do this for me. When she had finished packing, I heard her struggling to shut the case. It wouldn't close. I clung to my chair in the sitting-room. She continued to struggle with the case.

"I'm sorry, but you'll have to help me," she called.

If only she hadn't said "sorry".

I went into the bedroom, lifted the case from the bed, put it on the floor and closed it.

"Thank you. I enjoyed doing that. Can I come to the Air Terminal to see you off?"

I didn't look at her, but I saw her eyes were wet.

"Yes."

"Then we'd better be going. We can have some coffee there." She bent down to pick up the case resolutely.

As she thought that I wouldn't let her give me herself, she had given me this resolution. That, and her apologising because she couldn't close the case herself, was too much for me.

We never even reached the bed. I only just managed to get to the Air Terminal in time. After the bus left Victoria I saw her standing at a dark, wet corner of the road where she had waited to watch it go by.

"Let me know when you're coming back," she'd said, "and I'll meet you."

But I hadn't promised. Guilt consumed me. It was bad enough feeling guilt for the present, I couldn't carry guilt for the future too. My luggage was already overweight.

When arriving at La Guardia I heard my name being repeated over the loudspeaker in the waiting room. I went to the telephone as requested and dialled the number which a receptionist gave me. I announced who I was and somebody whom I had never heard of informed me that they hoped I would permit them to welcome me to America by giving me lunch at the Canadian Club at the Waldorf Astoria. He did not say who he was or who his friends were. I assumed he knew. I accepted the invitation, supposing it was something to do with the *Evening Standard*. Outside the airport a large Cadillac and chauffeur were already waiting for me. Another man looking like Al Capone stood by the car and got in beside me. He announced his name which I didn't catch, handed me a box of cigars to welcome me to the city. Whenever I am doing anything officially, such as opening a village book club or representing a newspaper, I feel an imposter. This may be something like fossilised modesty funking in me. It is not that I am unaware of my importance but I have so low an opinion of other people that I do not give them the credit of being able to appreciate mine. And as I observed my companion eating his cigar beside me as we sped into New York I realised that this five-star reception had obviously been laid on for somebody else. It occurred to me that I'd better clarify my identity.

"My name's Duncan," I said.

"Yeah, the poet," my companion commented without a trace of respect.

This confused me more. It seemed impossible to me that my reputation had penetrated this far, however regrettable that might be. After all, I had never had a book published in the States and though *The Eagle has Two Heads* and *The Rape of Lucretia* had been performed on Broadway, both had flopped. Yet this silent man beside me with his garish tie and his brash diamond tie-pin and diamond ring had a love of poetry somewhere beneath his uncouth exterior sufficient to make him drive to the airport to meet me. I was gratified, I smiled benignly at him.

"Have you read much of my poetry?" I asked him. He bit his cigar so fiercely the ash nearly singed his eyebrow. It was as if I has asked him if he had done much praying recently.

"Nope," he replied when he'd recovered. "Culture and me don't make no highball."

I savoured this remark, pondering since I had established that my welcome was not a case of mistaken identity whether I was being kidnapped, taken for a ride or any of those antics that I'd seen on the films.

"I suppose you're about to 'put me on the spot'?" I said jocularly.

"Yeah," he replied disapprovingly. "At 50 bucks a head. I hope you can eat as good as they say you write."

My bodyguard, or whatever he was, accompanied me into the Gladstone Hotel where I had booked and immediately hustled me round the corner to the Waldorf Astoria. The elevator flushed us to the twentieth floor where fifteen smart executives, each with a martini in their mitt stood to greet me. I observed a round table set for an elaborate meal.

Somebody made a brief speech welcoming me to New York and, to confuse further, referred to me by my own name. I had begun at that point to wonder whether the explanation to the muddle was not that they had mistaken me for somebody else but that I had. Probably I shall wake up in the morning and find I'm Field-Marshal Montgomery after all, who's just had a bad dream that he was an insignificant writer.

These thoughts were not allowed to develop as the stern features of Uncle Tom came before me as my hosts began to try to pelt me with lethal martinis. Thirsty, I abstained. The meal began. First I downed three dozen clams. Why had nobody told me about their seafood? The clams were followed by T-bone steaks of Rabelaisian dimensions. The food was as good as my appetite: enjoying the meal, I became quite careless of the question whether I was an impostor or not. Then one of my hosts began to engage me in conversation. It was clear that his remarks had been rehearsed, and that his pointed references to a few titles of my books had been supported, not by reading anything of mine, but by a hasty glance at a book of reference first before he'd met me. It was obvious that he was the gang's Public Relations Officer. Dubious as the relationship was which he established, he at least made me realise that however mistaken their hospitality might be, there had been no error over my identity. When coffee and liqueurs were served and I had lit a Churchillian cigar, I fell to pondering just what this football team of square-jawed tycoons could possibly want from me.

Then one of them got to his feet and made another brief, fulsome and fatuous speech welcoming me to America.

"And now that you are here with us in New York, we hope that you will not mind doing a little something for us...?"

He paused. During that instant I saw myself being asked to write a new National Anthem, to put Lincoln's Gettysburg Speech into Iambic Pentameter, or perhaps accept a commission to write a play about the Pilgrim Fathers.

I smiled benignly across the table, encouraging him to continue.

"What we want you to do for us," he said, "is to write just one sentence." He paused again. An immaculate pad of paper and new fountain pen miraculously appeared over my shoulder and was placed before me.

"Just one sentence," he went on.

"Saying what?" I asked feebly.

"How you like it, of course."

"You mean being in New York?"

"No, no," he said, incredulous of my stupidity. "How you like IT."

I picked up the pen wondering how I could comment on something so abstract. No doubt the metaphysical poets would have enjoyed the exercise. But I felt the need to have the conception limited a little.

"What particular aspect of IT?" I asked.

"Just a comment on the pleasure it gives you," he replied encouragingly. His colleagues all beamed in my direction.

I thought vaguely of Elinor Glyn. But surely they couldn't mean that?

"What do you mean by IT?" I asked timorously.

Their first reaction to my question was one of consternation on their collective jowls. But under their spokesman's guidance they decided that my question had been a tease and they all switched their masks to one of indulgence towards a Limey's attempt at humour.

"Just write one brief sentence saying how you like Pepsi," their spokesman said.

"Pepsi? Who is she?" I asked, genuinely not having heard the name.

"Pepsi-Cola," he boomed.

"I've never had it. I once tried Coca-Cola," I added, trying to be helpful.

Now confusion broke loose. The Public Relations Officer looked like an H. M. Bateman cartoon. The rest of the gang or board rose, looming like ghouls around me. The Chairman clapped his hands.

"Bring Mr Duncan a glass of Pepsi," he boomed at a waiter, "and make it smart."

Another waiter produced an empty tumbler. Something like order was restored. They sat down again waiting. I continued to hold my pen at the ready.

Then there seemed to be some hitch in the background.

310

Waiters whispered and eventually a *maître d'hôtel* appeared and approached the Chairman.

"We very much regret," he said, "but the Waldorf Hotel only stocks Coca-Cola."

They were too shocked to comment. Their reaction was one of stunned silence. It was as if they had just been told that the dollar had collapsed and found parity with the franc.

"Shall I bring a glass of Coca-Cola?" the poor misguided man asked.

None of them answered him.

"No, please don't do that," I said. "I drank Coca-Cola once, it tasted like warm ink or soiled bathwater."

Animation came back to them.

"What did you say?" their Chairman asked.

I repeated my slander.

"Just put that down on that piece of paper, Mr Duncan, and we'll be very grateful."

I did as I was told.

The document was taken reverently from me. Everybody seemed delighted.

"You've just given us a check for a million dollars," their Public Relations Officer confided in me.

"If I give you another cheque like that," I said, "do you think you could give me the change?"

This frivolous incident seemed, in retrospect, wholly appropriate as a beginning to my visit to the States. The rest of my stay had a bizarre note of garish fantasy about it. And though I didn't take to drink I had to take to drugs in order to survive, and then ultimately had to flee home from New York because they affected me so severely because I have, what doctors call, a low threshold. One ordinary sleeping tablet will not only put me to sleep but makes me sleep-sodden for twenty-four hours. In order to make myself capable of working the next day, I have to take something like benzedrine or dexadrine to wake me up. And these drugs will then stimulate me to fantastic energy and ridiculous optimism. In this state I can only sleep again by taking another sedative, from which I have to be woken by another stimulant. This was the doper's spiral to which I was reduced after twenty-four hours in New York. It was partially Lord Beaverbrook's fault and partially due to the difference in time between London and New York.

As soon as I had escaped from the Pepsi Waldorf Cola Convention I returned to the Gladstone Hotel where I found a message from Beaverbrook asking me to join him at his flat in the Waldorf Towers.

He was in his most mischievous mood: dictating tapes to every corner of the globe, dropping papers all over the floor, bullying his valet, watching television and, at the same time, threatening that we were going to have one hell of a time enjoying the circus of the Election.

I reminded him that I didn't know anything about American Politics and cared rather less.

"You haven't seen anything to care about yet," he said, "but you'll become indignant enough when you've seen something of this city. I dare say I'll have to file your savage teeth."

I told him gently that I had sat up all night flying the Atlantic, that I had lunched with the Board of Pepsi-Cola and felt so weakened by their hospitality that I would go back to my hotel, sleep and rejoin him the next morning.

"Tired? You can't be tired," he said. "Why, you're not half my age and you've no woman with you. Anyhow I've told London to hold their first edition for your article, so you must cable it by midnight."

"Won't tomorrow morning do?"

"You ought to wear two watches here," he said, "one to give you New York time, one to remind you London is six hours ahead."

"Is it?"

"How d'you think you managed to arrive in New York before you left London? Anyhow, you get out there and let me read your copy before you file it. I'm looking forward to reading it." He did his best to fire me to his mistaken enthusiasm. It was already six o'clock when I sloped off on my assignment. I went, of course, straight back to my hotel and had a bath, having decided to go to bed for at least a couple of hours. Before closing my eyes I foolishly switched on a television set at the foot of the bed. There were nine distinct nightmares, or channels.

The first programme I watched consisted of an oily gigolo in a satin dressing-gown. The camera held a close-up of this smooth ape. He faced the camera and whispered sticky, amorous endearments to the millions of female fans, each indulging in this verbal mass masturbation as they sat alone in their flats, all, no doubt, wearing dressing-gowns too. With morbid fascination I watched this dildoe till he brought his programme to its climax by kissing the screen. He then removed his dressing-gown as though getting into bed. I hoped fervently that he might, in fact, find himself beside the four million females he had aroused. The advertisement for Pepsi-Cola came as a relief. Beaverbrook had been right: ten minutes of American life had aroused my indignation and hurled me sleepless onto the streets. Somewhat naturally I went to Broadway; it reminded me of a sordid funfair, stinking of Hamburgers, brash, neon and neolithic. I decided to take a taxi to Madison Square Gardens where torch singers were arousing the political consciousness of a moronic mob by swinging their padded breasts at an inoffensive microphone. It occurred to me that I had, in fact, fallen asleep in my hotel and would wake up to find a less sex-obsessed city. After listening to Eisenhower I fled from the blare of his supporters and his own impotent emphatic platitudes. I then went to the Therese Hotel up in Harlem which had been recommended to me. It was owned by Joe Louis, the ex-heavyweight champion boxer. I don't know what I was looking for there, but I didn't find it. I sat in the bar and scribbled my first despatch and because I was conscious that I had been flown to New York to report the Election, I started the article off with my impression of General Eisenhower's Variety Show and quoted some of his patter from his own performance. But the political scene had bored me and I wrote almost as dully as the General had spoken.

When I had persuaded a girl in the Cable Office at the Waldorf to type my copy out in capitals I took it up to Beaverbrook before despatching it. He was waiting. He read the couple of pages, then dropped them on the floor.

"Now go and write what you want to write and not what you think is expected of you," he snapped. "Don't tell me you just spent the evening at this Meeting?"

It was already midnight. I found another bar and wrote a piece starting off with my reception by Pepsi-Cola and ending with a picture of Mass Masturbation I'd seen on the television, and some other impressions on Harlem from which I concluded that New York was a cesspit of the shoddy.

Even the typist in the cable office seemed to enjoy this piece of spleen. Beaverbrook, still wide awake, grabbed the copy and, deleting a couple of slanders, told me to cable it immediately.

"That's the way to treat 'em," he cried gleefully. "Come round after breakfast and we'll see what we can stir up together tomorrow."

By the time I had cabled my copy off and returned to my hotel it was three o'clock in the morning. I took a sleeping pill. I had not been to bed since I had left Devonshire. I was determined to sleep for eight hours. But after two the telephone rang and some breezy sub-editor who had just gone to work at the *Evening Standard* office in Shoe Lane rang me to make some footling check on my copy. After that interruption I couldn't sleep any more. And consequently the only way to get through the next day was to take some dexadrine.

At ten o'clock Beaverbrook was waiting impatiently for me, fresh and raring to tear the city in two.

"You look pretty jaded," he observed. "Don't overdo your research into New York night life. You must get some sleep."

I told him what had happened.

"Take the phone off the hook," he advised unfeelingly.

Thus sandwiched between a sleeping pill and a stimulant I tore round and round the city with Beaverbrook doing his best to dodge punitive hospitality and pouring pailfuls of martinis behind sofas, leading me further astray. And each night the precise pattern was repeated: taking the phone off the hook did no good—the London office merely phoned the hotel desk and a sleep-sodden Negro porter had to pad down the corridor to bang on my door.

I am unable to remember the name of the man who was the permanent New York correspondent of the *Evening Standard*. During the first week I was there, I met him frequently either in the office or in Beaverbrook's flat. He had been correspondent for many years, and, though a born Londoner, he could almost pass for an American. Beaverbrook seemed to think highly of him: he was in all ways except one a typical professional journalist, seedy and pale from endless late nights and snack meals, shabby from his daily crush in the subway with skinny elbows and grubby cuffs, and this battered appearance made his wife seem almost incongruous. She was an Italian, tall, very handsome and extremely well dressed. Until thirty-five she would have passed for a model; but when she came round to see me at my hotel, I mistook her for the wife of a diplomat until she introduced herself.

Her visit was unannounced; with admirable directness she went straight to the point.

"My husband has told me that you see a great deal of Lord Beaverbrook," she said, "and therefore, since he has an important appointment with him this morning, I thought I could ask you whether he's in a good mood? A great deal for us depends on this interview and I don't want it to be mis-timed, you see."

"His mood was all right when I left him at 3 a.m.," I replied rather sleepily, "but as you know, that's no indication what it might be like now."

The woman nodded and looked extremely worried. I thought she was going to get up and leave. Then she changed her mind and decided to confide further in me. She was, I suppose, trying to reassure herself rather than seek my advice.

"My husband's been on the *Standard* for fifteen years," she said, "but though it's a good job, it can lead nowhere. He's forty-five, he could go on for another fifteen years, and still be nothing but the London correspondent on somebody else's paper...don't you think I'm right in urging him to work for himself?"

"Rather a difficult thing for a journalist, surely?"

"Not in this case," she said fervently. "I know of a small town newspaper out here that's for sale, and I think my husband would be right to buy it. With his drive and talent he could build it up into an important paper which would be his own. Don't you agree?"

I thought of her husband's defeated, bent figure and his capacity to write paragraphs of platitudes. I was quite unable to see him as an embryonic tycoon.

"Surely buying a newspaper, even a small town newspaper, would cost a lot of money?"

"We've been into that, of course," she replied. "The banks will lend us a good deal to augment our savings. Of course, it will mean losing the steady income from the *Standard*, but don't you think I'm right in encouraging my husband to do it, even if it is taking a risk?"

"If it's what he wants to do?"

"It is," she said so emphatically that I concluded the resolution was almost wholly hers.

"And is your husband going to ask Lord Beaverbrook to invest in this paper?" I asked.

"No. Merely to give in his notice," she answered.

"That shouldn't be difficult whatever his mood."

"Then you don't know Lord Beaverbrook as well as my husband does; he's had to put it off time and time again."

The delay she mentioned confirmed my suspicions, but I said nothing and soon managed to excuse myself.

Later that morning I called in at Beaverbrook's flat just as her husband was leaving. Whatever Beaverbrook's mood had been before the interview he now appeared worried, impatient and depressed.

"Bloody fool," he muttered when the man had gone, and then told me the background I had already learned from his wife.

"And what did you do?"

"Refuse to accept his notice. Begged him to go off and think it over again. Told him that he would lose his shirt on this small town paper. Advised him to stick to his typewriter and leave newspaper finance to old devils like me."

"And how did he take it?"

"As you saw, he was secretly relieved. I've a hunch his decisions were all prompted by his wife, an ambitious woman."

I told Beaverbrook that I'd met the wife earlier that morning and his opinion confirmed my own. The matter was forgotten and I went about my dissipation.

About six o'clock the same day I called back to Beaverbook's flat. The couple were sitting there with him, each with a glass of champagne in their hand. They were celebrating; even Beaverbrook was trying to look happy. I was handed a glass and I found myself drinking the toast of something like the *Buffalo Gazette*.

Soon afterwards they left, the wife glowing with triumph, leading her husband off, and then turned back to make me promise to join them at dinner at my hotel to celebrate their new life. I agreed.

"Bloody fool," Beaverbrook repeated.

He told me that the man had returned an hour ago with his wife and had announced that he'd thought the matter over and was determined to go ahead.

"What did you do?"

"What could I do? I accepted his resignation, gave him two years' salary and..."

"Lent him some money to buy the paper?"

"No, I'm a realist. I gave it to him."

The dinner at the Gladstone was attended by half a dozen people. I made a mistake by not wearing a black tie; the journalist's wife was wearing a Paquin gown and looked happy and radiant. She thanked me repeatedly for listening to her that morning and announced that today was the happiest moment of her life. Her husband seemed pleased to see her so gay and during the evening he enjoyed himself by asking me if I would occasionally write for the *Buffalo Gazette* or whatever it was called. The evening ended on this triumphant note and I described the scene later that night when I took Beaverbrook my copy as usual before cabling it. He said he still wished the man hadn't resigned because "a second-rate journalist is better than a third-rate proprietor."

Early next morning the phone rang in my room. I cursed, thinking it was London, and found it was Beaverbrook himself.

"Come round," he said. "I want to ask you something." He sounded miserable.

"What happened last night at dinner?" he asked. "Anything you didn't tell me?"

"Nothing. They merely celebrated. She told me it was the happiest day of her life. Even he looked pleased."

"I don't know about the happiest," Beaverbrook said, "it was certainly her last. She went straight home and slashed her wrists in the bath. He's quite distraught. You haven't a clue why she did it?"

"Maybe he reproached her for forcing him to chuck his job?"

"I thought of that; he swears he didn't."

"Or possibly she realised that she'd forced him into a position he hadn't the talent to sustain?"

"Possibly. But we shall never know," Beaverbrook said. "The poor fellow is utterly broken."

One of the reasons why I had agreed to go to New York was that I thought it would be then easy for me to go down to Washington to see Ezra Pound, who had been detained there for many years. Not only did I want to see him—he had written to me every week since his "capture"—but I wished to explore what the possibilities were of getting him out of the mental hospital and to have the charge of treason against him dropped so that he could return to Italy. But it was one thing to get to New York, another to get to Washington. I had not calculated on Beaverbrook or realised that he expected me to dance or sleep-walk around him right round the clock.

After a week I had no alternative but to tell him I intended to go to Washington the next day.

"Waste of your time," he said. "The fun is here in New York. Washington's a dull city; you'll find nothing worth writing about down there."

"I'm going to see Ezra Pound."

He frowned. Pound had often attacked Beaverbrook.

"Well, don't get locked up too," he said, "and bring me your article as usual by midnight."

"That won't be difficult for you," he went on. "After all, if you can write a weekly column about a Devon farm from New York, what's to prevent you writing your daily report about New York from Washington? I dare say you'll invent it all going down in the train."

He was quite correct, of course. That was precisely what I did.

I found I couldn't visit Ezra till the afternoon. Peregrine Worsthorne gave me lunch and explained some of the legal difficulties of Ezra's case.

Eliot had seen Pound in St Elizabeth's, and had told me that Ezra's mind had gone. "He kept telling me to read Meredith," Possum had reported as though this was proof of insanity. But I was not convinced: the letters I received from Ezra were far from mad, though the thoughts they contained did not appear to follow each other. But this *non sequitur* had always been apparent in his letters and conversation. It derived from his ability to perceive where a conversation was leading and from his inability to realise that his listener would not always perceive the connection between subjects. And to Ezra everything was interconnected. What I wanted to discover by visiting Washington was whether Ezra was playing insane in order to evade trial, or whether the authorities were merely stating he was insane in order to avoid the embarrassment of condemning him for treason. And there seemed no doubt that by giving aid and support to the enemy by broadcasting from Rome, he was technically guilty.

Worsthorne was sympathetic and well informed: he thought Ezra's insanity was a convenient Government formula.

When I reached the large, grim asylum, I was interviewed by the principal, Dr Epstein, who wanted to know precisely why I wished to see Pound.

"He's an old friend of mine and I've brought a few books for him to read."

"I'm afraid I must examine them. I like to have details myself of all books he sees."

"But they're only *The Republic*, *The Gita* and a book about the Amazon."

"Nevertheless, please leave them with me."

They never reached Ezra.

An attendant or warder led me through miles of inhospitable corridors swarming with noisy inmates. The noise and echoes reminded me of a public swimming bath. As we approached Ezra's ward we passed a Negro who was comforting a girl who was crying. The Negro turned as we passed him.

"He's out," he said, indicating Pound's cell.

The warder then left me. The Negro left the weeping girl and led me along another corridor and pointed to a lawn outside.

Ezra and Dorothy were sitting there on a couple of deck-chairs.

Ezra got up quickly and erected another chair for me.

"They're very comfortable. One has to go nuts before you have the sense to buy proper chairs," he announced as an unassailable dictum.

His childish enthusiasm for something as ordinary as a deck-chair was typical of him. He always had the knack of making me see a familiar object for the first time.

"You'll understand why I like deck-chairs so much later," he said. "How's Rose Marie, Possum and Bunny?"

I hadn't seen Ezra since 1938. Thirteen years had not aged him particularly. He still looked leonine, big-chested and swarthy. Wearing a yellow sweater that gave him the appearance of a tennis coach yet, with his sloppy, loose-collared shirt and broad-brimmed hat, reminiscent of the Paris of Gertrude Stein, James Joyce and Hemingway.

Apparently Dorothy was allowed to visit him every afternoon for an hour. In spite of the environment and circumstances we sat and gossiped for half an hour. Dorothy always managed to carry an air of Henley and cucumber sandwiches with her. And in her company our conversation became appropriately frivolous. The poor woman was terrified of something. Her fear always frightened me. I was relieved when she rose to go. I promised to visit her that evening for dinner.

Ezra then led me, armed with a deck-chair, to his cell.

"You see why I like deck-chairs," he said, packing them flat against the wall and indicating the dimensions of his cell.

"Like a straitjacket," I thought. "Not big enough to swing a cat in," I said, looking round the 8 ft. by 5 ft. room which contained an iron bed, chaos of clothes and a muddle of magazines and paper.

"I've had six years in this to make myself at home," he shouted, gaily sweeping some papers under the bed with his foot.

We had to shout at each other even in his cell because a large television set outside in the corridor blared away.

"They try to reduce us idiots to the level of insanity outside," Ezra commented.

Outside the door of his cell which I noticed was made of chestnut, two inmates now sat each side in a rocking chair. They had inane grins on their faces and had taken up positions as though guarding us. One looked like Van Gogh.

Failing to hear each other in the cell, Ezra got out his deck-chairs again and set them up outside further along the corridor away from the television set.

"Have you written any poems in here?" I asked.

"Birds don't sing in cages."

We didn't mention poetry again.

"Any chance of your getting out of here?" I asked, when a very insane old man came and started to look down my ear.

"No," Ezra replied, "I'm too big to go down the drain. There'd be comment if they let me slip away. Maybe after the election things may be different...but I don't want to get out to be assassinated."

This fear of being assassinated was the first and only sign I noticed of Ezra's insanity. But it was not new. He had always imagined himself as the target of some international group of powerful bankers or warmongers, as he called them. Clearly this illusion that he was a menace to such power groups arose as a compensation for being ignored by them. I had never met any tycoon who'd even heard of Pound, let alone feared his influence.

"You see, they know I've tumbled them," he went on. "Wars are made solely to create debts."

"Yes," I replied, wondering how many men of genius I knew personally at that time who had been driven into some degree of paranoia or persecution mania by a world which ignored or persecuted them. There was Epstein, Stravinsky, Baird and Brancusi, each with their areas of "insanity" which derived not from the talents they had brought into the world, but from the treatment they had received from it. Eliot and Cocteau were exceptions. This was only because neither had been persecuted or ignored.

Poor Ezra seemed oblivious of his condition or his environment, unaware of a white-headed man beside us who was stroking the radiator and talking to it as if it were a cat.

"Gold is 4 dollars over price," he went on, venting his obsession with international finance, way above my head, but every remark pertinent.

"Of course that shit Roosevelt was always determined to take the British Empire to pieces. A pander to Stalin: a pity Winnie didn't or couldn't stand up to him."

Then he switched to asking me how Cocteau and Brancusi were and somehow got onto the subject of Vivien Eliot, whom I had never met.

"You should start *Townsman* again," he said, getting up and snatching a couple of teacups from a passing trolley. "Think of it while I go and see if any of my fellow maniacs can supply us with a couple of biscuits."

I went into his room, noticed he was still studying Chinese and had a photo of Mary by his bed.

"Try and get Olga out here to see me," he said, seeing the photo in my hand and passing me a cream cracker.

"You want to look into Roosevelt's perfidy," he said. "Of course it'll come out in time. The trouble is I spotted it way before time. Stalin and Roosevelt were nut-crackers to Winnie. The British Empire was the only thing that could stand up to Wall Street alignment with Marxism."

"Is there anything I can do for you?"

"Get me exact information. They stop my papers, censor my books. Write regularly if it's only a postcard. There aren't many of us. We must keep in touch."

I told him how I had disliked what I had seen of New York.

"The trouble with the U.S.," he said, "is they resent finding any other values than money. It's essentially a poor country. How can they understand anything when the function of education here is only to keep the young off the labour market. I see they can now take a Ph.D. in being an usherette."

We returned to our deck-chairs with our feet on a radiator, watching the evening die on our hands. An hour passed. He talked on, remembering details of previous conversations and incidents I had forgotten myself, jumping from one subject to another as associations which I didn't immediately perceive linked them. His mind, like the pick-up of a gramophone, played several discs at once. But this wasn't insanity: similar cross-references and associations are behind every page of the *Cantos*. The library of his mind had a different filing system from other people's.

"What d'you want me to do to get you out of here?" I rose to go.

"Pull strings. I couldn't stand trial three days, let alone three months."

"I'll see you soon," I said hopelessly.

We shook hands. Little did I guess then that I would see him again and it would be under even worse circumstances.

I walked up the long corridor to the door at the end. It was locked. The white-haired fellow who'd been trying to make the radiator purr informed me the warder had locked up half an hour ago and, I gathered, he wouldn't be opening the door till the morning. I turned and retraced my steps down the corridor towards Ezra's cell. A man came towards me.

"If you like," he said, "I'll clean your watch. I've got some black boot-polish here."

Then Ezra emerged and observed my predicament. Together we examined the locked door.

"Two bullfinches in the same cage now," he observed, "it's really more than Papageno deserves."

We continued to rattle the chain.

"Don't worry," I said, "it's much saner inside here than messing around with Beaverbrook. Besides, you've got a deck-chair."

"Yes," observed the white-haired man, "and not only has he got a deck-chair but a heart as big as Washington."

We heard heavy steps coming towards the locked door. It was opened.

"Not so much noise in here," the warder shouted. The door locked again.

"I want to get out," I said.

"You don't say!"

"I'm only a visitor."

"Sure. Next you'll tell me you're sane."

"No," said Ezra, "but he ain't been certified yet."

"I saw him come in," the white-haired fellow volunteered.

The key turned again.

"Didn't you hear the bell? Follow me, we'll soon check."

I turned and shook Ezra's hand again and watched him

shambling back down the corridor. '*Nel mezzo del cammin di nostra vita mi ritrovai...*'

I went to the address Dorothy had given me. It was a small rented bungalow in the suburbs.

"I thought you'd got lost," she said.

I told her how I'd missed the bell and got locked in.

"Poor Ezra sees so few old friends," she said. "I suppose he kept you talking."

"Do you see him every day?"

"Yes," she said. "Time passes and I read a lot. I try and read the same books he's reading so that I can follow what he's talking about."

Her loyalty was always touching. To her he could do no wrong. Wives are wonderful things. Blindness their virtue. Or perhaps only semi-blindness.

"Tell Olga that if she wants to come and see him," she said, "I won't stand in her way. He's only allowed one visitor a day, so while she's here, tell her I'll leave Washington."

I murmured something indicating that I thought that was generous of her.

We sat and talked for an hour, then went out to dine. During the meal I discussed ways and means of getting Ezra's case re-examined. She reacted without enthusiasm.

"I've been thinking," I said, "that it might be a good idea if I could persuade a dozen or so people who've been awarded the Order of Merit or the Nobel Prize for literature to sign a petition to the U.S. Attorney General appealing for clemency."

She thought this suggestion might be dangerous.

"Tom's doing something," she said. "He's thinking of getting a legal opinion."

I came sadly to the conclusion that Dorothy was resigned to Ezra's position. She knew where he was. She alone could visit him regularly.

But though I had written to Antonia from New York I had not told her I was returning. This self-restraint was easy: I didn't know. We left Idlewild at ten o'clock at night. Two hours later one of the four engines of the plane caught fire. A funnel of

324

flames flashed past the fuselage. The captain dropped his petrol from the tanks and announced that he was turning round and would try to make New York, then land on three engines. We were requested to remain calm and keep our safety belts on. The plane skimmed over the menacing black waves. The stewards instructed us to don our life-jackets in case we ditched, showing us that each jacket contained a small whistle and a torch for the purpose of attracting passing shipping.

I noticed to my surprise that I had no feeling of fear, merely a sense of the ridiculous at the image of myself floating in the Atlantic blowing a penny whistle, in the vain hope of arresting the passage of the Queen Mary.

We came down; I observed the fire engines on the runway. We made our landing and were given free drinks in the bar. Four hours later we took off again in another plane.

Even if Antonia had planned to meet me, seeing my name in the passenger list, this accident would, I thought, have prevented her. So I telephoned her from the airport and she met me at the Terminal. We went straight to the cottage. I immediately phoned Rose Marie. I was relieved to hear her voice. I never had any inhibitions about showing my feeling for Rose Marie to Antonia. And if she minded she never showed it. Rose Marie wanted to know if I'd remembered the food mixer which then couldn't be obtained in London. I was so anxious to get home to her that I said I would catch the midnight train.

It was then eight o'clock. But I was determined not to make love to Antonia. It was bad enough that she'd met me. Rose Marie was bound to ask if I'd seen her. I could not spoil my reunion with Rose Marie by going to her straight from Antonia. I had at least got that clear in my mind.

Odd that this resolve, which was, I thought, for the good, should have led me to do more harm that evening than I had done on the night I had left for America.

For on this occasion Antonia did not share my resolve. Perhaps my affection to Rose Marie on the telephone made her challenge it? Perhaps she had just missed me? I think it was that.

She had lit a fire in the sitting-room, made coffee, and now sat on the carpet leaning back against the sofa.

"Aren't you going to kiss me?"

Her tongue indicated that she had more than a kiss in mind. I broke from her embrace.

"Bitch," I said.

"You love women till they behave like women," she said.

I kept my eyes on the fire. It too was burning.

"No? So American puritanism is infectious, is it?"

I thought of the whistle "to arrest passing shipping". I said nothing. I was determined to return to Devon with a clean sheet, or at least relatively. That was, I thought, to be my present to Rose Marie. Perhaps it was to myself. I didn't know.

"Let's go to the station," I said.

As the train left, it was I who was apologising. It was always that way. I was like a shuttle between two looms of guilt.

As soon as I returned from America I went to see Eliot to tell him that I had visited Ezra in Washington. I felt that he was the one person with sufficient prestige on both sides of the Atlantic to be influential in obtaining a review of the case. While I described Ezra's tiny cell and how I had got locked in with the inmates, Eliot took up his usual stance, leaning forward in his chair and studying the pattern on the carpet as though it were an interesting Sanskrit text. It was his way of listening attentively: one got used to talking to the top of his head.

Ezra had already been confined for several years. Eliot and I had spent innumerable lunches discussing the matter. But my visit naturally gave me a new sense of urgency. It was not shared. Gently Eliot reminded me that Dorothy Pound's London solicitor, A. V. Moore, was attending to the matter, and had instructed an American counsel to produce an opinion. This sort of legal knitting had been going on for years and years.

I became impatient.

"I've read the transcript of the broadcasts Ezra made in Rome," I said, "and they don't contain anything treasonable or seditious."

"Yes," Possum said cautiously, "so have I. But he did broadcast and therefore committed technical treason by giving comfort to the enemy. And it is possible that if he were tried he would be found guilty on this technicality."

"He told me himself that he wasn't fit enough to stand a trial."

"Then there are two reasons for avoiding it, aren't there?" Tom was at his most cautious.

"But something must be done. This legal stalemate could last for years, meanwhile Ezra's in gaol," I cried. Tom looked up from the invisible script on the carpet.

"Perhaps in some ways that's the best place for him," he said quietly.

His remark shocked me. It silenced me. Was his caution mixed with indifference? My affection and respect for him had blinded me to something almost sinister in his attitude to Ezra's predicament. Was he being cautious, not on Ezra's account, but his own? I was bewildered. I could think of nothing to say. All I could see was that the man before me had received the Order of Merit and the Nobel Prize while *Il Miglior Fabbro* had been presented with nothing but a deck-chair.

"What I meant," Tom said, trying to soften the effect his remark had made on me, "is that at least Dorothy now knows where he is."

I smiled. The tension relaxed. But I knew that that was not all he had meant. And he knew that I knew. Tom was never quite as unguarded to me again.

For the next few years I felt hopelessly frustrated on this issue. Olga and Mary wrote to me urging me to do something for Ezra. I felt the initiative had to come from Eliot who whenever we met deferred to legal procedure. Delay seemed to mean nothing to him, though he was always particularly responsive to Olga's predicament and strangely bitter about Dorothy. I realised that there was some history to his attitude to her which I did not know about. Meanwhile Ezra continued to head his letters to me "Hell Basement of", and was becoming the man in the iron mask.

Eventually this feeling of impotency drove me to take a step without deferring to Eliot. I decided to write a letter to the leading figures in literature and politics, asking them to sign a petition for Ezra's release so that he could return to Italy and complete his Cantos. I wrote to Churchill, Picasso, Bertrand Russell, Smuts, Hemingway, Stravinsky, Epstein and half a dozen other international names. Some didn't answer; Churchill's reply was prompt and courteous: 'in his position he did not think he could interfere in a case concerning a national of another country'. Bertrand Russell refused categorically. Only Epstein and Hemingway offered to sign without reserve. This response amazed me. Nevertheless I addressed the appeal to President Eisenhower but had no evidence that it reached him personally. Whereas Eliot himself could have got into the White House.

Living at Orme Lane, Ashley Dukes was a near neighbour. We called him the Duke of Notting Hill Gate. This was apt. Ashley had always invested his royalties in freeholds. As the value of his properties rose, he had mortgaged them and with the money bought more. When I knew him he told me he owned property worth over a hundred thousand pounds excluding the Mercury Theatre. Wearing his ducal tweeds and buttonhole he used to drop in on Rose Marie as he took his daily constitutional which, even at the age of seventy, consisted of striding from Notting Hill Gate to the Garrick Club. Often he used to have a bottle with him, an unlabelled claret he'd bought in a lot at a city auction, a bottle of Madeira or a raspberry flavoured Moselle. He knew more about wine than anybody I ever met: and almost as much about women.

One day at Orme Lane, Ashley asked me why I never called to see Wyndham Lewis who, he told me, was living only a couple of hundred yards away in a flat at Notting Hill Gate. I replied that I had never met Lewis and doubted that he was the sort of man to welcome a stranger. Ashley pointed out that with Ezra as a mutual friend we had something in common.

"Besides," he added, "now that Lewis is blind, he never gets out to meet anybody. He's very miserable and very poor."

I went the next day. Lewis's flat was on the top of one of those sort of tenement blocks which were built by councils at the beginning of the century. The draughty stone staircase was built on the outside of the building without even windows for protection. Children played hop-scotch on the landings. Washing was pegged outside flat doors. I felt a little apprehensive about making this intrusion: but I had a debt to pay. *Blast* had influenced me considerably though I had failed to finish *The Apes of God* or any other book of his except *Tarr*. With Leavis as my tutor, I had had two minds about *Paleface*. But my admiration for Lewis as a draughtsman was unqualified.

The door was opened by a woman of about forty. She took my coat. I assumed she was a housekeeper.

Lewis greeted me warmly. He turned and asked the woman to bring us some coffee. But she had already left the room.

"And bring some brandy," he continued. He was obviously quite blind.

We talked furiously for an hour. I was very much reminded of Leavis. The similarity between them would have annoyed each considerably. Both were immensely intelligent, sharing the same passionate devotion to literature and lamed with a mutual bitterness.

"That coffee and brandy is a long time coming," Lewis complained.

While he talked to my empty chair, I tiptoed into the kitchen to tell the woman what he had wanted. When she brought it in, she put the tray down and left the room. The way she looked at Lewis told me she was something more than a housekeeper. But he did not introduce us.

Eventually I asked him if there was anything he needed or that I could do for him.

"Yes," he said. "I want to go to see my publishers. I can see my way down the stairs all right but I'd be grateful if you could put me into a taxi at the bottom of them."

Lewis's way of seeing his way down the stairs was to feel the wall with both hands.

I steered him to the kerb and waited in vain for a passing cab. None appeared. Eventually I told him that I was going to see if I could find one in Church Street. Like a monument, the blind artist stood surrounded by the unseeing pedestrians and the frantic traffic. The image stays like a symbol in my mind. Ezra sent me this poem on Lewis, which has never yet been published:

Preferring blindness to chance of having his mind stop,
                                        when European
mind does stop and has *stopped.*
A blown husk that is finished,
        but the light sings eternal
a pale flare over marshes
                where the salt hay whispers to tide's change.

I offered to accompany him to the publishers but he insisted that he could manage once he was seated in the cab.

The next day I saw Eliot and told him of Lewis's pitiful condition.

"He's quite blind now and Ashley says he's no friends. It's a sort of tenement flat without any heating. I don't suppose he sees anybody but his housekeeper."

"Housekeeper?"

I described her.

"That's his wife. He's very fond and wholly dependent on her, but some quirk makes him ashamed to introduce her to his friends."

I continued to stress the discomfort of his surroundings. Eliot's debt to Lewis was far greater than mine. And he'd won the Nobel Prize.

"We ought to do something to cheer him up," I said.

A few days later, Ashley told me that Tom had ordered a crate of champagne to be sent from the Mercury bar to Lewis every month.

Eliot had suggested that I should join the Garrick Club, but as he had only recently been elected there himself he asked Ashley Dukes to propose me while he seconded the application. We would sometimes lunch together in the backroom. During this time I saw that Eliot was both miserable and unwell. He aggravated his own unhappiness in small ways by denying himself small pleasures. Whenever I hailed a taxi he would look disapproving and trail off with his umbrella to the tube. Though he could afford luxuries, he pretended they were beyond his means. I remember having to persuade him that the smoked trout I had ordered was not an extravagant indulgence but cost only a few shillings on the Club menu. He came to like it. But he always took his wine flavoured with guilt. To add to his discomforts he decided to abandon his one pleasure: smoking. I tried to dissuade him. But a few weeks later he asked me to meet him for tea at Fabers. I arrived at 4.30. To my surprise I found Tom standing in the room looking very bad-tempered.

"You're late," he said shortly. "You said you'd come for tea."

"I have. It's only 4.30."

"I like my tea at 4.0."

"You didn't tell me that."

"Well, you'll know another time."

This was ridiculous. He was behaving like a *prima donna*. I began to sulk. Although I was nearly thirty years younger than he was I resented his talking to me in the tone of an elder brother. The tea tray came in. Tom grabbed the biscuits, passed them to me and hurriedly sloshed out two cups of tea.

"Hurry up, Ronnie," he said, "don't nibble the things as though you've got all the time in the world."

I assumed he was going dotty, and to please him wolfed the biscuits whole, and while they were still in my mouth drank my tea as though in a buffet running for a train.

"That's better," he said with a broad grin on his face, "now we've had tea."

"Wouldn't it be appropriate if I put my head in the pot?" I asked.

"You don't understand. Things are very difficult for me. You see, I promised myself not to smoke at all until after teatime, so I look forward to my first cigarette at precisely five minutes past four. That's why I was annoyed you were late."

He apologised and inhaled deeply.

This silly incident was serious because it was indicative of the way Tom was obsessed with punishing himself. His asthma, aggravated by his stoop and the ease with which he caught colds while trailing beneath his umbrella, required that he should winter abroad, or at least avoid the November fogs in which he invariably suffered from bronchitis. But though his friends urged him to go to Madeira or Andalusia, he would say he couldn't afford it. We knew, of course, that this was not true.

At other times when we asked him to dinner or to a theatre, he would say he couldn't come "because he couldn't leave John."

Hayward had become the stick which Tom used to beat his own back with. No doubt looking after him was to Tom a discipline in self-abnegation and humility, but many of us saw it as a kind of self-indulgent masochism.

Ashley Dukes and I often talked with some concern about our friend. Especially since Eliot began to affect many signs of premature old age. His stoop began to be accentuated, his umbrella trailed, he even started to cup his hands at remarks he he could hear perfectly well. The elation he had at receiving the Nobel Prize and particularly the Order of Merit, was short-lived.

"Unless we do something for Tom," Ashley said to me one day, "he'll die of melancholy or John Hayward."

As if I hadn't sufficient distractions, another now came upon me which absorbed me for almost a year. Ian Hunter, who had been assistant manager at Glyndebourne at the time of *Lucretia* and who managed the music agency, Harold Holt Ltd, had a scheme to introduce *Son et Lumière* into England. He asked me if I would write a script on Blenheim Palace. I became enthusiastic, especially when I discovered Rochester's association with Woodstock. I met a director of the English Electric Company, who was going to set up the technical side. The possibilities of using sound, light, music and words against architecture, fascinated me. Here was a possibility to revive the masque form again; Inigo Jones and Ben Jonson would have seized on it. I hurried off in the middle of a harvest to Versailles with Anthony Besch, to see what they were doing there, then went to Woodstock. Both the Duke and the librarian were extremely helpful. There was a mine of history to work on. I wrote half the script, and was then asked to write a similar masque on Hampton Court, as the plans for Woodstock had fallen through because of inadequate car park facilities. I now immersed myself in Wolsey, and became excited with the possibilities of light on Hampton Court Bridge. Within a week I had sketched what I thought was quite a good script. Unhappily, an old woman who had a Grace and Favour apartment in the Palace appealed to the Queen to prevent these "goings-on" and was successful. As if I had not taken punishment enough, I found myself agreeing to write yet a third masque based on Longleat. There was no difficulty there. Lord Bath was too much of a showman. He took me round his house, and revealed every family skeleton that he thought might make a dramatic point. These did not interest me, but the possibilities of light on the lake encouraged me enough to write yet a third script. But then the English Electric Company, who were underwriting the enterprise, decided that Longleat was too far from any centre of population.

A year went into the wastepaper basket.

While we were living at Orme Lane, George's son, David, began running over to the cottage to escape from his nanny. I used to make up stories for him. They were not fairy stories. I grew very fond of him; he was an attractive child. One day he told me that he wanted to go camping. I told him that tents were very expensive, and recounted the story of Robinson Crusoe.

"Will you come and live in a tent with me?" he asked. "If I start saving up for one?"

"How are you going to do that?"

"Collect money," he said.

This seemed a reasonable solution. I allocated a drawer in my desk for any pennies he could put into it. I suggested that the best way of saving money would be to take any odd change he might find in his mother's handbag. David used to scamper over every day and drop a few coins into the drawer.

"But we shall need other things besides a tent," I told him. "Forks, tin openers, spoons, glasses etc."

"How are we going to get those?" he asked, fearing that this difficulty might mean we might not be able to go camping.

"See if you can find such things about the house, and take them when nobody is looking." He clapped his hands with glee and ran back to the house. From then on my desk became a hiding place for odd pieces of Harewood silver, tin openers, pieces of string, knobs of sugar, bacon rind, and anything else this jackdaw could find. One day I showed the contents of the drawer to his parents. Marion naturally gave him a tent on his next birthday. I never saw a child so happy.

"Now there is nothing to stop us going camping," he announced. This was true. There was no way out of it now. Camping was a rigour I had never suffered; but neither George nor Marion would let me get off the hook. David and I travelled to Harewood and put the microscopic tent up in the park. All my Robinson Crusoe dicta came home to roost. With bits of bacon rind four months old, I found myself frying up magpies which, strangely enough, were quite edible. Meanwhile, David, to augment our larder, began fishing enthusiastically in the lake. For hour and hours he sat with a child's seriousness. I was moved almost to tears at this, and remembered an instance in my childhood. I asked Marion to go into Harrogate and buy some trout. That evening I placed one on David's hook when he was asleep, and then went to watch him draw the line in the next morning. He will never be as happy or proud again. Children deserve the kindness of deceit.

The lowest I have sunk, so far, in my life was when I became a dramatic critic. Beaverbrook had asked me to stand in for Beverley Baxter, who had written a weekly survey of the London Theatre in the *Evening Standard*. I agreed to do it for a couple of months while Baxter was away. I thought the job would give me the opportunity of saying something about the squalor of Shaftesbury Avenue. I hoped, too, that I would learn a few things from seeing a new play every night. And I told myself that I had a duty to do this because I had maintained that poetry could only be criticised by poets, music by composers and drama by dramatists. It would have been wrong of me, holding this opinion, to refuse to do the job for a time when given the opportunity. I was not that anathema, the pure critic, the person who, lacking creative experience gives the writer the benefit of it. Having had five or six of my own plays staged in the West End, I knew of some of the difficulties, the compromises, the playwright agrees to under pressure; the limitations placed on the producer under duress by the management; the restrictions placed on the actors' performance to please either the producer, the management or the dramatist. My hands were not clean, I felt fitted for the job. And I had some clear-cut criteria to apply. I wanted to blast the so-called poetic drama in which the poetry is used as decoration, stucco thrown on the wall of the action and not an integral part, evolving out of it. I wanted to torpedo the piffle of the new quasi-realistic theatre which is mere naturalism, never art. I repudiated all their false premises that the theatre should be only socially conscious: I wanted it to be wholly conscious. To say that man is only a social-political being is fantastic, not realistic. It is one of the contemporary fairy tales. Dialectics are true; the lie is maintaining that it is the whole truth. Another edifice I wanted to blast was the sickening way in which our truncated drama had been divided up into straight plays, comic plays, social plays, religious plays. Life is whole or it is not life. I was sick of the convention of the post office sorting house mentality. I wanted to see a play which contained all of these indivisible parts of humanity within one play. I had, of course, a subjective edge to this crusade: because my first play had been about a saint, idiots had tied a horrid tin label, or halo, round my tail calling me a religious dramatist, and expected me to spend the rest of my wicked life writing terrible little masques in which the characters wore beards and waved Biblical spears. I damned this division of the indivisible, the individual.

With a black tie permanently round my neck and armed like an anarchist with grenades of artistic principles bulging from every pocket, I joined my long-suffering colleagues at my First Night. However much the play bored me, remembering the critic who'd reviewed the whole of *This Way to The Tomb* after being in the theatre for only five drunken minutes, I resolved to sit it through and if possible read the script too, before writing about the play and judging it by its production.

I kept to this resolution; not even a migraine induced by a musical-comedy or a dose of Shavian superficial polemics, could budge me from my seat before the final curtain. And, believing that you should quote the text if you're going to tear it to pieces, I managed to scribble some of the dialogue down.

My first article was a blockbuster, savage and uncompromising. I used all my armaments: machine-gunning the audience for debauching the theatre, treating it as a digestive tablet, an after-dinner palliative; chucking a Mills bomb at H. M. Tennents for pandering to such offal and turning Shaftesbury Avenue into a bazaar of linguistic clichés and emotional platitudes, then drew my sharpest sabre to decapitate the producer, disembowel the playwright, and the cast I punished with pity or derision.

I wrote it carefully. Then I read it through and burned it. For I saw that if what I had written had been printed the play would probably have closed. I wanted it to close. I wanted to bankrupt the management, turn the playwright into some useful occupation such as ditching or bricklaying and, who knows, maybe the producer could be turned into a competent drapers' assistant? But I burned it. I had read too many cruel criticisms myself. I had seen too many little actors crumble pathetically, and perhaps deservedly, as they snatched the evening paper with hope, and put it down hopeless. A judge has to be indifferent. I knew too many actors to be able to punish even justly. So I rewrote the article half a dozen times. Finally producing something which read like a pastiche of Henry James rather than Swift, and was so full of conditional clauses and cautious parentheses that it said nothing, but it was just: it was also very dull.

Beaverbrook sent for me the next day after the article appeared. "What's up with you?" he asked. "You can do better than this." I made no reply. He continued.

"Look, Ronald, I didn't ask you to do this job because I wanted to know whether you liked or disliked a play. I wanted you to write a bright piece. I'm not interested in justice, but good journalism. A good critic has to attack, attack, attack."

His point was not lost on me. It was a brief interview. I went off, determined not to write any more "dramatic criticism" and when the next play was produced, not to read any either. "Attack, attack, attack," he'd said.

I phoned James Gunn, the editor of the *Evening Standard*, and asked him if he could replace me.

"I could, but I won't," he said.

Fortunately for my conscience, the plays that following week were so execrable I had no scruple in damning them and some of the performances too. Beaverbrook congratulated me on finding my cutting edge. John Gielgud wrote to me complaining of the unkind things I had written about Diana Wynyard.

During the next few weeks, I found to my horror that I was slipping into the habit which I had always suspected was routine with the regular critics. I discovered that I was thinking out an angle of attack even before I had seen the play. Sometimes as I drove to the theatre a line of fire, or a few satirical gimmicks, would come to my mind which I clung to whether the play deserved them or not. To think of an epigram was fatal: one became careless whose career it killed. Two or three witty remarks might occur to me at breakfast; I would realise that these would make my article; that evening the play would be executed before it was tried. As any journalist knows, his article is made or unmade by the impact he can obtain with the opening sentence or paragraph. This is the paragraph which critics cook up as they wiggle their toes in the bath and into which the play, the opera, the film or the person they subsequently see or interview is made to fit.

These dishonest habits are part of a dishonest trade. When you have to phone a considered judgement of a play in bright and witty prose to your paper within half an hour of the curtain coming down, you cannot risk being caught with your trousers down. Consequently you think out your angle of attack and even scribble a phrase or two long before the actors have applied their make-up. When I found that I was doing this with even more facility than my colleagues whom I despised, I felt I had caught a dose of cultural syphilis. Having obtained the dubious reputation of the Luther of Shaftesbury Avenue, I bolted back to my farm to cleanse myself mucking out pigsties again, much to the disgust of Roger and Briony, who had enjoyed these First Nights and seeing the tumbril carrying victims towards their execution.

I had taken my copy of Jan's Journal into the *Evening Standard* one day, when I saw Henry Williamson there. He often used to come over and see me at the farm. The editor had asked Williamson to go and interview Sir Oswald Mosley. Williamson asked if I would like to go along with him. I had never met Mosley but had seen several copies of his *Movement* newspaper. They had not impressed me. But as I had nothing to do, I thought it would be interesting to meet him. He received us very civilly in his flat in Westminster. Williamson had a list of questions which the editor had asked him to put to him. To each of these Mosley replied carefully and frankly. Listening to him, I was impressed by the moderation of some of his views and the extraordinary range of historical knowledge which supported them. And unlike any other politician I had met, Mosley admitted that he had been completely wrong on many major issues. There were several other questions which I would have liked to put to him, but it was Williamson's interview, not mine. When we returned to the office, Williamson typed out Mosley's replies.

"We can't print this," they said. "Nobody would believe us if we did." Williamson brought me in to corroborate that these were verbatim answers to the questions.

"Even so, we can't print this because it doesn't conform to the picture the Press have painted of Mosley." It was a depressing incident.

Like Luther, Eliot had a gut obsession. He came to lunch at Orme Lane one day and described to Rose Marie and me symptoms of his constipation and constriction through the entire meal.

I was therefore not surprised when he told me some weeks later that he was going into the London Clinic for an operation. I saw him a few days after he came out. He was ashen but voluble in describing every detail of his physical condition.

"Whatever you do, Ronnie," he wailed, "avoid piles, and if you get piles don't let them do to you what they've just done to me. They put a cork up my anus to prevent me from excreting. The pain was excruciating."

I allowed him the luxury of a minute description of his physical torments. Perhaps my sympathy would have been more genuine had I realised then that I was to undergo the same operation a few years later. When I did, I never told him that the cork had been a figment of his imagination.

After his operation I invited him to come to Devon to re-cuperate. He said he would like to do this, particularly as he wanted to have a look round Ashburton.

"I believe my ancestors originated from Ashburton," he told me.

But Eliot never came to Devon. So the next time I was motoring through the town I stopped and looked round the church and graveyard. I came across one or two graves inscribed with the name Elliott, copied the details down and sent them to him, remarking that there was still an Elliott in the town who kept a grocers' shop in the High Street.

Some weeks later Eliot told me that he thought these Elliotts were his ancestors.

"The spelling probably changed when they crossed the Atlantic," he explained.

I did not ask him how this theory fitted into his East Coker association. But I did see that he was concerned with "in my end is my beginning..."

About this time I became aware that I was attached to two obsessions. It would be false to say I suffered from either, since neither caused me any serious inconvenience. Nevertheless both were irrational and recurring. I realised that each derived from psychic disturbance but this realisation did nothing to diminish the obsessions themselves. For months, just before I fell asleep I imagined myself bowling at cricket. I would visualise myself running up to the wicket, swinging the ball then watching it pitch at an unidentified batsman. I would repeat this fantasy for about an over by which time I was in a deep sleep. Whenever I was sleepless, all I had to do was to conjure up this fantasy to relax and sleep almost immediately. I had indulged in this trick for a considerable time before I became aware of it or thought how odd it was that though I never liked cricket and had not played it since I was at school I should now create this particular fantasy. I wondered if the identity of the batsman contained any clue but though I bowled thousands of overs I never saw his face, nor did he hit the ball; he always disappeared just as the ball bounced on the pitch.

The other obsession came upon me about the same time and was equally inexplicable to me. One day walking along Queensway I suddenly woke up as though from a deep sleep to find myself standing outside a fish shop. I had been staring fixedly at a pile of prawns displayed on a slab. The fishmonger had offered to serve me but I had not even heard him speak. I wandered off feeling foolish, wondering what I had been thinking about when staring at the prawns. I didn't think that there was any significance in the fish itself. But a week or two later I had a similar experience and again found I was standing outside a fish shop; this time I was, as it were, magnetised by lobsters. But when I told Rose Marie of this she showed no surprise.

"You've been going dotty over shellfish for years," she said, "didn't you know? Whenever we've had a holiday we've had to keep to the coast so that you could move from oysters to *moules* or from lobster to crab. And when I cleaned the car out the other day I found it was littered with shrimp heads."

But awareness of my obsession brought no relief from it. On the contrary, it grew. Just as some people gape into motor car show-rooms or dress shops, I find I am fascinated by fish—on the deck, in seaweed-lined boxes on the quay, or when they are lying on the marble slabs, or in the frying pan. I can find no trace of this piscine taste in my childhood: the obsession seems to have emerged when I was about thirty.

I think one of the most beautiful, or at least fascinating, places I ever saw was the auction shed at Concarneau in Brittany. There were barrels of squids, slithers of eels, cascades of whitebait, fabulous skate, and crates of crayfish, crabs, lobsters and prawns. I enjoyed myself there much more than I had in the Louvre or the Prado. To me the smell of the sea—and I don't like the sea— which is carried on the slimy wet skin of a freshly-caught fish is infinitely more pleasing than any perfume—and I do like perfume.

I once told a practising psychoanalyst of this obsession. He said it was not unusual—though I don't recall ever joining a queue of voyeurs outside a Macfisheries. His interpretation for my fish obsession was that I was an emotionally defeated person who unconsciously wished to withdraw from life back into Mother Ocean from which I had once emerged.

Part Six

How mean thy hates
Fostered in falsity
      Pull down thy vanity
Rathe to destroy, niggard in charity

PEOPLE who wake up in the morning to find that they are worrying about their work or their debts are fortunate. I have always envied them: debts can, sometimes, be paid; work, somehow done. But it is my experience that however tangled my life is, or whatever muddle I achieve with my work, my sleeping mind discards those superficial matters and, at the instant of waking, always projects on to my consciousness the one problem it selects as being more urgent to my life than any other: my death. Before my eyes open, before I know what day it is; where I lie or with whom; what has to be done, or undone; I am aware that I am, and I experience the joyful accident of being which is instantly torpedoed by the dark certainty of my death. I lie for a moment transfixed on this cross of consciousness not daring to open my eyes. For I have one fear that is greater than the fear of death: it is that a part of me will be conscious after I am dead when I lie in a coffin which lies in a grave. So for a second I keep my eyes shut dreading that they should see no light, or that when I speak I should find my lips were set and my tongue was stone. Gingerly I move my fingers, relieved to find that they will move. Then I let the light laugh over me and immediately leap briskly out of bed, grateful and surprised that it is not my grave. This morbid and persistent obsession is a second skin to me: it does explain why I usually select the wrong neckties. Clothes seem unimportant when you are dressing with your very identity.

But within a few minutes I am immersed in my various roles: writing the end of a scene of a play, phoning my agent, and at the same time organising the combine to cut the barley, or the mason to mend a cottage lavatory; there are guests to greet, relatives to placate, not to mention the tethered horse whinnying to be ridden or my latest enthusiasm: the tobacco to be turned in the shed, or the golden pheasant fed. With all these distractions about me I must appear centred enough. But I am not: I clutch at life with all four hands to try to convince myself it's there. And I never succeed wholly.

However busy or involved I become, a part of me, the essential me, cannot take the business of living quite seriously because I am more concerned with the business of dying.

Just as before writing *Stratton* I had been obsessed with the idea of absolute evil, a few years later I found that I was constantly dwelling on the idea of betrayal. I was fascinated by the character of Judas, especially the suggestion in the New Testament that of all Jesus's disciples, Judas loved Him the most. I became convinced that there was something missing in the Gospel account that Judas had merely betrayed for money. It seemed more probable to me that love had been the motive. I knew a good deal about betrayal from love.

I found that I could not possibly hope to understand Judas's betrayal unless I could first come to terms with my own. On a rational level I was an agnostic. There had been a time when I had lifted the lid of Catholicism, and even had one or two sessions, at Rose Marie's instigation, at Farm Street. I had corresponded with Father D'Arcy, but this only led to the realisation that there was no possible way into orthodox Christianity for me, since I was unable to accept many of its dogmas. I could not believe in the physical resurrection: I could not believe that Christ had a unique relationship with God, which was not of his own spiritual achieving. I argued that if He had been "Son" in the sense that the Church claims, then His suffering on the Cross was diminished, since He knew that His transubstantiation was inevitable. If He were a privileged person by right of birth, then it seemed to me that the two thieves had to endure more suffering than He did. Nor could I accept many of the miracles, especially Lazarus. The more I read of other religions, the more I saw that supernatural powers were always attributed to a Deity, and were embellished by apologists for it.

The greater these intellectual gaps, the closer my emotional involvement with the story of the Passion became. I read and reread St John. Each reading convinced me that it was the most perfect and complete drama that had ever been conceived. My preoccupation grew. I tried to contain it. But the more successful I was in explaining away my intellectual interest, the more the emotional involvement came to the surface. This showed itself one day in a most embarrassing way.

I had gone to meet my agent, David Higham, at the Étoile. Arriving early, I had decided to wait and have a drink. I was reading a newspaper, or thought I was. A waiter came up to me and asked if I was all right.

"Quite all right," I replied, thinking he was referring to my drink.

"I mean, are *you* all right?" he said. I put my paper down, and only then realised that I was crying. I left the restaurant and walked up Charlotte Street, wiping my eyes as I did so. I had no worry that wasn't an old worry, nothing new had upset me, and there had been nothing in the paper to disturb me. Even if there had been, I am not a person who ever weeps. These involuntary tears were, I realised, from the unconscious. As I realised this, images of the Passion came painfully into my mind. I decided that I must, at some time, try and bridge some of the gap between my intellectual detachment and my emotional involvement. It was a big gap. Although I had written *This Way to the Tomb* it was written more from unbelief than from belief; it was a search, not a discovery. I had gone over some of the same road again when writing the long poem, *The Mongrel*. But none of this work had resolved the gap. I could not believe these doctrines. Looking around at the age I lived in, I saw that the average person found it impossible to relate their knowledge of elementary science with Christian dogma.

I decided. It was one of the very rare decisions I ever made. Generally I let the pressure of circumstances propel me. But this time, I decided. I decided to walk out of my life at least for a time. I realised that if I postponed my retreat until it was convenient to myself or others, it would never occur. Life is like a runaway bus. It doesn't stop. You have to fling yourself off ruthlessly. I explained this to Rose Marie and Antonia. They congratulated me. At least I had managed to make one decision. It gave them something to relate to: women like that. I said I didn't know how long I would be away or where I was going. And I didn't want to hear from either.

I told George and Marion that I was going to Devon. Then I stole back to the cottage at Orme Lane and bolted the door. I was besieged: fortunately there was coffee and cigarettes in the citadel. I kept the curtains drawn, took the phone off and put a couple of cushions over it to silence its complaint. I picked up the clock and stopped its irrelevant tick. I had not been allowed to be alone like this since my spell in gaol, which had been too brief. I had feared to be alone and had done everything to avoid it. I now knew why. For I felt such a release of physical and emotional energy that I literally shook with the excitement of it.

I got out a new notebook and without a line in my head sat down to write the entire Passion seen through the eyes of Judas. I had no books by me. I had no notes. But the entire poem seemed to be there; I wrote easily like a stenographer taking fluid dictation. I had had no idea what was there. Now I read a credible explanation of the miracle of Lazarus, how the Resurrection occurred by His rising in the hearts of His disciples, and in what sense He was the Son. And I read why I had betrayed Him, and why I could still weep at the mention of His name...I used to write, then rewrite till it was dark, then I would steal out of the cottage and walk from Bayswater down to the river, then return to write again. I drank coffee and ate chocolate I got from slot machines at a Tube Station on the Embankment. I spoke to nobody but myself. And for once I enjoyed the company.

I don't know how long I lived like this, since I had no time. Perhaps it was a fortnight. When I emerged with the poem, I didn't know what to do with it. I felt like a cub reporter who had stumbled across a great scoop, only to find that all the newspapers had gone into liquidation. But I didn't mind: the poem had been written for me. I sent a copy to Joan Blacksell, who for years had urged me to write something like it. And I posted another copy to Tom Eliot and one to Martin Browne. Then I put the phone back, got the clock out from under the bed. It had certainly missed a lot of time, the only time I had taken.

In the summer of 1954 Malcolm Muggeridge, who was Editor of

Punch, asked me if I would put a Punch Revue together. I had been writing a weekly column for *Punch* for about a year. Muggeridge is both ebullient and persuasive. He said that what the proprietors of the magazine wanted was to present a revue written by serious composers and writers. He thought it possible that such people had both the time and the ideas to write a short sketch, whereas they might not be able to produce a full-length play. As the idea of a so-called "high-brow" revue had been mooted some years previously, when Cochran had asked Eliot, Fry and myself to collaborate on one, I accepted Muggeridge's commission. I now invited Evelyn Waugh, Ustinov, John Whiting, Graham Greene and Auden to ferment savage sketches. They were all agreeable. It looked too easy. Indeed, the draft revue was so full that it looked as if it would be unnecessary for me to write any of the script myself. I spent weeks asking the various writers round to Orme Lane, and either listening to their ideas or suggesting one to them. Oscar Lewenstein had been engaged by *Punch* to act as the producer of the Revue and he had engaged Vida Hope, who had recently staged *The Boy Friend*, to direct. She was a flotilla of a woman, and had very set ideas on what made a musical comedy and revue. The more she looked at the ideas that I and others had proposed for the Punch sketches, the less enthusiastic she became. Gradually she began to cover up the shortcomings of these items by commissioning lyrics and sketches from the professional hack cabaret and revue writers. This was very shrewd of her, for when the time came to go into rehearsals, at least 80 per cent. of my writers failed to produce their material. As usual, only Ben had complied, writing an exquisite waltz, which should be resurrected. We started re-hearsals in London. By the time we went out on tour the revue had become like any other revue: full of topical references which did not echo further than Shaftesbury Avenue: a number of sloppy songs with the usual sentimental lyrics, and sketches not up to Footlights standards. When it opened at the Adelphi Theatre I felt the evening dying: the critics were not severe enough. Even so, the proprietors of *Punch* kept this revue running for several weeks, and considered the advertisement well worth their costs. As usual, I wrote off this interlude to the credit of experience. It served to burn up some of my energies which could find no adequate engagement anywhere. Whatever I did left me frustrated and unused. I felt like a gale canalised to cool a cup of tea or a load of ore being casually manufactured into a hatpin. A lot of my time was frittered away in London. I met many people and recognised fewer and fewer. This failing became a handicap.

One day sitting at the long table in the Garrick, a man came in whom I recognised as a well-known actor. As usual I couldn't think of his name. He started to talk to me about his rehearsals. Then we discussed Eliot's *The Cocktail Party*. I still couldn't think of his name. But we went on discussing the play which I had read.

"Did you ever see *Sweeny* or *Family Reunion*?" I asked him.

"No," he replied, "I'd like to read those."

"I'll send you a copy," I replied, trapping myself in my usual dilemma, "Mr...?" I queried.

A grin spread across the actor's face. Several members surrounding us smiled too. Then to help me out, he tapped the glass of beer in front of him.

"Worthington," I blurted, "Alec Worthington, of course... forgive me for forgetting your name."

I next tried to organise what I called the "Buskers". It was an attempt to find a bridge between the poet and the cabaret, and a long way from the troubadours. I had, a few years previously, been asked by an American cabaret singer, to write the lyrics for a song and had enjoyed doing this, though I had never received the payment of a new suit which she had promised me. Lavinia Lascelles and Cy Grant sang at the first performance at the Devon Festival and we planned to gather a repertoire of material, some from Kurt Weill and some other songs which would be written by contemporary poets and composers. Britten had written blues and boogie woogie for *This Way to the Tomb* and a waltz for the *Punch Revue*. It seemed possible that the Buskers might help to lift poetry off the page and give it its lighter and more satiric moments. But the Buskers failed to break into the night-club network where, as in the theatre, names alone count.

Another musical preoccupation I had at this time came from Imogen Holst, who was arranging a Purcell concert for Aldeburgh. She told me, when I was staying with Ben, that she wished to perform Purcell's *Cantata*, written "To Welcome His Majesty's Return from Newmarket." It is an exquisite piece of music. She wanted me to write new words. It was an extremely difficult job to fit words to Purcell and kept me absorbed for a fortnight.

During this period there was always a film producer in the shadows as a menacing distraction. There was a succession of them. They were always Hungarian, as Pascal and Korda had been. They used to arrive with presents, not only for me, but for Rose Marie and the children. They were always ingratiating, optimistic, and prodigal with my time. Their aim was always the same: that I should give them a synopsis for a film. This they hoped they could then resell to some production company. They were middlemen, peddlars on the periphery. If I had been a very successful playwright like Rattigan, for instance, I would not have been approached by these optimists. Rattigan, Ustinov, etc., had direct lines to Warner Brothers. I was in another category. I was the sort of person who could, they thought, be persuaded to work for the fabulous fruits they offered, and whose name was sufficiently well known to obtain them some entry into the film companies. Consequently I was, in my comparative obscurity, wooed by these aspiring film moguls more than if I had been entirely unknown, or if I had had a Hollywood reputation. They were not without shrewdness. One of these aspiring moguls was even more persistent than the others. He arrived at the farm, and announced that he would not leave until I gave him a draft of a comedy. What's more, he didn't. By the time he had revised my script with one eye on the box office, I was utterly nauseated by the result. The macabre ending of this sad story is that the producer left, delighted with his scenario and confident that he would be able to "set it up". Five years later I met him in the tube. He was still hawking the rubbish. He produced a copy from his valise. Having wasted three weeks of my life, his punishment had been to waste five years of his own. He is probably still doing it. Such incidents, and there were many, depressed me, perhaps unduly. I could not bear the pain of the image they conveyed: rows and rows of Bayswater lodging houses filled with tiny rooms, inhabited by lonely men with hopeless hopes. Consequently the next time one of these cigar-smoking gnomes appeared on my doorstep with a ballet scenario to turn into a play or a play to adapt for a film, he found me already softened towards him. Terrified of my own loneliness I became vulnerable to the suggestion of it in others.

Ben and I met frequently at Orme Square or at concerts; occasionally he came down to the farm, but we had not worked together for some years. Then quite suddenly he wrote to me suggesting that Rose Marie and I should join him for a ski-ing holiday in Switzerland. He had rented a chalet outside Zermatt. We arranged to share the rent. Pears, Ben's sister Beth, and Mary Potter made up the rest of the party.

The chalet was comfortable: we did our own cooking, or rather Pears and I did. Ben took the ski-ing very seriously and spent the evenings composing a suite for recorders. But I could see that there was something more serious on his mind. He became almost attentive, making sure I had tied up both laces on my ski boots and had got them on the right feet, waiting for me to emerge out of crevasses, and rushing to see which of my legs was broken; I began to suspect that somehow my survival and his music had become identical to him. Rose Marie reminded me that I was in the middle of a play.

Ben knew this. "You have your own work to do," he said, "and I mustn't distract you by asking you to write anything more for me."

"There are others you could work with."

"I've tried Eric, but he isn't a poet."

"Then what's wrong with Auden?"

"This," Ben said, handing me a wad of paper which felt as heavy as a novel or a rural telephone directory. "Wystan sent me this as a libretto for an oratorio. If I set it all, it would take three weeks to perform."

"Couldn't it be cut?"

"Read it. It's a thesis, not a libretto."

I took it off to a corner. Much of it was interesting philo-

350

sophically, but as a libretto Auden must have been suffering from some temporary aberration. It was as long as the *Ring* and almost as incomprehensible. Auden must have known it was unsuitable. He had been Ben's first librettist and knew as much about the needs of a composer as anyone did.

"You see what I mean?" Ben asked, taking the tome from me.

"Yes. Tippett would enjoy the metaphysics. Tell Auden to send it to him."

Ben put on his most pathetic look. "I suppose there's nothing for it, then, but for me to turn the commission down?" he said, without the slightest intention of doing so. He paused, expecting me to say "what commission?" but I refused his service and let the ball drop.

"Let's go up on the ski-lift," he suggested eventually, "and see if we can get all the way down in one piece."

"I thought you were beginning to value librettists," I said picking up my ski boots. "You know I'm sure to break my neck."

We mounted to the third stage, the cruel shoulder of the Jungfrau alone breaking the horizon. I felt frightened. It had seemed a long way up. I visualised my way down with indispensable limbs left casually wrapped round odd pine trees or dropped at every corner. But the snow was perfect: the first gradient looked temptingly gentle. Rose Marie, who had joined us, set off, Ben immediately followed her. Not wishing to emulate Mussorgsky, I allowed gravity to do its worst. After the first descent we reached an extensive plateau which was at such a gradient that we were able, to my surprise, to ski along relaxed without any vicious turns or sudden precipices to throw us off balance. The sun was setting and it was as if we were ski-ing not on snow, but over banks of pink clouds. Our skis hissed, movement without effort. Now I knew why people enjoyed ski-ing. My painful years on the nursery slopes had suddenly paid off. It was the most exhilarating hour I can ever remember.

When we reached the second stage down, Ben suggested that we had a drink at a bar overlooking the valley. This was very shrewd of him. He waited till Rose Marie had gone off with his sister.

"Yes," he said, passing me my second schnapps. "I suppose I shall have to turn this commission down."

I still refused his service.

"A pity because I've a special affection for York Minster. Have you ever seen it?"

"Tell me what you want," I said.

"I really can't ask you to do it. And you're the only one who could—so I'll turn it down."

"Well, let's ski to the next stage," I said, taking a leaf out of his book. "If I get down there safely my future activities will seem less hypothetical."

This part of the descent was fierce and suicidal; nothing less than a solid railway station or a hayrick could possibly have arrested me. We reached the next bar still whole.

"It would seem that destiny is on your side," I said. "Tell me what you want."

"York Minster want me to write an oratorio for them. The Minster is dedicated to St Peter. I wonder if you think St Peter would make a subject?"

"Very possibly."

"I want to write a very big work; large choir, big orchestra, the lot."

"Like Verdi's *Requiem*?"

"But I don't want to write a Mass. I want to set English poetry: your poetry."

"If we did St Peter," I said, "the thing would fall naturally into two halves. The first part could end with Christ's Crucifixion and the second half with Peter's. I shall enjoy doing the Quo Vadis."

For the rest of my stay in Zermatt, Ben and I talked of nothing else. My play, *Playback*, had to wait.

Rose Marie thought this was a pity. We did not discuss the matter further. It was a relatively unimportant issue between us at the time. There were others. Our own relationship still wandered in the morass to which the morality of "either/or" had reduced us. She could see that I was deeply attached to Antonia: my protestations that that didn't lessen my love for herself failed to convince her. And her own feelings for the girl were ambivalent and confused: convention told her she should hate her, but that response denied something in her own nature. In addition to this, she was undergoing psychoanalysis which intensified her emotional distress and self-awareness. Getting to know herself, she disliked what she saw and then projected that animus against me. I deserved a good deal of it, and what I didn't I still received. We had come to abuse each other's feelings, not because we didn't love each other but because we did. Indeed, we had become so inextricably tangled that we showed to each other as little respect as we showed to ourselves. For any woman, life with me during this decade was a kind of self-crucifixion. The best that could be said of it was that it was not dull. Secretly I longed for dullness. It seemed more remote than the unholy grail. At breakfast we would decide to part for ever: by luncheon we would be as gay and amorous as honeymoon couples are supposed to be; and by dinner, we would not be speaking. Of course any other woman would have left me years ago. Rose Marie didn't because, as she said, that would entail leaving herself. We were tied together at the ankles: consequently there were many spills.

I used to confide in Ben. He was then sympathetic and under-standing. He was fond of Rose Marie and had known her as long as I had. Perhaps it was my need then for his friendship that made me close my play I was writing based on Phaedra, and agree to write St Peter with him. What I told myself was that Lucretia had proved that Ben and I could work together successfully and that I mustn't let anything, even a sense of self-preservation, stand in the way of our creating another work together.

The more I worked on the subject the more enthusiastic I became. I read St John again, the Acts of Peter, the Apocalypse of Peter and the Acts of Pilate in the Apocryphal New Testament. and found enough yeast for four oratorios. I was now as excited as Ben. As soon as we returned to London I used to go round to his house in Chester Gate to shape the material with him. We always worked easily and quickly. We knew how each other's mind worked and how to give each other the opportunities, the spring-boards which we both needed. He had obviously thought very hard on the musical shapes and knew precisely what ensembles he required and where. Consequently within a week we had agreed a musical synopsis in detail indicating precisely where there were solos, duets, trios, and what should be carried by the chorus. With such a definite blueprint it only remained for me to find the words and he to find the notes. We both felt our work was done.

Ben urged me to let him have the libretto as soon as possible. I now made a decision which still astounds me by its degree of unusual resolution and strength: I decided to leave both Rose Marie and Antonia again to go to Spain alone to write the work without tears, reconciliations and wrangles to punctuate the text. I was able to make this apparent sacrifice of my emotional life only because I had become emotionally involved elsewhere: with St Peter. It was as if I had just read the Passion for the first time.

I left Rose Marie in the cottage in Orme Lane—she was having her portrait painted, and Antonia in her flat round the corner. I dimly hoped they'd keep one eye on each other. Then I flew to Gibraltar, cabling the Brenans to expect me. I felt very reckless. It's a great luxury to be able to leave two women. Monogamists deprive themselves of half the pleasure. But it was short-lived: as usual I felt homesick—for both—before I had reached Churriana.

I had known the Brenans for many years. Gerald had known Welcombe before I was born and had stayed at West Mill with Lytton Strachey in the party. He had later settled, after the Great War, as a writer in Spain where he had lived until he had had to abandon his home during the Civil War. He then returned to Welcombe and rented a house there. He had then gone to live in Wiltshire and returned to Spain after the war. I had become very attached to Gamel Brenan.

It was dark when I arrived by bus from Gibraltar. Gamel had waited up for me to give me some supper. It was delicious: small birds which looked like partridges. I ate two. She sat and watched me, looking as beautiful and sad as ever. Then I realised that there was something immediate about her sadness: I had just devoured two of her precious white doves. Knowing her affection for them this was one of the most succulent sacrifices any woman ever made me. I forbade the slaughter of any more doves and said I would eat only cats, as she had nearly twenty in the house not because she liked cats but due to the Spaniards' superstition about killing them.

It was late October: I worked at the bottom of their garden with ripe pomegranates, oranges and lemons falling from the trees around me. And as I worked I enjoyed hearing the two Spanish maids singing as they hung up the laundry. Without any interruptions except from myself, I worked at great pitch from breakfast till luncheon, then spent the afternoon striding about the countryside with Gerald swopping follies or picking his brain. And then in the evenings Gamel and I would pad quietly and slowly through the narrow village streets while I told her about my emotional troubles. It was impossible to shock Gamel. She did not believe in sin, but thought "people often did things which hurt themselves". It was easy to talk to Gamel. Perhaps that's why I had gone there.

In spite of feeling apprehensive about Rose Marie and Antonia I kept to my routine in the garden. Ben and I had planned the synopsis well: *St Peter* almost wrote itself. I thought it would take me six weeks to write: but it was completed in half the time. It was a relaxation for me to work: to concentrate on something outside myself. Only the post distracted me: letters from Antonia stressing her loneliness and telling me that she had called on Rose Marie who had seemed distant. She had asked her to go to a cinema: Rose Marie had refused. She had asked her to phone and heard nothing more. From Rose Marie herself I did not receive a letter: for the first two weeks, this did not alarm me: I had experienced the vagaries of the Spanish post before.

But it was while I was at Churriana that I received two letters by the same post which caused me considerable bewilderment and distress. One was from Eliot, the other from Martin Browne. Before leaving London, I had sent each a copy of *Judas*. Eliot had one, as my publisher: and I had sent a copy to Martin because Eliot himself had urged me to do so.

"I always let him see my work: he's one of the few people whose opinion I value."

The two letters took precisely opposite views of the poem. Eliot was profoundly shocked by it. He urged me not to publish it; accused me of "belittling the apostles by turning them into ordinary men and furthering a unitarian Christ." On the other hand Martin congratulated me on the poem. Their opinions were in complete contrast. I was tempted to send Eliot's letter to Martin and Martin's to Eliot, without comment. But I did not. I wrote at length to Eliot defending my attempt at making the apostles ordinary men and maintaining that that view, in fact, accorded with the scriptures and enhanced their spiritual achievements rather than belittling them. I also told him that I was bewildered by his opinion which differed so much from Martin whom I quoted. Eliot's letter distressed me: if I had received it earlier it would probably have discouraged me from writing *St Peter*. But thanks to the Spanish post, it had taken ten days to reach me, and the libretto was already finished.

Naturally I had shown both letters to Gamel and Gerald whose literary opinions I valued. Gerald, a great admirer of Eliot's, was almost as distressed by his letter as I was.

"He's playing Robert Bridges to your Hopkins," he said sadly.

For my part, I was not unaware that my perfidy against Robert Graves had now come home to roost. Indeed, Eliot could have quoted my own letter to him about Graves against myself.

But this battle of the books was now overshadowed by my worrying why I had not heard from Rose Marie. True, I had gone off to get away from my two women but it was disconcerting to have my intentions taken so literally. I could no longer blame the post. With *St Peter* finished I was tempted to fly back to London. But with some difficulty I held to the course I had chosen and left Malaga for Cordova, where I intended to stay by myself for a few days. As soon as I reached this city I rushed straight to the Post Office hoping that there would be a letter or two from Rose Marie waiting for me since I had told her of my intentions of going there before proceeding to Seville. But there was no letter. I took a room at an hotel. Then, instead of visiting the sights of the city, spent the next six hours waiting at the Post Office for the incoming post and bribing the sorters to do overtime. Perhaps Rose Marie had written direct to the Hotel d'Angleterre in Seville? I instantly abandoned Cordova and took a taxi all the way there. There was no letter from her: two from Antonia. This fact doubled my apprehensions. If one could write, why couldn't the other? All fears assailed me and instead of examining the cathedral, I found myself once again walking up and down the ugly, cold corridors of the sorting office. In such moments I suffer: my impatience persecutes me.

I finally got hold of the postmaster himself, and persuaded him to arrange a search. While this was taking place—the instigation of which was almost as much an achievement as defeating the Armada single-handed, I set off to console myself with food, having not eaten for twenty-eight hours. Confident that Rose Marie's letters would soon be found, I relaxed in a small restaurant and ordered the most successful meal I remember. It was a dish of small quail which I followed with a fruit I had not eaten before called Virgins Hair. Then I returned to the Post Office and surveyed the chaos I had caused. But there was no letter. Now in an agony of worry I hurried to my hotel and telephoned Orme Lane. There was no reply. I could hear the bell ringing on the stairway. Then I telephoned my sister in Devon to ask her when she had last heard from Rose Marie and if she knew where she was. She said that Rose Marie had gone down to Sussex to see Briony at her convent. This explained why she was not at home: but not why I had not heard from her. I decided to fly home the next morning. Decision is always a relief even when we make the wrong one.

For presents I bought Rose Marie an evening handbag lined in red silk: and, for Antonia, a fountain pen. Psychiatrists will smile at my choice, but they were in fact made because Rose Marie had asked me to bring her a handbag when I had told her I was going to Seville, and the pen was to encourage Antonia to write her novel. I also carried home my usual assortment of trophies: various vines which I hoped to grow somewhere; lengths of sugar cane which I had got from an agricultural research station outside Malaga and hoped they would withstand a Northern climate; innumerable tins of *paté*, packets of seeds, pods of oleander, besides a clutter of crude china, pounds of almonds and figs, an undrinkable liqueur and a tangle of cheap jewellery. My luggage always reveals both my interest in agriculture and my wish to please the natives. I travel back to this savage island like a Robinson Crusoe who hopes in vain to plant and eat better things. Customs officers examine my luggage with incredulity. Overwhelmed with my bushes and packets, they find themselves turning into valets, absent-mindedly searching to see if I have any clothes at all. I travel light in that respect: it has always seemed to me silly to take such things as socks, shirts and underclothes round the world: such dreary necessities can be purchased wherever you happen to be and then kicked under an hotel bed in order to make room for a precious lump of salami or a cutting of bougainvillaea. It is only the luxuries of life which are really necessary. On this occasion I had excelled myself: it took one taxi to convey me and my luggage and another followed to Orme Lane filled with sugar cane cuttings and bushes. I had been away a month. As usual I was intensely excited at getting home, and before the cabby was paid was shouting for Rose Marie to come and appraise my sticky prizes. But the cottage was empty. I had intended that my return should be a surprise. Yet I was annoyed she had not anticipated it. I could do nothing but set out my gifts and wait: it was an anticlimax. Life is a bad dramatist.

Waiting always punishes me: I take it as a personal affront. I like my characters to appear on cue and get intensely irritated when I discover that they have minor parts in somebody else's bad play. I waited an hour: then endured another. My friends say I am the most patient person they know: they do not realise I wait only when they allow me no alternative. And because I do not complain they mistake that for tolerance. The truth is when I am irritated, I tend to whisper; and when I am very angry, I merely become silent. Fury moves me not to a healthy violence but to a pained and sulky martyrdom. When I am at my worst, I look like St Sebastian on the Cross.

Consequently when Rose Marie finally appeared after another couple of hours my mood was almost saintly. Nor was it improved by her question.

"What are you doing here? I thought you intended to get women out of your hair and meditate for six weeks in Seville?"

"My return was meant to be a pleasant surprise. I see it is only a surprise."

Nor did my cheap jewellery please her, as it generally did.

My curiosity to know where she had been was such that I did not ask her. When she did not volunteer even an excuse, my curiosity hardened into suspicion.

"I only received one of your letters."

"That's because I only sent one. I didn't want to distract you from your monkish meditations. I guessed Antonia would be writing every day."

"Do you like your handbag?"

"Yes. Very much."

"You don't look very pleased."

"Your taste is impeccable. Sometimes I wish it weren't."

"Then take a look at this junk." I passed her the bird's nest of trinkets.

But they didn't interest her. Nor did any other of my assorted trifles succeed in distracting this mood. She was looking for something I had not revealed.

"What have you brought her?" she eventually asked.

"Nothing very much."

"A secret?"

"No, this pen."

"That'll be useful."

"I hope so," I replied casually.

"Does she know you're back?"

"No."

"No?"

"No."

"Then you'll have to take that pen round to her, won't you?"

"Yes..."

"Well, goodbye."

"...in the morning."

"Why not now?"

"I thought we'd go out to dinner."

"Yes. Let's do that," she said bitterly. "Then you can take the pen to Antonia in the morning and round we'll go again."

While she changed I went over to the house to tell George of the strange mood I had found on my return. He was always too good a friend to burden me with advice.

In the taxi I asked her how the portrait which Kenneth Green was painting of her was proceeding.

"Not bad. He wants you to see it. He's only painting me in order to interest you. That's always the way, I'm just a second fiddle."

"You imagine it."

"No, that's what he said this afternoon—'I can't wait for Ronnie to see it'."

So that's where she had been.

Our dinner was dull: our conversation monosyllabic.

"I've finished *St Peter*."

"Ben will be pleased."

I paid the bill. The waiters were staring at us. She was on the verge of tears. We marched round Leicester Square. There was no use going on and on like this. I was prepared to make a bargain, even a sacrifice, for this time it looked as if she had something to give up too.

"Let's make a fresh start," I said. "And devote ourselves wholly and completely to each other?"

As I said it, I knew it was an offer I had no moral right to make. You cannot give yourself to a person then take yourself away without doing a violence that is more immoral than the selfish morality you sometimes think it expedient to pursue.

"You mean you won't see her any more?"

"That would be cowardly. I will see her. I will tell her that I can't go round the roundabout any more."

The bargain in which another person was sacrificed on our matrimonial altar was agreed.

I telephoned Antonia the next morning. She asked me when I had returned. I told her. The fact that I had not phoned her the previous evening, told her a good deal more.

"How's Martha?" she said, which was her name for Rose Marie when she was excluded. She called her Mary, when included.

My pause was articulate.

"When am I going to see you? Or should I say, am I going to see you?"

Antonia was sensitive and quick. She knew from the tone of my voice that something was wrong. Her fears told her precisely what it was.

"Could we meet this morning, say in an hour's time?"

I had no need to say where. We had a secret little coffee shop near Leicester Square where we met when Martha ousted Mary at Orme Lane.

"If you're going to say goodbye to me again," she said, "this time it'll be for ever. I can't stand any more."

"In an hour, then," I said and hung up.

Antonia was the only woman who never kept me waiting. She was always there first, waiting for me. It was not that I was ever late: she was always early. She was lonely: and she lived alone. If I said I would meet her at quarter past eleven, she would be there half an hour earlier, fearful that I had said a quarter to eleven.

She did not see me enter the crowded coffee shop. From her posture I could see that she was feeling as sad as I was. But when I stood by her table it was as if tiny bunches of sweet peas waved from her eyes, unseeing and so sad a moment before.

"It's good to see you," she said unnecessarily.

Then the sweet peas disappeared. Her eyes looked worried.

"My God, you look terrible. Don't let's have any coffee. You need a brandy."

She got up and led me across the road to a pub.

"I haven't got any English money on me."

"I've got my last quid. We both need a double brandy. Don't tell me what's happened: I know. I guessed when she never phoned me back after I'd suggested we should go to a film together or something while you were away. Poor Rose Marie: she must be going through hell too."

That was typical. Half our age, she had twice our understanding. That is, she had the subtlety to stand under other people, to feel their feelings.

"No, don't say it, don't say you're sorry. I've always known it would come to this. You're incapable of making a choice between us, because you know if you did you would be destroying a part of yourself—maybe us too. This is the end. This time I must make some sort of life of my own and not wait in a cupboard for Mary to tell you you can take me out of it again...you'd better drink my brandy, too. I'm going now. Do me a favour, don't look up. I promise you not to look round."

I suppose I sat there for what is called an hour.

"Are you feeling all right?" the man asked.

"I forgot to give her the pen," I replied.

I went out and walked alone for what they measure as a mile. But it took me three years to tread it.

I suppose it was that day or the next day when I called on Ben at Chester Gate with the libretto of *St Peter*. He was excited by it and was particularly thrilled by the opportunities I had given him by the inclusion of the solos for the boy. He suggested some minor changes, an additional line here and there. I promised to let him have those revisions the same day. We went out to lunch to celebrate. But he soon saw that I was in no mood for a celebration. I told him that I had had to cut Antonia out of my life again.

"Poor Rose Marie," he said, echoing Antonia. Ben was fond of her.

During this breach, Antonia sent me a poem she had written. I thought it was very good but because of my emotional involvement in both the poem and the author, I decided that I was the last person to assess it. I wrote to her to tell her to send it to Princess Caetani mentioning my name. She did this. Margaret Caetani paid her £15 for printing the poem in *Botteghe Oscura*, and when it appeared, Eliot noticed the poem and asked his cousin if she knew anything about the author, as he would like to see more of her work. Margaret wrote to me, and I had the pleasure of telling Antonia to get in touch with Tom.

After Eliot had refused to publish my poem *Judas* and had begged me to withdraw it, I let it lie in a bottom drawer. When we met it was a subject he avoided. Friendship is not only finding points of contact but knowing where to stay apart. Though his strictures against this poem had hurt me, I bore no resentment. This was not due to any nobility in my character. I forgive people easily, not as a consequence of any spiritual grace within me, but as a result of my absent-mindedness: I forget. Though that may not be as difficult as to forgive, it is more reliable and equally effective. During the war, a man had offered to rent a cottage from me for £100 per annum. I let him move in without signing a lease. As soon as he was unpacked, he announced that he would appeal against the rent. The Tribunal assessed it on the rateable value and in consequence reduced it to £23 per annum out of which I had to pay the repairs and other outgoings. I felt I had been tricked: the law was on his side but business ethics were on mine. I resented his behaviour bitterly. But three months later, meeting him in Welcombe Woods I asked him and his wife to dinner. Everybody, excluding myself, was impressed by my forgiving nature. During the meal I knew there was something about the man I should remember but I couldn't recall what it was. So it was with Eliot and *Judas*. And I might even have forgotten having written the poem if Martin Browne and Edward Blacksell had not insisted that it was published. Martin also recorded the entire poem at the BBC. And eventually John Piper who had read the poem, offered to do a series of illustrations for it. With these splendid drawings as a standard, I decided to have a limited edition published. The book was designed by Christopher Bradshaw and printed by letterpress on rose-tinted Abbey Mills Glastonbury paper. The text was handsomely set in 13 point Poliphilus with Gaudier figures and titling. A thousand elegant copies were printed: thirty were sold. But how does one measure success? Surely not by numbers?

In the autumn of 1955 I went with the Harewoods to Jugoslavia to attend the Dubrovnik Festival. We had enjoyed the round of operas, concerts and plays, but felt we would like to see something of the country itself. Marion suggested that we should drive out to a village. We hired a car and drove in the direction of a place called Cilipe, about a couple of hours' drive from the city. Setting off that morning, I remember making some pessimistic remark about whether we should get back in time for luncheon. It was a Sunday; and when we arrived, the villagers were just coming out of church. We stood admiring their costumes. Marion asked one of the girls if she would mind posing for a photograph. The girl was flattered; and her family were so delighted at meeting some people from England that they asked us if we would like to see their smallholding on the outskirts of the village. Of course we didn't understand a word of the invitation but could see that it was warm. We were literally frog-marched from the church, down the village street, with the entire colourful congregation following. It looked like a religious procession. George and I were getting increasingly apprehensive about whether we should get back to Dubrovnik in time for luncheon.

We were led into a kitchen with a low ceiling and a long white scrubbed table. A bottle of Rakiya was produced; we drank innumerable toasts; one of the girl's brothers produced a guitar, and another a clarinet. Marion suddenly appeared from a side room wearing the girl's costume. Another bottle of Rakiya appeared. We became less apprehensive about missing our luncheon. Indeed, when we saw how the table was now loaded with food we began to worry just how we were going to acquit ourselves, especially when we saw several dusty bottles being added to the meal. We realised that our hosts were giving us the hospitality which they felt was due to our country. It was a test; we were not batting for England but drinking for her. And both of us took it in turns to drink for Marion. The meal over, we were taken to look at pigs and cows, then glanced longingly at our car. But the villagers had other ideas. Apparently they had agreed among themselves that the first family should be allowed to give us lunch if the other farmers had an opportunity to entertain us after the meal. It was, as it were, a unilateral agreement: we knew nothing of it, nor, when we staggered off to another farm to be given seed cake and more Rakiya drinks in the living room, that there were another five buxom and hospitable housewives round the corner all waiting to slaughter us with kindness. It was a day none of us will ever forget. About seven o'clock that evening we were at last allowed to walk through the village to our car. And that we used our own feet will always be a matter of considerable pride.

This happy incident had a somewhat sad sequel. Marion suggested that we should show our gratitude to the villagers by asking two or three of them to dine with us at the Villa Argentina, our hotel in Dubrovnik, and then accompany us to one of the Festival events. We decided to send a car to Cilipe and to entertain the two sisters at whose farm we had lunched so well. We went into a huddle about what we should give them for dinner.

And eventually agreed that, as the village was a long way from the sea, lobster might be a treat for them. We planned the rest of the meal on similar lines and Marion arranged with the head waiter to have a little bouquet for each of the girls. They arrived looking incredibly pretty but not in peasant costume. Heaven knows what frantic improvisation and expense our invitation had put them to. They seemed very shy but we were confident that we could break that down and make them enjoy themselves, and their dinner. To our dismay, as each course was laid before them, so was it removed; they never touched a single mouthful throughout the meal. We wondered whether, since there are many Mohammedans in Jugoslavia, we had made a gaffe by asking them to dine out on some fast day. But a question soon dispelled that fear. We could not understand their abstinence. Though they might not have liked lobster, surely they should have enjoyed the artichoke or the pineapple flambé? We were nonplussed by their refusal to eat and worried about it through the entire play to which we took our presumably hungry guests. Marion was particularly distressed over this incident, and asked the Festival Manager for a possible explanation. He was unable to give one himself but he promised to make a few discreet enquiries. Several days later he told us that the only reason our guests had not eaten a mouthful at dinner was that they did not know how to use the knives and forks and didn't wish to make fools of themselves. It was all rather Chaplinesque. We felt very sad.

It was at Dubrovnik that Marion saved my life. I had been swimming: no more need be said. We decided to take a boat from Dubrovnik and have a luxurious and leisurely cruise up the Adriatic towards Venice. My sense of luxury was somewhat dampened by noticing that the boat was called the s.s. *Proletariat* and that the whole craft was swarming with comrades in shorts calling for bottles of beer. Our cabins were over the engine room: we endured four days of miserable discomfort before reaching Venice on my birthday. From Venice we went to stay with Igor Markevich and his wife at their villa in Vevey. Igor took us to the *Fête de Vignerons* in Geneva. It was held in a large stadium. He had made some muddle with the tickets and asked me if I would go in by myself and wait for a relative of his who was also unable to accompany the main party. I waited by the turnstile and the girl never turned up, having gone in by another entrance. Markevich came to me at the end of the performance and asked if I had found his friend. I told him that she hadn't appeared: he assumed I had forgotten or omitted to meet her, and upbraided me in the most ridiculous fashion. In fact, he was so rude that I felt I could not continue to stay in his house. I returned to the villa, and making some excuses about feeling indisposed, told George and Marion that I was going to fly home before I went down with flu.

I took a train to Lausanne and hurried to the air terminal. I took my seat in the bus and, about ten minutes later, was surprised to see everybody getting out of it again. I had not thought the aerodrome was so near. Then I noticed that we were not filing into an airport, but being shepherded into a restaurant. I assumed there had been some kind of breakdown: I ordered a drink and then found I was watching a striptease act. A quarter of an hour later we trouped back into the bus. I assumed we would now be proceeding to the airport. A second stop occurred, precisely like the first; and I was again subjected to a cabaret act. I thought I had better ask why we were being delayed. I knew that the plane took off in ten minutes. I found the bus conductor.

"When do we get to the airport?" I asked. I discovered that I had inadvertently got on the wrong bus. It was doing a tour of the night-spots of the city. This is the reason why I never reached London that night. Nobody ever believed it.

If Antonia had returned to her husband, I might not have worried about her. But she did not. They had separated months before. So she had taken a room in London. Visualising her world of the gas ring and the slot machine telephone, I couldn't bear her loneliness. I missed her and I sulked. But I didn't write to her or telephone her. I hoped, or pretended to myself that I hoped, that the feelings between us would lessen. Though everything in me resisted turning her into a casual *affaire* which was what I was appearing to do by not seeing or communicating with her. The fact that I did not hear from her either helped, if that is the word when we vulgarise our feelings by conforming to convention which is itself unfeeling.

Then about a month later, I went up to London, and, at the Garrick, was handed a large envelope. It contained two school exercise books. They were written in pencil. It was her diary since she'd left Mead.

"I have to write this," she wrote, "because I cannot go to sleep at night, unless I am talking to you." Her loneliness was intense; so was her misery, not for herself, but for the unhappiness she had caused Rose Marie. "I love her too," she explained, "for you two are inseparable and if I love you, I have to love Rose Marie too. And I hate myself for making her jealous."

I sat in the Club and read these diaries through three times. Not because I was personally involved: one reading told me what she was suffering. But the second and third convinced me that here was writing of the highest order. Antonia had a genius for feeling and an equal capability for articulating it. She was only twenty-four, but her maturity was infinitely greater than my own.

I telephoned her. We met that evening for a cup of coffee. I told her to go on writing to me. She was grateful and said she would send the letters to the Club.

"Writing to you will help. You are the only window I can look out of myself through."

I returned to Devon. Rose Marie and I were alone there: the children were away at school: we wintered besieged by our own company. And mine was bad. But after some months the pain seemed less. We say time is callous, but it is not: it is we ourselves who are. Or when our feelings are hopeless something in us makes us give up hope. And that was my condition when Rose Marie confounded me as she always managed to confound me. She had gone up to London to do the Christmas shopping. She telephoned me.

"I'm meeting Antonia for a drink this morning. And I shall bring her down for Christmas. Does that make you happy?"

"What makes you think she'll come?"

There was a gay snort.

"Meet us at Barnstaple," she said.

I did. I have never been so happy to see two people. Two people. There was no tension, no recriminations, for the next couple of

367

weeks while Rose Marie and Antonia gossiped happily in the kitchen. I felt secure, released, again able to bear my own company, be alone to work. I continued writing *The Death of Satan* which was the contemporary sequel to *Don Juan*, and completed it while the going was good. For most writers, this domestic life is a background to their work. I was not unaware that I had unwittingly reversed the condition. My desk swayed in a gale of emotions which I had created about me. But this was a brief interlude: there were no scenes. I wrote quickly, anticipating the ink to fly in my face and the paper hurl itself out of the window.

But Antonia did not make the mistake of outstaying her welcome. Rose Marie was sorry to see her go. I was not so sad, for her visit had brought Rose Marie and me together. The sense of siege was over.

After a month or two Antonia asked if she could go to West Mill. She stayed down there alone for some time, to try to write a novel. I used to ride down to the valley to see what she had written. It was difficult not to make love but often we succeeded. I found I had repeated Pound's pattern with a trivial geographical variation. It worked for a time. Antonia used to ask Rose Marie and me down to West Mill for dinner. At other times Rose Marie would invite Antonia up to Mead for a meal. On these occasions they got on well together. I was happier seeing that than I was with either. For alone with one, I felt guilty about the other. It was not that I was a born bigamist, but a born Sultan.

But the tension returned. I did not tell Antonia to go. But when she suggested it, I did nothing to stop her. Her tears hurt me, Rose Marie's destroyed me. I noticed whenever a row occurred, that it had been triggered off by some person outside the situation pitying one of those within it. Pity is convention's most lethal weapon and is fired invariably when the citadel of conformity is threatened. Sometimes Rose Marie was pitied, sometimes the sympathy was for Antonia. The effect was always instantaneously destructive. Nobody, of course, dared to commiserate with me. In many ways my life looked like a hell of my own making but I knew it was the only heaven I'd ever know.

Even so, I again tried to become reconciled to not seeing

Antonia any more. Or at least to restrict our meetings to hurried cups of coffee, whenever I was in London. Antonia too tried to pick herself up and took a job.

That spring George and Marion, who had observed the round-about without vicariously sympathising with anybody in it, agreed to come to Mead. George thought he could cheer me up. We could poach my trout and the four of us could play poker. It was to be a house party of two conventional couples.

The day before George and Marion arrived, Rose Marie telephoned Antonia to ask her to come down to help with the cooking. She gave me George's Edwardian appetite as a reason. I did not doubt the appetite: I should have doubted the reason. But one doesn't enquire deeply into what causes happiness: it is only our unhappiness which prompts us to ferret down to the causes until we unearth the bone of despair. So I went to meet her. Her job had been temporary, she said.

When George and Marion arrived, they did not raise an eyebrow. They were good friends. And now that Rose Marie and I were gay again I knew we must be both wise and moral.

Before we could pay for the debts of the first Devon Festival, the second was round again. Again George, Marion, Ben and Peter came down for the marathon; again George introduced an opera concert, Ben and Peter gave a recital. The English Opera Group presented Arthur Oldham's realisation of *Love in a Village* and a one-act opera by Lennox Berkeley, *A Dinner Engagement*. And again we managed to put an ad hoc theatre company together which staged *The Cocktail Party* and *The Death of Satan*. We had also enlarged the Festival to cover films, wine tasting, pottery, and, what I was particularly glad about, a reading of Sydney Goodsir Smith's poems. But once again the Festival was a financial failure: that is to say, as far as box office organisers' pockets were concerned. But the public relations officer worked out that if Bideford and Barnstaple had had to pay for the press mentions the Festival obtained for them, it would have cost the Councils £25,000 each. In addition, tradespeople of the towns had taken another £50,000 over the counter. Even so, when faced with these figures, the local Chambers of Commerce did nothing to bail us out.

The difficulty of finding a management to stage *Don Juan* at the first Devon Festival had been repeated the following year when *The Death of Satan* was produced. The problem was that no London managements were interested in festivals, or in staging plays that were "experimental". The only exception was Henry Sherek who had staged *The Cocktail Party* at Edinburgh but, with Eliot as the author and Rex Harrison in the cast, he had not risked very much. Apart from the Old Vic Company, subsidised by the Arts Council, and Martin Browne's Pilgrim Players, the theatre was wholly in the hands of the commercial managements who were only interested in innocuous little plays which would provide a vehicle for a star to achieve a long and tedious run. The most successful managements, such as H. M. Tennant, kept rigidly to this formula.

"There's no place for Poetry in the Theatre," Beaumont's partner had exclaimed when I had submitted *Stratton* to them, only a few months before *The Cocktail Party* settled down for nearly a year on Shaftesbury Avenue. But such managements were, of course, quite right in pointing out that playing a week or fortnight at a Festival was uncommercial: they could not recoup production costs; festival guarantees were insufficient to cover their inevitable deficit and, in addition, actors disliked committing themselves to a date in the country. They tour under protest, wishing to be available for the odd television serial.

Against this background, it seemed to me imperative, if the sort of theatre which I was interested in was to persist, for a management to be formed which would stage non-commercial plays. First I urged my agent, Margery Vosper, to form such a company. I told her that Eliot, Fry and I would support it, write for it and give the company options on all our plays. Again I found myself eating my way through innumerable lunches, trying to convert others to my own enthusiasms, with one hand on the phone to my farm and the other making sure I had some alka-seltzer in my pocket. But my digestive marathon proved to no avail. My agent, perhaps wisely, decided to remain purely an agent. I then tried to get Martin Browne to start another company based on the Mercury Theatre. But Ashley Dukes would not grant a lease.

Sadly I realised that there was no alternative but to do the job myself. This realisation infuriated me: it meant less writing, more yattering over meals, more dashing up to London and leaving my farm and horse. The Devon Festival already dissipated enough of my time. I resisted the thought of another venture which would put me in debt and depress me with committees. For weeks I hesitated. Then Rose Marie and Antonia, sensing my frustration, encouraged me and said they would help, which entailed the usual round of sending out begging letters, drafting brochures and Deeds of Covenants. Edward Blacksell readily supported the company and was soon drafting an appeal to the Arts Council.

Because I had been associated with the formation of the English Opera Group, I decided to call this new venture the English Stage Company and hoped it would achieve for the theatre what the Group had done for chamber opera. I also wanted to encourage serious composers and artists to write and design for the stage again. Ben, Topolski, John Piper and Epstein endorsed the plans. I wrote to Cocteau: he promised a new play. Bébé Bérard offered to paint sets himself. Fry approved, even Eliot was mildly enthusiastic within the limits of that habitual caution which was a second skin to him. Useful as these names might be on a brochure, they didn't make the chore of addressing envelopes and paying for the printing any lighter. That privilege added to the chaos on my desk and the hole in my pocket.

Earlier in the summer I had vaguely thought of renting the Royal Court Theatre to do a season of four plays there. The theatre was mostly dark: Alfred Esdaile, who leased it, was prepared to let it. But these negotiations came to nothing. However, through this abortive scheme I met Oscar Lewenstein, who was then manager of the theatre. He was enthusiastic for the idea of forming a new company. I immediately shanghaied him to Devon. We sat up most of three nights, drawing up lists of plays which had never been seen in England though they'd been produced on the Continent a generation previously. Brecht, Montherlant, Betti, Sartre, Cocteau, and many more. Lewenstein was a ferret of a man with a terrier's energy. I liked his methodical mind and practical approach to every problem. With him in the company I felt sure it would succeed in staging one or two plays at least. Lewenstein told me he was a Communist, but our different political views did not prevent us from agreeing that something had to be done to revitalise the theatre. We decided to try and stage the *Threepenny Opera* first, to be followed by a new play he'd brought down to show me, *Waiting for Godot*. He told me that every commercial manager had rejected this play and that the rights could be bought for £100. The play stayed on my desk for months while we tried to raise the money to stage it. Lewenstein returned to London and immediately busied himself writing letters to anybody I thought might send us a donation. Olivier failed to answer my letter. He, like very many others, reserved his approval for the company till it had become fashionable to support it. John Gielgud gave me tea in his dressing-room and told me that he thought The *Threepenny Opera* was a trifle sordid and a tedious bore. I didn't argue, but tried to arouse his interest in *Waiting for Godot*. He thought the theme was fatuous. I let that pass. Finally I gave him the list of dramatists whose works were unknown in England, or at least never pro-duced in any theatre in this country larger than a cellar. His reaction to this was to trot out the effete notion that if a play was really worth while it reached the West End anyhow.

"When?"

"Eventually."

"Possibly. But the purpose of the English Stage Company is to cut that interval down by twenty years and also to cause new plays to be written."

"How?"

"By commissioning them."

"If a man wants to write a play, he does so. A commission doesn't help. If an artist has got anything worth while to say, nothing will stop him."

"I don't agree."

"Shakespeare didn't need a commission."

"But he got one."

"Great artists compose from an inner necessity."

"Agreed. Released by an occasion, or a commission."

"Don't try and tell me that Marlowe, Sheridan, Congreve and Wilde wouldn't have written without the equivalent of your English Stage Company to encourage them."

"Possibly. But those names are known. I suspect comparable

talents failed to create because their work was never encouraged..."

To argue further was a waste of both our time. I often noticed that artists who, by accident, had had their talent recognised, believed stoutly that merit was alone sufficient. Those at the top were complacent about the frustration of those who were ignored, consoling themselves with the fatuous belief that merit always got through, was always recognised, even if unpublished, unhung and unproduced. This romantic fallacy always infuriated me. It was, and is, my hunch that there are more undiscovered talents than those that are known. Indeed, I've often thought that the most serious artists would inevitably remain unknown aloof from the rat-race which has perhaps always been the filter, letting only the more insensitive through. Survage and Picasso had shared a similar talent and the same studio: the former was the better draughtsman; he had a sensibility that recoiled from the publicity parade and social charades which canonised the latter. Taste and fashion are not the same thing. Most of Schubert had remained unpublished for a century. And how many Schuberts, Hopkins, and Rochesters are there whose names I cannot mention because the accidents of fashion condemned them to oblivion? "I do not believe that genius is always recognised," I told Gielgud, "indeed, I think there is probably just as much good music that has never been played as there are plays that have never been staged."

I was becoming a bore. I rose to go.

"Anyhow, Ronnie, let me know if you find a good modern comedy. I'm looking for one."

"But you don't wear clothes off the peg," I said. "Why don't you give some dramatist a few fittings?"

"Even dramatists have to be inspired. I don't think my figure would inspire anybody."

"Nonsense," I replied to his first assertion. "I'd write a play for a camel and three hunchback Turks if someone commissioned it."

"You astonish me," he said, unconsciously echoing Diaghilev, and passing me another thin sandwich.

A pity Gielgud always hides himself in a frivolity which he had borrowed from Wilde, but without the wit.

Peter Ustinov, of course, was more helpful. He came to dinner and delighted us with his anecdotes. Easily the best conversationalist in London, he always made me feel like a country bumpkin. As usual he sang so well for his supper that I didn't even get a chance to mention the English Stage Company. Nevertheless he sent a cheque and a new play round in the morning. John Whiting, too, came to Orme Lane and said he would support the new company in every way. But by far the most constructive conversations I had at that time were with Pierre Rouve. I cannot recall how I came to meet him. He was an Albanian who had settled in London as a young man. Like Ustinov, he spoke many languages. He had produced plays in Sofia and had ambitions to continue his career in London. He knew more about European drama than anybody I ever met. He bristled with ideas fifteen years before the *Sunday Times* had heard of them. He was and is unknown in London: no management used his gifts; he drifted into films and eventually produced Peter Sellers in *The Millionairess*. A waste: only Michel St Denis knew as much about the theatre as Pierre Rouve. The trouble was he was too serious to push and sufficiently philosophical not to complain when pushed out. In Fleet Street only a man with the soul of a pirate can survive: in Shaftesbury Avenue you need to be a swordfish. A process of devolution: the survival of the witless. Darwin's thesis also explains the triumph of mediocrity. Perhaps universal dullness is the ultimate pattern to which destiny, like an illiterate librarian, moves? *The Dunciad* is our epitaph.

With one eye optimistically on the Royal Court Theatre, Oscar Lewenstein thought it would be tactful if we invited its lessor, Alfred Esdaile, to join the Board of the English Stage Company. He accepted with alacrity and suggested that he should give a large party at his flat to which he would invite his monied friends and relatives, including Charles Clore, the property tycoon. Esdaile's only condition was that George should address his guests.

"They'll come with their cheques already signed if they've a chance to meet a member of the Royal Family," he said. Esdaile was a Jonsonian figure. I liked him as one likes Mosca, Sir Epicure or Falstaff. George agreed to attend his champagne beano, but said he would prefer not to make any speech. He was then very shy. But Esdaile insisted, and he finally agreed to make himself ridiculous for the sake of the *Threepenny Opera*.

To strengthen the board I also asked Eric Bessborough and Greville Poke to join. Both had, I vaguely remembered, been interested in the theatre when we were up at Cambridge. I asked them because both were sympathetic to the Arts without any axe to grind of their own. They were the sort of people in whom the Arts Council finds confidence.

When I told Edward Blacksell that George had thought it better if he were not Chairman of the Company, and had suggested we looked for a rich businessman, he surprised me by having a suggestion. He told me that he had been in the R.A.F. during the war and, with the plastic surgeon Sir Archibald McIndoe, he had helped to found the Guinea Pig Club, which patched up and rehabilitated airmen who had been badly burned during operations. One of the supporters of the Club was a Manchester wool manufacturer, Neville Blond, who lived at East Grinstead. He had helped the Guinea Pig experiment, and with his wife Elaine had raised considerable funds to help found the Victoria Hospital.

"Blond is a man of extraordinary executive ability," Blacksell told me. "The Treasury used him in Washington to negotiate a lot of lease-lend during the war. He received the C.M.G. for that work. He's a rich man in his own right, and married to Elaine Marks, the chain store millionairess."

"Yes," I said very dubiously. "I know such people exist, but the question is to find one who is interested in the theatre."

"Neville Blond used to back shows."

"What sort of shows?"

"C. B. Cochran, I believe."

"That's a long way from wanting to promote a non-profit making theatre company which wants to stage uncommercial plays."

"Yes."

We both felt depressed. It looked as if I would have to continue in the chair and that the company would grub along and we would be lucky if it ever succeeded in doing much more than to stage one play a year at some theatre such as the Embassy at Hampstead, and then only for a week or two.

"I could give you a note to Neville Blond, or you could write to him and mention my name," Blacksell said hopelessly.

I wrote a brief note and asked him to lunch with me at the Garrick if he'd like to hear more about the English Stage Company. He accepted.

"You say the Earl of Harewood is on your Board?" he asked before we had sat down. He was, I observed, a warm teddy-bear of a man with heavy-lidded eyes which, when he was interested, were suddenly undipped like the headlights on a car. He was direct. There was no small talk. I told him of our artistic plans. He had not heard of any of the dramatists I listed. I mentioned my idea of getting well-known artists and musicians to work for the theatre: he remained unenthusiastic. But when I started to talk of our financial problems his eyes immediately shone with interest.

"I don't know much about the theatre," he said frankly, "but I do know something about business. What you've got to realise is that it falls into two stages: first to produce a saleable commodity; secondly, having somewhere to show your commodity to the public. I assume that you and Lord Harewood can produce the goods and that you want me to market them?"

"Yes, that's precisely what we do want."

"Very well, but there's no point in running a production company if you don't have a theatre."

"They're very expensive," I murmured. "We thought of renting a theatre by the week."

Blond was very unimpressed at this proposal and seemed to withdraw his interest altogether.

"I'll join your company," he said eventually, "on condition you buy a theatre or, failing that, take a long lease on one. Do you know anybody who's got a theatre for sale?"

"As a matter of fact I do. Alfred Esdaile who leases the Royal Court and also owns the Kingsway Theatre."

"Well, let's go round and see him after lunch," Blond said, "and see if he'll sell it."

I was beginning to ponder whether I should emulate the Mad Hatter, order a tea pot and put my head in it. At any moment I expected to see a large white rabbit enter the Garrick. After all, I had just exhausted myself for the best part of six months raising less than £500, in addition to a possible grant from the Arts Council of a further £500.

"The Kingsway Theatre was bombed. But Esdaile has applied for a licence to rebuild it."

"Has it a good position?"

"Very."

"How much does he want for it?"

"I've no idea."

"How much would it let for, when rebuilt?"

"£300 a week."

The headlights undimmed. "Then he'll be asking about £70,000," Blond said. "You'd better phone him and tell him we're coming round."

"But we've only got about £500 in the kitty," I said, trying for once in my life to be business-like.

"We'll soon raise the rest," he informed me.

"How?"

"Mortgages."

"On what security?"

"The theatre."

"But it's not ours."

Blond smiled indulgently. "I'll deal with that. You and Harewood find the plays."

We drove to Esdaile's office in Park Lane. They understood each other's language. I didn't. But I could see that Blond had almost bought a theatre which neither of us had seen.

"You're on the Board of the English Stage Company, aren't you?" Blond asked Esdaile as we rose to go.

"Yes," he admitted.

"Then I shall expect you to guarantee £1,000 of the first mortgage. Three or four of the Directors will surely do the same." I heard Esdaile agree to contribute this guarantee to the purchase of his own property.

"There you are," said Blond as though he'd just given me a toy. "Now we're in business."

Blond's performance had impressed me as much as listening to Richter. I was silent with both gratitude and respect.

At a Board Meeting a day or two later I hurried out of the chair for Blond. Architects, surveyors, were appointed; mortgages arranged, and all this business transacted casually and quickly as the new Chairman sped between one Board Meeting and another. With the executive side in such good hands, George, Lewenstein and I were appointed to an artistic Sub-Committee. Our first task was to find a manager or a full-time director of productions. Lewenstein had suggested George Devine months before. I had not met him or worked with him. I now invited him to lunch.

I told him how I had come to form the company—the necessity of having a management which could stage plays for festivals, produce uncommercial works and commission others. He was enthusiastic. I told him who had promised plays: he approved. I told him that I was interested in a theatre that was not lifelike but bigger than life: he endorsed these views. I said that to my way of thinking the theatre was only important if it was universal, poetic but not poetical, providing a point of growth in consciousness and not a mere after-dinner digestive or a sectarian platform for temporary polemics. He said he was in complete agreement. I believed him. I was never a judge of character.

I had acquired a theatre at one luncheon. I lost it at another.

George Devine was appointed artistic director of the English Stage Company. He immediately showed that he was extremely talented. His gifts lay wholly in administration. He was adept at handling the Council. His brief-case always bulged with production estimates, schemes for commissions and budgets, and long-term programmes. He was shrewd enough to know that the way to handle a Board of Directors was to feed them paper and confuse them with more paper and go on his own way while they were left consulting memoranda that a subsequent estimate or programme had long ago made irrelevant. But his white hair, black horn-rimmed glasses and persistent pipe smoking lent him an authoritative, almost episcopal air. The Arts Council, impressed with our established Director, doubled their grant. Devine would have made an admirable civil servant or a Colonial administrator.

But of course in conversation at dinner at Orme Lane, Devine was anything but an Establishment figure. Then the words "experiments", "avant garde" and "progressive" were in every sentence. He was for The Method, against racial discrimination and thought that anybody who was as intelligent as he assumed he was, shared all his views, including vintage socialism inspired by Canon Collins and the late Beatrice Webb. Indeed, his ideals were so broadly based that I was really shocked driving him home one night shortly after his appointment when he confided in me that he didn't care whether his programme and estimate eventually bankrupted the English Stage Company.

"If we get a year out of it and stage three plays," he said, "we shan't have done too badly and Blond and his rich friends can easily pay the bills. Jews always help each other out."

I should have reported this declaration of high socialist principles direct to our Chairman. I didn't know how to do so. I hoped that Blond's own shrewdness would perceive the type of man Devine was and that if given rope enough he would soon hang himself. The contrary occurred: he hung me.

Meanwhile I tried to work with him in and outside the Artistic Committee. This body, still consisting of George Harewood, Oscar Lewenstein and me, had been empowered to read and choose the plays and select the programme. I naïvely thought that this would mean the Committee had effective control of what plays were produced. But Devine out-manoeuvered the Committee on every issue. This was easy. All plays which were submitted for production were sent, in the first instance, to his office. He had been instructed to weed out those manuscripts which were not worth our consideration. Consequently we only received those plays which had the polemic slant of which he approved. I discovered that Fry's play *Curtmantle* was returned without reaching the Committee. There were many more. And if I suggested a play for production, Devine frustrated it, not by expressing disapproval, but by reporting back that either the rights were unavailable or it had proved impossible to cast. Consequently Eliot, Fry, Whiting and Ustinov, to name only a few whom Devine secretly dismissed as reactionary writers, never had a play considered. If, on the other hand, a play appeared with a working-class background, however illiterate it was, the rights were quickly acquired and a cast engaged.

I hoped that the English Stage Company would have opened

with *Waiting for Godot*, or the *Threepenny Opera* which had never been performed in England. But another management took an option on the Becket play; Oscar Lewenstein got a company together to stage the *Threepenny Opera* under his own management. George and I had always been enthusiastic for Kurt Weill. When the work was staged, I was convinced that the success of the piece was due more to Weill than Brecht.

Blond had spent several months negotiating with Esdaile for the Kingsway Theatre. There were difficulties with the L.C.C. Finally, during a Council meeting, Blond passed me a note: "Would you like the Royal Court Theatre?" "Yes, please," I wrote underneath and passed it back. Esdaile was the lessor of that theatre too, but under Blond's expert financial guidance we managed to take a lease, mortgage it, and thus raise the money somehow.

We had not long moved into Sloane Square before I became apprehensive of the direction the theatre was going to take under Devine. When I had first met him he had shown enthusiasm for our aims: to stage new plays, and in order to be able to do that, to use stylised settings and keep the production costs beneath £2,000 per play; not to rely on star names but build up a repertory company of good actors; to use serious artists in the theatre.

I had two or three lunches with Eliot to discuss the play he was going to write. The theme was the impossibility of making a true marriage. Eliot's ideas were vague, but then so are any artist's until a commission precipitates them. Devine failed to approach Eliot. Epstein was never approached, and although Topolski had already done the sets for *Don Juan* and *The Death of Satan*, he, too, was considered reactionary. When the first productions were discussed, Devine put forward *The Mulberry Bush* by Angus Wilson. As the Company had hoped to try to persuade novelists such as Evelyn Waugh and Graham Greene to write for the theatre, we read *The Mulberry Bush* with some sympathy. That was all the enthusiasm I could find. It was donnish, flabby, with a New Statesman & Nation primness about it. But the next play he passed me was more exciting. It was *Look Back in Anger*. I read it and immediately wrote to Osborne to congratulate him. But it was *Cards of Identity* by Nigel Denis that struck me as the most original script. This play was based on his novel of the same title. The satirical idea behind it was worthy of Ben Jonson.

But Devine's own choices were usually the only ones that went forward. The Artistic Committee became little more than a rubber stamp. These tendencies were reined until *Look Back in Anger* became a success. Its original reception was poor. We had several meetings to discuss whether to take it off. Then George Fearon, our publicity agent, had the inspiration of coining the phrase "Angry Young Man"; consequent to this piece of frivolity, public interest was aroused until it became a vogue. With this fashionable breeze behind him, Devine felt his policy was justified and Blond, who wanted "success" at any price, was convinced that Devine's policy was right. If I voiced my views I was merely placated. It is only fair to both to record that George did not then share my differences of opinion with Devine, nor would he now subscribe to my evaluation of Devine's artistic criteria or character. And it is also fair to say that since Devine and I did not see eye to eye, he worked closer with George, who was consulted over most of the artistic decisions and enjoyed being a very active chairman of the Artistic Committee. But George and I had a *modus vivendi* which was elastic enough to stretch around these artistic differences. Though we often disagreed we were still often of the same opinion.

Filling the sails in the wings was Mr Tynan with his facility for reaching the wrong conclusions. He eventually propagated the idea of the Committed Theatre. This was not precisely novel: Brecht had discussed the notion thirty years before. But it provided a talking point. It now became fashionable. Nobody worried about what one was committed to so long as the commitment was apparent. The language in a play was not noticed so long as it had the tone of protest within it. I observed sadly that the protests were always prompted by social envy, and though the trappings of privilege were disparaged by the playwrights, they copied them as soon as they had received their royalties. Socialists of the Savoy Grill, angry young men with silk shirts and sports cars. I pondered the integrity of a Gandhi, recalling his pushing a cart through the villages and loading it up

381

with his own hands filled with human shit. I could not take any of these new characters seriously, either as artists or reformers. I had no objection to the Left Wing play, but was worried when they were exclusively biased in that old corner. Why is it that the theatre always attracts the most superficial minds?

After this financial "success" the values of Shaftesbury Avenue merely shifted to Sloane Square. The use of stars became the order of the day: Olivier jumped on the band-wagon and Osborne wrote *The Entertainer*. The script was sent to me act by act; I disliked it act by act. The lyrics seemed as witless as *Punch*. The sentiment behind the piece nauseated me. I expressed my disapproval but only isolated myself further as a consequence. Osborne and Olivier were names not to be criticised. With this strength behind him Devine now manipulated the Council to alter the terms of reference for the Artistic Committee. Instead of having the veto in choosing plays, we now became a merely consultative body to which Devine could go if he wanted advice.

By this time Brecht had become the apostle at the Royal Court. I used to sit there listening to the awe that surrounded his name, recalling the man I had known who sat stuffing his face with chocolate éclairs. But the New Establishment was now established. I felt like a python who had given birth to a mongoose. But stayed on, hoping in vain to influence rather than withdraw. It was a mistake. When you realise a bus is going the wrong way, you save time if you get off immediately.

I cannot remember how I came across the French play *Un homme nommé Judas* by Claude Puget and Pierre Bost, but since it gave a contemporary twist to the Judas legend, I decided to make an English version.

George and I had flown to Paris in search of Puget. Neither of us had heard of him. I found his address and telephoned him from the Hotel Castille in my execrable French, while George busied himself by knocking down all the wire coathangers in the wardrobe. I tried above the din to explain my purpose. Puget saw us that evening; we discovered that he was a very considerable author, whom the fashion for Sartre and Anhouilh had excluded. He agreed to my proposal, and I wrote the play during the following winter. Henry Sherek agreed to produce it, and as Martin Browne had directed Eliot's two plays for him, he readily agreed that Martin should be asked.

The play opened first at the 3rd Devon Festival and later at the Kings Theatre, Edinburgh, in April 1956. I went up there for the last weeks of rehearsals. Yvonne Mitchell played Leah and Duncan Macrae was Judas. It was a good cast, and Martin Browne produced it sensitively and showed great imagination, especially in the lighting cues for the final scene. But in spite of Yvonne Mitchell's excellent performance, the play was not well received at Edinburgh by an audience that had been brought up on the lethal mixture of John Knox and Sir Walter Scott. Nevertheless, Sherek intended taking the play to London, if he could re-cast the part of Judas. Duncan Macrae's Scots accent would have been too conspicuous in London. Sherek wanted Michael Redgrave. When it became apparent that this actor was not available, the plans for a West End production dissolved, irrespective of the merits of the play. The theatre was star-bound: I found it impossible to take it seriously. My farm was a distraction, a distraction from insanity.

One of the memories of the Devon Festival which I relish occurred when I arranged for a production of Yeats' *Purgatory* as a curtain raiser. Eliot had drawn my attention to this piece of Yeats' some years before. I had always wanted to see it. It is the best of Yeats and, unlike his other dramatic work, entirely free of Gallic moonshine and feyness.

After the first performance, the Mayor of Barnstaple gave a reception in the Guild Hall for the cast and the author. George and I went to this, and his Worship asked me what I had done with Mr Yeats. I looked a little bewildered.

"The party was for the cast and the author," he explained. "You really ought to have brought him along with you."

Tom Eliot had a reputation for caution. Ezra had nicknamed him Possum and occasionally referred to him as the Reverent Thomas. He was generally very circumspect, especially in print where his sentences are punctuated by conditional parentheses. But there were many times when he delivered the most incautious dicta to me. I remember meeting him one day and he told me he had just come from a ceremony in Tite Street, Chelsea, where the Mayor had unveiled a plaque commemorating Wilde's residence in the house.

"I didn't know you admired Wilde?" I said.

"I don't," he spat. "Nobody would have remembered him if he hadn't committed sodomy."

As my own opinion of Wilde differed so completely, it was a waste of time to argue.

"I wish I had written *The Importance of Being Earnest*," I said.

"Don't undervalue yourself," Tom said. "It's a form of conceit."

Tom was always doing these sort of literary chores, even when his health didn't permit them. Once when he was stooping almost double with asthma and cold, he told me that he was busy writing a paper on Goethe as he had to go to Germany to receive the Goethe Prize and an honorary degree. He already had over twenty.

I thought his visit was unwise at the time and I had never been able to be sympathetic to Goethe after I had read that he had not even acknowledged Schubert's letter when he had sent the poet his settings of his poems.

"Isn't it a bit of a grind for you to write about Goethe?"

"It is. I can't stand his stuff."

Sometimes our opinions clashed completely. I was on one occasion praising Charlie Chaplin to him. Tom listened, looking hard at his plate.

"I divide the world into two parts," he said solemnly. "Those who like the Marx brothers and those who like Charlie Chaplin. I like the Marx brothers and I'm disgusted with you for liking Chaplin."

He respected few of his contemporaries other than Gabriel Marcel, Stravinsky, Santayana and one or two obscure philosophers. He would frequently tease me over my wasting my time adapting Cocteau or doing something with Britten. Though he respected Tippett.

He was embarrassed by being bracketed with Christopher Fry. He felt that Fry had queered the pitch. Eliot and I had tried to make verse in the theatre a pliable vehicle of our contemporary feeling. We had both turned our backs on *Murder in the Cathedral* and *This Way to the Tomb* and set ourselves the task of writing modern plays in which the verse was not decoration upon the theme but simple, unrhetorical and lucid. In *The Cocktail Party* and *Stratton* we felt we were moving towards language which had the discipline of prose but could carry the charge of a hand grenade when required. But the success of Fry's *The Lady's Not for Burning* put the clock back. We deprecated these verbal fireworks, this concern with imagery for the sake of coining it. My own aversion to this was tempered by my knowing Fry personally and liking him considerably. But Eliot had no inhibition here.

"He'll get over this style," I said.

"But the damage will be done."

He was quite correct. The damage was done. Fry's brief success associated poetry on the stage with rhetoric and verbal puff again. Within five years both Eliot and I found it difficult to get a production—Fry himself found it impossible.

My real difference with George Devine and his supporters on the Artistic Committee of the English Stage Company was on what drama should be about. There are two kinds of problems: those which can be solved and those to which there are no possible solutions. In the first category lie ephemeral matters of a social or political nature: questions of wages, working conditions, and so on. To such political or social issues there are, of course, social or political solutions. But in the second category, lie such matters: how man faces up to old age, death, loneliness, and his existence as the only conscience being in an unconscious universe. These issues I maintained, were the proper subjects of drama—unless it was to be reduced to being as transient and essentially frivolous as yesterday's newspaper. Temporal matters which can be solved by the raising of wages or the laying of sewers are, in the last analysis, trivial. As a dramatist, I am only interested in those problems to which there are no possible solutions: Faust, Lear, Hamlet and Macbeth are on the rack of their own humanity. It is the dilemma of being, the limitations of humanity, the frailty of our nature, yet the strength of our vision, which are the proper themes for plays. Devine had a different measure. And mine was derided and dubbed the stuff of religious drama. Occasionally I would ask these Fabian-conceived intellectuals, who stood with one hand on the bible of Brecht and the other on the *Observer*, to consider the derivation of the word "religion". It derives, I reminded them, from the Latin 'to connect'. Surely every man, the scientist doing research, or the individual fumbling towards some attitude to the universe, is therefore religious? But the elks equated religion with the singing of Hymns Ancient and Modern, and consequently ran from me as though I were a leper.

In this atmosphere of puritanical disapproval, Devine found himself committed to produce my plays *Don Juan* and *The Death of Satan*. It was as if Cromwell had found himself saddled with the distasteful job of acting as valet to Charles I. Devine wriggled and tried his usual gambit of finding the plays impossible to cast. But there was a contractual obligation. When I had founded the Company, Sir Reginald Kennedy-Cox had joined the board and subscribed £2,000 to the funds, on condition that my two plays should be produced, with the rider that a friend of his, George Selway, should be cast in them. This proviso was as embarrassing to me as it was to Devine. He proceeded eventually to cut the two full length plays so that they could be performed in one evening. This operation gleefully performed by a sadistic surgeon removed all the flesh and reduced my text to a skeleton of stage directions. His next move was to sabotage my intentions by inspired miscasting. For Don Juan he found an actor who had rightly found his place in musical comedy, for Doña Aña a lady who would have made an adequate Mother Courage, and for the frivolous and amorous Isabella, an actress who might have passed as an officer of a Marriage Guidance Clinic. The only mistake Devine made was to appoint John Minton to do the décor for both plays. Perhaps he had assumed that Minton would not be sober enough to complete them? But Minton's enthusiasm for the plays acted as a Fernet Branca upon him. His designs were excellent and so economical that nobody could discard them. What's more, the artist made most of the props himself and worked furiously to paint the sets. With Minton's encouragement and the sympathy which Tom Eastwood, who was composing the music, gave me, I allowed the production to proceed. This was a mistake: I should have glanced at the cast and withdrawn the remnants of my plays at the first rehearsal.

It is fair to say that Devine handled the technical problems which the plays contain, such as the ghost scene, with more than average competence. I could not fault the surgeon though he was removing my guts and heart. The rehearsals continued with Devine inspiring the cast with the feeling that they were helping him to perform a contractual obligation.

George, Marion and Rose Marie accompanied me to the first night at the Royal Court. I felt like a holed barge being towed out to be torpedoed. I had laboured hard towards this fiasco. I had eaten my way through dozens of terrible meals to form the English Stage Company. I had suffered the company of bores, panders, pimps and profiteers. And the result was a production as lamentable as that which *Stratton* had received.

Not without reason, the critics were unenthusiastic or derisory. My plays had been reduced to a costume melodrama. Bent over Sloane Square with my trousers down, I received a beating of expletives. The audience was sparse. After ten days, Neville Blond phoned me and said that since the plays were not making money he felt they should be withdrawn. The advantages of a non-profit making production company were temporarily shelved.

Once again, I had to wait for a German production before these plays were given a fair chance and established themselves successfully in spite of the difficulties of translation.

After reading the criticisms, I found myself indulging in the fantasy of giving a banquet for all the dramatic hacks of the London Press. My plan was to send each an invitation to meet some internationally famous nonentity, and with this gentleman's name as bait I visualised them all trooping in holding their card and wearing a black tie, into some banqueting hall, preferably in a remote castle in Kent. When they were all seated, the portcullis would drop, the door would be bolted and the greedy little men would be left to eat each other. In idle moments I consoled myself with the sight of Tynan as he chewed a haunch of Harold Hobson.

Part Seven

Here error is all in the not done,
all in the diffidence that faltered

WE now moved a step nearer to the green baize door when Rose Marie decided to make some pocket money for herself by taking in, quite literally, a few paying guests during the summer. She started making plans in April. As usual, our schemes to make money led from one extravagance to another. This particular method towards solvency nearly landed us in Carey Street. Our trouble was not that we didn't get any paying guests, but her being new to the business made her so nervous about failing to give value for money, that she ended up by subsidising every visitor who came for a holiday to the house by at least £5 per week. It would have been considerable economy to my pocket if I had taken these people for a tour round the Swiss Alps and kept my own house closed. The failure was not because Rose Marie was a bad housekeeper but because her standards were too high to be profitable. Like any amateur starting a business, they are at first always nervous that they are overcharging, and end up by under-charging.

A few weeks before the first guests arrived in May, Rose Marie and I stayed up night after night drafting and re-drafting menus, happily quite oblivious to their cost. I would recall dishes I had eaten in Italy or Spain and she would remember delicacies which had delighted her in other parts of Europe. Between us we managed to evolve menus which would have done credit to any four-star hotel. Harrods and Fortnum & Mason's received long orders. Duck and geese were ordered from neighbouring farms; butchers were asked to hold back their best undercut. In spite of this extravagance Rose Marie was almost on the point of tears with nerves when she banged on the gong for her first dinner. Doing an involuntary imitation of Chaplin, I helped her carry in the trays. Our mouths watered, we returned to the kitchen hoping there were no complaints, praying that there might be a little of the paté left over for our own supper. This often proved the case and I found the sacrifice of the rest of the house worth some of the scraps we gobbled up in the kitchen.

Unhappily there were no complaints. Our guests recommended others. Each party that came cost me a little more. To add insult to injury, my own literary agent had spotted Rose Marie's advertisement in the Personal column of *The Times* and gleefully booked for the whole month of August. It is one thing to pay 10 per cent. of one's royalties to your agent: it is hard to have to keep them and their family on top of that. The news of this Michelin guide oasis in the deserts of Devonshire spread far and wide. It soon became necessary for Rose Marie to have some help with this catering, and as we couldn't get any local woman, we advertised and finally employed a dèbutante who had done a spell at the Cordon Bleu. The bills became even more expensive, not because the menus were increased, but with this kind of domestic in the kitchen it was necessary to serve the same kind of food each side of the green baize door. As the butchers' bills reached double figures a week I had the temerity to suggest to Rose Marie that she raised her fees of full board per person to twelve guineas per week. But she had not the confidence to do this. She felt that this would be over-charging them and much preferred to subsidise their holidays herself. Fortunately the summer season in Devonshire ends abruptly in the middle of September. If it had been longer I would have gone bankrupt.

It was Antonia's birthday. She complained that I had never taken her away. The complaint was justified but ill-timed. My conscience troubled me. As usual, I made a ridiculous compromise. Being fond of both of them, I thought they should be fond of each other. They had been on many occasions, but this was not to be one. We stayed at the Hotel Castille in Paris where I had first met Cocteau, but the weekend was a disaster. Yet the visit was not entirely wasted because I tracked down Leopold Survage, whose work I had admired for many years.

One evening I decided to take Rose Marie and Antonia to the theatre. They chose the play. It was *Le Seducteur* by Diego

Fabbri. Anna had, I remembered, played in the original production in Venice when Visconti had produced it a year or two before. It was about a man who, happily married, complicated his life by keeping a mistress and also having an *affaire* with his secretary. But as he tells the audience, he is not a philanderer, but simply fond of women. Deceiving the three of them wears him out; he decides that his life would be less complicated if the three girls could accept the situation. After all, he argues, he loves them, so why shouldn't they therefore all love one another? He organises a series of accidents so that the girls get to know one another without realising that they each know him. They get on well together. The wife talks about her husband, Fred, to the secretary, who returns her confidence by telling her about her lover, Michael; and both chatter eventually to the third girl who is kept by a man called Thomas. The little man sees that the girls have much in common, and finally engineers a scene where he alone appears when the girls are going to introduce each other to their men.

I felt deeply sympathetic to this comic character and decided, before the first act was over, to adapt the play into English, which I did.

That evening was a success, but the *à trois* visit to Paris was a failure. But nobody's failure. I was distraught with worry: racked with guilt. I should not have allowed Antonia to be thrown up and out of my life. The thing which actually broke us was when I stopped her from working as a secretary to the English Stage Company. I should have been weaker in my weakness, stronger in my strength. I had compromised with my feelings. Rose Marie and I should have shared our life completely with her, instead of picking her up and dumping her as though she were a thing. Should, should, should. But at the time we were only dimly conscious. Most of life is sleepwalking, a dream few of us wake up from, then only momentarily.

The morality of either/or had triumphed. For me, this was a failure. I felt amputated: I had been amputated. Rose Marie missed Antonia too. After several months she made a last, humble approach to her: it was rejected. I felt sorrier for Rose Marie than I did for myself. We were both unhappy, not because we did not love one another, but because we had both lost somebody we had loved too. I suppose it was good to know that we were respectable members of conventional society again, but this was no consolation. Perhaps immorality and happiness are sometimes the same thing?

Why was I so involved? Was I trying to prove myself, like some lecherous (and probably imaginative) Frank Harris? Was I sexually frustrated? Or just unable to resist a pretty girl? None of these are true. I was full of self-confidence and happily married. What then made me so vulnerable? It was because I could not stop myself from responding to the pathetic vulnerability which is what I find in all women. Girls are such sad and insecure creatures: even the prettiest are like beggars—begging to be admired, grovelling for appreciation, so easily hurt and, by indifference, destroyed. Sometimes they expose a hard exterior, but it is superficial: they are all pathetic, sad and uncertain at the centre, children trying so hard to please. Like my own sister who, when she was in the nursery, was given a toy cooking stove on which tiny pots were heated over nightlights...one day she announced that she had cooked my dinner: the bits of meat tasted of candle grease, the potatoes were still quite raw. But her little face was radiant with pleasure. I swallowed it all: I even swallowed my own sickness. This I believe is the reason why I am so vulnerable, because they are so vulnerable too.

And to add to my sadness, I realised that the theatre was not going my way and that poetry was becoming less accepted again, delegated to odd corners in magazines circulating only to contributors. As Cole Porter has it:

> Good writers too
> Who once knew better words
> Now only use four letter words;
> Writing prose
> Anything goes.

The emotional failure was supported by intellectual hopelessness. Glancing round the cultural deities of the late fifties I felt like a traveller in a strange city, or a relic from a previous age. My misery was deep-seated. I felt isolated, insulated and useless. It is one thing to miss a bus, another to miss one's own Age. But I had not, in fact, missed it: I had got off. It was going where I didn't want to go. Like a salmon, I would swim up-stream against the current, exhaust myself and spawn in a lonely pool and shed the sea-lice on the gravel. Like a wolf I would pad the woods alone. I resolved:

> To sing high and aloof
> Free from the wolf's black maw
> And the Dull Ass's hoof.

I returned to the country and picked up my farm again, and found consolation in the profligate use of cement. There is as much art in ploughing or building as on any damn page. Art is not a thing, but a method. Beetroot became my poems: rows of lettuce my lyrics. And when words intruded into my mind, I would seldom bother to write them down. At this time, as at other times, only he could console me. No, not the carpenter, nor Dante, nor Donne, but the little man they called "Fatty", the ridiculous-looking figure who once shuffled round Vienna dropping songs out of his pocket.

That is the best of failure: it makes one grateful for life itself. When we are intensely unhappy it is a consolation to realise that one has two feet, two eyes and ears to hear Schubert. Indeed, unhappiness is necessary, if consciousness is to grow. We must pray not for happiness but the amount of unhappiness we can bear. If happiness is unconsciousness and unhappiness alone induces consciousness, then I choose unhappiness. For consciousness is all: it's the pain that makes our being.

Most people buy a house because they need it to live in or because it appeals to them. But I bought "The Hermitage" at Welcombe, not because I wanted to live in it, but because I thought it so extremely ugly. It was not that I had a perverse taste and wanted to collect examples of hideous architecture. I had known the house since I was a child. It had been built originally in 1890 as a place of retreat for Roman Catholic priests. It sat two hundred yards from the cliff, plonk in the middle of the valley, and spoilt the view. Every time I passed it as a child I thought what fun it would be to blow the house up. Later, as I became less reckless it occurred to me that if I owned this box-like building which was so unrelated to the surrounding countryside, I would immediately lengthen it so as to improve from its proportions. Later I became keen on what I called landscape architecture, maintaining that every building should be designed to fit to the surrounding countryside. Houses in flat country should be lower and longer than those which are surrounded by hills. There was no excuse for the squareness of buildings. This reforming zeal eventually led me to bid for "The Hermitage" when it came on the market in 1945. I did this to prevent anybody else buying it, then leaving it in the shape that annoyed me so much, with no plans of improving its appearance before selling it again. But having bought it I found that I, too, was unable to do any of these things. To begin with, the Town & Country Planning Act prevented me from making any architectural alterations without an adequate reason. The walls which I had planned to build flanking each side of the house were regarded as frivolous and had to be abandoned. Disgruntled, I put the house up for sale. It remained empty for several years and on the lists of half a dozen agents. I did not get a single bid. The agents reported that it was a waste of time trying to sell the house until it was connected to main water and electricity. Neither of these services were available, and their appearance in Welcombe seemed remote.

For another year the great house stood gaunt and empty. But it was not unused. For a whole summer it became a hermitage in fact. Though the house was now entirely unfurnished I decided to use it as a vast echoing study. Sitting on an oil drum which I found in the garage and using a window-sill as a desk, I wrote there. Two friends, Frederick Tomlin, the philosopher, and his brother who had given up his job as a master at Eton in order to take up medicine, took over adjoining rooms as studies, each improvising a seat and using a window-sill to write on. This used the place, but it was an expensive study: no rent came in.

There was nothing for it, but to decorate the place the following winter, install a small electric generator to light it and a water pump, and then try and find a tenant for the house I had wished destroyed.

Eventually, after showing innumerable people round, a timid

woman without any family or even a pet to keep her company, took the enormous building for her own occupation at £80 per year. We wondered what she was going to do with it. Then a tiny notice appeared on the front door: *Visitors Taken In.* It could not be read from the road. She never thought of hanging it on the gate. She sat for a whole season in the large kitchen which had once been used as a servants' hall, meditating on a row of dusty lemonade bottles which nobody came to buy. Not a single visitor put up at the Hermitage during her tenancy. The poor woman left. I had not the heart to hold her to the lease. The white elephant was now on my hands again.

As it was only two hundred yards from a sandy beach, I decided to capitalise on this fact and turn the nine large bedrooms into flatlets for holiday-makers. This, of course, entailed an enormous amount of capital expenditure which, in optimistic moments, I called an investment. It meant putting a kitchen unit with hot and cold water into every room, Calor gas cookers, and furnishing each flatlet with two single divans, cupboards, tables, chairs, blankets, and the whole range of kitchen equipment. But I discovered that turning a bedroom into a flatlet according to the Planning Officer constituted a structural alteration. He would only give us permission for this if we made each flatlet fireproof from the adjoining one, by lining the door panels with asbestos; running separate pipes for drinking water, and arranging to ventilate the food cupboards. This entailed more "investment". Next we had to find means of heating the water for each flat by an immersion heater run on the electric generator, costing another £300. Having met the limit of my overdraft, Rose Marie and I had to improvise a good deal of the furnishings. We attended sales of bankrupt hotels, bought Army blankets which we decorated with braid, and improvised lampshades from frames which we threaded with dishcloth wool. Her sewing machine worked into the night making curtains to separate the kitchen from the bed-sitting room, making bed covers, cushions, from cheap material called crash, and unbleached linen. But eventually, with the slave-labour that one is able to find by employing oneself and one's own family, "The Hermitage" stood equipped down to its last coffee-strainer and tin-opener. The rooms looked light and bright, and if anybody did not like my drawings which I had hung on the walls they always had the view of the sea from the window.

The next step was to design a brochure describing the property and its amenities, and advertise the place. We were not prepared for the response. A single advertisement brought something like a couple of hundred replies. Replying to these became a major chore. We discovered, as anybody in the hotel or letting business finds out, that at least 80 per cent of the enquiries are made from mere curiosity. There must be many people who never intend to take a holiday other than looking at brochures. Even so, in our first season we were booked up for July and August. Before the first visitors appeared, Rose Marie was so nervous lest the holiday-makers complained that she insisted on sleeping in several of the flatlets to make sure the beds were comfortable, and discover whether any article of kitchen equipment was missing. Reassured, we were still nervous when the first tenants arrived. If one of them told me they enjoyed the view from the window, or appreciated the decoration of the room, I immediately ran to Rose Marie with the glad news, and when another tenant complained over some detail to her, I had to stand by to console. I don't suppose the people who take rooms realise how worrying their holiday is to the people to whom they pay the rent. Indeed, worrying about their holiday, most of us need a holiday.

Though we had equipped each flatlet carefully and had remembered even such details as coathangers, ironing boards, bedside lamps, and a large airing cupboard in which parents could hang their children's clothes, we knew that one thing was missing. That was reliable electric light. Our Achilles heel was a solenoid. It was this small piece of equipment which kept us awake at night. The entire house was dependent on the electricity generator, both for lighting and heating. I had installed what is called a Startomatic, which was fixed in the garage. The solenoid was part of the gadget which started the engine when anybody switched a light on in a flatlet, or whenever the immersion heater turned itself on automatically by means of a thermostat. This wretched solenoid had a vice-like grip on the Hermitage. When the float switch in the cold water tank up in the roof went below a certain level, the electric pump was theoretically switched on automatically, but the solenoid was temperamental. Angry tenants would telephone us to say that the hot water was running cold and then five minutes later they would ring again to say that there was now no cold water. Or that the entire house was plunged in darkness. I would rush down to the garage, hoping in vain that it was merely a fuse, or that the wretched engine had run out of diesel. I would find tenants wandering about the house holding matches in their hands as we had omitted to equip them with candles. Generally I discovered that the solenoid had blown. This entailed getting an electrician from seventy miles away: no one nearer was an agent for this particular make of generator. Rose Marie and I used to hold devoted little prayer meetings in which we would pray to the South Western Electricity Board to connect us to the mains; not relying on prayer from experience, I held meetings in Parish Halls, lobbied M.P.s, and organised a petition with the locals. This little exercise took five years.

But to our utter amazement we discovered, in subsequent years, by noticing the names of the people who booked again for a holiday in the Hermitage, that those who returned were the same families who had been plunged into darkness several times and gone without a hot bath on more than one occasion. This intrigued me sufficiently to ask one couple from Birmingham why they chose to return, knowing these hazards.

"It gives the holiday a sense of adventure," I was told. "The children love being plunged into darkness and having to find odd bits of candles. They think it's like Christmas."

Perhaps enterprising boarding-house keepers should equip themselves with unreliable solenoids, pumps that have faulty valves and taps that run dry?

Out of timidity we only charged eight guineas a week for a flatlet with beds for two or three people, with precarious light and heat thrown in. It was not expensive, especially since many of the tenants brought camp beds and we often found five people sleeping in a room.

But of course not all of them were satisfied. Rose Marie often came back from the Hermitage in tears when she had just shown some new tenants into a brightly tidied room on a fine day, because they had complained about some detail. I began to analyse these complaints, and found that they had only one feature in common. Sometimes they would come from one flat, sometimes another. It was nothing to do with the weather on the day the tenants arrived. Nobody complained about the erratic electricity. The common cause was the distance the tenants had travelled; many, to save money, had driven almost non-stop from such distant places as Carlisle and had arrived exhausted. The wife had been crushed in the back of the car with two small children, the remnants of ham sandwiches, spades, surfing-boards and a folding pram, and was generally in such a temper that even if she had been shown into the Ritz she would have found it necessary to vent her rage on the *maître d'hôtel*. They would complain that the house was isolated, when we had advertised it as being secluded; or begin to pack their things again when they discovered that the North Devon coast had not got a promenade fitted with slot machines. Generally these people who blew up when they arrived were all smiles and contentment after they had had a good sleep. But it took us several years to learn this and to anticipate the long distance motorists' inevitable malaise.

Having converted the Hermitage and a couple of cottages, the stable at West Mill seemed to pose no problems. The stone walls and the roof were there. The horse was gone. All that was necessary was to put in half a dozen windows, a floor, a bathroom partitioned off, leaving the building as one large studio which could be divided off into kitchen and two bedrooms. Instead of erecting hardboard partitions, Rose Marie had the bright idea of putting up curtains on runners which divided the studio at night, but turned it back into one big room during the day. We tackled most of this conversion ourselves, using our friends as forced but willing labour. While I knocked a window out where my horse used to stand, Lord Queensberry, who had come down for an idle weekend with us, found himself happily decorating the bathroom and painting up an old lavatory seat. Our first tenants at the studio moved in three weeks later. They were a French nuclear physicist with his wife and four children. They stayed for three weeks. The valley was perfumed with garlic. When they were about to leave he came to pay the rent, and presented me with three bottles of Hennessey brandy. I thought this generosity was excessive and asked him why he was making such a gift.

"We really felt," he said, "that you have undercharged us, because the snails we have picked up were alone worth twice the rent. Do you realise that the cliffs here are littered with the yellow escargots which in Bordeaux we value more highly than any other? We have been able to pick up at least half a pailful a day, and indeed, I am taking several kilos back to France with me, if you don't mind?"

That is the best of tenants from the Continent; they appreciate England so much more than the English, especially the foods that they can pick up. It was a family from Belgium that taught me that we had at least twenty varieties of edible fungi on the farm, all of which made the most delicious salads. It was a couple from Switzerland who showed us that the churns of sour milk returned from the dairy should not be thrown to the pigs but turned into paprika cream cheese.

Campers are a side-line. They usually drive into the farmyard in a very expensive car and ask if they can put their tent up somewhere on the farm. They often resent paying anything for the privilege. They do not hesitate to knock on your door and ask to borrow the bathroom. Consequently we do not encourage them, especially as they litter the hedges with tins and bottles which are dangerous to the horses. My prejudice against campers accounts for the fact that I never met Mr Moore, although he put up his tent in the valley and endured the discomforts there for almost a week. He had told me that he was a sculptor but failed to give me his first name. He gave this to Rose Marie yet failed to inform her that he was a sculptor. Consequently neither of us knew who he was until he had left, taking with him several pieces of interestingly shaped driftwood which he had picked up from the beach.

After Rose Marie's two extravagant seasons taking paying guests, she had to return to Yorkshire to nurse her invalid mother for a year. During this time my daughter Briony suggested that we should turn the farm house into three flats, live in one and let the other two. This entailed putting up a few partitions and installing another bathroom. But I was a dab hand at fixing lavatories. I think I knew as much about the construction of water-closets as I did about sonnets. Probably the former is more useful. I looked on this new venture with more confidence. We were not going to do any catering. Each flat was provided with its own kitchen, though I observed that Briony, like her mother, was becoming increasingly nervous as her tenants were about to move in. She started to run off to Bideford, buying another set of cushion covers and replacing a new frying pan with an expensive non-stick variety. The day her first tenants appeared, she had decorated the flat with bowls of flowers by every bed, and foxgloves festooned the sitting-room. I congratulated her on her efforts and felt that my profit from them was the look of radiant pleasure I saw on her face when she showed the couple into the flat. Half an hour later I went out to drive the cows in, and came back to find Briony crying her eyes out. Apparently the woman had accosted her land-lady of seventeen with vile abuse because the teapot lid was cracked. Furious that all Briony's pathetic efforts should have been appreciated in this way, I went to interview the woman. I replaced the teapot lid, then told her of the effect her impatience had had on my daughter, who had spent a whole week preparing the flat and then decorated it with flowers. To my astonishment the woman herself then burst into tears, not from rage but remorse. This couple enjoyed their holiday and left, leaving a box of chocolates for their landlady.

Financial greed can make you put up with the most extra-ordinary physical discomforts. Encouraged by my bank manager to reduce the mounting overdraft I had incurred by making the two flats at Mead Farm, I persuaded myself that it would be little sacrifice to me if I let the remaining part of the house where I now lived by myself as Briony had taken a job in the BBC. If I did this it would bring in another twenty guineas a week for at least three months. This prospect blinded me to the discomforts that I would meet living in a tent behind the tennis court. I argued that I was not only making a financial gain but my health would improve from sleeping out in the fresh air and it would be a move towards monkish simplicity. I saw myself as a desert father sleeping on the turf with my manuscript book on one side and and a bowl of rice on the other. I hurried up to London and found a shop near Victoria that dealt in Government Surplus stores. I asked the man behind the counter if he could sell me a small tent. He must have been a practical joker. He put a canvas bag on the counter and assured me that it contained everything including a mallet to knock in the pegs, and that the whole thing cost only £6 10s. I thought this was very cheap. I had no real idea how much tents were but assumed that I had made a saving by going to a surplus store. I hurried back to Devonshire the day before my tenants were moving into the flat. The next day, having shown them into my bedroom, I gaily marched out to erect the tent, holding a leaflet of instructions in one hand. When I had disentangled myself from knitting with the various ropes, I eventually discovered that I had bought a tent which is generally sold to cyclists and carried on the back of their bike. My home for the summer was two feet high, three feet wide and five feet long. There was not even room for the bowl of rice. Nevertheless, with the thought of my twenty guineas a week coming in from those who slept in my bed, I endured these rigours, waking some mornings to find the wet canvas flapping against my cheek. At this time the BBC had commissioned me to write a play on the Pilgrim Fathers. It was a wet summer. The tent was not water-proof. I had turned my study into a sitting room. There was nothing for it now but to set up my desk in the greenhouse. Sweltering amongst the humidity of tomatoes, I wrote this play when I was not interrupted by my visitors' children, who enjoyed coming to look at the maniac who sat all day behind glass, knowing that he should have been behind bars.

After running the Hermitage with nine flatlets for several years, we decided to convert it into four self-contained flats, each with a kitchen, bathroom and three bed-sitting rooms. This meant sinking another couple of thousand pounds in the house, but we thought it was worth it as we could then raise the rents and have fewer tenants, and therefore less work. And by now the mains had arrived. I celebrated this by smashing the electric generator with a large axe, and Rose Marie went gay by buying refrigerators, fires and electric cookers and kettles for every flat. Equipped with every so-called modern convenience we thought that we were now out of several woods, but my theory about the long distance motorists still proved correct.

The first family came into a spruce flat which had just been equipped with a forty guinea refrigerator, electric stove, fires etc. It even had bunches of primroses by every bed. But the two young couples that had taken the flat had motored from Middlesbrough. The two girls looked rather drab, having sat up all night. Their mascara had slipped half-way down their cheeks. Their husbands (we do not ask for marriage lines) had taken turns in driving and appeared very disgruntled. As usual I showed them in and told them we delivered eggs and milk from the farm, and countered their comment that there was no sand on the beach by my usual observation that this was only true when the tide was in, but was rectified when the tide was out. Two hours later they appeared at West Mill, where we were again living, to inform me that they were so dissatisfied with the "Nunnery" as they miscalled the Hermitage, that they intended to report me to the *News of the World*, and blithely admitted that as a gesture of their appreciation they had thrown the cups against the wall. I offered to go with them to their flat to examine any article which was not up to standard, fearing that a fuse had blown on the refrigerator, or another tenant had swiped their electric kettle.

"It's nothing to do with the flat itself," one of the girls complained, "the place is so horribly quiet. There's no cinema anywhere about. The pub's two miles away, and there's this silence on the beach—not a gramophone or a transistor to keep the place cheerful."

Taking visitors in, you eventually become philosophical. You learn a great deal about people. You discover that couples who are unhappy with each other will divert some of their disatisfaction onto you. Though people who are happy themselves will put up with chipped plates and eventually leave a box of chocolates on a table in an extremely tidy room. And I can make other generalisations too. The people who are flush with money are miserable unless they can spend it. They resent having had to work hard through the year and then find that the fivers in their pockets are meaningless tokens on a beach where only the waves break. It is as if their life's efforts are suddenly made null and void and they resent you for making this fact apparent to them. They hate the loneliness of the countryside and the values that it insists upon. The axiom that people who have worked hard in the factory all the year would appreciate a quiet country holiday more than anybody else is not true. Those who have worked in Coventry need a holiday in Blackpool. Too great a change between the environments comes only as a dislocation rather than relaxation.

In a few years, in spite of these trials and tribulations the "letting lark", as Rose Marie called it, had grown from an indulgence, to a hobby, and from a hobby, into a business. We now had seven flats and three cottages to let for the summer. Our winters were spent painting, making lampshades and repairing. I became a do-it-yourself addict, because we could not afford builders: plumbers are non-existent in North Devon and carpenters seem to be wholly employed making coffins. But I am ham-handed, a clumsy carpenter and a lethal electrician. But in spite of that, our visitors seemed to appreciate the décor that we achieved. They are tired of the dull rooms of English hotels, with their grim beds, beastly dressing-tables and cupboards, mere closets for sleeping in which you are unable to sit without feeling imprisoned.

Having waited so long for the electric mains we were over-extravagant with electric equipment. Tenants kept their fires on all night if they had children, and I suspected they toasted bread merely to feed to the gulls. But after a year or two of enormous electricity bills I was told that there were such things as meters. I had these installed. I may be particularly childish, but all the heartbreak I had suffered in building up this business has been worth the pleasure I now obtain by opening these meters—when I can find the right keys – and scooping out a hatful of two-shillings and then scampering off to count them. I am well aware that these two-shillingses only represent the electricity I have sold, but somehow or other it gives me the same pleasure as finding mushrooms on the cliff or kegs of butter on the beach. I have now become an addict of slot machines, and am considering installing them in my own house merely for the pleasure of opening them and seeing a heap of my own shillings in the little drawer. Indeed, I have already installed a cigarette machine in the hall of the Hermitage. Rationally I know that it will take me ten years at ¼d. profit per packet to pay for the machine, but fortunately I have another method of accountancy, in which childlike pleasure is an asset that will balance any budget.

Besides the joy of emptying slot-machines there are other pleasures to which we professional dustbin emptiers lay claim. Every flat or cottage has to be cleaned immediately the tenants leave, sometimes only two hours before the next move in. We rush in with vacuum cleaners and polishing materials, but before we get to work, like any other char, we make a bee-line for the perks. In our terminology perks constitute anything that has been left behind and which we shan't be asked to forward. It is irritating when things like wellingtons are found behind doors and hairbrushes are discovered in bedrooms. We know that these will be missed and we then have to go to the trouble of doing up a parcel. But the perks that are ours for the keeping are the foodstuffs left in the kitchen. During the season we never have to buy any cornflakes, marmalade, sugar or jam. Packets half full are left as a matter of course, but sometimes we do better than this. A whole pound of butter or a forgotten tin of lobster constitute a prize and gives a ridiculous amount of·pleasure in proportion to its value. I am sure some holidaymakers who have been back year after year realise this, and order a few tins of sardines the day before they leave so that I can have the pleasure of finding them after they have gone. The fun of finding something extra to the profit you have budgeted for makes all the difference to the usual drudgery of this trade. I remember one summer we had a well-known film star staying with us. She used to go round with Rose Marie and help clean up the cottages. She was never recognised in her rags and on one or two occasions was actually tipped. The half-crown piece pressed into her palm gave her much more pleasure than the thousands of pounds she received for her film work.

One of the necessary attributes for a hotel keeper or *restaurateur* is, of course, his ability to recognise people. I try hard but make serious mistakes, such as last year when I saw a woman drive into the farmyard, and thinking she was a new arrival immediately hurried to her car and piloted her towards a flat.

"This is your kitchen," I said, showing her round and giving her the key. The poor woman looked bewildered, wondering why she had to move since she had been staying in another flat in my house for more than three weeks. Sometimes these lapses can be more serious, as for instance, when a couple took Mallow Cottage for their honeymoon, and I failed to notice that the people who asked me the way to the place were, in fact, not my tenants but the girl's husband and the husband's real wife. But how was I expected to know that? Even so, no crockery was broken and difficult though it may be to explain, the four stayed on in the cottage until their tenancy expired.

In time, of course, one gets to know which couple are having an illicit relationship, though it is hard to say what gives them away. Genuine honeymooners seem to have a sense of anticlimax about them; the couple is often bad-tempered and irritable. But this is seldom the case with the illicit liaisons. They are gayer. The man carries the suitcases in and then goes back for the parcels. From these people we get the most perks. And whereas the married couple seem disappointed if the post has not left them anything, the fugitives are relieved when there is no letter. These are the small points one notices.

The other thing which we observe is that loneliness is now the most serious and prevalent contemporary disease. Affluence does nothing to lessen it. I am thinking of a middle-aged man who took a cottage a couple of years ago. When I showed him in he told me that his wife was joining him in a day or two. He drove to the station to meet her: she did not arrive. He went in on several other occasions. I began to wonder whether she existed. After a week he gave up waiting for his wife and started to look for a companion on the beach, wearing an immaculate blazer and white trousers. But he was far too shy to speak to anybody he didn't know and he didn't know anybody. By the end of his holiday he had got into the habit of taking sugar and bars of chocolate out to the horses and talking to them...and of course we see many examples of the holiday which is made up of two or three girls who are looking for male companionship. What often happens is that two of them find it and the third does not. Perhaps that is why the farm animals receive so much affection.

Just before he died, Somerset Maugham admitted that he had

learned practically everything he knew about people from the period when he was a medical student at Guy's Hospital. Some people think that my running Welcombe Estates is a distraction from my profession as a playwright, but it is not. One learns a great deal about people when you "take them in" and clear up after them. Having done this now for some years I can make some generalisations about the English on holiday. One is that the women, for the most part, are fractured by timidity and so used to the tyranny of their routine of running their home that they cannot free themselves from all the worries that go with it. I have actually seen women on holiday mending a tear in a curtain they did not cause, or tidying out cupboards in a house that they have rented. Their husbands are often crippled with boredom. Suddenly removed from the routine of their office, they wander aimlessly about the cliffs in a sort of daze, feeling that they ought to be keeping an appointment and wondering whether they have forgotten one. By the time they have unwound, most of them are packing to go back to the treadmill, just when they are starting to enjoy themselves. There are many who, having motored a couple of hundred miles to get to Devon, spend their fortnight in a sort of mechanical St Vitus' dance. Such people don't feel that they are seeing Devon unless they are on the road going from one town to another, viewing the back of lorries for most of the day. Many of the tenants only return to the cottage to garage the car at night. They leave after their holiday more exhausted than when they arrived. But there are others who are more rewarding. It is gratifying to see how a few days on the beach improves them and oddly enough, watching these is one of the profits from our chores.

Soon after I had completed the first act of *The Catalyst* Devine telephoned me and asked if I would be willing to make an English version of *Apollo de Bellac*. I did not know the play, although I admired Giraudoux. When I had been in Paris for the production of *This Way to the Tomb* at the Studio des Champs Elysées, his widow had asked me if I would make an English adaptation of another play of his. I was utterly enchanted by *Apollo de Bellac* and immediately dropped my own play as Devine had already scheduled a production and cast some of the characters. I enjoyed doing this adaptation immensely. I was pleased with the script: the production proved a fiasco. This was largely due to the producer's mistake of casting Esmé Percy as the old man. All the rehearsals were held up by Percy's inability to remember his lines. After a week it was clear that the star should have been dropped, but this was not done. Heather Sears as the girl was only adequate, and lacked an ingenuous charm which this play particularly required. Richard Pascoe as the man from Bellac had to carry a great deal. During rehearsals it was quite apparent that the whole production was being sabotaged by Esmè Percy. On the first night this proved to be the case, when no actor knew whether Percy was going to speak lines from Scene I or Scene II. Indeed, sometimes Mr Percy spoke other people's lines instead of his own. He had, by bringing fantasy into his performance, taken it all away from the play.

George was enthusiastic about *The Catalyst* and I was confident that Devine could not dislike it for any "religious content". And I had had it so typed that the idiomatic verse was not apparent. Even so, he showed little enthusiasm for the play because none of the characters came from a working class district, nor were they concerned whether their neighbours had got a better car than they had. He thought the play lacked social consciousness, and was consequently more than relieved when the Lord Chamberlain refused to give the play a licence. On George's advice I went along to St James's Palace to see whether this difficulty could be overcome.

"We liked the play, we enjoyed reading it," they said, "and if it is staged we hope you will send us tickets, but we can't possibly give a licence to a play which deals with a homosexual theme."

That this was between two women did not lessen their objection. I was reminded of the story George had told me, why homosexuality between women was not an offence in Law. Apparently Gladstone had taken the draft of the Act to Queen Victoria at Windsor Castle. Her Majesty had glanced at the document and noticed that homosexuality included sexual acts between men and also between women.

"But that is impossible," she had exclaimed, and struck the last clause out. Even so, though it was not recognised as an offence in Law, it was still an offence on the stage.

For the next year it looked as if *The Catalyst* would not be staged at all. Then somebody proposed that the English Stage Society should present it at the Royal Court since it had Club membership, but Devine thought that this was dangerous as it might confuse the general public whether or not they had access to other productions. Another year was allowed to elapse. Eventually prodded by the Council, Devine agreed to stage the work at the Arts Theatre. I suggested various producers. None seemed available. The same difficulties obtained with the casting. My first choice for the man had been Trevor Howard. Devine told me Howard had turned the play down, though a year later I discovered he had never been sent a script. This blocking, which amounted to sabotage, continued. Eventually, an American actor called Phil Browne was engaged to produce the play. Renée Asherson was cast for the wife. Four days before rehearsals were due to start, the only male character in the play, Charles, had still not been cast. The inevitable seemed unavoidable. Phil Browne took on the lead as well as producer.

These must be the last pages in this book. For after them, I was not the same man and therefore were I to continue, it could not be the same book. A book I haven't the courage to write. It looked as if it were going to be an ordinary evening. My life divides on that evening. Two volumes of preface: the play unwritten.

I had spent the day with George Devine and Phil Browne trying to cast *The Catalyst*. The usual sort of day, flicking through *Spotlight* and phoning agents, having bright ideas and then being realistic. It had been abortive. To cheer me up, George and Marion offered to take me out to supper to the Shangri-la, a Chinese restaurant in the Brompton Road. We had just started our meal when I was telephoned by Phil Browne. He asked if I could meet him immediately to see a young actress whom he wanted to read the part of Leonie.

"But we haven't heard from Mary Ure yet," I told him.

"It's a good thing to have this girl up our sleeve in case Ure and the others turn the part down. I have a hunch she's absolutely right."

"What's she done?"

"Nothing much on the stage. But she's made quite a name on the films."

I grunted. "Then let's see her tomorrow."

"She's leaving for Spain in the morning for three weeks' holiday. She lives quite near. I could come round to the restaurant and drive you to her. As I say, if she's right it would be good to have her up our sleeve in case the others on our list turn the part down." It was already eleven o'clock. But George thought I should go. I abandoned my supper and promised to have a drink with him later before going to bed. It seemed an ordinary evening.

Browne picked me up. I was not enthusiastic. I had met these hunches from producers before. He drove to Earls Court, then had some difficulty in finding the house in the dim-lit street. He led me down some wooden steps to a flat in the basement. I tripped over a dustbin lid. A girl opened the door. She was wearing blue ski trousers and a shirt in large red checks. She was about twenty-one. She had chestnut hair. She led us into a bed-sitting room, then sat on a pouffe by a gas fire. I stood while she read some pages from the part of Leonie. Every intonation, every movement she made carelessly as she squatted on the pouffe was precisely as I had imagined when I had written the part. I felt I had written her. I let Browne do the talking. When she had finished her reading my play was a long way from my mind. I heard her say that she was flying to Barcelona in the morning. She showed us out. We hadn't stayed longer than twenty minutes.

"You were very quiet. Didn't you like her?"

"She's perfect. It doesn't matter if the others turn it down."

"We must wait till they do. Meanwhile we'll keep her up our sleeve."

"Yes, up our sleeve," I said.

He drove me to Orme Square. George was waiting up for me, playing the gramophone. He turned it off, then offered me a drink.

"Well, what was she like? I said: what was she like? You look as if somebody's run over you."

"They have."

"What was her name?"

"Virginia. Her name was Virginia."

I haven't the strength now, or the courage, to write the rest.